The Appropriation of Cultural Capital

China's May Fourth Project

Harvard East Asian Monographs 207

Contributors

Milena Doleželová-Velingerová
Oldřich Král
Leo Ou-fan Lee
Stephen Owen
Rudolf Wagner
David Der-wei Wang
Ellen Widmer
Catherine Vance Yeh
Ying-shih Yü

The Appropriation of Cultural Capital

China's May Fourth Project

Milena Doleželová-Velingerová
and
Oldřich Král, editors
with
Graham Sanders, assistant editor

Published by the Harvard University Asia Center
and distributed by Harvard University Press
Cambridge (Massachusetts) and London 2001

Printed in the United States of America

The Harvard University Asia Center publishes a monograph series and, in coordination with the Fairbank Center for East Asian Research, the Korea Institute, the Reischauer Institute of Japanese Studies, and other faculties and institutes, administers research projects designed to further scholarly understanding of China, Japan, Vietnam, Korea, and other Asian countries. The Center also sponsors projects addressing multidisciplinary and regional issues in Asia.

Library of Congress Cataloging-in-Publication Data

The appropriation of cultural capital : China's May Fourth project / Milena Doleželová-Velingerová and Oldřich Král, editors ; with Graham Sanders, assistant editor.

p. cm.

ISBN 0-674-00786-7 (alk. paper)

1. Chinese literature--20th century--History and criticism. 2. China--History--May Fourth Movement, 1919. I. Title: China's May Fourth project. II. Doleželová-Velingerová, Milena, 1932- . III. Král, Oldřich. IV. Sanders, Graham Martin.

PL 2302.A66 2001

895.1'09358--dc21 2001039402

Index by Mary Mortensen

Printed on acid-free paper

Last figure below indicates year of this printing

11 10 09 08 07 06 05 04 03 02 01

To continue the legacy of

Professor Jaroslav Průšek

Contents

Part III: The Dialectic of History: May Fourth and Contemporary Chinese Literature

Part IV: Neither Renaissance nor Enlightenment

Preface

This volume contains a collection of papers originally presented at the conference "The Burdens of the May Fourth Movement," held at Charles University in Prague from August 29 to September 1, 1994. For Czech sinology this international meeting of prominent scholars was a milestone because, after two extremely unpropitious decades, it was once again possible to revive the legacy of its founder, the late Professor Jaroslav Průšek. As much as he extended the horizons of European sinology—in his day much centered on classical Chinese culture—by establishing the studies of modern Chinese literature at the Oriental Institute and at Charles University, so, too, our conference aimed at embarking contemporary studies of Chinese culture and literature on less traveled paths. The organizers of the Prague conference were convinced that with the knowledge gained during the preceding three decades, we could afford to open new vistas through studies that confront the principal tenets of the May Fourth cultural project, which has profoundly shaped the present understanding of Chinese culture and modern culture as a whole.

It is fair to say that the idea of the conference was Milena Doleželová's. The project was, however, not born overnight. It had been afloat for several years before the Prague conference was possible and was kept alive for an extended period thanks to the encouragement of her friends and colleagues. Special recognition should go to Merle Goldman, who so generously offered support to organize the workshop "The Burdens of the May Fourth Movement" on May 11, 1991, at the John King Fairbank Center for East Asian Research, Harvard University. This is, then, the occasion to express to her our heartfelt thanks.

The new and large-scale conference in August 1994 could not have been realized without the extended assistance of two broadminded benefactors who were, after 1989, intensively engaged in the rapid renascence of Chinese studies at Prague. Charles University generously hosted the conference and let us use the Carolinum, the oldest, fourteenth-century quarters of the school, for this auspicious occasion. Meanwhile, the Chiang Ching-kuo Foundation for International Scholarly Exchange provided an ample grant to organize the conference and devoted extraordinary attention to its preparation and realization. We thus hope that this volume expresses our sincere gratitude to both institutions for securing a befitting ambiance for ardent debates among scholars concerned with a further revitalization of studies of modern Chinese literature. Our thanks also go to all staff members and students of the Institute of East Asian Studies at Charles University, who enthusiastically assisted in the preparation of the conference and prepared a cordial and inspiring milieu during the days of our gatherings.

Yet the fact that a confrontation between May Fourth doctrines and today's research resulted in revelations of novel aspects of the May Fourth project is to the credit of the participants of the conference themselves. It is to them—the leading scholars from Europe, the United States, Canada, Taiwan, and Hong Kong—that we owe our most profound thanks for their willingness to participate in this Prague venture. Our special thanks go to those participants whose papers are not, for one reason or another, included in this volume. These include Chang Han-liang, Christoph Harbsmeier, Oldřich Král, and David Pollard. Our thanks go to those participants invited without papers, including Martin Hála, Zdenka Heřmanová-Novotná, Dana Kalvodová, Olga Lomová, Helmut Martin, Lucie Olivová, Augustin Palát, and Hua Laura Wu. We wish to express a special word of gratitude to Professor Ying-shih Yü for his inspiring closing statement at the conference and his generous consent to add his post-conference essay to this volume.

In conclusion, we wish to acknowledge those scholars whose professional skills, wisdom, and striving for perfection contributed to the implementation of this volume. Milena Doleželová has shouldered the heaviest burden as its editor. Graham Sanders, assistant editor of this volume, used his mastery of computer intricacies to match the content of the book with a higher order of technical execution, while his scholarly erudition enabled him to keep a watchful eye over matters stylistic and sinological. We are much indebted to Dr. Henri M. Day, whose profound understanding of the text and good humor served him in good stead to tame the misbehaving English of some of the contributions and other writings connected with this project. To John R. Ziemer, the Executive Editor of Harvard University's Asia Center Publications, we owe deep gratitude for his continual encouragement in bringing this volume to a proper end and for professional advice that greatly enhanced the clarity and precision of ideas formulated in this volume.

Finally, on behalf of both editors, we wish to express thanks most heartily to our families. Without their tolerance, support, and understanding the conference would not have been realized and this book would not have been finished.

Oldřich Král

Contributors

Milena Doleželová-Velingerová, Professor Emerita of Chinese Literature at the University of Toronto, earned her Ph.D. at the Oriental Institute of the Czech Academy of Sciences. She has published numerous articles on twentieth-century Chinese fiction, medieval Chinese storytelling, and premodern Chinese theory of fiction and drama. She is the editor and coauthor of *The Chinese Novel at the Turn of the Century* (1980), *A Selective Guide to Chinese Literature 1900–1949,* vol. 1, *The Novel* (1988); and *Poetics East and West* (1988/89). She translated, with James I. Crump, the *Ballad of the Hidden Dragon* (*Liu Zhiyuan zhugongdiao*) (1971).

Oldřich Král is Professor of Sinology and Comparative Literature at Charles University, Prague. He earned his Ph.D. for research in Chinese fiction at the Oriental Institute of the Czech Academy of Sciences. He has written several studies on the classic Chinese novel *Rulin waishi* (1964) and was one of the co-authors of *Rise and Development of Modern Literatures in Asia* (1965). He has published Czech translations of *Rulin waishi* (1962), *Honglou meng* (1986–88), and *Wenxin diaolong* (2000).

Leo Ou-fan Lee is Professor of Chinese Literature at Harvard University. His most recent book is *Shanghai Modern: The Flowering of a New Urban Culture, 1930–45* (1999).

Stephen Owen is James Conant Bryant University Professor at Harvard. He works in classical Chinese poetry and poetics. His most recent books are *The End of the Chinese Middle Ages* (1997) and *An Anthology of Traditional Chinese Literature: Beginning to 1911* (1997).

Graham Sanders is an Associate Professor of Chinese Literature at the University of Toronto. In his research, he concentrates on the narrative depiction of producing, performing, and receiving poetry as a socially engaged form of discourse. His book, *Words Well Put: Poetic Competence in the Chinese Tradition*, is forthcoming.

Rudolf G. Wagner is Professor of Chinese Studies, University of Heidelberg. He has done research on early medieval Chinese philosophy, nineteenth- and twentieth-century political and cultural history, and modern Chinese literature. Publications include *Inside a Service Trade: Studies in Contemporary Chinese Prose* (1992); "The *Shenbao* in Crisis: The International Environment and the Conflict Between Guo Songtao and the *Shenbao*," *Late Imperial China* (1999); *The Craft of a Chinese Commentator: Wang Bi on the Laozi* (2000). He is finishing a book on Ernest Major, the editor of the most important early Chinese-language newspaper.

David Der-wei Wang is Professor of Chinese and Comparative Literature at Columbia University. He specializes in late imperial and modern Chinese literature and comparative narratology. His recent publications include *Fin-de-siècle Splendor: Repressed Modernities of Late Qing Fiction, 1849–1911* (1997), *Chinese Literature in the Second Half of a Modern Century* (co-edited, 2000), and *The Monster That Is History: History, Violence, and Fictional Writing in Twentieth Century China* (forthcoming).

Ellen Widmer is Professor of Asian Languages and Literatures at Wesleyan University. She is the author of *The Margins of Utopia: Shui-hu hou-chuan and the Literature of Ming Loyalism* (1987) and the co-editor with David Der-wei Wang of *From May Fourth to June Fourth: Fiction and Film in Twentieth Century China* (1993) and with Kang-i Sun Chang of *Writing Women in Late Imperial China* (1997).

Catherine Vance Yeh, Ph.D. in Chinese Literature, 1990, Harvard University, is a Research Associate at the Institute of Chinese Studies, Heidelberg University. She has worked on Shanghai entertainment culture. Her publications include "Reinventing Ritual: Late Qing Handbooks for Proper Customer Behavior in Shanghai Courtesan Houses," *Late Imperial China* (1998);

"The Life-Style of Four *Wenren* in Late Qing Shanghai," *Harvard Journal of Asiatic Studies* (1997); and a book manuscript "City, Courtesan, and Intellectual: The Rise of Shanghai Entertainment Culture 1850–1910."

Ying-shih Yü is Professor of Chinese History at Princeton University. He has published extensively in both Chinese and English on China's intellectual, cultural, and literary history.

The Appropriation of Cultural Capital

China's May Fourth Project

Introduction

Milena Doleželová-Velingerová
and David Der-wei Wang

The May Fourth era (1910s to 1930s), together with the last thirteen years (1898–1911) of the Qing dynasty, constitutes the crucial period for the formation of a Chinese discourse of modernity. During this period, the Chinese intelligentsia imported Western culture and institutions with great zeal, critiqued their own legacies, and reassessed their positions vis-à-vis the national crisis. Thus they laid the ground for China's initiation into the global period called the Modern Age. To understand modernity in a Chinese context, it is necessary to understand the Chinese discourse on modernism, the historical conditions under which it was formed, and the aims and ideas that guided its formation.

Studies of the May Fourth era appeared as early as the 1930s, and by the early 1960s one could speak of a "tradition" of May Fourth scholarship. This discourse was undertaken primarily by scholars who were contemporary with the New Culture movement (later known as the May Fourth movement) or even direct participants in it. Although they provided a picture of the movement based on ample first-hand evidence, they were generally unable to view the period from a perspective that differed from that of its proponents. For these first-generation scholars, the May Fourth movement remained unquestioned as the awakening moment of radical iconoclasm, revolution, humanism, science and democracy, progress, individualism, and nationalism—a Chinese Enlightenment or Renaissance. A good example is Chow Tse-tsung's *May Fourth Movement: Intellectual Revolution in Modern China* (1960). A monumental work that continues to inspire scholars, the book nevertheless takes for granted all the assumptions of the May Fourth leaders and unreservedly endorses the consequences of their actions. The reluctance of this earlier generation of scholars to rethink the legacies of the May Fourth movement was perhaps due as much to the awe-inspiring scholarship of the May Fourth leaders as to their political charisma. These early scholars still had, like their May Fourth objects, an emotional investment in the success of the movement. By writing affirmatively of the May Fourth movement, they, too, were bolstering China's continued march toward modernization.

One finds a similar tendency to canonize the May Fourth movement in scholars' accounts of the rise and development of modern Chinese literature. Despite their differing ideological and methodological positions, these critics rarely call into question any of the basic May Fourth tenets. Studies written at the height of the Cold War by Chinese, Japanese, and Western scholars (e.g., Wang Yao 王瑤 [1951, 1953], translated into Japanese by Sanetō Keishū 實籐惠秀 [1955–56]; Shimada Masao 島田政雄 [1952]; Ding Yi 丁易 [1955]; Jaroslav Průšek [1955, 1964]; C. T. Hsia [1961]) were of course not as single-minded in their ideological evaluations as the studies of the 1930s and 1940s (e.g., Chen Bingkun 陳炳坤 [1930]; Wang Zhefu 王哲傅 [1933]; Fu Donghua 傅東華 [1937]; Henri van Boven [1946]; O. Brière [1948]; Joseph Schyns et al. [1948]). Yet, as in the case of Chow Tse-tsung, these literary historians tend to accept the protagonists' views of the May Fourth period. In their accounts, the ideas outlined in a series of essays and letters written in the late 1910s by several young, Western-educated Chinese intellectuals, most notably Hu Shi 胡適 (1891–1962) and Chen Duxiu 陳獨秀 (1879–1942), are deemed most influential. The views of Hu Shi, Chen Duxiu, and a few others on Chinese literary history became indisputable.

Thus, modern Chinese literature was presented as arising in consequence of a rapid and radical renunciation of the Chinese heritage. The enlightened literati is said to have replaced a worn-out tradition with a new one, one that had abandoned dysfunctional Chinese linguistic and aesthetic norms, one based on values, ideas, and forms appropriated from occidental literature and culture. In "On Literary Revolution" ("Wenxue geming lun" 文學革命論, 1917), Chen Duxiu propagated the concept of a nation breaking from its past, so as to make way for the "new civilization" (*xin wenming* 新文明). Hu Shi advocated similar views. Because of Chen's and Hu's prestige, this powerful fiction was imposed on the realities of Chinese literary modernization. Since the 1920s, literary historians have tended to treat Hu's and

Chen's conceptualizations as dogma and created a historiographical paradigm that duplicates the May Fourth claim of radical anti-traditionalism. This paradigm was so powerful that it obscured alternative views, particularly the argument that modern Chinese literature resulted less from a Western-inspired revolution than from a tortuous evolution from China's own tradition. Representative moments of these more sophisticated views of "evolution" can be found in works by Zhou Zuoren (1932) 周作人 (1885–1967) and Jaroslav Průšek (1957 [1980]; his views in this study differ remarkably from those expressed in the works of 1955 and 1964 mentioned above).

However, new scholarly initiatives have brought changes in our view of a subject once thought to be satisfactorily understood. These initiatives returned to the May Fourth cultural project and re-examined its anti-traditional claims, and they arrived at conclusions radically opposed to certain fundamental May Fourth tenets. These new directions of research are traceable to two scholars based in Prague. As early as 1957, Jaroslav Průšek suggested in his well-known essay "Subjectivism and Individualism in Modern Chinese Literature" (1957 [1980]) that subjectivism and individualism, the most innovative trends in Qing fiction, were the prime driving forces behind the modernization of Chinese fiction. Meanwhile, in 1964 Oldřich Král, in his studies of the artistic devices of the classic Chinese novel, argued that *The Scholars* (*Rulin waishi* 儒林外史) represented a new, sophisticated type of Chinese narrative created by literati.

Both Průšek's and Král's researches pioneered a new approach to the relations between modern and premodern Chinese literary conventions. In 1981, Patrick Hanan demonstrated in *The Chinese Vernacular Story* how short-story writers in the early Qing played deftly with both the classical and the vernacular languages in relation to genre and subject matter; he thus challenged, perhaps inadvertently, the antagonistic dichotomy between the classical and vernacular Chinese discourses held by the May Fourth practitioners of literature. In 1987, Andrew H. Plaks argued persuasively that the four masterworks of the Ming novel—*Romance of the Three Kingdoms* (*Sanguo zhi yanyi* 三國之演義), *Water Margin* (*Shuihu zhuan* 水滸傳), *Journey to the West* (*Xiyou ji* 西遊記), and *The Plum in the Golden Vase* (*Jin Ping Mei cihua* 金瓶梅詞話)—represent the literati's sophisticated modulation of the popular genre of prose fiction, an undertaking that predates the May Fourth intellectuals' promotion of "popular literature" (*tongsu wenxue* 通俗文學) by almost three centuries.

New research in modern literature also began to rethink the validity of May Fourth canons from thematics to stylistics, from authorial intention to ideological concerns. A volume edited by Merle Goldman, *Modern Chinese Literature in the May Fourth Era* (1977), though focusing on the achievements of the May Fourth, shows no less concern about the multiple paths through which modern Chinese literati have negotiated their claims to nationalism or womanhood. In the same spirit, the volume edited by Ellen Widmer and David Wang, *From May Fourth to June Fourth* (1993), challenged the May Fourth canon by examining how writers of later generations rewrote the May Fourth legacies. In *The Limits of Realism: Chinese Fiction in the Revolutionary Period* (1990), Marston Anderson reassessed the May Fourth literati's reception of European realism and concluded that writers such as Lu Xun 魯 迅 (1881–1936), Ye Shaojun 葉 紹 鈞 (1894–1988), Ba Jin 巴 金 (1904–), and Mao Dun 茅 盾 (1896–1981) started out with a realist project based on national restoration (*jiuguo* 救 國) and enlightenment (*qimeng* 啓 蒙) only to end up with works that contradicted their premises.

David Wang's *Fictional Realism in Twentieth Century China* (1992) takes up the polemic of realism by arguing that, for all its claims to be an unmediated, authoritative representation of reality and truth, Chinese realism from the outset spoke in various voices in response to the fractured realities of China. Meanwhile, the achievements of late Qing and pre–May Fourth Republican literature have received increasing attention, starting with the articles in Milena Doleželová's pathbreaking *The Chinese Novel at The Turn of the Century* (1980) and Theodore Huters's articles (see, e.g., Huters 1988) on the formation of the modern discourse of literature in the nineteenth century, Chen Pingyuan's 陳 平 原 voluminous treatments of the changing narrative formats of late Qing fiction (1989), and David Wang's *Fin-de-Siècle Splendor: Repressed Modernities of Late Qing Fiction, 1849–1911* (1997). Equally notable is the scholarly attention give the popular or middle-brow vein of modern Chinese literature, such as Perry Link's *Mandarin Ducks and Butterflies* (1981) and Ts'un-yan Liu's (ed.) *Chinese Middle-brow Fiction* (1984).

The desire to probe the discrepancies between received views concerning the May Fourth era and actual results was further fueled by a number of more recent studies. These studies, though not focused solely on the May Fourth, have questioned the movement's claims to be the voice of enlightenment, progress, science, nation, feminism, and the like. Prasenjit Duara (1995) alerts us to the fact that modern Chinese historiography has been overshadowed by the obsession with nationalism, and Wang Hui (1995) highlights the ideological and political motivations of such sanctioned notions as science, justice, democracy, and individualism. Both Lydia Liu (1995) and Ying Hu (2000) look into the complex "translingual practice" behind the rendition of foreign thoughts and discourses into Chinese society. Xiaobing Tang (1996) ventures a remapping of the late Qing political and intellectual configuration in his study of Liang Qichao 梁 啓 超, and Joan Judge (1997) uses *The Eastern Times* (*Shibao* 時 報) to study the rise of journalism and the media industry at the turn of the century. John Fitzgerald (1996) examines the dynamics of politics, culture, and class that constitute the backdrop of the May Fourth era, and Mau-sang Ng (1988) traces a genealogy of Russian models in the Chinese imagination of national identity.

Finally, increasing attention has been paid to the counterdiscourse in Chinese modernity, thanks to the publication of books on arguably "conservative" scholars such as Wang Guowei (1877–1927) 王 國 維 (Bonner 1986) and those of the National Essence school (*Guocui xuepai* 國 粹 學 派), and to the unearthing of such thought-provoking historical materials as *Discourses on New Knowledge and National Heritage* (*Guogu xinzhi lun* 國 故 新 知 論, 1995), which clarify the views of the members of the Nanjing literary journal (and society of the same name) *Critical Review* (*Xueheng* 學 衡). Until recently these voices had been silenced merely because they sounded radically contradictory to mainstream May Fourth discourse.

The current volume is inspired by, but not limited to, these recent efforts to re-examine the origins of Chinese literary and cultural modernity. By approaching the May Fourth problematic from hitherto little-studied perspectives, this volume seeks to play a part in the ongoing critique of the movement. Unlike studies that probe the topics of May Fourth discourse—realism, selfhood, revolution, enlightenment—on their own terms, the present volume is centered on the intellectual and cultural/historical motivations and practices through which such a discourse became possible. In other words, it highlights issues such as the strategies of discourse formation, scholarly methodologies, rhetorical disposition, manipulation of historical sources, and, above all, the construction of modernity by means of the reification of China's literary past. By analyzing these practices, this volume intends to disclose elements of modern Chinese literature and culture long hidden from view.

The volume consists of four parts, each revolving around a particular topic prevailing at one or another stage in the evolution of the Chinese discourse of modernity. Part I discusses the formation of the May Fourth movement both as a discourse and as a practice. It touches on the contested notion of *public sphere*, treating it not only as a rhetorical locus in which plural voices and opinions are brought into play but also as a physical arena in which organizational forces are mobilized to substantiate cultural and political agency. Part II, the central part of the volume, furthers the discussion in Part I by focusing on an extremely polemical issue—the *rewriting of literary history*—in the period. It stresses the motivations behind the canonization of a certain type of Chinese literature at the expense of others and dissects the fundamental aspects of New Culture—language, rhetoric, and literature—by examining the circulation of the "symbolic capital" of the May Fourth and its ideological bearings. By trying to clarify how certain components of Chinese modernity were effaced by the May Fourth, it seeks to demonstrate the impact of this "act of erasure" on contemporary Chinese acquisition of the literary past. Part III compares the New Culture movement with literary and cultural production in the wake of the Cultural Revolution. It ponders the similarities and differences between these two periods in terms of cultural dynamics, ideological debates, and the imperatives of rewriting literary (and national) history. The volume concludes with Ying-shih Yü's essay "Neither Renaissance Nor Enlightenment: A Historian's Reflections on the May Fourth Movement," in which Yü argues that the way in which the May Fourth movement itself became reified was a ground on which competing factions carried out incompatible projects.

Part I of the volume challenges the common wisdom that the May Fourth was an era of intellectual emancipation and social polyphony. It features a dialogue between two veteran scholars, Leo Ou-fan Lee and Rudolf Wagner. The May Fourth opened up a multitude of new possibilities for Chinese intellectuals, relieving them from traditional epistemological and behavioral shackles. Looking back from the beginning of a new century, one nevertheless finds numerous gaps between what the May Fourth advocates professed and what they truly achieved. From very different perspectives, Lee and Wagner deconstruct the "mythology" of the May Fourth. Whereas Lee focuses on the rhetorical constructs that facilitated May Fourth as a *discourse* (i.e., a communicational circuit informed by a distinct *episteme*), Wagner reveals the institutional maneuvering that gave rise to May Fourth as a *movement* (i.e., an organized mass action masterminded and mobilized by a calculating leadership). Despite their methodological differences, both share the understanding that the May Fourth was premised as much on a new mode of knowledge as on a new mode of cultural politics. Moreover, both advocate that in addition to studying the symbolic repertoire evoked by the May Fourth, we need to give equal attention to the material aspect of the movement.

In "Incomplete Modernity: Rethinking the May Fourth Intellectual Project," Leo Lee contemplates the contributions of May Fourth discourse by harking back to the late Qing moment. His examples include a newspaper, the *Shanghai News* (*Shenbao* 申 報), and a journal, *Eastern Miscellany* (*Dongfang zazhi* 東 方 雜 誌). Lee suggests that long before the May Fourth advocacy of liberal thought and open communication, the late Qing journalists and literati had already cultivated a "public sphere" of their own. The literary supplement of *The Shanghai News* must be regarded as a discursive space, however unlikely it may seem, in which the serious and the frivolous, the conservative and the radical, could be articulated. Ironically enough, with the establishment of the May Fourth discourse, one finds less tolerance in publications and other public venues dedicated to the encouragement of free thought. Thus, despite its negative images, the last years of the Qing may prove among the more liberating moments of Chinese modernity.

Lee next studies a debate between the editors of two journals, Du Yaquan 杜 亞 泉 (fl. 1918), editor of the *Eastern Miscellany*, founded in the late Qing, and Chen Duxiu, editor of *New Youth* (*Xin qingnian* 新 青 年), founded on the eve of the May Fourth. The debate dealt with the key issue of the day—the modernization of China—but the views of the discussants, both proponents of modernity, were diametrically opposed. Whereas Chen Duxiu advocated immediate, total Westernization, Du Yaquan favored amelioration based on the traditional heritage. Like most of his contemporaries, Du regarded continuity and national traditions as necessary for the country's stability. With his strident rhetoric and vociferous style of argumentation, Chen appeared to have won the debate, but the way in which he promoted his agenda reveals a trait of the May Fourth movement that is anything but tolerant. Lee concludes that journals in the May Fourth promoted their agendas to the exclusion of opposing views; they were in reality neither liberal nor pluralist. Specific issues aside, Lee stresses that the May Fourth intellectuals were able to utilize a new rhetoric and polemic in making their case; the linguistic form manifested itself as a new source of power.

Lee's essay leads one to rethink the cultural scene of the late Qing. At first sight, the turn of the century and the first two decades of the twentieth century do not appear propitious for a venture so vital and so risky as the integration of Chinese culture into the global framework of modernity. Politically, this was a bleak moment for China, a once supreme power mired in a series of military defeats, failed political reforms, economic problems, and educational crises. Even more disheartening to China's political leaders was the recognition that Chinese culture—that millennia-long adhesive of Chinese territorial integrity—was dissolving as Chinese cultural superiority lost ever more ground in the face of Western material, cultural, and intellectual importations. But political disorder may have fostered an unexpected locus for communication between China and the West. Shanghai rose in the midst of national turmoil to become the first Chinese metropolis and the mecca for new-style cultural industries. Its cosmopolitan and polyglot atmosphere made possible the appearance of the Chinese "public sphere."

Lee's invocation of the close ties between the burgeoning printing industry and the dissemination of a new national imagination naturally leads one to think of Benedict Anderson's (1991) by now-familiar theory of "imagined communities." But he expands Anderson's model by suggesting not a parallel but a contradiction between the progress of technology and the advent of national consciousness. For Lee, it was the "backward" late Qing, rather than the new Republican society, that was more ready to espouse the concepts of modernity. Behind Lee's argument is therefore a critique of the linear, teleological program that underlies the traditional May Fourth scholarship. Lee associates the late Qing media with the "public sphere" conceptualized by Jürgen Habermas (1989) in the context of eighteenth-century European society, which Habermas understands as a realm of freedom of private and collective activity to be defended against state intrusion and domination. However, whereas the "public sphere" in France and England consisted of journals and salons that were to contribute greatly to the formation of a civil society, in China at the turn of the century the "public sphere" was, as Lee points out, "mainly confined to journalistic discourse, the overriding theme of which was, as in the case of other spheres of cultural life, nationalism—what new China should be like."

The volatile nature of the debate—the battle for hegemony over the cultural, and later political, life of the newly emerging Chinese nation-state—led to the abandonment of the tolerance found in the late Qing discussions.

Lee demonstrates that Chen Duxiu's harsh tactics prefigure those used in later periods of Chinese journalism and political debate. Lee concludes that the proponents of the New Culture were neither liberal nor pluralist, and hence the modern project became highly suspect. To Lee, the debate manifests "the rise of a new culture elite" motivated by "a desire to seize hegemonic power in the field of culture" and engaged in what Antonio Gramsci would later call, in another context, a battle for "positions."

Rudolf Wagner's "The Canonization of May Fourth" complements Lee's essay by addressing the practices through which the May Fourth advocates asserted their hegemonic power. Like Lee, Wagner is interested in the linguistic indices of modernity, but he also presents new historical evidence that strips the May Fourth movement of many long-established myths, and he reveals a pattern of the "desertification" of the Chinese cultural landscape. Wagner details how a political takeover, executed primarily by the educated elite, was represented throughout the whole of the modern era as the emergence of a "new era."

Wagner begins by tracing the origin of the word *yundong* 運動 (movement). He concludes that the word was most probably introduced into the Chinese language via Japan only in the 1910s. This neologism, once introduced to China, was quickly implemented in a political way. *Yundong* became a magical incantation that was skillfully used during the student demonstrations of May 4, 1919, to convey the general yearning in China for "action." By demonstrating how rhetoric and political power were mutually implicated, Wagner provides yet another example of Lee's argument.

Historians of modern Chinese history and politics will be even more interested in Wagner's demonstration that the May Fourth movement did not arise from a spontaneous outburst of discontent among the masses. Rather, the movement was consciously crafted by activists after the model of earlier movements (especially the Korean Independence movement of March 1, 1919) in order to strengthen its position in public and state organizations and to legitimize its activities. "The participants in the May Fourth demonstrations," Wagner argues, "assumed and arrogated the role of national vanguard, spokesman and teacher for themselves." Once in this position, the cultural elite, irrespective of its standpoint—Confucian, May Fourth, Cultural Revolution—stakes its claim to being the legitimate purveyor of the national political orientation, with a view to eliminating every remnant of the past or of local thought or tradition that inhibits a modern, centrist orientation.

Prasenjit Duara argues forcefully that the current historiography of the early modern era tends to endorse the May Fourth agenda of streamlining the multiple development of Chinese experience into a unified goal of nationalism (Duara 1995: 91–92). This is where Wagner's observation becomes most pertinent. The May Fourth intellectuals organized a movement in the name of the people even as they made inspiring the people their goal. Thus, "the break with history especially dramatized the need to *make* the people the foundation of the nation. The nation had already emerged in the name of the people, but the people who mandated the nation would have to be remade to serve as their own sovereign. It was no longer a question of reawakening the nation and the people, but rather, making them from scratch. *Who* would be responsible for making the people?" Hence the necessity of more, and even better organized, movement.

For Wagner as for Lee, the May Fourth movement became a burden for those who helped initiate it. Wagner concludes his contribution with the following statement: "The early iconoclasm that was a polemical reaction to society seen as decrepit and corrupt turned into a liability once the movement's perception had in fact become the dominant discourse in the intellectual world and had made the Chinese intelligentsia a partner, and all too often an active participant, in the desertification of the lands they themselves were called upon to till." Therefore, to use Leo Lee's words, the May Fourth can at best be regarded as a project of "incomplete modernity."

Leo Lee's and Rudolf Wagner's treatments of the May Fourth as a discourse that incites a radical movement and as a movement that fostered a hegemonic discourse point to the dynamic exchange between symbolic yearning and social mobilization, imagination and its materialization, at a time when China was trying to define its future. Both, however, are keenly aware that this national pursuit of the future was rooted in the national re-vision of the past. By observing how the May Fourth advocates carved out their new projects in discourses as well as in actions, Lee and Wagner at the same time examine how they undid their cultural and political heritage. Modernity cannot assert its legitimacy without first renegotiating history. Lee's and Wagner's essays thus pave the way for the central part of this volume: the tactics with which May Fourth scholars affirm their positions as *the* moderns by rewriting their literary tradition.

Part II consists of three essays, each touching on one aspect of the May Fourth enterprise of rewriting (literary) history. One of the most polemical issues in the May Fourth discourse is the formation of a new historical consciousness. At a time when Chinese literati came to realize that China was no longer the supreme world power and that Chinese history must be understood as part of a global configuration of temporalities, how to represent *national literary history* became an urgent task. In a seminal article, "The New Way of Writing" (1988), Theodore Huters points out that the search for a new and different format for Chinese literary history started as early as the mid-nineteenth century. Dynastic adversities served as the breeding ground for intense intellectual activity and drove intellectuals to devise new formulations of the national imagination, in which literature stood out as its most prominent sign. In this "monumental transformation of literary discourse" (Huters 1988: 247), solutions were sought in the past in proposals, for example, to restore archaic prose (Tongcheng school 桐 城 派) or parallel prose (Wenxuan school 文 選 派). But more challenging were the attempts to break the mold of the past, as exemplified by Liang Qichao's various attempts to modernize cultural communication.

Liang discerned that nationalism would be the "glue" that would replace the adhesive of traditional culture. Thus not only did Liang introduce a "new prose style" (*xin wenti* 新 文 體) and advocate the novel as a vital medium of social and political reform, but during his exile in Japan (1898–1912) he, together with Zhang Binglin 章 炳 麟 (1868–1936) and Liu Shipei 劉 師 培 (1884–1919), introduced the concept of "national history" to Chinese historiography. This concept of "national history," according to Ying-shih Yü (1994), derived from the model provided by the new generation of Japanese historians. Liang's progressive replacement for the traditional historiographical format enabled him to create the first *modern* Chinese history in narrative. Called "the narrative of the Enlightenment" by Prasenjit Duara, this historiography "made it clear that a people could not become a nation without a History in the linear mode" (Duara 1995: 33). Liang Qichao's reification of national history through literature is particularly demonstrated by his own theory about fiction. For Liang, the "four powers" (*si zhong li* 四 種 力) of the novel could provoke the reader out of a state of inertia and into one of national awakening. He thus provided a strong rationale for the production and discussion of fiction as a new method of disseminating national consciousness and national history.

The authors of the studies presented in Part II observe numerous lacunae in May Fourth accounts of Chinese literary history, lacunae that nevertheless facilitated the May Fourth interpretation of the Chinese literary past. This "act of erasure," to use Ellen Widmer's term, was employed by New Culture proponents for purposes other than merely rewriting Chinese literary history. Thus, Hu Shi, when writing his "Chinese Literature of the Past Fifty Years" ("Wushi nianlai zhi Zhongguo wenxue" 五十年來之中國文學) in 1922, proclaimed the late Qing period "a very significant period in the history of Chinese literature," but only because it witnessed the demise of literature in classical language and the ascent of vernacular literature (Hu Shi 1923: 96–97). At the same time, New Culture leaders, such as Zheng Zhenduo 鄭振鐸 (1898–1958), Mao Dun, Zhou Zuoren, and Lu Xun (Link 1981: 7, 17–18), launched a campaign to devalue the work of the writers of the 1910s as commercial romantic kitsch by labeling them the "School of Mandarin Ducks and Butterflies" (*Yuan yang hudie pai* 鴛鴦蝴蝶派), the clichéd symbols of lovers.

Other examples can be mentioned. In 1922, Lu Xun and Hu Shi refused to engage in discussion with a group of American-educated professors in Nanjing, who in the newly founded journal *Critical Review* (1922–33) had expressed well-grounded doubts about the historical veracity of Hu Shi's appraisal of late Qing literature and his concept of Chinese language as rigidly separated into vernacular (*baihua* 白話) and classical Chinese (*wenyan* 文言) (Sun and Guo 1995). And in 1935, the ten-volume *Compendium of Modern Chinese Literature* (*Zhongguo xin wenxue daxi* 中國新文學大系), compiled by New Culture leaders (such as Hu Shi, Mao Dun, Zheng Zhenduo, Lu Xun, Zheng Boqi 鄭伯奇[1895–1979], Zhou Zuoren, and others), established the new canon of Chinese literary modernity (L. Liu 1995: 214–38) through exclusive inclusion of May Fourth writings, while other works of the period, such as those by Mu Shiying 穆時英 (1912–40) and Liu Na'ou 劉吶鷗 (1900–1940) of the avant-garde School of New Sensibilities (*Xin ganjue pai* 新感覺派), active in Shanghai in the 1930s, and numerous other outstanding writers, such as Shen Congwen 沈從文 (1902–88), were silenced and fell into oblivion. As is the case in any other period when literary history was edited to suit a specific agenda, the gaps in the history of modern Chinese literature were not filled till generations later as a result of shifting paradigms or canons.

In his essay "Zheng Zhenduo and the Invention of Chinese Literary History," drafted in 1991 but unfortunately not fully elaborated before his untimely death, the late Marston Anderson vividly captured the intellectual ferment of the early 1920s, centered on the May Fourth re-evaluation of China's cultural heritage and literature. As early as 1919, shortly after his return from the United States, Hu Shi had launched a campaign for "systematic reorganization of the national heritage" (*zhengli guogu* 正理國故) in which scholars were encouraged to systematize old Chinese theories and give them new interpretations in the light of Western thought. In contrast to the opposition of certain scholars, particularly those gathered in the newly formed *Critical Review*, Zheng Zhenduo, then head of the Association for Literary Research (*Wenxue yanjiu hui* 文學研究會) and later to become the foremost May Fourth literary historian, took this slogan to heart. When he took over the editorship of *The Short Story Monthly* (*Xiaoshuo yuebao* 小說月報) in 1923, Zheng devoted part of the first issue for which he was responsible to essays dealing with this subject. As Anderson points out, "the contributors generally agreed that, properly practiced, research in traditional literature was fully consistent with the goals of the New Culture movement." "Zheng," writes Anderson, "in particular focused on literary history as the appropriate tool for such revision and his ultimate resolve was to produce a literary history that, as he later put it, 'would show the readers the complete process of development of Chinese literature, as well as its complete, true face'" (Zheng 1932).

According to Anderson, Zheng took as his mission the formulation of a comprehensive, "unified" view of the literary tradition because for him traditional China lacked not only literary history but a proper understanding of literature as well. But, as Anderson also points out, the May Fourth intellectuals "viewed literary history not merely as a pedagogical tool, but as a new way of envisioning the tradition. . . . May Fourth both established literary history as a legitimate (indeed as the dominant) way of writing about literature and, in more general terms, fundamentally altered readers' perceptions of the relationship between literature and history." If literary history constitutes, as nineteenth-century European literary historians thought, the "national biography" of a people, the Chinese national biography, as Zheng wrote in 1938 in his influential *History of Chinese Popular Literature* (*Zhongguo su wenxue shi* 中國俗文學史), was to be found not in the "toadying and whining of the literati," but in the tales of popular heroes and lovers that circulated among the common people (Zheng 1938: 4).

The three studies included in Part II, first drafted at the same time as Anderson's essay, also deal with May Fourth literary history, but their authors have since been able to attain a more radical rereading of May Fourth literary historiography than that formulated by Anderson. Despite dealing with different subjects, the three studies—"Literary Historiography in Early Twentieth-Century China (1904–1928): Constructions of Cultural Memory" by Milena Doleželová-Velingerová; Stephen Owen's "The End of the Past: Rewriting Chinese Literary History in the Early Republic"; and Ellen Widmer's "The Rhetoric of Retrospection: May Fourth Literary History and the Ming-Qing Woman Writer"—arrive at a similar conclusion: that May Fourth literary histories and anthologies are not so much accurate accounts of historical reality as hypothetical constructs that reify the Chinese cultural past in order to legitimate May Fourth cultural policies. This interpretation differs radically from the received view of May Fourth modernity. But, as we shall see below, the nature of the investigations on which this novel interpretation is based also differs from that of its predecessors.

These three studies look into the methods and cultural practices through which May Fourth historians and literary anthologists effaced historical reality and replaced it with an "artificial," imaginary reality that would sustain the May Fourth present. In her essay, Milena Doleželová closely reads three early Chinese literary histories all entitled *History of Chinese Literature* (*Zhongguo wenxue shi* 中國文學史)—by Lin Chuanjia 林傳甲 (1904), Huang Ren 黃人 (1905), and Zeng Yi 曾毅 (1915)—and questions May Fourth scholars' claim that their literary histories laid the groundwork for literary historiography in China. By comparison, Doleželová argues, Hu Shi's *History of Vernacular Literature* (*Baihua wenxue shi* 白話文學史), published in 1928, presents itself as a new breed of Chinese literary historiography. Whereas, however, literary historiography in early twentieth-century China had by and large been based on the empirical study of a large number of literary works and related materials, Hu Shi's *History* and its May Fourth successors were based on theoretical speculation.

Doleželová acknowledges that some of the May Fourth literary histories, such as Zheng Zhenduo's *History of Chinese Popular Literature*, present a great amount of new material. But the criteria of compilation derived from prevailing May Fourth axioms concerning the distinction between the classical and the vernacular and the primacy of the latter as the "literature of the people." Works that did not fit these conceptions were ignored or, perhaps better, simply not seen. Thus, despite the fact that this new method of writing literary history allowed an innovative and comprehensive treatment of Chinese literary history, it could not but reinforce a powerful and ultimately nese literary history, it could not but reinforce a powerful and ultimately distorting ideological conceptualization of literary development. The closer the histories approached the present day, the greater loomed the achievements of vernacular literature.

Doleželová finds that the May Fourth literary historians organized historical facts into a causal narrative that replaced the customary temporal arrangement of facts in historical writing. This new narrative format highlights and legitimates the vernacular language, which for centuries was the vehicle of eventful fiction and verisimilitude, as opposed to the classical language, previously the linguistic register reserved for historical writing. With the sanction of the vernacular language and genres in vernacular form, the new literary reality was called on to reflect a new vision of national reality.

In a similar vein, Stephen Owen's essay examines the ideology and practices of the May Fourth reinvention of Chinese literary history. He observes how the May Fourth reinterpretation of the Chinese literary past was so efficiently disseminated that it became the unquestioned and unquestionable canon of our times. Certainly, the publicity for and distribution of May Fourth studies on traditional literature by the great publishing houses, such as the Commercial Press in Shanghai, were effective means of establishing this canon. But Owen marshals evidence to show that it was, in fact, the use of the May Fourth anthologies of classical literature in school education systems that served to fix this new reading of the Chinese literary heritage in the minds of young people. Owen's argument thus touches not only on the institutionalization of literary history as such but also on issues ranging from pedagogical rationales to the commercial production of literary heritage at a time of radical re-visioning of the Chinese past.

To clarify how the landscape of classical Chinese poetry was impoverished by the moderns, Owen compares three literary anthologies (published in 1924, 1927, and 1962) so compiled and arranged as to make the literary production of the past increasingly consonant with May Fourth conceptual literary histories. He also cites Hu Shi's *History of Vernacular Literature* as an example of the May Fourth conceptualization of the Chinese literary legacy. Hu's history upholds the vitality of the vernacular language, the exuberance of popular genres, and the inevitability of literary evolution. While Hu (and fellow critics such as Zheng Zhenduo) should be credited for incorporating into their canon hitherto less prestigious genres such as mythical narratives, *yuefu* 樂府, and *sanqu* 散曲 poetry, they show no less dogmatism in asserting their discoveries. To authenticate this new history, Hu works hard to emplot the past by imposing a beginning, middle, and end on the narrative, together with a full cast of protagonists and antagonists. "The enemy is an elite, rhetorical, and ornamental writing." His scenario has since become an orthodoxy in the modern curriculum of classical literature. Owen indicates much reservation about Hu's and his colleagues' methodology, which he believes is deeply ingrained in ideological motivations. For him the richness of classical Chinese literature can never be reduced to any formulaic dichotomy such as elitism versus populism or a "vital" style versus a "sick" style. With Yuan *sanqu* poetry as his example, Owen wonders that "except by the criterion of 'vitality,' which is one stylistically coded value within a tradition that had many values, it is very hard to maintain that Yuan *sanqu* has much to offer the reader of poetry" when compared to the bulk of "elite" and "ornate" works rejected by the May Fourth readers.

Owen's survey draws attention to the May Fourth literati's predilection for the "narrative" and the "polemical" in rewriting literary history. He thus echoes the argument made by Leo Lee on the rhetorical nature of the May Fourth discourse in general. The May Fourth literary history "required new heroes, polemics, and complex negotiations with the inertia of earlier judgments. It required new anthologies with guiding headnotes to make these new judgments 'self-evident.'" On the other hand, his argument resonates in a subtle way with Wagner's observation that the seemingly spontaneous project of enlightenment is motivated by a calculated endeavor, one grounded in the material disposition of cultural and symbolic capital. Owen concludes on an ironic note: "Now the enemy is dead; [the May Fourth scholarship] has supplanted that tradition. But since the values of the May Fourth critics and scholars were so deeply tied to their narrative of struggle, we must wonder what remains when the Antagonist is dead."

The final contribution to Part II, Ellen Widmer's study of the May Fourth rewriting of the history of China's female authors and the literature they produced contradicts the claim of May Fourth intellectuals that they possessed a special enlightenment concerning the question of women. Widmer begins with Hu Wenkai's 胡文楷 1957 work, *Research on Chinese Women's Writings Through the Ages* (*Lidai funü zhuzuo kao* 歷代婦女著作考), which lists "at least three hundred women who published their poems during the Ming dynasty and over four thousand for the Qing." The boom of feminine literary creativity in late imperial China and its impact on modern Chinese women writers, nevertheless, was downplayed in the hands of May Fourth scholars, arguably *because of* their own feminist agenda. Widmer's survey indicates not just that May Fourth leaders disregarded evidence that might have made their feminism look less pathbreaking, but rather that "the 'burden' of their break with feudalism was so total as to submerge evidence of this old system's own efforts at self-reform." The force of this repression, Widmer argues, "lends credence to a recent formulation by Homi Bhabha on national myth-making to the effect that 'disavowal, displacement, exclusion, and cultural contestation,' along with 'affiliation and establishment,' are crucial to the process through which late blooming nationalisms assert themselves."

Widmer examines three histories of Chinese women's literature by famous May Fourth scholars of the 1930s, Zheng Zhenduo's *History of Chinese Popular Literature* (*Zhongguo su wenxue shi*, 1938), Tan Zhengbi's 譚正璧 *Historical Discussion of Chinese Women's Literature* (*Zhongguo nüxing wenxue shihua* 中國女性文學史話, 1930), and Liang Yizhen's 梁乙真 *History of Qing Dynasty Women's Literature* (*Qingdai funü wenxue shi* 清代婦女文學史, 1925). She focuses particularly on the rise of the *tanci* 彈詞 narrative, a genre perfected in the hands of women in the late Ming and Qing periods. She notes that although both Zheng Zhenduo and Tan Zhengbi warmly espouse women's literature, they are not lacking in bias. Zheng highlighted women and the *tanci* tradition to the exclusion of their achievements in other genres; Tan ignored the role of male sponsorship in women's creative process as if overcompensating for the unbalanced record of female writing in the past. By comparison, Liang Yizhen's research on Qing women poets appears less impeded by a "gendered" agenda. Still, Liang is to be faulted for obscuring the role that Manchu scholars and aristocrats played in fostering women's literary activities. As Widmer points out, this "act of erasure" enabled May Fourth leaders to submerge evidence that many women became writers under Manchu rule, lest the Manchu reign appear more tolerant than a Han Chinese government.

Widmer's examination of these and other May Fourth editorial strategies attests that, as in the case of May Fourth literary histories in general, the history of women's writing was made subject to May Fourth ideological constructs. In this regard, she reiterates Doleželová and Owen's arguments. What distinguishes Widmer's article is her analysis of the skewed dialogue between literary history, gender polemics, and nationalism. Although she pays due respect to the May Fourth historians' revisionist works, she sees their contribution to Chinese literary modernization as lying not in their success but in their inability to articulate the complex relations between men and women, modern and classical, literature and national politics. These historians, accordingly, demonstrate what Leo Lee calls an "incomplete modernity."

In Part III, Catherine Vance Yeh and David D. W. Wang reopen the dialectic of history and its literary representation by venturing into the world of contemporary literature. Whereas Yeh deals with one of the most contested discourses of the 1980s—the search for roots literature—David Wang explores the many trends in fictional experimentation in the 1990s. Both link their subjects with literature of earlier periods. Yeh ponders the ties between roots literature and the May Fourth legacy of New Culture, and Wang examines late twentieth-century fiction in light of late Qing fiction. In this way, they engage themselves in the unfinished May Fourth project of rewriting literary history while at the same time critiquing the "blindness and insight" of their May Fourth predecessors.

In "Root Literature of the 1980s: May Fourth as a Double Burden," Yeh observes the surge of the "Search for Roots" (*xungen* 尋 根) literature after the death of Mao Zedong. As Yeh points out, the decade after the Cultural Revolution was a challenging time for the young generation of Chinese writers, particularly those who had grown up in the "ten-year turmoil," for they were no longer taken in by the party mythology and party leadership. Denied access to the multiple roots of Chinese modernity by the success of the May Fourth movement in asserting its vision of the past, they tend to see the May Fourth as the harbinger not of enlightenment but of hegemony on the political, cultural, and intellectual fronts. To them, the destruction of Chinese culture during the Cultural Revolution may amount to an uncanny repetition of the May Fourth rejection of the past. This limited view of the May Fourth demonstrates to a considerable extent the negative legacy of the New Culture movement. As they come to terms with their literary and cultural identities, late twentieth-century Chinese writers confront three challenges. First, long confined by a monolithic political rule, they have to rediscover the plural strains underneath Chinese modernity. Second, they need to cross the May Fourth threshold and re-enter the immense world of premodern Chinese literature. Third, after years of being denied access to foreign resources, they are obliged to catch up with literary trends in the rest of the world.

The ties between contemporary Chinese writers and their May Fourth predecessors are ambivalent. Despite their vehement attacks on the radical revolutions and movements traceable to May Fourth, they are now engaged in a process that is not too different from that celebrated by their May Fourth predecessors: a belief in the multiple roots of the Chinese humanities, a critical reassessment of a classical heritage, and an espousal of Western treasures. Yeh poses the question: How did it happen that contemporary writers are trying to sever their ties to (the official version of) the May Fourth on the one hand while recapitulating an agenda reminiscent of that of the May Fourth on the other? Yeh argues that this ambivalence was compounded when these writers confronted what they saw as a worldwide trend of "seeking cultural roots." The desire for "national culture," therefore, was intensified as no more than a "response to the West." Hence Yeh's observation that the "search for [cultural] roots" was impeded by strong tendencies to return once again to the archetypal May Fourth pattern—adulation of foreign literature, didacticism, appropriation of "popular" culture—all inevitably leading to a familiar dead-end.

Yeh carefully traces out the "roots" of roots literature by delineating the post-Mao writers' interactions with the party line as well as their dialogue with the May Fourth agenda. She notes that literature served for the root writers and critics as a metaphor for a more comprehensive construct of Chinese culture. While Yeh gives full credit to these writers' and critics' commitment to their newly found cause, she expresses reservation about their goals. For all its courage and instinctive drive to find a means to rejuvenate Chinese culture, the root movement, argues Yeh, was doomed from the outset. Like the May Fourth writers, the roots writers also tried to use the novel as a means to build a new national cultural consciousness, but compared with their forerunners, they were badly equipped for such a task. After years of being denied linguistic and literary resources, the cultural construct they so eagerly tried to grasp may be no more to them than a mirage. For example, the classical language, which they had been taught to reject in the name of modernization, now became, in their hopes and fantasies, the very tool that would enable them to discover new strengths in ancient Chinese culture. But because of a lack of knowledge of how to use this tool, the door that might have led to a rediscovery of new values in the past and thereby to the resurrection of Chinese culture remained locked. "The 'cultural revival' accordingly is not born out of a living link with this tradition, but comes from the search for literary inspiration outside the overdefined social realities of contemporary mainland China." As both a totem and a taboo, the May Fourth legacy constitutes a double burden for the young writers.

Chinese fiction of the 1990s, from Taiwan and Hong Kong as well as mainland China, has flourished, resulting in a flood of bizarre, baroque, and grotesque products. With its attractive ugliness, this literature has prodded critics to rethink the ambiguous energy of this literary outburst. Unlike most contemporary scholars, who, as a rule, attempt to grade Chinese modernity by the degree of its identity with Occidental counterparts, David Wang suggests an alternative approach: to show how Chinese contemporary literature is both modern and different, pointing out that "not all modernities were exhausted in Western practice." In so doing, Wang refuses to regard the May Fourth era as the sole source of literary modernization. Instead he chooses to compare late twentieth-century Chinese fiction with that from the late Qing period, seeking clues and traces that enable us "to recognize anew the complex voices in the formation of modern Chinese literature."

Specifically, Wang describes four of the dominant late Qing and late twentieth-century fictional discourses—social exposé, chivalric and court-case cycles, depravity romances, and science fantasy—and examines how these discourses, later suppressed by the May Fourth master narrative, have lent themselves to the dialogue on contemporary Chinese modernities. As Wang puts it, these genres have significantly "undermined the traditional (May Fourth) approaches to modern China and modern Chinese literature, approaches that were bound by a mimesis-oriented canon of realism, a yearning for a total equation between ink and blood, a censorious impulse to redirect libidinous consciousness into an ideologically sanitized space, writing, and revolution, and a reinforcement of History and Truth at the expense of an understanding of individual dreams and fantasies."

As does Catherine Yeh, Wang uses fiction as a reference point in the more comprehensive issue of modern Chinese cultural renovation. For him the four genres under discussion have to be understood as fictional representations of four discourses of most concern in Chinese modernity: desire, value, justice, and truth/knowledge. By setting late twentieth-century and late Qing Chinese fiction side by side, Wang is not arguing for historical causality; rather, he means to invoke an allegorical reading of modern Chinese literary history and to ask: "If late twentieth-century Chinese literature recapitulates some of the highlights of late Qing literature, does it mean that we have not gotten very far beyond the program of the first generation of modern writers? Or does it mean our modernist endeavor has taken us full circle since May Fourth, back to where we started a century ago?"

Wang argues that the energy exhibited by these fictional modes arises from the inversion and negation of the canonized May Fourth model, just as late Qing fiction gained energy through negation and inversion of hitherto prevalent aesthetic norms. Wang's initiative "to look not only into areas whose modernity has been admitted but also into areas whose modernity has been denied" should prove especially significant for future studies of modern Chinese literature. To recognize the modernities in twentieth-century Chinese literature is again to engage in literary history not as a linear construct but as one involving multiple traffickings. Western stimuli notwithstanding, Wang concludes, Chinese literature derived its modernity no less from the inherent dynamism of its own tradition.

In the concluding essay of this volume, "Neither Renaissance nor Enlightenment: A Historian's Reflections on the May Fourth Movement," Ying-shih Yü examines how the concept of the May Fourth movement itself became a foundation on which competing factions carried out incompatible projects. Yü surveys the origins of the two characterizations most often associated with the May Fourth—the Chinese Renaissance and the Chinese Enlightenment—and concludes that both "Renaissance" and "Enlightenment" were imposed on the May Fourth to serve specific purposes, with long-lasting cultural and political consequences. The notion of May Fourth as the "Chinese Renaissance" was promoted by Hu Shi on a lecture tour in England in 1926; the term itself originated with the English subtitle, *The Renaissance*, of the magazine *New Tide* (*Xinchao* 新潮), founded by Hu Shi and his friends in 1918. The notion of the "Chinese Enlightenment" stems from the New Enlightenment movement mobilized by Chinese Communists in 1935, particularly the political activists Chen Boda 陳伯達 (1904–89) and Ai Siqi 艾思奇 (1910–66). Yü notes the fundamental difference between these two appellations in terms of motivation and subsequent political significance. Whereas "Chinese Renaissance" is conceptually rooted in Anglo-American liberalism, with an emphasis on progressive, modern

Western institutions and learning in the most general sense, "Chinese Enlightenment" refers to a well-orchestrated *movement*, precisely as defined by Rudolf Wagner in his chapter, concocted in the service of Communist propaganda.

Yü's survey of the invention and implementation of Chinese Renaissance and Chinese Enlightenment demonstrates that however distorted the way in which the two Western notions were appropriated by Chinese intellectuals, the Chinese (mis)representations deserve serious study. For Yü, Renaissance suggested to Hu Shi and his followers "renovation rather than destruction of the Chinese tradition." Despite his image as a total iconoclast, "central to the notion of Renaissance was Hu Shi's belief in the possibility of breathing new life into the old civilization of China." In contrast, "Enlightenment" was invoked by the Communists to facilitate both a well-planned political project and the single timetable prescribed by Marxist historicism. This Enlightenment project "was ultimately revolution-oriented, with the emphasis squarely placed on patriotism and national salvation," as opposed to the Renaissance project, which highlighted intellectual autonomy. Both, however, failed to achieve the utopian goals promised by their leaders, and it became apparent that parallels drawn between these two terms and their Western counterparts were inadequate.

Moreover, Yü ponders the paradox that those who appeared to hold to the radical agenda in the heyday of the New Culture movement might harbor conventional thoughts, whereas those who have been labeled conservatives might be responsible for some of the most innovative achievements. Based on evidence of newly published correspondence, Yü finds "conservative critics of the May Fourth movement to be no less critical [of Confucianism] and no less Westernized than their 'progressive' rivals." Yü aligns himself with the growing demand to place the cultural conservatism of Mei Guangdi 梅光迪 (1890–1945) and Wu Mi 吳宓 (1894–1978), along with the radicalism of Chen Duxiu and Lu Xun and the liberalism of Hu Shi, in the same discursive structure of May Fourth New Culture (see Lin 1979: 396–402; and Yue 1990: 264–66). Only with such multiple entry points to May Fourth can one really appreciate it as "an age of cultural contradictions," an age of "multidimensionality and multidirectionality."

Ying-shih Yü's essay, pointedly subtitled "A Historian's Reflections," uncovers a plurality in the May Fourth movement that is not apparent in its proclamations and cultural policy on literature and language and thus provides an alternative way of looking at the May Fourth movement as a historical event. His essay throws the thrust of this book into relief, demonstrating that its aim rests in the clarification not so much of the May Fourth movement per se but of what it came to mean as a cultural legacy.

This book argues the double bind of the May Fourth legacy. Taking up where Chinese literati and intellectuals left off in the late Qing and the 1910s, the May Fourth advocates did open a ground of pluralism that promised modernities. But at the same time they sowed the seeds of monologic hegemony that eventually dominated the literary, cultural, and political discourse of modern China. How this double bind arose and how its establishment, its reiteration, its transmission, and its aftereffects have influenced the way we inscribe the Chinese modern across most of the twentieth century constitutes this volume's true subject.

We emphasize that we do not mean to deny the rich contribution of May Fourth. Rather, we believe that once the "burdens of May Fourth" are better understood, we can engage ourselves in an even more resourceful dialogue with its legacies. We hope that Chinese literary works can be read anew from wider perspectives and that cultural and political issues once denigrated can be brought back for deliberation. These include the thriving short story of the 1910s, the sophisticated literary theories of the same period, classical Chinese poetry of modern times, avant-garde and popular literary genres, the fusion of literary and non-literary texts, and literature from Chinese communities other than the mainland. We hope that, in turn, these newfound territories for research will foster a revival of studies of this period and reinstate the goal of openness and pluralism of the New Culture movement. From this viewpoint, the history of twentieth-century Chinese literature will no longer be constricted by the narrowly defined discourse of the May Fourth Movement but will finally expand to cover the full variety and momentum of the May Fourth and all that followed upon it.

Works Cited

Anderson, Benedict. 1991. *Imagined Communities*. London: Verso.

Anderson, Marston. 1990. *The Limits of Realism: Chinese Fiction in the Revolutionary Period*. Berkeley: University of California Press.

———. 1991. "Zheng Zhenduo and the Invention of Chinese Literary History." Unpublished paper delivered at the "The Burdens of the May Fourth Movement" workshop, held on May 11, 1991, at the John King Fairbank Research Center, Harvard University.

Bonner, Joey. 1986. *Wang Kuo-wei: An Intellectual Biography*. Cambridge, Mass.: Harvard University Press.

Boven, Henri van. 1946. *Histoire de la littérature chinoise moderne*. Peiping: n.p.

Brière, O., S.J. 1948. "Les tendances dominantes de la littérature chinoise contemporaine." *Bulletin de l'Université de l'Aurore* 3, no. 9 (1948): 248–69.

Chen Bingkun 陳炳坤. 1930. *Zuijin sanshi nian Zhongguo wenxue shi* 最近三十年中國文學史 (A history of Chinese literature of the past thirty years). Shanghai: Taiping yang shudian.

Chen Duxiu 陳獨秀. [1917] 1954. "Wenxue geming lun" 文學革命論 (On literary revolution). *Xin qingnian* 2, no. 6: 1–4 (paginated separately). Reprinted—Beijing: Xinhua shudian. See also *Hu Shi wencun* 胡適文存 (Hu Shi's collected works), 1: 24–28. Shanghai: Yadong tushuguan, 1921.

Chen Pingyuan 陳平原. [1989] 1997. *Ershi shiji Zhongguo xiaoshuo shi, diyi juan (1897–1916)* 二十世紀中國小說史, 第一卷 (A history of twentieth-century Chinese fiction, vol. 1. 1897–1916). Reprinted—Beijing: Beijing daxue chubanshe.

Chow Tse-tsung. [1960] 1969. *The May Fourth Movement: Intellectual Revolution in Modern China*. Cambridge, Mass. 1960. Reprinted—Stanford: Stanford University Press. 1969.

Ding Yi 丁易. 1955. *Zhongguo xiandai wenxue shilüe* 中國現代文學史略 (A brief history of modern Chinese literature). Beijing: Zuojia.

Doleželová-Velingerová, Milena, ed. 1980. *The Chinese Novel at the Turn of the Century*. Toronto: University of Toronto Press.

Duara, Prasenjit. 1995. *Rescuing History from the Nation: Questioning Narratives of Modern China*. Chicago: University of Chicago Press.

Fitzgerald, John. 1996. *Awakening China: Politics, Culture, and Class in the Nationalistic Revolution*. Stanford: Stanford University Press.

Fu Donghua 傅東華. 1937. "Shi nian lai de Zhongguo wenyi" 十年來的中國文藝 (Chinese literature of the last ten years), in Fan Zhongyun 樊仲雲, ed., *Shi nian lai de Zhongguo* 十年來的中國 (China of the last ten years), pp. 659–86. Shanghai: n.p.

Goldman, Merle. 1977. *Modern Chinese Literature in the May Fourth Era*. Cambridge, Mass: Harvard University Press.

Habermas, Jürgen. 1989. *The Structural Transformation of the Public Sphere*. Cambridge, Mass.: MIT Press.

Hanan, Patrick. 1981. *The Chinese Vernacular Story*. Cambridge, Mass: Harvard University Press.

Hsia, C. T. 1961. *A History of Modern Chinese Fiction*. New Haven: Yale University Press.

Hu Shi 胡適. 1921. *Hu Shi wencun* 胡適文存一集 (First collection of Hu Shi's collected works). Shanghai: Yadong tushuguan. 2 vols.

———. [1923] 1924. *Hu Shi wencun* 胡適文存二集 (Second collection of Hu Shi's collected works), Shanghai: Yadong tushuguan. 2 vols.

———. 1928. *Baihua wenxue shi* 白話文學史 (A history of [Chinese] vernacular literature). Shanghai: Xin yue shudian.

Hu, Ying. 2000. *Tales of Translation*. Stanford: Stanford University Press.

Huters, Theodore. 1988. "A New Way of Writing: The Possibilities for Literature in Late Qing China, 1895–1908." *Modern China* 14, no. 3: 243–76.

Judge, Joan. 1996. *Print and Politics: "Shibao" and the Culture of Reform in Late Qing China*. Stanford: Stanford University Press.

Král, Oldřich. 1964a. "Several Artistic Methods in the Classic Chinese Novel *Ju-lun wai-shih*." *Archiv Orientalni* 32 (1964): 16–43.

———. 1964b. "Some Artistic Methods in the Classic Chinese Novel *Ju-lin wai-shih*." *Acta Universitatis Carolinae—Philologica* 3 (1964): 79–102.

Lin Liyue 林麗月. 1979. "Mei Guangdi yu Xin wenhua yundong" 梅光迪與新文化運動 (Mei Guangdi and the New Culture movement). In Wang Rongzu 王榮祖, ed., *Wusi yanjiu lunwen ji* 五四研究論文集 (Collected studies on May Fourth), pp. 383–402. Taibei: Lianjing.

Link, E. Perry. 1981. *Mandarin Ducks and Butterflies:. Popular Fiction in Early Twentieth-Century Chinese Cities*. Berkeley: University of California Press.

Liu, Lydia, H. 1995. *Translingual Practice: Literature, National Culture, and Translated Modernity—China, 1900–1937*. Stanford: Stanford University Press.

Liu, Ts'un-yan, ed. 1984. *Chinese Middle-brow Fiction*. Hong Kong: Renditions.

Ng, Mau-sang. 1988. *The Russian Hero in Modern Chinese Fiction*. Albany: State University of New York.

Plaks, Andrew H. 1987. *The Four Masterworks of the Ming Novel: Ssu ta ch'i-shu*. Princeton: Princeton University Press.

Průšek, Jaroslav. 1955. *Die Literatur des befreiten China und ihre Volkstraditionen*. Prague: Artia.

———. [1957] 1980. "Subjectivism and Individualism in Modern Chinese Literature." *Archív orientální* 25: 261–83. Reprinted in idem, *The Lyrical and the Epic: Stud-*

ies of Modern Chinese Literature, ed. Leo Ou-fan Lee, pp. 1–28. Bloomington: Indiana University Press.

———. [1964] 1980. "Introduction to Studies in Modern Chinese Literature," in idem, ed., *Studies in Modern Chinese Literature*, 1–40. Berlin: Akademie Verlag. Reprinted in idem, *The Lyrical and the Epic. Studies in Modern Chinese Literature*, ed. Leo Ou-fan Lee, pp. 29–73. Bloomington: Indiana University Press, 1980.

Schyns, Joseph, et al. 1948. *1500 Modern Chinese Novels and Plays*. Peiping: Catholic University Press.

Shimada Masao 島田政雄. 1952. *Chūgoku shinbungaku nyūmon* 中國新文學入門 (Introduction to new Chinese literature). Tokyo: Hato shoba.

Sun Shangyang 孫尚揚 and Guo Lanfang 郭蘭芳, eds. 1995. *Guogu xin zhi lun—Xueheng pai wenhua lunzhu jiyao* 國故新知論—學衡派文化論著輯要 (Discourses on new knowledge and the national heritage: essential discourses on culture by the *Critical Review* group). Beijing: Zhongguo guangbo dianshi chubanshe.

Tang Xiaobing. 1966. *Global Space and the Nationalist Discourse of Modernity*. Stanford: Stanford University Press.

Wang, David Der-wei. 1992. *Fictional Realism in Twentieth-Century China: Mao Dun, Lao She, Shen Congwen*. New York: Columbia University Press.

———. 1997. *Fin-de-Siècle Splendor. Repressed Modernities of Late Qing Fiction, 1849–1911*. Stanford: Stanford University Press.

Wang Hui. 1995. "The Fate of 'Mr. Science' in China: The Concept of Science and Its Application in Modern Chinese Thought." *positions* 3, no. 1: 1–68.

Wang Yao 王瑤. 1951 and 1953. *Zhongguo xin wenxue shi gao* 中國新文學史稿 (A draft history of China's new literature). Vol. 1: Beijing: Kaiming shudian; vol. 2: Shanghai: Xin wenyi.

Wang Zhefu 王哲甫. 1933. *Zhongguo xin wenxue yundong shi* 中國新文學運動史 (A history of the new literary movement). Beiping: n.p.

Widmer, Ellen, and David Der-wei Wang, eds. 1993. *From May Fourth to June Fourth: Fiction and Film in Twentieth-Century China*. Cambridge, Mass.: Harvard University Press.

Yü, Ying-shih. 1994. "Changing Conceptions of National History in Twentieth-Century China." In Erik Lönnroth, Karl Molin, and Ragnar Björk, eds., *Conceptions of National History: Proceedings of Nobel Symposium 78*, pp. 155–74. Berlin: Walter de Gruyter.

Yue Daiyun 樂黛雲. 1990. "Shijie wenhua duihua zhong de Zhongguo xiandai baoshouzhuyi" 世界文化對話中的中國現代保守主義 (A survey of *Critical Review*: modern Chinese conservatism in the dialogue on world cultures). In Li Funing 李賦寧, Sun Tianyi 孫天義, and Cai Heng 蔡恆, eds., *Diyi jie Wu Mi xueshu taolunhui lunwen xuanji* 第一屆吳宓學術討論會論文選集

(Selected papers from the first scholarly conference on Wu Mi), pp. 253–75. Xi'an: Shaanxi renmin jiaoyu.

Zheng Zhenduo 鄭振鐸. [1923] 1985. "Zhengli guogu yu xin wenxue yundong de faduan" 正理國故與新文學運動的發端 (Reorganization of the cultural heritage and the beginnings of the New Literature movement). Reprinted in Jia Zhifang, Su Xingliang, Liu Yulian, Zhou Chundong, and Li Yuzhen, eds., *Wenxue yanjiu hui ziliao* 文學研究會資料 (Materials on the Association for Literary Research), 1: 275–76. Henan: Henan renmin.

———. [1932] 1982. "Zixu" 自序 (Preface). In *Chatuben Zhongguo wenxue shi* 插圖本中國文學史 (Illustrated history of Chinese literature), p. 1. Reprinted—Beijing: Renmin wenxue.

———. [1938] 1954. *Zhongguo su wenxue shi* 中國俗文學史 (History of Chinese popular literature). Reprinted—Beijing: Zuojia.

Zhou Zuoren 周作人. 1932. *Zhongguo xin wenxue de yuanliu* 中國新文學的源流 (Origins of new Chinese literature). Beiping: Renwen shudian.

PART I

Formation of the May Fourth Cultural Project: Discourse and Practices

CHAPTER ONE

Incomplete Modernity: Rethinking the May Fourth Intellectual Project

Leo Ou-fan Lee

To place the May Fourth intellectual project in a framework of modernity requires some preliminary reflections on the problem of modernity itself: What does the word mean in its Western and Chinese contexts? How can we justify the usage of this amorphous term, with its complex historical underpinnings, instead of a term much preferred by Hu Shi 胡 適 (1891–1962) himself, "The Chinese Enlightenment"? And why did Hu Shi prefer this term to a more radical term, "revolution," which appealed to Chen Duxiu 陳 獨 秀 (1879–1942) (and later, Chow Tse-tsung)? Should we still follow the May Fourth leaders in considering this "movement" as marking a clear break with the past—and with Chinese "tradition"? In tackling these broad questions, I would like to offer some interpretive narratives based on my own reading of the historical sources of that period.

The Modern Background

In a way Chinese modernity was achieved, in Stephen Owen's phrase (see Chapter 4 in this volume), through a "performative declaration" as articulated by the word "new," *xin* 新. Ever since the late Qing there had been a proliferation of journal titles and terms including the word "new": from Liang Qichao's 梁 啓 超 (1873–1929) *New People* (*Xin min* 新 民) to Chen Duxiu's *New Youth* (*Xin qingnian* 新 青 年) to such ubiquitous compounds as "new tide," *xin chao* 新 潮, "new literature and art," *xin wenyi* 新 文 藝, "new life," *xin shenghuo* 新 生 活, "new society," *xin shehui* 新 社 會, and "new epoch," *xin shidai* 新 時 代. What makes for the qualitative difference in the

May Fourth formulation is that "the notion of newness is defined in a context of unilinear time and a unilinear sense of history" that was itself derived from the Chinese reception of a Western Darwinian concept of evolution. In this new temporal scheme, "present," *jin* 今, and "past," *gu* 古, became polarized as contrasting values, and the obvious emphasis was on the present moment "as the pivotal point marking a rupture with the past and forming a progressive continuum toward a glorious future" (Lee 1990: 110–11).

This new mode of time consciousness was, of course, a Western derivation and represented a concurrent desire on the part of some leading intellectuals to embrace a larger space, the modern world, in order to make China part of it. There can be no better early evidence than a prefatory entry in Liang Qichao's "Travels to Hawaii" ("Xiaweiyi youji" 夏威夷遊記), written in 1899 in diary form, in which he declared his own transformation from a provincial person to a national citizen and a man of the world, as his ship crossed the Pacific Ocean (1900: 185). To accompany his melodramatic declaration, he chose to date subsequent entries in his diary in the Western calendar, "for the sake of convenience" (Liang 1900: 186–87) as well as to mark off a crucial date when China entered the modern age (through the vision of a single man!). By sheer coincidence, Liang's gesture also ushered in the twentieth century. Seventeen years later, Chen Duxiu made an equally melodramatic proclamation in an essay called "The Year 1916" ("Yijiuyiliu nian" 一九一六年):

> The epoch in which you are living, which epoch is this? It is the beginning of the sixteenth year of the twentieth century. The changes of the world are evolutionary, different from month to month, year to year. The shining history is unfolding, faster and faster. . . . To live in the present world, you must raise your head and proudly call yourself a person of the twentieth century: you must create a new civilization of the twentieth century and not confine yourself to following that of the nineteenth. For the evolution of human civilization is replacing the old with the new, like a river flowing on, an arrow flying away, constantly continuing and constantly changing. (1916; quoted in Lee 1990: 114)

This twentieth-century consciousness signaled a concept of modernity as both evolution and rupture. The critical task for Chen and the May Fourth generation was to "create a new civilization"—a constructive project much more mammoth than their iconoclastic destruction of Chinese tradition. Although the two tasks formed integral parts of the same project to be carried out simultaneously, the iconoclastic one seems to have been given an undue weight. Much scholarship on the May Fourth has been preoccupied with, hence "wasted" on, its anti-traditionalism. In historical hindsight, it now seems quite clear that the May Fourth revolution did not destroy Chinese tradition; the leaders won an ideological battle, but not necessarily their war against tradition. But what about their constructive urging: "You must create a new civilization"? What constitutes a "new civilization," and how does one create it? This brings us to much thornier issues of modernity, which most scholars in Chinese studies seem unwilling and unprepared to tackle. The situation is further complicated at the present moment (at the turn of the twenty-first century) by the discourse of post-modernity, which has likewise been appropriated by another generation of Chinese intellectuals. How are we to reconstruct that historical discourse in China in full awareness of the current debate in the West: are we, inevitably, situated in a "post-modern condition" or should we still consider modernity an "incomplete project"? I am prepared to argue, although for reasons quite different from those of Habermas (1983: 3–15), that the Chinese project of modernity is also "incomplete" and that the entire May Fourth movement may be seen in this light.

To return to Chen Duxiu's statement, what does he mean by the words "new civilization"? As is well documented by now, the Chinese word *wenming* 文明 is a direct borrowing from the Japanese word *bunmei*, which in the Meiji discourse refers to modern Western civilization, especially in its manifestation of science and technology (Masini 1993: 204). By the time of Chen's call for a new civilization, the Meiji example had been in full view of Chinese intellectuals for at least two decades. According to Vera Schwarcz, even the May Fourth discourse of "enlightenment," *qimeng* 啓蒙, was taken from the Meiji experience: "Chinese intellectuals were so taken by this phenomenon [i.e., what was known as Japanese enlightenment], in fact, that they borrowed the word for enlightenment, *qimeng*, from the nineteenth-century Japanese intellectuals, who had called themselves 'enlightenment scholars,' *keimō gakusha*, which in Chinese is *qimeng xuezhe* (啓蒙學者)" (1986: 30). As the Japanese example shows, wholesale institutional reform must be "matched by a new worldview." Thus, one of the principal tasks of enlightenment in both Japan and China was to formulate a new worldview with which the leaders could then seek to enlighten the people. It was also obvious that in both countries the principal medium for such a task was seen to be education: the Chinese phrase itself, in particular, invokes the beginning of education in which a child received his first lesson from a teacher (often the first tutor) in learning how to read and write. That the term *qimeng* underwent a radical transformation and took on the added meaning of being awakened to a view of modernity should by no means eclipse its underlying implications of education. As Lu Xun's 魯 迅 (1881–1936) famous "Madman's Diary" ("Kuangren riji" 狂 人 日 記) indicates in its first sentence, written in the modern vernacular, the experience of enlightenment could be achieved through an epiphany, an act of sudden "en-lighten-ment" aided by moonlight (with its implications of lunacy).

If a new worldview could be declared at a single moment in a new vision, the construction of its new intellectual content and a new language to describe it was a more laborious task. For that entails not only the historical and intellectual "baggage" of European modernity but also China's sociopolitical and cultural situation at that moment—both mediated by the discourse of the intellectuals. I would like to suggest that Chinese intellectuals, while borrowing certain Western terms (via Japanese translation) to articulate a sense of Chinese modernity, were not engaged in the full semantic context of modern Western modernity. (Nor could we expect them to do so, because of obvious linguistic and cultural barriers.) For instance, the philosophic term "subjectivity" in the modern Western sense did not exactly exist in the late Qing and May Fourth vocabulary. The Japanese term *shutai* was used by philosophers perhaps in the 1930s; the Chinese term *zhuti* 主 體 was popularized in the 1980s by the literary theorist Liu Zaifu 劉 再 復. Recent scholarship has shown that the late Qing discourse of *gong* 公 and *si* 私 by Zhang Binglin 章炳 麟 (1868–1936) and the early Lu Xun was not only a far cry from the Japanese usage but differed considerably from that of the Western enlightenment tradition. The concept of *gong* was by no means the equivalent of the English word "public," whereas the words *si* and *ji* 己 had Confucian and Buddhist implications (Wang Hui et al. 1994: 598–605). (The views of Zhang and Lu Xun were more influenced by the latter and, in Lu Xun's essay "The Power of Mara Poetry" ["Moluo shili shuo" 摩 羅 詩 力 說], mixed with his reading of a strand of European anti-enlightenment ideas from Nietzsche and Max Stirner.) Thus, to construct a modern "subject" in China on the basis of partial knowledge of the West proves to be a most difficult task, certainly one more daunting than to "deconstruct" a Chinese tradition.

At the same time, ideas as articulated by intellectuals must not be separated from their own institutional background. To be sure, the reform of political institutions received top priority at the Qing court, but equally urgent was the creation of social institutions. (Again the term for "society," *shehui* 社 會, was probably coined around the same time from a Japanese term, which itself was an inversion of the more traditional term *kaisha* 會社 [Masini 1993: 195]. Needless to say, there was no conceptual demarcation between state and society in the late Qing.) We are reminded by Max Weber that the history of Western modernity involved a long process of rationalization in several realms of human activity, of which the government-initiated modernization effort was but a part. The consequence of such a process, which Weber calls "disenchantment," is by no means positive. According to recent critics, it has resulted in the triumph of *Zweckrationalität*, or "purposive-instrumental rationality" and the creation of an "iron cage" of bureaucratic rationality from which there is no escape. In a sense, Kafka's world of Joseph K could be read as an eloquent artistic evocation of Western modernity.

This familiar message did not, however, make a strong impression on early Chinese proponents of modernity. They were more concerned with the initial task of "envisioning"—of trying to draw the broad contours of a new China and to disseminate such a vision to their audience—a newly constructed "public" that consisted by and large of newspaper and journal readers and students in newly created schools. Like eighteenth-century French Enlightenment thinkers, whose ideas were popularized and vigorously disseminated by a network of printing and journalism, Chinese thinkers of the late Qing and early May Fourth period had to explore and invent new channels to reach their target audiences. The rise of commercial publishing, particularly large companies such as the Commercial Press (Shangwu yinshu guan 商 務 印 書 館) and the "Enlightened" Bookstore (Kaiming shudian 開 明 書 店), which made fortunes principally by compiling new textbooks and dictionaries, was by no means a historical accident. The large compendium *Eastern Repository* (*Dongfang wenku* 東 方 文 庫), sponsored by the journal *Eastern Miscellany* (*Dongfang zazhi* 東 方 雜 誌), was a clever publishing venture that transformed the traditional repository into a new device to introduce and popularize new knowledge. In so doing, it also served to recategorize the old. All these publishing enterprises are in some ways comparable to the French "Business of Enlightenment" as described by Robert

Darnton (1979).[1] A remarkable point of difference is that these Chinese books were quite cheap, whereas during the early phase of the French Enlightenment the cost of books was high, which severely restricted their initial readership, which consisted of liberal aristocrats and priests (Hampson 1982: 132–35).

In reaching out to a new audience, the late Qing print industry also succeeded in carving out a societal space "beside" the one dominated by the government. Whether it can be considered a new Chinese "public sphere" in the making is a hypothesis requiring careful thought and research. The late Qing socioeconomic background was certainly different from that of modern Europe where the thriving market economy provided a basis for "print capitalism." In China there were no salons in which to conduct free discussions of politics without governmental interference. (Chinese teahouses were not intended to foster a democratic spirit.) But we also find something extremely exciting in the late Qing project: these writers and publishers were defining a new nation at the same time as they sought to define a new reading public. However, among recent Western theorists, neither Benedict Anderson nor Jürgen Habermas has seen fit to connect the two phenomena. Anderson has drawn our attention to the crucial function of newspapers and journals in establishing the "imagined community" of the modern nation (1991: 24–25). Habermas has pointed to the close connection between journals and salons, which in turn contributed to the formation of the public sphere and civil society in England and France (1991: 40). In the late Qing period, it would seem, the overriding concern of public discourse was not so much civil society as nationalism. Late Qing newspapers and journals became important precisely because they served to establish a new "public space" for the relatively open discussion of envisioning the modern nation—what a new China should be like—against the background of present sociopolitical reality.

It is in this regard that I find my research turning increasingly from ideas to institutions—from the selected texts of a few famous men to the larger

1. The following conclusion by Darnton about the publishing business is especially relevant: "The publishers emphasized that their customers would get a compendium of modern knowledge and a synthesis of modern philosophy, all in one. In this respect, they carried out the strategy of Diderot and d'Alembert, who wanted to promote *philosophie* by identifying it with knowledge" (1979: 523). The equivalent Chinese term at this time was "new knowledge," *xin zhi* 新智, and publishing ventures like the *Dongfang wenku* served to promote new knowledge by a massive compendium.

context of cultural production. In my view, the project of Chinese modernity was both intellectual and "material"—a societal task initiated by a few elite scholars but carried out by a large number of people: publishers, editors, writers, and translators in a mushrooming number of new governmental and nongovernmental institutions. These "organic intellectuals" and their new "media" not only laid the groundwork for the May Fourth intellectual movement but also accounted in large part for its success. This is a familiar thesis, but to unfold the details of such a story requires several monographs, even a team research effort. In this chapter, I can only use the two most successful journalistic enterprises as a starting point of comparison with the May Fourth journals: the newspaper the *Shanghai News* (*Shenbao* 申 報) and the popular journal *Eastern Miscellany*.

It is worth noting that both the *Shanghai News* (founded in 1872) and the *Eastern Miscellany* (founded in 1904) had enjoyed several decades of popularity before the journal *Youth* (*Qingnian* 青 年) was established in 1915 (retitled *New Youth* by Chen Duxiu in September 1916, the year that marked his adoption of the Western calendar). To reiterate a point made above, the success of the two journalistic publications means that an urban print medium had made it possible for intellectuals to conceive of a new "imagined community" of the reading public. In the case of the *Shanghai News*, that community of readers was defined in a new format, the literary supplement page called "Free Discourse" ("Ziyou tan" 自 由 談). It marked the beginning of a new feature in modern Chinese journalism (the term more common today, *fukan* 副 刊, was probably first used in the early 1920s by the *Morning Post* [*Chenbao* 晨報] of Beijing). I have written elsewhere about this interesting feature, in which we find discussions of current politics, issues such as "strengthening the [Chinese] race" (*qiang zhong* 強 種), Western science and technology, and ways of imagining a new nation (Lee 1993). Some of the columns in this page, written in the "literary language," *wenyan* 文 言, and deriving their persuasive power from clever reinventions of traditional literary genres (poetry, commentary essay, *yuefu* 樂 府, as well as the serialized novel), contain sarcastic critiques of the new body politic: for instance, one feature was called "Playful Compositions" ("Youxi wenzhang" 遊 戲 文 章) and aimed both to entertain and to enlighten readers.[2] Although it is

2. These columns can be compared to the *feuilletons* that emerged in the 1840s in Europe, which are also a part of the contents of newspapers and journals designed to entertain and enlighten the general readers. Interestingly, it was not until the early 1930s that Qu Qiubai 瞿

still uncertain how many of the pseudonymous authors of these compositions were mere disguises of the editor(s), the paper published as early as 1911 an "open call" for contributions from its readers in the form of poetry, *ci*, songs, and anecdotes, as well as playful and humorous pieces. Thus something of a public domain of letters was formed, in which a dialogue in literary forms was made possible. The "Free Discourse" page had another noteworthy feature (a practice the paper had adopted years earlier): both Chinese and Western dates were printed on top of the columns—the Western date on the left, the Chinese date on the right. Thus on the eve of the Republican Revolution, a silent revolution in print was already under way: the editors of the newspaper had clearly followed Liang Qichao's example and imprinted a modern time consciousness in the popular imagination. The "homogeneous, empty time" that Anderson (1991: 25) attributes to the functions of the modern novel and the modern newspaper is achieved without great generic flourish in the daily pages of the *Shanghai News*.

The principal editor and author of the "Free Discourse" page in those years was Wang Dungen 王 鈍 根 (b. 1888), a founder of the so-called Saturday School (Libailiu pai 禮 拜 六 派), who was also in charge of two other journals, *Playful Magazine* (*Youxi zazhi* 遊 戲 雜 誌) and *Saturday Weekly* (*Libailiu zhoukan* 禮 拜 六 週 刊) (Zhang 1938: 34–35). Wang had sponsored the writings of Zhou Shoujuan 周 瘦 鵑 (1895–1968) and together with Bao Tianxiao 包 天 笑 (1876–1973) and others had dominated the literary publication scene in the 1910s. The "Saturday" School also controlled *The Short Story Monthly* (*Xiaoshuo yuebao* 小 說 月 報) until Mao Dun 茅 盾 (1896–1981) assumed power in 1920 and turned the journal into a vehicle for the New Literature. The received account of this celebrated episode is as misleading as it is self-serving: for nearly half a century we have been led to believe that the Saturday School of writers espoused a traditional outlook since they were denigrated by the May Fourth leaders like Mao Dun. Recent "revisionist" scholarship has shown that the establishment of the Association for Literary Studies, together with Mao Dun's assumption of the editorship of *The Short Story Monthly*, was a well-calculated power play by Mao Dun to establish cultural hegemony (Wang Xiaoming 1993: 149–85). The writers and edi-

---

秋 白 (1899–1935) formally used the French term to describe Lu Xun's *zawen* 雜 文, or "miscellaneous essays," thereby giving the word a high degree of seriousness. As a consequence of Lu Xun's style and the changed sociopolitical situation of that time, the connotation of "entertainment" was lost.

tors of the Saturday School were cast into an ideological backwater and given the disparaging epithet School of Butterflies and Mandarin Ducks, Yuanyang hudie pai 鴛鴦蝴蝶派 (see introduction to Link 1981). As will be apparent to anyone who reads the pages of "Free Discourse" produced under Wang Dungen and Zhou Shoujuan, these journalist-litterateurs behind the *Shanghai News*, *Short Story Monthly*, and *Eastern Miscellany* were by no means behind the times; rather, they were pioneers of Chinese modernity, whose contributions were intentionally eclipsed by the May Fourth leaders through a series of polemics (see Hsia 1982; Fong 1982 as summarized in Doleželová-Velingerová 1988: 19). One of the earliest instances of such a polemic revolves around, in fact, the issue of modernity itself. It began in 1918 with Chen Duxiu's devastating critique of three articles published in *Eastern Miscellany*, an act that pitted the newcomer *New Youth* against an old established journal. The debate has been all but forgotten.

Power Through Polemics

Like the *Shanghai News*, *Eastern Miscellany* may be considered a "middlebrow" publication brought under the aegis of the Commercial Press for an urban readership. Its table of contents shows its eclectic quality: journalistic reports and political commentaries are combined with cultural critiques, translations, and, occasionally, learned articles. The editor from 1911 to 1920 was Du Yaquan 杜亞泉, a "transitional" intellectual very much in the late Qing reformist mode: a pioneer thinker who had translated several books on modern science and philosophy but who was unwilling to embrace total Westernization. In April 1918, Du (using the pseudonym Cang Fu 傖父) published in his journal an article entitled "The Confusion of the Modern Mind" ("Miluan zhi xiandai renxin" 迷亂之現代人心), which was apparently inspired by an article from a Japanese journal, "A Critique of Chinese and Western Civilizations" ("Zhongxi wenming zhi pipan" 中西文明之批判), translated probably by Du and published two months later together with another article written by Du's friend and successor as editor, Qian Zhixiu 錢智修 (1883–1947), titled "Utilitarianism and Scholarship" ("Gonglizhuyi yu xueshu" 公利主義與學術). The three articles elicited two pointed rebuttals from Chen Duxiu in his journal, *New Youth*, in September 1918 and February 1919, both entitled "Questioning the Editors of the *Eastern Miscellany*" ("Zhiwen *Dongfang zazhi* jizhe" 質問東方雜誌記者). Not only did Chen's eloquence and scathing critique seem to win the battle, but the polemic apparently cost Du his job: he was forced by circumstances to resign as editor in 1920 and stopped writing for the journal altogether.

The three articles are not exceptional in manifesting their professed disillusionment with the outcome of Western modernity: like many other articles published in the same journal, they were a reaction to World War I, which in Du's view caused spiritual bankruptcy and confusion in Europe. What made Du's article an obvious target was his strong defense of the continuity of Chinese tradition. In his opinion the history of Western civilization was marked by confusions and contradictions caused by the displacement and destruction of one intellectual strand by another. "Therefore," Du wrote, "although the Westerners have achieved success in wealth and power, spiritually they are extremely troubled—like a rich man who wears brocade and eats meat, and calculates about his fortune but is deeply worried about his unsettled family and household. He is ill in both body and mind" (Cang 1918: 6). This Western crisis, according to Du, has also led to a kind of spiritual bankruptcy in contemporary China, where "the spirit of the majority of the people has been utterly engulfed in material life" (Cang 1918: 3). Du's main point, the salvation he offered to his compatriots to deliver them from their spiritual malaise, was a conservative one: "We should put our hopes not on the Western civilization imported from abroad but on the inherent civilization of our own country." Confronted with the West's disintegrating influence, Du seemed to yearn for a strong government to clear away all the confusion and reinstitute a Chinese orthodoxy. Although he still welcomed the importation of Western ideas, his intention was rather "to merge them into our own civilization. For the fragments of Western civilization are like small coins spread on the ground, and our own civilization is like a cord that can bind them into one string" (Cang 1918: 6).

Interestingly, Du's reflections were caused by an article in the Japanese journal *Light of East Asia* relating the news of a certain Chinese named Hu who had published two books in Germany at this critical juncture of the European war, attacking European materialism and avarice and calling on its intellectuals to learn from Chinese Confucianism. In Chen Duxiu's view, Mr. Hu could be none other than the notorious conservative Gu Hongming 辜鴻銘 (1857–1928) (Chen 1918: 206). The article in Chinese translation quotes H(G)u as saying that what the Europeans learn in their schools was nothing but knowledge, whereas "the Chinese in their schools learn about the way of becoming a gentleman (*junzi zhi dao* 君子之道)" (Chen 1918: 5).

This apparently led Du's friend Qian Zhixiu to issue a severe warning against his countrymen's preoccupation with practicality and utility—the result of their embracing Western utilitarianism—to the neglect of genuine spiritual concerns. Qian also faulted cheap popular books for their lack of interest in profound and original scholarship (Qian 1918).

These views seem to prepare the ground for the more famous debate on science and metaphysics in 1923, in which prominent intellectuals from Hu Shi to Zhang Junmai 張君勱 (1886–1969) took part. The trope of two polarized civilizations, East and West, embodying two diametrically opposed categories of values (in this case spiritualism versus materialism) had become a commonplace. Liang Shuming 梁漱溟 (1893–1988) used it in his series of lectures entitled "Eastern and Western Civilizations and Their Philosophies." Chen Duxiu himself employed it in his famous article "Call to Youth" ("Jinggao qingnian" 敬告青年) (see Chow 1960: 45–46, 328–32). What divided the two camps was obviously the value judgment behind this dichotomy of cultural characteristics. The three *Eastern Miscellany* authors, as Du acknowledged, were not categorically opposed to Western values; rather, they bemoaned the excesses of indiscriminate assimilation. However, in Chen Duxiu's rebuttals, this stance was seen as self-contradictory and illogical. Chen also faulted the *Eastern Miscellany* authors for equating Confucianism with the totality of Chinese tradition; he then charged them with tacitly supporting "restorationism" (restoring the emperor system) and opposing the Republic, for this was precisely Gu Hongming's position. When Du in his response argued that quoting Gu Hongming did not mean endorsing his ideas, that good Confucian government was a matter of historical fact and should not be glossed over by the moderns, Chen Duxiu leveled more challenges and accusations in his second article. Above all, he charged that his opponent's admiration of a monolithic orthodoxy as a solution to intellectual chaos was itself a despotic stance and detrimental to the development of intellectual freedom. "This is the public opinion of all those with an inkling of common knowledge in the modern age." Above all, "to attempt a unified orthodoxy (that is, the unification of scholarship and thought)—its damaging impact on progress and evolution can be evidenced in China in the Han dynasty's exclusive privileging of Confucianism and [in the West in] the singular espousal of [Christian] religion" (Chen 1919: 153). Finally, in large characters and bold print (a kind of "big-character" style) at the end of the article, Chen presented his own reading of his opponent's "real" position and challenged Du to respond (having also charged that Du had failed to respond to a number of questions raised earlier). According to Chen, Du was arguing (1) that "the importation of the chaotic and contradictory Western civilization has destroyed the ethos and norms (名教綱常) of the way of emperor and minister in our country's civilization, thus causing the loss of the national essence, the bankruptcy of the spiritual realm, and the impending extinction of our country;" (2) that "the salvation of our lost ways must be the preservation of the ethos and norms of the way of emperor and minister"; and (3) that "in order to preserve this inherited civilization we must eliminate the republican system, which has no emperors and ministers," lest it lead to "the loss of the national essence, the bankruptcy of the spiritual realm, and the impending extinction of our country" (Chen 1919: 160). This overemphatic coda not only simplified Du's argument but also showed it in the worst possible light. By putting it in bold characters, Chen certainly wanted to draw his readers' attention and arouse their anger. It was a brilliant polemical stroke of co-optation.

These excerpts for this debate reveal the rhetorical mode of the arguments on both sides. Chen Duxiu obviously gained the upper hand by putting Du Yaquan on the defensive. Chen also won by a strategy of forced allegation: by rearranging some of Du's sentences at the end of his second article, he basically reduced a discussion of Chinese and Western civilizations to a difference of political ideology. Although Chen showed more analytical acumen than Du in his understanding of Western civilization, he also took for granted the correctness of certain Western values such as progress, democracy, freedom, and utilitarianism (his opponents made similar assumptions about Chinese tradition). Most significant, Chen assumed self-righteously as "common knowledge of the modern age" the Western background of modernity, without critical reflection. However simplistically Du Yaquan and his colleagues may have justified Chinese culture and denigrated Western civilization, they nevertheless positioned themselves as concerned and critical observers of the Western cultural scene instead of being its unreserved proponents. By contrast, Chen Duxiu cast himself as an unquestioned proponent of Western modernity and took the contrary view about the impact of the European War: "Since the war there has been extremely speedy progress in science, society, and politics" (Chen 1919: 159). This statement, with no elaboration, is tantamount to a declaration of belief. As Jiang Menglin 蔣夢麟 (1886–1964), another Westernized modernist, pointed out in his critique of Du Yaquan, "new thought is an attitude—an attitude toward the direction of progress. Those who embrace such an attitude view the life of our country with discontent and cannot be intellectually pleased fully with its thinking" (quoted in Wang Yuanhua 1994: 7). On the other hand, Du differentiated between attitude and thought, the former a form of feeling and the latter a function of the intellect—and argued that the two must not be confused. In a recent reassessment, the Chinese scholar Wang Yuanhua 王元化 has solidly sided with Du's position and considers it to be relevant to contemporary China: in his view, what Du opposed and Jiang and Chen espoused is precisely what Weber would call the "ethic of intentions," and Qian Zhixiu was probably the earliest Chinese critic of "instrumental rationality" (Wang Yuanhua 1994: 8, 13). That this critique of Western modernity should have taken a conservative thrust and a bipolar East versus West scheme is, in my judgment, regrettable. But I agree with Wang that Du Yaquan cannot be taken as an anti-reformist reactionary who had fallen behind the times.

If we look into the institutional makeup of the debate in terms of cultural capital, the stakes are higher. The first two volumes of the *New Youth* magazine were printed by two smaller publishers, as compared to the giant Commercial Press. Until January 1918 its sole editor was Chen Duxiu; afterward a six-man editorial committee was in charge. But Chen seemed clearly the leader: in 1919 he organized the New Youth Society and published a new manifesto and "Rules of the Organization." This continued until the Society split in the summer of 1920 and Chen resumed sole editorship. The society was later reorganized and became an organ of the Chinese Communist Party (Chow 1960: 45–46). Thus the journal was shaped by one powerful personality, not a powerful publishing enterprise. But Chen could claim the intellectual backing of some famous professors and students from the elitist Peking University. The rise of this new culture elite, therefore, was both a phenomenon of institutional development (which led also to the rivalry of academic Beijing versus commercial Shanghai) and a feat of self-engineering. From Chen's critique of the *Eastern Miscellany* writers, we can easily surmise his displeasure with the *Eastern Miscellany*, which may well have been too eclectic for his taste. This sense of dissatisfaction may also reflect an anti-establishmentarian mentality and a desire to gain hegemonic power in the field of culture. In other words, strategically it was comparable to what Antonio Gramsci would later call, in a different context, a battle for "positions."

In this connection, a document written by Luo Jialun 羅家倫 (1896–1969), a student at the time, in the April 1919 issue of *New Tide* (*Xinchao* 新潮), another early May Fourth journal that was closely affiliated with *New Youth* through its Peking University connections, is revealing. Here is what Luo had to say about *Eastern Miscellany*:

> This is a journal belonging to the past-and-present school. At times it is about industry, at times political commentary, or agriculture and commerce, or spiritual matters—it's truly diverse and bizarre. If you say it's old-fashioned, it looks new; if you say it's new, it does not really qualify. . . . Now, as I look at it for a while I feel really at a loss: with such an unopinionated, characterless, and unsystematic method [of editing], we can truly say it exerts no impact on society and fulfills no obligation to inculcate new knowledge. I sincerely hope that the person in charge of this journal will change directions. For one must know that when everyone can read it, it's the same as no one is reading it; and when it contains everything, it's the same as containing nothing. I hope that it will no longer be necessary for our society to have such a deservedly "miscellaneous" journal. (1954: 81–82)

Luo also wrote that the journal had looked better in 1913–14 when it was under a different editor, not knowing that for the past decade (1910–20) the same editor, Du Yaquan, had been in charge. According to the memoirs of Zhang Jinglu 張靜廬 (1898–1969), the famed scholar and practitioner of modern Chinese publishing, in its early phase the journal was merely informational and consisted of excerpts and translations from other newspapers, domestic and foreign. Its first reform in fact occurred when Du was assigned the editorship: commentary had crept in together with translated articles (Luo 1954: 86). It is ironic that Du managed to maintain the eclectic nature of the journal despite his own desire for unified orthodoxy. Luo Jialun's view betrays a radical's penchant for staking out a clear position. A singular self-righteous position eloquently proclaimed seemed to endow *New Youth* with symbolic power. In order to sustain it, as we now know, the editors had to fabricate criticisms in order to gain more power from rebuttals. Thus, when the old translator Lin Shu 林紓 (1852–1924) fell into this trap, one could well imagine the glee with which they greeted Lin's inadvertent contribution to their cause.

Still, the polemic mode proved to be a powerful weapon. It is not necessary for us to compare the views of Lin and Du to see their differences of opinion. Nor did it really matter for the leaders of the *New Youth* and their followers, for in the polemic mode of discourse the line of battle is clearly drawn: you are either for or against us, and a strong offensive is always better than a weak defense. However, the monological implications of such an either/or position are also obvious. Not only does it not allow room for pluralism (which was *not* a part of the May Fourth position on democracy), but it also bequeaths a legacy of polemics in the name of "debate," often with a foregone conclusion as to who would be the winner. In hindsight, we can see that it led inevitably to the radicalization of modern Chinese intellectuals.

Language and Authority

By inventing this assertive polemic mode, instead of the more passive and cynical satirical commentary employed in the "Free Discourse" pages, the New Culture leaders succeeded in establishing their own cultural authority to replace that of the "transitional" generation of intellectuals. However, it would be erroneous to suggest that the May Fourth leaders won by rhetorical strategy alone. As Ying-shih Yü 余英時 has reminded us in his long introduction on Hu Shi, there also existed an intellectual vacuum that a new generation of largely foreign-educated students was able to fill (Yü 1993: 10). The prime movers of the late Qing reform movement were scholars and officials who knew only Chinese and had to rely on translations, mostly from Japanese. As Liang Qichao later recalled, the intellectual shallowness of the reform movement was caused by the lack of participation of Western-educated students (see Yü 1993: 13). To be sure, Japan claimed the largest number of Chinese students abroad at the turn of the century. It was not until the early twentieth century that more students went to America and Europe, among whom the elite members were supported by the prestigious Boxer Indemnity funds. Hu Shi was a typical product of this elite education, and as his diary of his days in America reveals, he worked hard to prepare himself for a future mission.

There is no need to delineate Hu Shi's familiar biographical profile—a profile constructed largely by his own autobiographical writings—to be aware of his unique gifts. According to Yü, these gifts enabled him to establish a new "paradigm" of intellectual method based on his knowledge of Dewey and Huxley (Yü 1993: 19–20, 43–44). With this new method, Hu was emboldened to undertake the critical task of the "transvaluation of all values." I will not concern myself with the content of these values, old or new, as Yü and others have already done so well. Rather, I would like to explore one of Hu Shi's unique gifts—his apparent gift for language.

To begin with, we should state the obvious: Hu Shi was not a trained linguist. Unlike his friend Y. R. Chao 趙 元 任 (1892–1982), Hu was unequipped with, and uninterested in, the skills of linguistic analysis. Hu's special gift lay in relating language to something else—that is, its relationship to literature and social life. The familiar story of his insights about vernacular literature in the Chinese literary tradition is a case in point. There was nothing terribly original about this insight, except that Hu reconstructed a whole vernacular tradition out of it. In present-day scholarly language, his project represents a "re-reading" of the history of Chinese literature, which he later subjected to a "rewriting." What makes his reading more noteworthy than other readings, as recent scholars have pointed out, lies in his purposeful application of the concept of evolution. While abroad, especially during his stay in America, Hu Shi had apparently adopted the notion of evolutionary progress (which was included in several textbooks of modern philosophy). In translating it into Chinese literature, he indeed broke new ground: his is a "modern" interpretation in that he believes not only that each country and each epoch had its own literature (echoes of Vico perhaps),[3] but also that literature develops and matures and dies, like a living organism. Consequently, in attempting to bring the vernacular strain of Chinese literature to the forefront of this developmental scheme, he labeled it a "living"—as opposed to a "dead"—literary tradition. This bold claim, a reflection of Hu's modern convictions, allowed Hu to bypass some thorny issues: the relationship between the oral and the written (especially in a language with an ideographic script only partially based on sounds); the problems of privileging one genre (such as fiction and drama) over other genres (such as poetry and prose, although, like all traditional elites, Hu was interested in poetry); and the possible biases of favoring certain periods over other periods in order to substantiate his scheme. Thus, as one recent study has shown, Hu Shi's book on the history of Chinese literature is more an intentional thesis than a general coverage.[4] But then, he was among the first Chinese scholars to con-

---

3. Whatever Hu may owe to Vico, the idea of artistic and literary evolution was already a commonplace in the late Ming. In late Ming painting theory, evolution is explained in terms of a dynastic scheme, but the philosopher Li Zhi 李 贄 (1527–1602) and the three Yuan brothers of the Gong'an school operated with the Buddhist notion of "transformation," *bian* 變. Still, it is clear that Hu's argument is buttressed by his newly acquired Western concept of evolution.

4. I have learned much from a master's thesis on Hu Shi's writings on Chinese literary history by my student Wang Chaohua at UCLA (1994).

ceive of literary history in terms of a temporal and developmental scheme rather than a dynastic one.

From the very beginning, Hu Shi's scholarly project was mixed up with something else. His own sense of mission as a student seems to have preordained his future role as more than a professional scholar. Unlike most American-educated students who brought back from their training a sense of professionalism derived from their specific academic disciplines, Hu Shi was determined not to be narrowly confined. From his diaries we know he had broad interests and was widely read. A psycho-historical study would perhaps focus on this rather unusual personal ambition: he wanted to become an intellectual leader, but not necessarily a high official by climbing the traditional ladder of success. Although the abolition of the civil service examinations in 1905 had destroyed this established channel, the intellectual prestige attached to high education remained unchanged. (The Boxer Indemnity scholarship examinations were quite rigorous, and the prestige of winning one could be compared to gaining a Rhodes scholarship; both moreover derived from a "colonial" bequest.) Still, Hu Shi, unlike his contemporary Lu Xun, was more fortunate in finding the "right" thing to do at the right time. Both men gave up a training in science (agriculture and medicine, respectively) for literature. A few years earlier, however, Lu Xun had languished in depression in Japan, after failing to get a literary journal, *Nuovo Vita* (*Xin sheng* 新生), off the ground; in contrast, Hu Shi wrote one tentative essay on literary reform, which was sent first to a Chinese student journal in America (Lu Xun had also written for student journals in Japan), and became an overnight celebrity. As Hu recounted in one of his celebrated memoirs, he also sent a carbon copy of the article to *New Youth* (1934: 118). The *timeliness* of Hu's argument for the vernacular did not escape Chen Duxiu, for whom the modern vernacular (*baihua wen* 白話文) was now a necessary medium because of changed socioeconomic conditions: "If people like Hu Shi had championed the modern vernacular thirty years ago, one article by Zhang Xingyan 章行嚴 [Zhang Shizhao 章士釗] would have rebutted it into nothing" (quoted in Yü 1993: 31).

As is well known, Chen Duxiu turned Hu's "tentative suggestions" into slogans for a literary revolution—another rhetorical strategy that served Chen's purposes perfectly. Whereas Chen seemed happy to sound the clarion calls for a new realistic, social, and national literature, Hu Shi had a pragmatic bent and supplied the details of practice. Not only did he attempt to experiment with writing poetry in the modern vernacular—with results far from artistically satisfying—but he also discussed in several articles the practical problems of how to write in the vernacular. As we reread these how-to essays from a present-day perspective, his limitations are ample and self-evident. Despite his modern, Western orientation, his examples are drawn mostly from classical Chinese literature, and his literary judgments are obviously biased by his belief in evolutionism and the "living" vernacular tradition. At the same time, he fervently prefers the short story to the long, sprawling, and "badly structured" narratives he found in traditional Chinese literature (Hu 1918: 66). Yet for the new fictional form he could offer only such vague ideas as structure and detail and neglected to mention what Lu Xun did best in his short stories: the invention of a narrator and narratorial points of view. Hu's own "modern" literary taste in both fiction and poetry seems to have been limited to realism, and throughout the 1920s and 1930s he was apparently unaware of Western modernist trends (apart from a shaky knowledge of American Imagism). Drawing on the precedent of Renaissance Italy, he boldly announced in his famous essay of 1918, "On a Constructive Literary Revolution" ("Jianshe de wenxue geming lun" 建設的文學革命論), that his purpose in advocating the modern vernacular was to realize a grand vision: the creation of "a literature of national language, a literary national language (國語的文學、文學的國語)." Since this ambition bears on his notion of literature and language, it deserves some analysis.

Hu argued that the purpose of the Literary Revolution was to "create for China a literature of the national language," without which there could not be a "literary national language" (1918: 57). In other words, he believed that a new language cannot be constructed by linguists but only through literary practice. How did one create a literature in a "national language" in a country with numerous dialects? Hu bequeathed modern Chinese writers a most burdensome task: to create a corpus of literature on which a national language can evolve. The contradictions between his revolutionary goal and evolutionary belief are self-evident: since, as he said, the effect of evolutionary progress is cumulative and gradual, sometimes even set back by obstacles, it may indeed take several generations to realize his dream of "a literature of national language." Hu's concrete suggestions for this grandiose literary task consist merely of a few rudimentary "tools" and "methods"—such as reading exemplary vernacular literatures of the past, using *baihua* for all genres of writing, expanding the scope of materials, and paying more attention to actual experience and observation. These are, as he admits, preparatory "methods" for the education of a modern writer, not a primer of literary technique. Hu's discussion of literary technique seems outmoded even by the yardsticks of his own time and consists of rather amorphous notions of "structure" and "depiction," which seem to be what he means by imagination. In sum, the consequence of Hu Shi's pragmatism was, ironically, a separation of theory and practice—so much so that the literary scene since the late 1920s has been beset by numerous ideological debates in the name of theory, with little concern for nurturing literary creativity.

Although in his later deliberations Hu did pay some attention to the artistic values of literature written in regional dialects, in this early period his goal was less regional and more national. Implicit in his project is the loaded issue of nation-building through language. However, nationalism seems to be absent from Hu Shi's literary agenda. His examples of Dante's Italy and Chaucer's England bypass the ideological issue of power—of how a unified language was closely related to the consolidation of monarchical power. In the case of early modern France, the process of language unification can be seen in the elevation of the Parisian dialect to the national level and relegation of other dialects to the status of *patois*. That a modern Chinese nation must be constructed on the foundation of a modern Chinese language unified by the modern state is something that Hu Shi chose *not* to emphasize, even in his summary reflection on the entire May Fourth movement in lectures given at the University of Chicago in the early 1930s, which bore the English title of "Chinese Renaissance." Hu was clearly awed by this historic landmark in premodern Western civilization, which seemed to offer, in Hu Shi's eyes, a more glorious precedent for the May Fourth movement. But in choosing the historical epithet "Renaissance" (instead of Enlightenment), he also, in effect, privileged the literary and artistic dimension of the movement—and his own contributions—at the expense of the ideological. The standard Chinese translation for "Renaissance" is *wenyi fuxing* 文藝復興, literally, the "revival and reflourishing of literature and the arts." It was clearly attractive to Hu.

That literature and arts, particularly fiction, performed a seminal role in the formation of modern nationalism is a commonplace acknowledged by Liang Qichao and many others since the late Qing period. Instead of Renaissance Italy, Liang had chosen to focus on modern Italy as "constructed" by its three national heroes: Cavour, Mazzini, and Garibaldi. Other late Qing and early Republican litterateurs—Su Manshu 蘇曼殊 (1884–1918), for instance—paid attention to modern Greece, and in particular Byron's heroic sympathy for the patriotism of the Greeks. Had Hu followed suit, he would have realized that the battle for the use of the modern spoken vernacular was by no means limited to China alone; modern Greek writers and intellectuals had experienced a more prolonged language conflict in their effort of nation-building. The battles between the demotic, a form of modern spoken vernacular, and more archaic forms such as the *katharevusa*, had extended from the cultural to the political realms and involved the entire nation (Jusdanis 1991: 41–46). The Greek phenomenon of *diglossia*, or the coexistence of two forms of language and their competition for cultural hegemony and national legitimation, yields an interesting "mirror" with which to reflect on the Chinese case. Although *baihua* gained an easy victory officially—legitimized by the Ministry of Education, which decreed in the early 1920s that *baihua* was to be used in all primary school textbooks—*wenyan* did not exactly die off either. Classical-style poetry continued to be written, even by modern fiction writers like Lu Xun and Yu Dafu 郁達夫 (1896–1945). Large quantities of popular works were written in mixed, half-classical and half-vernacular (*banwen banbai* 半文半白) styles. Some of the most learned scholarly books on Chinese philosophy and classics were written entirely in *wenyan*. It was on the ideological front that the vernacular movement seemed to carry the day. But on a deeper level problems remain unsolved: whether the semantic field of *baihua* is adequate to encompass the full range of Chinese cultural sensibilities and thereby effect a total transformation of the Chinese mode of thinking (as Hu Shi and Chen Duxiu had wanted) is a question that cannot easily be answered without full-scale research into the linguistic and philosophical implications of *baihua* in all its complexities.[5]

Despite all these reservations, however, we should not belittle Hu Shi's contributions. In a way, the superficiality of his ideas in "On a Constructive Literary Revolution" bespeaks their persuasive power. Most Hu Shi scholars

5. Not being a linguist and philosopher myself, I am not qualified to comment on the question, which in the Western case is more self-evident, whether the modern Chinese language is indeed capable of representing a new paradigm of thought: for instance, subjectivity in terms of both linguistic construction and philosophical formulation. The mere invention of the word *wo* 我, or "I," and its semantic insertion still seems to be inadequate. Another issue may be the expressive capacity for abstractions.

agree that the hallmark of his prose and public lectures is precisely their clarity: it is, as Ying-shih Yü perceptively points out, the language of an "enlightener" and not necessarily an erudite scholar (1993: 62). This chosen role is perfectly in line with Hu's ambition to be a pioneer, to open up new avenues of inquiry so as to initiate new intellectual trends. In this regard he succeeded brilliantly. It could be argued that despite his obvious indebtedness to traditional Chinese methodology, especially that of mid-Qing philology, Hu was able to look at Chinese and Western cultures in a new light—or at least to couch them in a new (somewhat) popular language. Written *baihua* was used by Hu Shi not as a language of creative literature but as a means to construct a new mode of intellectual discourse and communication, because the "grammar" of late Qing discourse had proved by this time to be inadequate. That Hu repeatedly argues against the use of old clichés and traditional references is a case in point, for they inevitably invoke a cluster of old cultural associations that constrict the reader's receptivity to new ideas. In the late Qing period, new ideas from abroad were still phrased in the traditional semantic context combined, however, with certain invented words and terms (e.g., "freedom," "society") often from Japanese. It is still a device of putting new wines in old bottles.[6] By the time of the May Fourth period, it was definitely being found to be insufficient. Hu Shi's singular contribution, based on his insight that language is more than a discipline of linguistics, was to persuade his readers of the need for a new language as the foundation of a new discourse. This insight has a close relationship with social and cultural conditions. Whether Hu Shi's language reform constitutes a new intellectual "paradigm" is an issue that requires further research and analysis. But from the perspective of literary and cultural history, it is easier to see how a reconfiguration of intellectual power and prestige had indeed taken place in the May Fourth period, for which language was a harbinger. As mentioned above, Chen Duxiu's polemical strategy in editing the *New Youth* had contributed to such a power shift, which edged out both conservatives like Lin Shu and transitional moderates like Du Yaquan. Hu Shi's "invention" of a new language enabled this new power elite to articulate its

---

6. Still, the post–May Fourth translations continued the practice of coining new words and phrases: such as *xing er shang xue* 形而上學 for "metaphysics" and *benti lun* 本體論 for both "ontology" and "subjectivity"; sometimes it even resorted to direct transliterations, for instance, *aofuhebian* 奥伏赫變 for *aufheben*, as popularized by the Creation Society (Chuangzao she 創造社).

central "authoritarian" significance. In addition, the mushrooming of a great number of intellectual journals, together with newspapers and their literary supplements, formed the institutional base for this new power elite.

Spheres of Influence

In a recent talk on the "transitional" period of modern Chinese intellectual and cultural history, Hao Chang 張 灝 (1994) cited some impressive statistics about print media.[7] Before 1895 there were some fifteen newspapers and journals; the number increased to 64 in the period between 1895 and 1898; by 1913 it had increased to 487; down to the May Fourth period, the numbers ranged anywhere from 840 to 2,000 (Chang 1994). Not all of them, of course, rallied to the new causes, but it is safe to say that by the early 1920s May Fourth intellectuals commanded a great majority of these media. Not the least significant is the fact that a great majority of the newspapers and journals began to use *baihua*. It would seem obvious, therefore, that the May Fourth elite succeeded in carving out an enlarged print space in which they could freely voice their new ideas and command public attention. Compared to the late Qing publication scene, did this May Fourth print media better serve as the "public sphere" in the way that Habermas conceives? Or to put it simply, did the May Fourth elite succeed in furthering the cause of Mr. Democracy in the intellectual arena?

This question was the central concern of a number of learned articles written by Chinese scholars and intellectuals in 1989—the seventieth anniversary of the May Fourth Movement (see Lin et al. 1989). The discourse of most such articles is, like those by their May Fourth predecessors, highly elitist—that is, the authors attach great significance to the ideas and writings of a few leaders and thus take for granted the elitist premise that the words of a few individuals indeed shape history. At the same time, most such articles focus on content analysis of a few privileged texts and pay little attention to voices in that broader space, the print media. This may be more than a methodological bias; it could also be the consequence of self-promotion by the May Fourth leaders themselves, who, fully confident of their own mis-

7. I am much indebted to and influenced by Chang's research on the "transitional" period intellectuals. Since we share similar ideas, in this chapter I have adopted his term "transitional," which could also mean a period of transformation, but use it to refer to the period from 1895 to 1915. The May Fourth period, then, covers roughly the decade 1916–26; the "post–May Fourth" period roughly 1927–37.

sion, wrote profusely about the historic significance of their own project as it was happening. Although they may have inherited this sense of self-confidence from leaders of a previous generation—Liang Qichao and Yan Fu 嚴復 (1853–1921)—their self-assertive rhetoric was certainly a far cry from the language of the late Qing journalist-litterateurs. The debate between Chen Duxiu and Du Yaquan is an illuminating example. Thus if we attempt to enlarge our perception of the May Fourth field of discourse to include works published in newspapers and journals as well as the writings of members of the mushrooming "study societies" as a background of measurement, the picture to be drawn, even from sketchy preliminary research, may not look so bright and glorious.

First, we must briefly examine the composition of the May Fourth elite and their relationship to the intellectual press. The crucial difference between them and late Qing intellectuals lies of course in their educational background. The May Fourth generation was the first to arise from the modern school system, especially universities. The curricula of higher education since the 1920s have essentially been modeled after those of American universities because of the direct impact of American missionaries and American-educated Chinese students. A sizable number of intellectuals had also been educated in Japan, where they studied the Japanese language and Western subjects such as medicine and mining. This foreign-derived educational makeup became the crucial part of their modern outlook, which set them apart from what they considered to be traditional-style intellectuals. But this educational boundary could be more apparent than real, especially in arenas outside the educational system. It is worth noting that the Western division of town and gown—the line that separates and encloses academia from the outside—was not clearly marked in modern China. Many May Fourth intellectuals may have had an academic base in the universities as professors or students, but their intellectual activities certainly exceeded the confines of scholarship. In their frequent writings for journals and newspapers, they projected a public persona that did not necessarily reflect their academic role. Moreover, in view of the thriving publication industry since the late Qing, more and more educated men and women were able to carve out a living as writers, translators, editors, and publishers without attaching themselves to an educational institution. Some famous young writers, like Ding Ling 丁玲 (1904–86) and Shen Congwen 沈從文 (1902–88), did not have a formal educational status or degree (sometimes they merely audited classes at universities, as Mao Zedong 毛 澤 東 [1893–1976] did). What makes this situation different from the late Qing case is not only the assumption of symbolic power on the part of self-styled new intellectuals but also their perpetuation of an image of group solidarity in their own journals. In other words, journals were regarded as mouthpieces of a few colleagues in the same group or society (*tongren zazhi* 同 仁 雜 誌). And if some members of the group came to disagree with the journal's stance, they would branch off and publish their own journal, with an even narrower position. Thus, the mushrooming of journals did not mean a broader sphere for free public discussion, since there were hardly any general-interest journals in which opinions from different sides could be voiced in the same issue. In other words, the typical May Fourth journal was more self-important, less tolerant, and often more ephemeral than the commercial journals. In literature the only major exception was Shi Zhecun's 施 蟄 存 *The Contemporary* or *Les contemporains* (*Xiandai* 現 代) magazine, which was initiated not by a literary society but by a publishing firm, the Xiandai shuju 現代書局.

Thus the significance of the *Eastern Miscellany*, the target of attack by Chen Duxiu and Luo Jialun, must be reaffirmed precisely because of its eclecticism and popularity. The roster of authors of the eighty-odd pamphlet-sized volumes of the *Dongfang wenku* is very impressive, and it includes both academic and nonacademic intellectuals representing a wide spectrum of backgrounds and positions. The subjects and titles (mostly translations) are even more impressive, since they cover an immensely wide range. For example, Du Yaquan's contribution, "A Philosophy to Cope with the World" ("Chushi zhexue" 處 世 哲 學), is a translation of a Japanese rendition of a Schopenhauer book. It is collected in a box (volumes 32–50) which also includes works on journalism, East-West cultural criticism, Chinese society and culture, ethics, psychology, contemporary philosophy (mainly on Dewey), Bergson and Eucken, Kropotkin, Gandhism, the philosophy of war, two volumes of Bertrand Russell's essays, and fundamentals of science. Some of these volumes were originally published in the *Eastern Miscellany*. In terms of the diversity of its introduction of new knowledge, therefore, these two publication enterprises of the Commercial Press, the journal and the repository, certainly surpass that of *New Youth*, *New Tide*, and other May Fourth journals—except in terms of intellectual prestige.

Another important case deserving close study is the literary supplement of the *Morning Post* of Beijing, which first occupied a portion of the newspaper's seventh page. From February 1919 the supplement underwent a major reform; three special columns were added: a "Free Forum" ("Ziyou luntan" 自由論壇) inviting outside contribution of articles containing "new morals, new knowledge, and new thought"; a "Translation Series"; and a column on literary and theater criticism (see *Wusi* 1979: 99, 398). This reform measure, according to a latter-day study, formally turned this supplement into an arena for the New Culture movement, and a number of prominent May Fourth intellectuals began to contribute (*Wusi* 1979: 99). Lu Xun's "The True Story of Ah Q" ("A Q zhen zhuan" 阿Q真傳) was first serialized there, with some goading from his friend Sun Fuyuan 孫伏園 (1894–1966), the supplement's editor. Another writer to appear here was Li Dazhao 李大釗 (1889–1927), who contributed several articles on Marxism and socialism. From October 12, 1921, the supplement became an independent sheet attached to the newspaper, like a small literary journal, and from 1925 it was dominated by members of the Crescent Moon society.

A mere glance at the table of contents of the "Free Forum" column from 1919 to 1921 indicates that its contributors constituted virtually a who's-who of Beijing's New Culture elite: from Chen Duxiu, Li Dazhao, Hu Shi, Lu Xun, Zhou Zuoren 周作人 (1885–1967), and Cai Yuanpei 蔡元培 (1868–1940), to the woman writer Xie Wanying 謝婉瑩 (1900–) (otherwise known as Bingxin 冰心), the early Marxist Qu Qiubai 瞿秋白 (1899–1935), the poet Kang Baiqing 康白情 (1896–1945), and the literary scholars Yu Pingbo 俞平伯 (1900–1991) and Zheng Zhenduo 鄭振鐸 (1898–1958) (*Wusi* 1979: 474–77). With such an impressive list, we can imagine the intellectual impact on readers. But did the "Free Forum" indeed provide a "forum" for a free discussion of ideas? One notable fact is that intellectuals from other camps did not participate: some of Liang Qichao's speeches, including one on the May Fourth, were published, but not in the "Free Forum" column. Since its basic injunction was to introduce new knowledge and thought, a general guideline had been set. Within the parameters of the new, the literary supplement of the *Morning Post* as a whole from 1919 to 1925 was more "liberal" and open-minded than the *New Youth* of the same period. But it also had a more elitist profile by virtue of its contributors in comparison to the column of a similar name in the *Shanghai News*: "Free Discourse."

Obviously the *Morning Post*'s "Free Forum" owes a debt to the "Free Discourse" page of the *Shanghai News*, which continued without interruption under a succession of new editors—the most prominent was Li Liewen 黎

烈文 (1904–72), a French-educated scholar who solicited Lu Xun's contributions in the mid-1930s. From the 1910s to the 1930s, a "paradigm shift" certainly took place in the "Free Discourse" page. Instead of playful social commentary from the sidelines (as I have characterized its general features of the 1910s), articles published on the same page in the early 1930s were dead serious; the satiric tone of Lu Xun's *zawen* 雜文 contributions was miles apart from the humor of the anonymous authors two decades earlier. To be sure, a new temper and a new epoch had set in. But a new question arises: given the post–May Fourth temper, did the "Free Discourse" page serve its new public function—and what was its public function?

What indeed should have constituted the "public sphere" of the May Fourth and post–May Fourth period? As the May Fourth elite began to occupy and dominate the print media, what was their main purpose in intellectual journalism? A simple answer to the question may well be that they wished to propagate their ideas to a broader audience, very much in the same way as their predecessors in the late Qing had. However, the reading public at the turn of the century was being formed at the same time as the "societal intelligentsia" (educated intellectuals who chose not to hold government positions); together they formed a preliminary "imagined community" in their attempt to define the new nation. By the 1920s, a reading public had been established, for whom and to whom the May Fourth leaders wished to address their new knowledge. But this readership of the urban newspapers had also become less homogenized, and the relationship between the New Culture elite and its audience had likewise become more complex. Some urban readers preferred more eclectic journals and entertaining news; others, mainly students, were die-hard converts to the May Fourth causes. Both, however, had accepted the general premise of modernity and would not revert to a traditional past. The dilemma of popularity in late Qing journalism—to provide a serious message or entertainment?—was solved by the practitioners of the trade through sheer formal inventiveness. They provided entertainment even as they tried to inculcate new messages by expressing serious social and political critique in a purposely playful mode. But in the literary supplements of the *Shanghai News* and the *Morning Post* in the 1920s and 1930s, that spirit of popularity was somehow lost. What replaced it was a highly elitist notion of populism: to elevate the cause of the people and to speak on their behalf. Meanwhile, the practical project of enlightenment became increasingly elitist. Small groups of thinkers competed with one another in order to propagate their own causes or otherwise pontificate what they considered to be the truth to their imagined audience of followers. This factionalism of intellectual societies and literary groups had in fact split and shrunk their audiences. Thus the sound and fury of the debates that raged since the 1920s did not in my view expand the scope of the "public sphere"; nor did they contribute constructively to the spread of "democracy" (however we wish to define the term).

Elsewhere I argued my case by using the celebrated example of Lu Xun's contributions to the "Free Discourse" page of *The Shanghai News* (Lee 1993). These *zawen* pieces were collected by Lu Xun in a book called *A Book of False Freedom* (*Wei ziyou shu* 偽自由書). As I reread these essays, my impression is mixed: although containing some ingenious formal devices due to Lu Xun's battles with the government censors, they suffer nevertheless from a shrill self-righteous tone and a stance of fortuitous duplicity. One of Lu Xun's satirical devices was to copy an article or news dispatch verbatim and to insert an occasional sarcastic note. In asking the reader to judge the falsehood of reported reality, he insinuated his own sketchy interpretations as "truth." Living in a condition of "false freedom" in Shanghai's Japanese section, Lu Xun succeeded only in masking his own observations under the veneer of cynicism and indirection. This served to make his commentary, written in the sharp tones of personal attack, equally suspect—especially for readers who are not "true believers" of his ideological position. Thus the participation of this renowned writer ironically rendered the "Free Discourse" page not so "free" because voices other than Lu Xun's were trashed beyond recognition.

As Lin Yu-sheng 林毓生 (1985: 123) has argued, Lu Xun's political stance derived from what Weber called the "ethic of intentions": the belief that good intentions and sincerity of will ultimately bring about good results. But this ethical stance also led to a sense of moral absolutism: not only did Lu Xun believe in one truth but he allowed no alternative paths to it. By the 1930s, when he turned leftist, Lu Xun's skepticism was turned against his enemies but seldom imposed on himself, as had been his penchant before. This hardened stance of radicalism was characteristic of most leftist intellectuals of the time. The direct impact of this stance on the print media was to turn China's modern newspapers into not a Habermasian "public sphere" but spheres of power and influence controlled by different political interest groups. The May Fourth intellectuals contributed their share to this political quagmire, ironically, by their own self-righteous ethic of intentions.

Conclusion: The "Incomplete Modernity of the May Fourth Intellectual Project"

Where did journals and polemicists gain this absolutist sense of self-righteousness and self-confidence? Lin Yu-sheng (1985: 123–25) has linked it to the influence of traditional Chinese epistemology. In my view, it is also the intellectual outcome of the Chinese project of modernity.

In a previous article I referred to the effusive usage of the word "epoch," *shidai* 時 代, which, according to Lung-kee Sun, had become a catchword by 1927, especially among radical intellectuals: "*Shidai*'s most important connotation came to be 'the present time' or 'our time,' always with the implication that it is a time of breathlessly rapid changes and incessant innovation" (quoted in Lee 1990: 120). The present epoch was, by definition, a new era radically different from all past periods, bringing "new tides" that could not be resisted. This excessive emphasis on the present moment is, of course, a sign of Western modernity as well. But the May Fourth intellectuals, with few exceptions, did not choose to view the present, as Baudelaire did, as fleeting and contingent; rather, in seizing the present "epoch" they also invested their own project with epoch-making significance. Thus by the late 1920s, a cluster of grandiose metaphors had entered into the modern Chinese literary vocabulary: "the great wheel of the epoch or history," "on the crest of the new epoch," "facing the new dawn." These clichés reappeared in the "revolutionary" novels of the 1930s. (Conversely, the government's increasing oppression turned the present into a long "dark night before dawn" and rendered the revolutionary endeavor equally heroic, if also tragic.) More research in leftist revolutionary fiction written around this time should indicate that something of a grand narrative tends to govern the plot of the work. The story unfolds as if according to a preconceived plan, of which the resolution or "closure" is left to the future. It is, in other words, a narrative constructed in the light of a historical teleology. Still, the details of such a "telos" were left vague; some of this was due to government censorship, but a more significant reason is the utopian frame of thinking that accompanied it. If we look through the numerous manifestos in the inaugural issues of May

Fourth journals, this utopian frame of thinking is already evident, but it was still couched in the new catchphrases of that period. It would not be hard to see the same rhetorical trope infusing most of these manifestos.

The following is a mosaic of selected passages from eight journals of the May Fourth period, as collected in volume one of *Introduction to Periodicals of the May Fourth Period* (*Wusi shiqi qikan jieshao* 五四時期期刊介紹; 1979: 383–422; all page references are to this collection). My purpose is to show how together they conjure a collective image of dedication to vaguely defined goals. The ethos of reform is expressed in a sentiment of utmost sincerity, which becomes all the more touching and tragic because of the youthful naiveté of its utopian vision. Still, the recurrent motif of awakening and progress somehow enabled these dedicated activists to fervently embrace hope for the future.

Let us ask what is the trend of contemporary thought? What is the place of China in such an intellectual trend? (*New Tide*, Jan.1, 1919: 394)

What kind of world is the world today? What kind of responsibility is our responsibility for the present? The world today is no longer the world of the past; the world of the past is passé! Our responsibility today is no longer the same as in the past. The "self" from the past has long been disowned and transformed! In this age of "changing the environment and renewing the self" . . . we have decided to establish this small journal. . . . For the convenience of our study, we cannot but establish at the outset a certain *tendency*. What follows is our tendency, not our *ism*. [The words in italics were originally printed in English.] (*Jiefang yu gaizao* 解放與改造 [Emancipation and reform], Oct. 15, 1919: 418)

We use the words "light of dawn" [as the journal's title]; its meaning is easy to understand. For the present society is in a "long lingering night" of "muddled dreams." Without the warning of a "cockcrow of dawn" that "the east is already light," how can we have the feeling of awakening? (*Shuguang yuekan* 曙光月刊 [Light of dawn monthly], Nov. 1, 1919: 407)

The waves of "awakening" are fiercely raging in the new tides of the twentieth century. . . . All those which do not conform to modern progress . . . must be eradicated and changed. . . . To "awaken" step by step, and to "progress" step by step; "awakening" is boundless as progress is limitless. (*Juewu* 覺悟 [Awakening], Dec. 29, 1919: 415)

The intent of this publication is that we hope our four hundred million people, as they slumber at midnight, can touch their hearts and begin to think and ponder: in this new tide following the end of the European War and the extinction of the emperor species, how do we plan for our individual lives, our social life, and our national life? (*Xin shenghuo tongsu zhoukan* 新生活通俗週刊 [New life popular weekly], Aug. 24, 1919: 406)

A youthful society is a society filled with youthful spirit and air—a progressive society. Societal youth is youth with feelings for social life—the helping youth. . . . How do we realize our motto? To launch a movement for youth in a spirit of helping: study, criticism, struggle, creativity. (*Shaonian shehui* 少年社會 [Youth society], Dec. 1, 1919: 405)

We think that reforming China—which is part of reforming the world—must take three measures:

The first step is to study modern trends of thought with a scientific spirit so that the Chinese will have a clear idea of the tendencies of modern intellectual trends.

The second step is to record in detail the facts of evolution of modern intellectual trends, so as to give Chinese a more profound challenge.

The third step is to draft a concrete plan to reform China based on the tendencies of these trends and facts. (*Shaonian shijie* 少年世界 [Youth world], Jan. 1, 1920: 403)

Our ideal new society in the new age is honest, progressive, positive, free, egalitarian, creative, beautiful, good, peaceful, mutually loving and helping, laboring and joyful, and for the happiness of the whole society. (Old manifesto of *New Youth*, Dec. 1, 1919: 383)

The revolutionary nature of *New Youth* is not because it likes revolution in particular or it likes to "voice radical opinions"—it is because in modern society there is already a material foundation for the solution of social problems. Therefore a social science is born, and a study and investigation based on its scientific objectivity makes us aware that revolution is inevitable; besides, the proletarian class naturally occupies the leadership position in social relations. And therefore, the intellectual institutions of the proletariat suddenly but expectedly reveal a clear revolutionary color. . . .

The *New Youth* has been a pioneer of China's real revolutionary thought.

The *New Youth* will from now on become a compass for China's proletarian revolution. (New Manifesto of *New Youth*, June 15, 1923: 387)

This last manifesto of the *New Youth* magazine bespeaks also its new revolutionary direction, which it shared with many other groups and journals. Thus it provides a fitting finale to the first phase of this youthful intellectual saga. There is no need to belabor the obvious conclusion that the Chinese Communist revolution brought this revolutionary saga to a close by providing the most grandiose and devastating "meta-narrative" for the nation. The vague telos in the May Fourth narratives of History as metaphor and "absent cause" became terribly "present" in the Thought of Mao Zedong.

It could be argued that the Maoist revolution represents a betrayal, not a continuation, of the May Fourth legacy, whose liberal orientation was carried on after the ideological split among the *New Youth* leaders in 1923 by Hu Shi and his friends. This narrative was, of course, provided by Hu and has a certain validity. Hu's views after the May Fourth period were indeed characterized by a discourse of reason, in sharp contrast to the hyperbolic effusions on the leftist front. In this chapter, I have reached a somewhat different conclusion by studying the general *rhetoric* of May Fourth journals. I have also argued that the success of the May Fourth leaders (including both Hu Shi and Chen Duxiu) lies to a large extent in their rhetorical power—the power of their words, with which they were able not only to defeat their intellectual enemies but also to invent several new narratives: in particular, the linear and developmental view that can readily be seen in their conceptions of history and literature and that is in turn grounded in the premise of a grand "rupture"—of modernity's total break with tradition. This polar dichotomy between tradition and modernity was easily equated with the dichotomy between China and the West. This has been a familiar "story" retold with slight variations in many non-Western countries. The underlying theme is temporal, signifying the need to catch up with the West. This narrative of "belated modernity" also carries the problematic of incompletion. In a study of the national literature of modern Greece, Gregory Jusdanis gives the following apt characterization:

> Belated modernization, especially in nonwestern societies, necessarily remains "incomplete" not because it deviates from the supposedly correct path but because it cannot culminate in a faithful duplication of western prototypes. The imported models do not function like their European counterparts. Often they are resisted. The project of becoming modern thus differs from place to place. This is why it is possible to speak of many modernities. Peripheral societies, however, internalize the incongruity between western originals and local realities as a structural deficiency. The lack of modernity is seen as a flaw. Hence, "incomplete" attempts to catch up with the West are followed by calls for a new phase of modernization. Ironically, however, the flaw lies not in modernity's absence but in its purposeful introduction, ignoring autochthonous exigencies. (1991: xiii)

I see the May Fourth project likewise as a purposeful introduction of Western modernity by the *New Youth* leaders. In a way the "autochthonous exigencies" were pointed out by their opponents—by people like Du Yaquan and other authors of the "popular press." However, the story of Chinese "belated modernity" differs from the modern Greek case in two notable respects. First, unlike modern Greece, China—past or present—never considered itself to be on the margin of Western Europe; this served to heighten the sense of trauma at the point of introduction. Second, Chinese modernity did not go through a phase of "aestheticization" of literature and culture—there was no assumption of an aesthetic of autonomy "as a cure for failed irredentist and wrecked hopes for a modern, democratic, and modern state" (Jusdanis 1991: 79). Instead, as I have repeatedly argued, whatever traces of aesthetic modernism one finds in modern Chinese literature had been subsumed under the larger narrative of modernity of which nationalism provides the central impetus. This conflation of the two modernities—historical and aesthetic—has deprived modern Chinese intellectuals of the power of critical reflection necessary to fully flesh out the ambiguities immanent in the Western legacies of modernity as well as its inevitable incongruities with autochthonous cultures. In this sense, Chinese modernity also remains "incomplete." It has only been in recent years, when China has become truly embroiled in globalism, that some initial efforts at critical self-reflection have been undertaken, but they tend to be, once again, conflated with the current Western discourses of post-modernism. A new "cycle" of confusion seems to lurk on the intellectual horizon.

It must also be pointed out that the meta-narrative of Chinese modernity should not be equated with the state's project of modernization. It definitely contains a crucial component of societal culture that should be, at least conceptually, at some critical remove from the state, as the May Fourth rhetoric implies. The "burden" of the May Fourth legacy, as I see it, lies again in its de facto confusion of the two realms, which in turn leaves little space for the emergence of a "civil society." Rather, this conflation of state and society in the name of nationalism gave May Fourth intellectuals both an exalted self-image and a self-assigned task of some enormity: to lead both state and society toward the grand vision of what Chen Duxiu called "a new civilization of the twentieth century." In hindsight, when the global problems bequeathed by Western modernity remain unsolved and incomplete, the incessant talk of responsibility and mission in the early May Fourth manifestos sounds like a utopian dream.

Works Cited

Anderson, Benedict. 1991. *Imagined Communities.* London: Verso.

Cang Fu 傖父. 1918. "Miluan zhi xiandai renxin" 迷亂之現代人心 (The confusion of the modern mind). *Dongfang zazhi* 15, no. 4 (Apr.): 1–7.

Chang Hao 張灝. 1994. "Zhuanxing shidai (1895–1920) zai Zhongguo jinxiandai sixiangshi yu wenhuashi shang de zhongyao xing" 轉型時代在中國進現代思想史與文化史的重要性 (The importance of the transitional period in modern Chinese intellectual and cultural history). Paper presented at Academia Sinica, Taibei, July 12.

Chen Duxiu 陳獨秀. 1916. "Yijiuyiliu nian" 一九一六年 (The year 1916). *Qingnian zazhi* 1, no. 5 (Jan. 15): 1–4.

———. 1918. "Zhiwen *Dongfang zazhi* jizhe" 質問東方雜誌記者 (Questioning the editors of the *Eastern Miscellany*). *Xin qingnian* 5, no.3 (Sept. 15): 206–12.

———. 1919. "Zai zhiwen *Dongfang zazhi* jizhe" 再質問東方雜誌記者 (Questioning once again the editors of the *Eastern Miscellany*). *Xin qingnian* 6, no.2 (Feb. 15): 148–61.

Chow, Tse-tsung. 1960. *The May Fourth Movement: Intellectual Revolution in Modern China.* Cambridge, Mass.: Harvard University Press.

Darnton, Robert. 1979. *The Business of Enlightenment: A Publishing History of the Encyclopedia, 1775–1800.* Cambridge, Mass.: Harvard University Press.

Doleželová-Velingerová, Milena, ed. 1988. *A Selective Guide to Chinese Literature 1900–1949,* vol. 1, *The Novel.* Leiden: E. J. Brill.

Fong, Gilbert Chee Fun. 1982. "Subjectivism in Xu Zhenya (1889–193?) and Su Manshu (1884–1918): Chinese Fiction in Transition." Ph.D. diss., University of Toronto.

Habermas, Jürgen. 1983. "Modernity—An Incomplete Project." In Hal Foster, ed., *The Anti-Aesthetic: Essays on Postmodernism,* pp. 3–15. Seattle: Bay Press.

———. 1991. *The Structural Transformation of the Public Sphere.* Cambridge, Mass.: MIT Press.

Hampson, Norman. 1982. *The Enlightenment: An Evaluation of Its Assumptions, Attitudes and Values.* New York: Penguin Books.

Hsia, C. T. 1982. "Hsü Chen-ya's *Yü-li hun*: An Essay in Literary History and Criticism." *Renditions* 17/18: 199–240.

Hu Shi 胡適. [1918] 1953. "Jianshe de wenxue geming lun" 建設的文學革命論 (On a constructive literary revolution). In *Hu Shi wencun* 胡適文存 (Collected works of Hu Shi), 1: 55–73. Taibei: Yuandong.

———. [1934] 1967. "Bi shang Liangshan: wenxue geming de kaishi" 逼上梁山：文學革命的開始 (Forced into outlawry: the beginnings of the literary revolution). In idem, *Sishi zishu* 四十自述 (A self-account at forty), pp. 91–122. Reprinted—Taibei: Yuandong.

Jusdanis, Gregory. 1991. *Belated Modernity and Aesthetic Culture: Inventing National Literature.* Minneapolis: University of Minnesota Press.

Lee, Leo Ou-fan. 1990. "In Search of Modernity: Some Reflections on a New Mode of Consciousness in Twentieth-Century Chinese History and Literature." In Merle Goldman and Paul A. Cohen, eds., *Ideas Across Cultures: Essays in Honor of Benjamin Schwartz*, pp. 109–35. Cambridge, Mass.: Harvard East Asian Monographs.

———. 1993. "Critical Spaces: The Construction of Cultural Criticism in Modern China." Unpublished paper. A revised Chinese version was published as Li Oufan 李歐梵, "Piping kongjian de kaichuang" 批評空間的開創 (Opening up a critical space). *Ershiyi shiji* 19: 40–51.

Liang Qichao 梁启超. [1900] 1967. "Hanman lu" 汗漫錄 (A record of wandering afar). In *Qingyi bao* 清議報 35: 2280–83. Reprinted in *Yinbingshi zhuanji* 飲冰室專集 (Special collection of the Yinbing studio), no. 22: 185. Taibei: Chengwen.

Lin Yu-sheng 林毓生. 1985. "The Morality of Mind and Immorality of Politics: Reflections on Lu Xun, the Intellectual." In Leo Ou-fan Lee, ed., *Lu Xun and His Legacy*, pp. 107–28. Berkeley: University of California Press.

Lin Yu-sheng et al. 1989. *Wusi: duoyuan de fansi* 五四：多元的反思 (May Fourth: pluralistic reflections). Hong Kong: Sanlian.

Link, E. Perry, Jr. 1981. *Mandarin Ducks and Butterflies: Popular Fiction in Early Twentieth-century Chinese Cities.* Berkeley: University of California Press.

Luo Jialun 羅家倫. 1954. "Jinri Zhongguo zhi zazhi jie" 今日中國之雜誌界 (The magazine world of today). In Zhang Jinglu 張靜廬, ed., *Zhongguo xiandai chuban shiliao jiabian* 中國現代出版史料甲編 (Historical materials on modern Chinese publishing, first collection), pp. 79–86. Shanghai: Zhonghua.

Masini, Federico. 1993. *The Formation of Modern Chinese Lexicon and Its Evolution Toward a National Language: The Period from 1840 to 1898.* Journal of Chinese Linguistics Monograph Series, no. 6. Berkeley: University of California.

Qian Zhixiu 錢智修. 1918. "Gonglizhuyi yu xueshu" 公利主義與學術 (Utilitarianism and scholarship). *Dongfang zazhi* 15, no. 6 (June): 1–7.

Schwarcz, Vera. 1986. *The Chinese Enlightenment.* Berkeley: University of California Press.

Wang Hui, Leo Ou-fan Lee, and Michael Fischer. 1994. "Is the Public Sphere Unspeakable in Chinese? Can Public Spaces Lead to Public Spheres?" *Public Culture* 6, no. 3 (Spring): 598–605.

Wang Xiaoming 王曉明. 1993. "Yifen zazhi he yige shetuan" 一份雜誌和一個社團 (A journal and a society). In Chen Guoqiu 陳國球, ed., *Zhongguo wenxue shi de xingsi* 中國文學史的省思 (Reflections on Chinese literary history), pp. 149–85. Hong Kong: Sanlian.

Wang Yuanhua 王元化. 1994. "Du Yaquan yu dongxi wenhua lunzhan" 杜亞泉與東西文化論戰 (Du Yaquan and the East-West cultural debate). *Xueren* 5 (Feb.): 1–24.

Wusi shiqi qikan jieshao 五四時期期刊介紹 (Introduction to the periodicals of the May Fourth period), vol. 1. 1979. Beijing: Sanlian.

Yü, Ying-shih 余英時. 1993. *Zhongguo jindai sixiangshi shang de Hu Shi* 中國近代思想史上的胡適 (Hu Shi in modern Chinese intellectual history). Taibei: Lianjing.

Zhang Jinglu 張靜廬. [1938] 1984. *Zai chubanjie ershi nian* 在出版界二十年 (Twenty years in the publishing world). Shanghai: Shanghai zazhi.

CHAPTER TWO

The Canonization of May Fourth

Rudolf G. Wagner

In this chapter, I argue the following points:

1. That the events on May Fourth were the first in China to be consciously crafted in a new form of social action, the "movement."

2. That this notion of the "movement" implied self-assertive action from citizens on self-chosen topics considered to be of national importance and badly mishandled by the existing political powers and parties.

3. That the effectiveness of this type of action was to rest on its capacity to stimulate broad public response and thus exert pressure on the government.

4. That the notion of the "movement" as a Japanese/Western concept implied a closed modernist, moralistic, and rational agenda, which could not legitimately be challenged from other discursive modes.

5. That in their specific performances on May Fourth the activists relied heavily on precedents in other "oppressed nations" that were reported in the Chinese press, in particular on the Korean events on and after March 1, 1919.

6. That in the eyes of the ideologues of May Fourth, the political elite as well as the populace at large were caught in traditional befuddlement and, as a consequence, had not shifted from being members of the species "slave" or "cattle" to being members of the species "man," which alone qualified for participation as mass in a mass movement.

7. That, as a consequence, what was later termed the New Culture movement was an integral part of the May Fourth agenda, because only by

Ms. Natascha Vittinghoff, Ms. Nanny Kim, and Ms. Andrea Janku have been my research assistants locating sources for this paper. I am exceedingly grateful for their valuable work.

radically transforming the elite ("Confucian") and mass ("superstition") cultural trappings could the Chinese become "men" and have a chance to survive in an environment of Social-Darwinist selection.

8. That the subjective legitimacy of May Fourth was derived not from a demoscopically or electorally gauged local mass appeal but from the internationalist logic of nations struggling for supremacy and the historical role of the educated as remonstrators.

9. That, as a consequence, the appeal of May Fourth was not populist and that its protagonists assumed the roles not of spokesman and representative but of teacher, avant-garde, and guide for the rest of the populace.

10. That this elitist structure embedded in the notion of the "movement" gave rise to two alternative definitions of the "spirit of May Fourth": the first according the role of the elite to the young educated members of the political class; the other to political parties willing and able to stay tuned to, direct, and instigate such "movements."

11. That the protagonists of May Fourth set out to establish this date of May 4 against other contenders such as National Shame Day, May 7, and the Day of the Republic, October 10, as an important anniversary in the national calendar as a recurring reminder to both the public and the government of the enduring legitimacy of such movements and as a prop to the legitimacy of their own political standing as the participants in the movement they described as a watershed in modern history and as administrators of the "spirit" of this movement.

12. That this struggle to fill the new republican calendar was part of a larger struggle to eliminate the peasant calendar organizing the "backward" productive and "superstitious" religious life of the large rural majority of the country.

13. That there was a struggle for hegemony over the definition of May Fourth and the control of the political capital it represented; the main fault line ran between the party in power—the Guomindang (GMD) or Chinese Communist Party (CCP)—and independent, mostly young, and educated contenders. The parties in power would claim for themselves the role of the avant-garde and would reduce the role of youth to a minor support prop. Independent political articulation was criminalized as "counterrevolutionary." The youths, often supported by opposition parties or illegal groups, would claim the legitimacy of May Fourth in times of a perceived national crisis to independently and publicly articulate their vindications in

order to exert pressure on a national government seen as unable to handle the crucial problems of the land.

14. That one of the specific manifestations of this struggle was the recurrent parallelism and contention between state-organized and citizen-organized celebrations of this day.

15. That the canonization of May Fourth with its strongly nationalist agenda as the core obliterated other possible priorities such as the setting up of a unified parliament negotiated during early 1919 between Beijing and Canton in Shanghai or the organizing of a sober assessment of China's economic development needs.

16. That the priority given to this nationalist agenda reflected the traditional commitment of the imperial elite to national unity as their area of professional circulation as well as the generalist dilettantism of former times perpetuated by the students and precluding sophisticated assessments of either political, economic, social, or cultural problems.

17. That the priority given to this nationalist agenda also reflected a lingering regret for China's loss of great power status and the hope of reestablishing this claim.

18. That the price paid for this nationalist priority was the hectic search, be it in literature, the economy, or revolution, for shortcuts to a world leadership that was assumed to be China's traditional due, with the result of a deep provincialism made up of cheap borrowings, heightened self-righteousness, and the claim that all of China's problems were due to imperialist evildoings.

19. That the self-righteousness encoded in the "spirit of May Fourth" prompted its protagonists to use a state power they were otherwise often critical of in order to effect the re-education of their benighted countrymen; in this process they did not refrain from resorting to terrorist methods especially with regard to popular religion.

20. That the shift from cultural remonstrance with the citizenry through the public sphere to the use of state power dramatically curtailed the leeway of the citizenry. Through the state policy of "partified" cultural re-education, the citizens were required not only to silently tolerate state action, as they had been in the past, but to actively verbalize and express their new cultural consciousness as the progressive "mass." At the same time the integration of a large part of the intelligentsia into this re-education effort deprived the populace of articulate and legitimate spokesmen for their woes.

21. That the May Fourth movement with its radical break with Confucianism, Christianity, and popular beliefs legitimized and systematized the cultural self-destruction of China, which had its antecedents in the relentless battles of the Confucian elite against popular "superstition" and the radical Christianization policies of the Taipings 太平 with their large-scale destructions of all other religious artifacts, buildings, and structures. The cultural desertification of China pursued by the Nationalist government during the "destroy superstition" movement of the late 1920s as well as by the Communist government after 1949 (and not only during the Cultural Revolution) were well within the May Fourth agenda.

22. That the May Fourth movement with its undiscriminating attack on the moral values upheld by the various belief systems present in China unwittingly helped to create a moral vacuum into which the diverse governments moved with a value propaganda running directly counter to some of the core tenets of May Fourth, especially the need to foster the development of a self-assertive and independent-minded individual. The core notion of the "new morality" spread by the Communists was Mao Zedong's 毛澤東 (1893–1976) "serve the people," which, under the particular institutional circumstances in which it was spread, preached the unquestioned subordination of the individual under party orders as opposed to the individual social commitment originally promoted by Hu Shi 胡適 (1891–1962) with this slogan. The core notions of the "new morality" spread by Chiang Kai-shek 蔣介石 (1887–1975) were patriotism plus the Confucian values of "humaneness," *ren* 仁, and "filial devotion," *xiao* 孝.

The Notion of the "Movement"

The May Fourth movement did not end up with this name. It had it before it started.

On May 3, 1919, Zhang Guotao 張國濤 (1897–1979)—a student later to become an important Communist military figure—made a speech at a mass meeting at Peking National University in which he spoke of the event planned for the next day as a "mass movement," *qunzhong yundong* 群衆運動 (1971: 50).[1] On the morning of May 4, the head of the organizing com-

1. Zhang inadvertently mentions the use of this term in recalling his first big speech at Peking University on May 3, 1919: "I have quite a strong Pingxiang accent and my pronunciation,

mittee at Peking National University, Di Fuding 狄福鼎 (1895–1964), stormed into the office of the journal *New Tide,* also known by its English subtitle *The Renaissance* (*Xin chao* 新潮), then edited by Luo Jialun 羅家倫 (1896–1969), and declared: "Today's movement cannot do without a public appeal" (note added to Luo 1943: 2). On May 26, 1919, Luo (then still a student but later to become the president of Qinghua University) published his famous "The Spirits of the May Fourth Movement" ("Wusi yundong de jingshen" 五四運動的精神), which fixed the term in print. With his opening rhetorical question "What is called the May Fourth movement?" he claimed in fact that the recent events had already been widely "called" this way and that he would offer now a description of their "spirits."[2] The organizers of the rally and demonstration on May Fourth were thus making a programmatic statement when they spoke of it as a "movement." They were selecting one form of action over another, and the term they used, "movement," gave to all participants enough guidelines to understand how to behave in this form of action; for example, that one could not do without a public appeal, a manifesto. To my knowledge, this was the first use of this form in China. Newspapers such as the *Shanghai News* (*Shenbao* 申報) in 1872 printed statements of purpose in the first issue and would do so again after major shifts in orientation. Reformers such as Liang Qichao 梁啓超 (1973–1929) and Kang Youwei 康有為 (1858–1927) had written articles or memorials to the emperor to state their purpose. But a public and political manifesto addressed not to scholars and officials but to people on the street and calling them to action belonged to a new brand of movement literature, which sported a new rhetoric and a new form of communication.

The conscious and positive use of the term *yundong* 運動 as representing a deliberate choice of action becomes still clearer when confronted with the other names given to these events. The newspapers spoke of "activities," *huodong* 活動 or *judong* 舉動, in order to stay on the neutral side, and a government spokesman is quoted by the Tianjin *L'Impartial* (*Dagongbao* 大公報) of May 6, 1919 (p. 1), as saying that things had quickly developed from *huodong* to *baodong* 暴動—from patriotic "activities" to "turmoil" (*Dagongbao* reprint, Beijing 1982: 45.53), a terminology again used by the government in

---

for example, of the all-important term 'mass movement' (群衆運動這個重要名詞) was quite different from the Beijing dialect (普通話) so that it was hard to understand."

2. In a letter on June 20, 1919, Dewey also referred to the May Fourth events as a "big cleanup reform politics movement" (quoted in Chow 1960: 102).

1989 to justify its crackdown. By planning and defining their activities as a "movement," the students claimed for it a positive evaluation.

The effort to revolutionize literature had already established the notion of a "movement" for this field, which was taken from descriptions by Chen Duxiu 陳獨秀 (1879–1942) and others of literary "movements" in Europe.[3] These movements shared some of the key characteristics of the political and social movements. They were not government instigated; they operated through the public sphere to find supporters; they brought about often dramatic changes in the public sphere without relying on parties or government organs.

As far as I have been able to find out, the events on May 4 are indeed the first in China to be defined by participants in this manner. From then on, the term quickly became popular for a certain type of political action, and by September 1919 the term was even widely used for the New Culture movement, *Xin wenhua yundong* 新文化運動.[4] By the mid-1920s, many political, cultural, and religious activities claimed the status of a "movement," which was also retroactively awarded to such currents as the "Yangwu 洋務 movement" of the 1860s and 1870s with its emphasis on a self-strengthening of China. Eventually the term became enshrined in the official denominations of a large number of such events in PRC parlance.

The notion of "movement" was a relative newcomer on the international political and social scene. It was first introduced as a scholarly concept by Lorenz vom Stein in 1851 in his *Geschichte der sozialen Bewegung in Frankreich von 1789 bis auf unsere Tage* (History of the social movement in France from 1789 to our days). Since this time, many social scientists have dealt with political and social movements, their relationships to political parties or simple social fashions, the variety of their internal organization and the structure of their leadership, or the scholarly definitions of this term (Heberle 1951; Deltgen 1969a, 1969b). However, this use of the term was imposed by definition and not derived from the way in which the participants described themselves.

---

3. Cf. the use of *wenxue geming yundong* 文學革命運動 in Zhongmi 1919: 445–46.

4. In July 1919, Cai Yuanpei spoke of a "movement to save the nation" 救國之運動 in his "Second Letter Addressed to the Students of Peking University Concerning 'May 4'" (printed in *Zhuanji wenxue* 傳記文學 14, no. 5 [May 1969], p. 86). For its use in the "New Culture movement" see, e.g., the advertisement for the journal *Young China* (*Shaonian Zhongguo* 少年中國) in the September 1919 issue of *Jianshe* 1, no. 2 (reprinted—Beijing: Renmin, 1980: 428), which claims its only purpose is to provide material for the "culture movement," *wenhua yundong* 文化運動.

This is evident from the fact that participants in the French social and political battles after the Revolution of 1789 did not define themselves as a "social movement."

The European term *movement/mouvement/movimiento/Bewegung*, however, is not a scholarly creation. It was and has remained to this day a term used as a self-definition of people involved, both in China and elsewhere. They were a "movement," and they knew they were. The plethora of studies of "social movements" notwithstanding, I have not been able to locate a single study dealing with the question of what the participants thought when defining themselves as a movement, what they communicated to the public with this term, and to what extent this notion gave them guidance for the particular kind of issue to take up, of action to undertake, of alliance to form, of authorities to address, and of structures to develop. We have thus the burden of outlining on our own a history of this notion and its implications.[5]

It seems that the term became a conscious self-definition only in the latter half of the nineteenth century. By 1885 Zola would speak of the *mouvement socialiste*, and it seems that the term started to be used in the sense of "our movement" for (presumably) broadly based "popular" and public vindications around a given topic or issue.

5. The specialized dictionaries of political and social terminology, for the French Revolution or Marxism, for example, do not provide the required material. The European historical dictionaries are of uneven reliability, and there are no historical dictionaries of language for either Japanese or Chinese. According to the *Dictionaire historique de la langue française* (1992), there are some early French uses of *mouvement* for an upheaval since the middle of the thirteenth century and for a collective reaction of a group translating itself into some collective behavior in the seventeenth century, but no social action defined itself as emanating from a *mouvement*. The term does not belong in the political dictionary of the French Revolution, although the long and detailed article on *mouvement* in d'Alembert's *Grande encyclopédie* makes it into a core notion of modern physics and astronomy and thus gives to a social movement the potential status of being in conformity with the universal laws of the cosmos. Early in the nineteenth century, the term was used in this sense for the movement of history and eventually ended up as a term used for collective and public actions that would bring about this movement and progress of history. The notion of movement could acquire positive implications only in the context of a dynamic worldview in which movements were thought to correspond to objective laws of development. The *Oxford English Dictionary* lists Benjamin Disraeli as the first on record to speak in one of his political novels of a "political movement" (1828) and quotes De Quincey decrying in 1835 the French *parti du mouvement*, a grouping of radical reformers whose program it was to bring about the objectively necessary "movement" of history.

For Japanese, the *Comprehensive Dictionary of the Japanese Language* (*Nihon kokugo daijiten* 日本國語大辭典, 1972) shows the early incorporation of this meaning into the Japanese vernacular as *undō* 運動. Possibly taking the term from the translations of Disraeli's political novels into Japanese, Yano Ryūkei 矢野龍溪 (1850–1931) used it as *undō* in his *A Noble Tale of Statesmanship* (*Keikoku bidan* 經國美談, 1883–84), speaking of "the center guiding the movement of the mob" 亂民の運動を支配する中心は, although the context makes it clear that the connotations here are negative. Tsubouchi Shōyō 坪内逍遙 (1859–1935) repeated this usage but this time in a more positive sense in his *The Character of Modern Students* (*Tōsei shosei katagi* 當世書生氣質, 1885–86) when he wrote of "making movements in the living society" 活社會に運動して, these movements being "generally devoted to political reform" 大に政治の改良で (*Nihon kokugo daijiten* 1972–76: 2.118, s.v. *undō*). By 1890, a coded propaganda song for the Freedom Party (Jiyū tō 自由黨), referring to it with the homophonous Bean of Freedom (Jiyū tō 自由豆), started with "It has begun, it has begun, the movement of the valiant has begun" 壯士が運動始めたよ, the movement referring to that for a constitution.[6]

It is thus very likely that the term as a translation of the Western "movement" reached China through Japan. The first evidence I have found for the term in China is in the title of a work *The Most Recent Chinese Revolutionary Movement* (*Zuijin Zhina geming yundong* 最近支那革命運動). I know nothing more about it than that it was banned in Sichuan in 1905, that it must have referred to the agitation surrounding the railway concessions and the railway loans, and the use of *Zhina* for China in the title suggests that it is a translation from the Japanese.[7] I cannot trace at this stage the exact history of the concept in Chinese. Liang Qichao did not translate the section of

6. "Mameuta (Yazuzukeko setsu)" (1890) in Soeda 1963: 19–20. A recording with textual notes is available on the record *Meiji ka to in de tsuzuru* 明治歌と音でつづる, King Record Ltd. Japan, 1967. I am exceedingly grateful to my learned Heidelberg colleague Wolfgang Schamoni for making these references available to me.

7. The banning of *The Most Recent Chinese Revolutionary Movement* is said to have been reported in the Shanghai paper *Jingzhong ribao* 警鐘日報. This information is given in *Shinmatsu shosetsu kara* 清末小說から, no. 46 (July 1997): 20. The date given there, however, Feb. 14, 1905, is not possible because by then the paper had stopped publishing. A check through the entire reprint also netted no results.

Keikoku bidan in which the term appeared. To my knowledge, it came into use in the above meaning only after the end of the Qing.[8]

The notion of "movement" is set against that of calm, of immobility. In the polemical vocabulary of the first years after the founding of the Republic in 1911, these latter terms received ever worsening press. China was characterized as immobile, stagnant. In a reader's letter by Zhu Ruyi 朱 如 一 in April 1917 in *New Youth* (*Xin qingnian* 新 青 年) entitled "Activity and Human Life" ("Huodong yu rensheng" 活 動 與 人 生) the cosmology of political movements is nicely argued:

Everything in the cosmos moves. According to Newton, a moving body does so eternally if not influenced by something else. The cosmos started with movement and will end with it. The world may go under and the cosmos be smashed, but matter in space cannot be annihilated and this continues to move. All that moves changes, and once there is change, the old and new separate and this and the other are separated. Without movement nothing in the cosmos could change, and with eternal stagnation no individuation could take place. Without movement (活 動) neither cosmos nor entities exist; thus movement (活 動) is the basic nature of the cosmos, the root and source of the ten thousand kinds of entities. We men . . . pride ourselves to be the most operative (靈) of the ten thousand kinds of entities. And what makes us into the most operative? That we alone excel at moving (活 動). . . . [The Neo-Confucian philosopher] Cheng Yichuan [1033–1107] says, "Heaven and Earth accumulate essence [of Life]; that which receives the most excellent of the Five Agents is man. As to his basic [nature], it is pure and tranquil (靜)."[9] I dare to replace this "calm" with "moving" (動). . . . The basic character of man definitely is movement (運 動). Without movement, he will be weak and fearful and cannot live out his human character, and that is called "a deformed person" (畸 人); deviating from Heaven and going against his nature without being able to fully live out his endowments, he is called a "sick body." . . . The purpose of mankind is movement (活 動). Without movement, knowledge finds no application and ethics is only empty words. . . . Now people are saying that the culture of our land is a culture of tranquillity, which enjoys pleasant rest and cherishes peace, puts the emphasis on cultural behavior and treats martial virtues lightly; and that it is different from the European culture of movement (動), where proceedings in society are fought over

8. The *Hanyu wailaici cidian* (1984: 398) lists *yundong* 運 動 in the meaning of "sports" as an import from Japan; it fails to note that the meaning in the sense of a sociopolitical movement also comes from there. The term is not listed in Masini 1993, because this work includes new terminology only through 1898.

9. Quoted in Zhu Xi, comp., *Jinsi lu* 近 思 錄, Sibu beiyao, 2.1b; see also Wing-tsit Chan, trans., *Reflections on Things at Hand* (New York: Columbia University Press, 1967), p. 36.

and the states devote their energy to war. They are pleased and satisfied with this. In fact, however, our country has been the pinnacle of progress over thousands of years, and this progress was the result of our movement. As long as movement does not stop, progress does not come to a halt. . . . Progress without halt definitely is our ideal. . . . [In short,] the success or failure of an individual is determined by checking the strength of his motive power (活動力); extrapolated from this, the flourishing or demise of a state can be determined by checking the strength of the motive power of its citizens. The weakness of our state lies in the fact that the Chinese do not appreciate movement. (Zhu Ruyi 1917: 193–94)

The argument links the principle of the universe—motion—with that of human life. With the capacity for conscious action, humans are the only ones able to consciously go against this cosmic principle and espouse quietism, which is seen here as personal and national stagnation. Against this, motion on all levels had to be and was propagated, especially in the pages of *New Youth*. Movement meant the strengthening and martialization of the body, the enlivening of the mind, the change and reform of the state, and a shift from weak obsequiousness to a combative self-assertion for the purposes of change for progress. A year after the May Fourth events, Luo Jialun was to return to this theme and claim that May Fourth had in fact "got China moving" (1920: 846).

The first, to my knowledge, to take up the notion of "movement" as a form of collective social action with regard to China was Chen Duxiu in 1916 in his article suggestively entitled (in arabic numerals) "1916." In this keynote article for the New Year issue of 1916 of the periodical later well-known under the title *New Youth* (*Xin qingnian* 新青年) but at that time still called *Youth* (*Qingnian* 青年), Chen Duxiu proposed to his readers—"the young gentlemen whose burden is heavy and whose way is long"—to make a clean break with the past year. There should be clean breaks between centuries and "if the culture of the twentieth century does not contribute something beyond that of the nineteenth century, the existence of the twentieth century is worthless, and twentieth century history is empty" (1916a: 371).

The same sort of break should now be made between 1915 and 1916. The main reason was the rapid change in the world due to the war. *Youth* had reported with enthusiasm about the Young Germany Association (Jung Deutschland) with its stress on patriotism, education, and physical training (Xie 1915: 243–45), and Chen 1916a: 371–74) envisaged Germany as the rising new power, symbolizing "the replacement of the old by the new," *xinchen daixie* 新陳代謝, in a programmatic phrase often reappearing in his writings at the time. The old powers like Turkey were going under and the newer powers, England, France, and Russia, were helplessly looking on as the "hearts of the Muslim world were turning toward Germany" with the possibility of the colonies being lost.

The shame of China in the previous year, in which its government accepted Japan's Twenty-one Demands, could not "even be washed away by the combined waters of the Yangzi and the Han River." The "heart blood had to be renewed" as a way to renovate the human character, the state, society, the family, and the nation. According to Chen Duxiu, the young should do three things to achieve this renovation:

> 1. Put yourself into the position to conquer and not into one to be conquered. In all of mankind, the men are the conquerors, and the women are the conquered. The white man is the conqueror; all the non-whites are the conquered. Among the nations in the Far East, the Manchus and the Japanese are conquerors, and the Han race are a conquered nation. Within the Chinese race, it is especially along the Yangzi valley where the conquered nation of this conquered nation is living, with the law-abiding citizens to the south of Suzhou and the Yangzi [i.e., the people of Shanghai] as their representatives. What kind of people are conquerors? They are good at valiant fighting and are so fierce that they cannot be subdued. What kind of people are the conquered? They are fearful and submit to the powerful; they strive only after the safety of their present life and property, and they even meekly submit to the plundering by enemies and eunuchs from another nation, and praise them. They are what is called "obedient people. . . ."[10]
>
> 2. Emulate the character of independence and self-mastery in the individual; don't become an appendage of others. . . . If an individual becomes an appendage of another individual, he loses his character of freedom and self-respect and sinks into the position of the conquered, the women, slaves, prisoners of war, or domestic animals. . . . The Confucian theory of the three relationships . . . makes the people an appendage of the prince without any freedom and self-mastery.
>
> 3. Pursue citizen movements (從事國民運動); don't get entangled in factional movements (勿囿黨派運動). Man from birth is a private being (私) and cannot do without parties. For politics to use parties is the best. In criticizing parties there are two opinions:

---

10. It is interesting that Chen Duxiu takes verbatim the key features of this characterization of his compatriots as "striving only after the safety of their life and property" and "submitting to the powerful" from a Japanese article "The National Character and Social Organization of China" 支那之民族性與社會組織 in the Japanese journal *Valiant Youth* (*Giyu seinen zasshi* 義勇青年雜誌), quoted by Chen in *Youth* 1, no. 3 (Nov. 1915): 2–3.

a. Political party politics is a leftover (長 物) from 1915 not fit to be used in today's China. Pure political party politics can be seen only in London, England, and even there they are not secure. That England is able to continue with this system is due to the fact that its citizens are almost all [members of] political parties. The rich and noble belong to the Conservative Party, the poor and downtrodden belong to the Labour Party, if they do not belong to the Liberals. The political parties are something like a transfiguration of the citizens themselves. . . . Great policies of the state are generally decided by means of the three "Cs," namely "contest," that is party contest, "conference," that is negotiation, and "compromise." Few other states can match this.

For us [Chinese] this is even more difficult. The political parties have become shallower by the year and month, and what they represent is too narrow. They are being regarded as a special class within the citizenry and also consider themselves as a particular kind of profession. In the distribution of privileges they might accommodate each other, but in the craving for monopolies they battle each other without end. That is why [I] say: the politics of political parties are not fitting for today's China.

b. For years there have been only party and faction movements (黨 派 運 動) in our country, but no citizen movements (國 民 運 動). The French revolution was the revulsion (惡) of the French citizenry (國 民) against the monarchy and the power of the church. The independence of America was the revulsion of the people of the thirteen provinces against vexatious taxes. The Japanese [Meiji] reform was the revulsion of the Japanese citizens against the Tokugawa autocracy. These [three], accordingly, were citizen movements of the French, Americans, and Japanese and not the success of the pretensions of the people of one party or grouping.

What the people of one party or grouping maintain but what does not come from the movement of the majority of the citizens in fact is hardly to be brought to a successful end. And even if successful, it will not agree with the basic progress of the citizenry.

The reform (維 新)[11] of our country, its return to olden times (復 古), its becoming a republic (共 合) or a monarchy (帝 政)—these are propositions maintained and fought over by the governing party and the opposition parties (在 野 黨), but the citizenry follows [these squabbles] like a fire on the other shore, they look on with interest but not with concern. The result [of these squabbles] is but the victory or defeat of a party or grouping and has definitely nothing to do with the fundamental progress of the citizenry. Let us take it upon ourselves to be the young men and women of 1916! That each may make efforts to be a strong and resourceful citizen so that the party movements of our state get ahead and become citizen

---

11. Note that this is the term designating Japanese reforms.

movements from 1916 on! And I dare predict to our young ladies and gentlemen that 1916 will also be the year when the political situation is such that the minority of excellent policies of political parties develops into a majority of excellent policies of the citizenry. (Chen Duxiu 1916a: 371–74)[12]

Already in his introduction, Chen had mentioned that even in England the "weakness of its party politics becomes ever more evident." In view of the Chinese experience with factional politics, this option seemed even less attractive. Further, according to Chen, none of the major turnabouts in modern history, the French Revolution, American independence, and the Japanese Reform, came about through "movements of parties and factions"; they were all the result of "movements of the citizenry." Only in this manner could politics be turned from being the affair of a few politicians to being that of the citizenry at large. The awakening of the citizens to their duties and possibilities created the subjective conditions for a successful conquest or defense of self-rule.

From this reference as well as the polemics against the parties, we can infer what Chen Duxiu saw as the particulars of such movements:

1. The movement is a form of political action used all over the world, especially where grand and successful social changes have come about. This implies that China's problem can be fully defined in terms of an international political experience and that much can be learned from such international experience as to specific procedures.

2. It is the appropriate form to bring about fundamental changes in society like the "reform of our country," China, which has to do with all three issues at stake in North America, France, and Japan, namely, independence, social reform, and political reform.

3. It is a relatively short-term social activity focused on a particular issue, which is the reason why Chen could speak of "citizen movements" and "party movements" in the plural.

4. It involves very broad sectors of the populace, not just a group or faction, around issues of national importance, such as independence and basic political and institutional reform. The change in basic attitude which this involvement presupposes will come at different speeds for different segments of the population. The addressees of the essay are the "young gentlemen whose burden is heavy and whose way is long," the youth who will be pro-

12. On the general importance of this article in Chen's work, see Zhu Chengjia 1989.

grammatically called "the new youth" from September 1916 on. As the section of the adult populace with the longest life ahead of them, the greatest "power of resistance," openness to new things, and willingness to change, they are the natural candidates for sparking off such a movement.

5. These American, Japanese, and French reforms were not granted by the men in power through the established channels of social negotiation, but had to be pushed through against them by the "movement," which thus brought about a fundamental change in the citizens themselves, in the leading personnel, and in the institutional structure of the state.

6. A movement presupposes individuals willing and able to resist the established order of things, to dedicate their lives to the movement, and to acquire the necessary knowledge and skill to make the enterprise successful. This presupposes a break with those elements of tradition that instill docility and obedience into the young as key virtues, in the Chinese case the "three net-ropes," *san'gang* 三 綱. The first two attitudes recommended by Chen, "put yourself into the position of the conquerors," and "emulate the character of independence and self-mastery in the individual; don't become an appendage of others," are thus the essential personality features for the participants in such movements.

A month later, in February 1916, Chen spelled out these ideas in more detail in the article "Our Ultimate Consciousness" ("Wuren zuihou zhi juewu" 吾人最後之覺悟) (1916b), in which he outlined the changes of Chinese consciousness in six stages of Sino-Western interaction. Until now, the Republic is but an affair of a few political leaders without any involvement by the larger segments of the population. With the impulse coming from the young, this has to change. A "political awakening" of the multitude of citizens is needed; they have to live out the fact that they are "political animals"; they have to follow "the international path" 世界系之軌道 to move "from autocratic politics to free politics, from individual politics to politics of the citizenry, from bureaucratic politics to self-administered politics"; but the "single basic condition for the realization of the 'constitutional system' and 'politics of the citizenry' is simply whether the majority of the citizenry is able to take an active position of being the master with regard to the political consciousness." In this framework, the "New Culture" movement with its attacks on the Confucian code of social behavior and of "popular superstition" is an essential part of and underpinning for the development of political movements in China.

7. The "movement" envisaged here is not a spontaneous outburst. In fact, the masses who are supposed to get involved need much previous education and guidance so that the "movement" can fulfill its potentially progressive functions. The factual mental state of the citizenry is thought to be one of narrow self-interest, disregard for the interests of the nation, spiritual weakness, and meek obedience. Luo Jialun would complain a year later that in fact no real knowledge existed about the mental state of the "masses," quite apart from the fact that there were still only a few thousand students who seriously qualified as "masses" (1920: 847). The movement would thus come about through the guidance of an educated, progressive, and informed elite, which for itself would already fulfill these qualifications and thus had the legitimacy to guide the others. This elite was to be the young intelligentsia addressed in *Youth / New Youth, New Tide, Weekly Review* (*Meizhou pinglun* 每週評論), and other similar journals.

8. The movement does not seem to replace the party as an essential organizational form. The initial statement that "man from birth is a private being (私) and cannot do without parties. For politics to use parties is the best" remains in force, and even after the scathing condemnation of Chinese political parties and factions, Chen only suggests "that the party movements of our state get ahead and become citizen movements from 1916 on!" However, the only purpose parties seem to have is to promote citizen movements, because only in this manner can they prevent themselves from becoming distribution networks for privileges and ensure that the changes wrought are also those in the attitude of the citizenry.

9. Although movements might have a military component, this is decidedly not essential. And if there was a strong military component as in America, this would not come in the form of individual terror, as had been advocated by the Chinese anarchists, but in that of an armed mass uprising.

The emphasis on the urgent need for citizen movements in this article was not transitory. After the events of May 4, *New Youth*'s program of December 1919 upgraded the importance of "popular mass movements" 民衆運動 while reducing that of the traditional parties to zero: "What we advocate is a social transformation through popular mass movements, and we absolutely break off all relationships with the past and present political parties of the different factions" 我們主張的是民衆運動社會改造和過去及現在各派政黨絕對斷絕關係 (*Xin qingnian* 7, no. 1 [1919]: 4).

Sun Yat-sen's 孫中山 (1866–1925) new journal *Construction* (*Jianshe* 建設) also recognized the particular organizational form that was the "movement," when writing in October 1919 that upon the news of the loss of Shandong, "everyone got together and made use of the method of demonstration movements (示威運動) to express the true and honest will of the people. The ensuing student strikes and shop strikes were all continuations of this movement and are included in this term 'May Fourth movement.' The Beijing papers have coined the special term 'May Fourth movement' for this movement" (Shen 1919: 599). Such "demonstration movements," the article continues, were "quite common in the West" and even the Japanese had not been able to avoid them. In China, however, there had not been any such movements prior to May Fourth, which was "a new beginning that helped 'progress' and 'the life of mankind'" (Shen 1919: 600).

Given the wide circulation and the influence of *Youth / New Youth* and Chen Duxiu among the young intelligentsia, there can be no question that the organizers of the May Fourth events understood their own action in the context of the "citizenry movement" outlined in Chen's article in this journal. Its argument that the North American, French, and Japanese reforms had all sprung from such movements lent it the double strength of being the "world current" that China should definitely join and of being successful. The two slogans at the end of the only public appeal distributed during the May Fourth demonstrations attest to this influence: "It may be that the land of China is conquered, but it may not be that it is given away. It may be that the people of China are slaughtered, but it may not be that they bend their heads." This combative summary expresses in a very succinct form the new core virtues for which Chen Duxiu had pleaded in his two articles.

The use of the "movement" mode of political action rejects other forms of political action that had been tried and found unfitting. In particular, these outmoded forms of action were other elite forms like party politics as an instrument to influence government policy, individual armed terror against leading representatives of the state as advocated earlier by the anarchists, and spontaneous, diffuse types of mass action like the Boxer uprising (Yihe tuan 義和團), which lacked a "progressive" orientation. This rejection became quickly evident in 1919 when the May Fourth activists refused not only to join the May 7 commemorative activities for "National Shame Day" but also to join in the various petitions to the government coming from different circles and regions. Petitions and mourning over one's shame were meek and helpless articulations used only by slaves and defeatists (cf. Onu 1989).

We can thus make a first assertion: the leading activists of the May Fourth demonstrations were making a conscious decision when opting for the form of the "movement" for their action. It stressed independent, essentially unarmed, civic action of broad sectors of the populace enlightened as to the essential interests of the nation. It rejected other established forms of political action as ineffectual and damaging, even if successful.

Although the general framework of the May Fourth activists certainly was established by the arguments advanced by Chen Duxiu as well as the role envisaged for the intelligentsia in this scenario, the articles quoted above were still not specific enough to function as guidelines for action in such movements.[13] It was not at all evident what to do in such hectic moments, whether and how to go public, whom to address, how to behave toward the government, the police, or the foreign legations, what form to choose—the rally, the indoor meeting, the demonstration—what symbols to craft, what clothes to wear, what speeches to make, and how to define the targets. For this type of social action, the Chinese had no "modern" domestic precedents and were in urgent need of advice. Many revolutionaries found themselves in the same quandary then, before, and after. The French Revolution therefore drew its precedents from Republican Rome, the European, American and Asian student movements of the 1970s eagerly copied each other, including the Red Guards, and the civic mass movements in Iran, South Africa, the Philippines, Korea, and Japan showed themselves keenly aware of one another's forms of action down to the headgear, the slogans, and the organizational forms. Were there models of behavior, speech, and action on which the May Fourth demonstrators could and did draw?

The March 1, 1919, Korean Precursor of the May Fourth Movement

In an assessment of the May Fourth movement a week after the event, Luo Jialun seemed to refer to such models, asking: "Are we Chinese not even a match to the Koreans and Indians?" (1919: 3). In a similar manner, a text circulated after the event but perhaps drafted before, claimed: "The French in

13. For studies using a similar methodology for the role of such precedents for the performance of social action, cf. Wagner 1982, 1991, 1992; and Esherick and Wasserstrom 1990.

their struggle for Alsace-Lorraine cried, 'Give us our wish or give us death.' The Italians in their struggle for the Adriatic Strait cried, 'Give us our wish or give us death.' The Koreans in their struggle for independence also cried, 'Give us our wish or give us death.' We now face a crisis in which our country is threatened with subjugation and her territory is going to be ceded" (quoted in Chow 1960: 107). In his first assessment of May Fourth in August 1919, Mao Zedong bluntly linked this movement with the international currents. After describing the strikes and other social movements in Europe during the preceding months, he wrote: "The furious waves rolled toward the West and then turned and came about to the East. England, France, Italy, and the USA saw many big workers' strikes, and quite a few revolutionary upheavals occurred in India and Korea. With the upsurge of these armies elsewhere, there finally occurred, between the Chinese Great Wall and the Gulf of Zhili [i.e., in North China], the 'May Fourth' movement!" (Mao 1919: 390).

A glance at the Chinese papers during the period immediately preceding May Fourth will quickly substantiate the point that the activists were quite aware of "movements" elsewhere, were well informed about them, and had a fair number of models to borrow from. By adapting their gestures, symbols, and forms of struggle, they joined in a common agenda and could hope to garner similarly friendly responses in the Chinese media as had these other movements. At the same time the public, which read the same papers, would be able to identify them from these trappings as patriotic heroes risking their lives for their fatherland instead of mistaking them for a bunch of youngsters who instead of studying were disturbing the public order and arrogating for themselves the right to speak for the nation.

During this period, the Chinese papers had been full of reports about anti-colonial and anti-imperialist stirrings from all over Asia, in many cases in direct connection with the Versailles peace negotiations. They ranged from a letter written in blood by Vietnamese to the negotiators in Paris to movements in India that led to the imposition of martial law (*Dagongbao*, Mar. 23, 1919),[14] from an "independence movement" in Mongolia presumably engineered by the Japanese government (*Dagongbao* 1919, March 13), to, most important, the independence movement in Korea, which was reported in

---

14. On March 29, 1919, the *Chenbao* also printed, on p. 3, an appeal of the Vietnamese Independence Party ("Yuenan dulidang zhi huyu" 越南獨立黨之呼籲).

much detail, especially by the Beijing *Morning Post* (*Chenbao* 晨 報), but also in the Tianjin *L'Impartial* and the *Shanghai News*.[15]

The terminology for "movement" remained unstable. During the early phase the term *yundong* was closer to the notion of "agitation." It was often used as a verb—"movementing" or "agitating"—and only gradually acquired the distinct meaning of a social movement in the sense of a loose social formation to which one could belong. This element became firmly established only when the generation of participants came of age, and it became a distinguishing part of their vita and status to have been part of this movement. From the beginning, however, *yundong* had a positive ring. The term "independence movement," *duli yundong* 獨 立 運 動, for Mongolia appeared only in a Japanese government statement rebutting the charge of Japanese involvement. Thus, by calling it by this specific term, this Mongolian "movement" got an authenticity and dignity of its own in terms of its supposed popular support, which was to lend credibility to the Japanese rebuttal of the charge that it had been their creation.

L'Impartial reported on March 1, 1919, the "independence activities," *duli huodong* 獨 立 活 動, in different Korean cities. The next day, it reported on the harsh repressive measures by the Japanese authorities against this agitation, which later was called the March 1 movement, and about the provisional government set up by the "leaders movementing for independence" 運 動 獨 立 之 領 袖. On March 3, the *Shanghai News* reported, on the basis of an Osaka news report, the (shocking) participation of women in the demonstrations and said: "Those movementing for the rallies distributed their propaganda sheets, and there were students who made speeches to passersby." The Beijing *Morning Post*, which was associated with Liang Qichao's faction and also printed Liang's reports from Versailles, took up these various reports on March 6 with an article, "A Detailed Report about the Revolutionary Movement in Korea" ("Gaoli geming yundong xiangbao" 高 麗 革 命 運 動 詳 報), the title of which elevated the Korean protests into a "revolutionary movement" (*Chenbao*, March 6, 1919, p. 2).

From then on, the newspaper carried extensive news about this movement nearly every day; it also made great efforts at newsgathering outside

15. The Korean events are listed by Chow (1960: 10) among the examples showing "possibilities of change by popular uprising" to the Chinese. Jansen (1975: 241–47) juxtaposes the "stirrings" in Japan, Korea, and China but does not go into the details of their parallels and mirroring.

the channels of the Japanese colonial authorities and their news releases. According to the article "Independence Movements in Different Regions of Korea" ("Gaoli gedi zhi duli yundong" 高麗各地之獨立運動), the Korean movement made best use of the fact that people from all over the country were streaming into the capital to pay their last respects to the late emperor, who was widely rumored to have been killed by the Japanese. The women students "also came out in formed ranks and distributed leaflets," and male students made speeches on street corners. In this way they reached a receptive national audience and were able to spread their movement throughout the country, Japanese censorship and police notwithstanding. Many educational institutions in Korea were run by missionaries and the large Korean Christian community. This provided a vital channel of information and organization for the students, many of whom were in these schools. The article also reported that the demonstration started with a rally in front of the Korean imperial palace and had gone from there to the French and American embassies (not to the Japanese colonial authorities) (*Chenbao*, March 27, 1919).

The *Morning Post* at this stage had to use many hostile Japanese reports for news. These reports spoke not of a movement but of "disturbances," *luanshi* 亂事, "upheavals," *panluan* 叛亂, "incidents," *biandong* 變動, or "havoc," *bianluan* 變亂. Reading them against their bias and inserting its own, the *Morning Post* looked for counterbalancing tidbits from other, unnamed sources. To show that the participants were decent human beings, this first long *Morning Post* article ends: "According to information, there was no disturbance whatever during the funeral cortege [for the emperor]" through the streets packed with weeping onlookers. On March 12, it reported that the movement had spread through the entire country and that there had been over 3,500 arrests.

On the same day, it printed the entire text of a letter sent in February 1919 to the Japanese Diet by the Korean Youth for Independence League (Kŏryŏch'ongnyon kuklip tuan 高麗青年獨立團). The letter described Korea as an old civilized nation with every right to independence, declared that with the changes in Russia and China there was no need for "protection" from Japan, and that as a consequence of Japanese policies of suppression and appropriation of the Korean national wealth "there had been agitation for independence (運動獨立) everywhere during the last few years." This document, quoted in the article "Supporting the Struggle of Korean

People Agitating for Independence" ("Zai feng Hanren yundong duli zhi anchao" 在奉韓人運動獨立之暗潮), is also the first I have seen which clearly uses *yundong* as a noun: "thus in Korea arose a kind of movement" 發生一種運動 (*Chenbao*, March 12, 1919, p. 3). On March 13, *L'Impartial* reported that women students had paraded on March 3 and sung religious songs and the Marseillaise, and said that elsewhere in the country there had been "demonstration movements," *shiwei yundong* 示威運動; the *Morning Post* was able to interview a European with twenty years' experience in Korea who was fluent in the language and had just come from Seoul. He reported about the tremendous importance of the Korean Proclamation of Independence of March 1, which was "spread throughout the country," claimed independence for a republican state of Chaoxian (instead of the old imperial Kŏryŏ) and advocated civil not military means to reach this goal. This European used the term *yundong* in the Western sense as a loose social formation that one could "join," *jiaru* 加入.

The article ended with another full document brought by the European informant, in this case from the Korean Citizen League for Independence (Kuklip kukmin tuan 獨立國民團). Finally, on March 14, the *Morning Post* came out with a strong editorial simply entitled "[Our] shame" ("Can" 慚) (Xing Mu 1919). The state of Korea, it said, had disappeared like a stone sunk in the sea. But unexpectedly there "finally were some valiant men (志士) lifting it out from the depths and restoring it to its original form. For this many lives have been sacrificed, and they braved the greatest dangers, but they were not discouraged, they really have a courage and uprightness to be applauded." The Koreans furthermore had understood that the Paris conference was the crucial moment they had to use to turn around their fate. Even if they were not entirely successful, Japanese rule would never be the same. In all three areas, the behavior of the Chinese was a "shame." They did not care about the dismemberment of their fatherland, "our country disregards the crucial moment" [of the Paris conference], and as "China at present is already half dead and continuing in the same manner as hitherto, it could only expect the collapse." "Seeing these activities of the Koreans and looking back at China's situation can really make one ashamed."

On March 20, the *Morning Post* printed on its op-ed page (Free Speech Forum, Ziyou luntan 自由論壇) a piece entitled "New Lessons from the Korean Independence Movement" ("Chaoxian duli yundongzhong zhi xin jiaoxun" 朝鮮獨立運動中之新教訓), which claimed that this movement, weak as its material forces were, was so strong in its spirit that it "marked the beginning of a new era in revolutionary circles." The Koreans were unarmed, could only distribute leaflets and hold rallies, they fought against impossible odds, and they proved that "every revolution in history was inseparably linked to the students" and drew its strength from nothing but the consciousness of these bookworms. In all this they were in agreement with world trends and would eventually gain victory, which the author wished them by inviting his readers, "we have to loudly exclaim 'Long Live the Spirit of the Korean Independence Movement.'" In the end, the article took on the Chinese students—just over a month before the May Fourth events!

> When thinking of China, one really must be ashamed. About those without consciousness, we do not even have to talk. But even those who do have consciousness are so feeble and weak in their resolve! They babble about anarchism, have golden rings on their fingers, and pen articles promoting individualism, and they get closer and closer to the powers-that-be. The regular university students throw themselves into studying to become bureaucrats or political operators, and when the students today are like this, we can image how society will look tomorrow. That is why at present I do not hate the bureaucrats, but the students; I don't hate the deadwood with their deplorable ignorance and greed but the "new personalities" with their straight words and crooked hearts. (*Chenbao*, March 20, 1919, p. 2)

On March 27, the *Morning Post* reported on the further spread of the movement that had started on March 18 with shop owners closing their shutters. Since then the paper had daily published a long column on events in Korea showing large numbers of common folk and students continuing to battle Japanese military and police forces undeterred, it seemed, by torture, wanton brutality, heavy casualties, and many arrests. Although the reports also mentioned attacks on military installations, demonstrators did not use arms, but by and large used forms of civil disobedience, which secured them much international acclaim and support. A Western observer, quoted in the *Morning Post* on April 13, claimed that the "upsurge of [the demand for] independence was an extremely civilized and peaceful agitation that did not exceed crying out loud 'long live independence.'" On April 5, the *Morning Post* reported that students in Seoul had stoned the house of Yi Wanyong 李 完 用, who nine years before had "sold the country [to the Japanese]." On April 12, the same paper reported that Korean students refused to take the Japanese examinations and wanted to take Korean examinations "after independence." On April 20, the first appeal of the Korean Provisional Government was quoted in full. On April 25, the paper carried a report about the careful planning of the March 1 events as well as the broad social base of the movement. There were four segments in this movement, students in the Christian schools, workers and farmers, Confucian scholars, and the royal family and aristocracy. On May 2, the word was given to a missionary who sent a report to President Wilson on the brutalities he had witnessed in Korea. He ended by claiming that "Korean independence is not a matter of a minority of radicals bent on overthrowing the government but the activity of eighteen million Koreans opposing the brutal military suppression by Japan." On May 6, 1919, the paper published "A Comparison Between Korea and China" ("Gaoli yu Zhongguo zhi bijiao" 高麗與中國之比較) with the telling subtitles "Today's Korea Is the Forerunner of Tomorrow's China" ("Jinri zhi Gaoli wei weilai Zhongguo zhi xiandao" 今日之高麗為未來中國之先導) and "The Korea of the Past Is the Miniature Image of Today's China" ("Guoqu zhi Gaoli wei jinri Zhongguo zhi xiao ying" 過去之高麗為今日中國之小影). It is a reprint of an editorial from the *China Press* (*Dalu bao* 大陸報) that argues that the Koreans had in large part only themselves to blame for falling under Japan's rule. The traitors who would sell their fatherland did have their way in Korea, as they were now having in China. And Korea showed the direction in which to move. The article does not make a direct comparison with the events on May Fourth, which still seemed to be on an altogether different dimension. However, the guarded optimism in this article as opposed to the harangues in the earlier ones suggests a change in climate.

The Korean independence movement culminated just a few weeks before May Fourth with the realization that the Versailles negotiations would not bring independence to Korea. The turning point was March 1, 1919, "Independence Day," when an independent government was announced and a new constitution secretly promulgated in the midst of great rallies and demonstrations. This "movement" seemed to have gained very widespread popular support among students, both male and female, the business classes, workers, and even in villages across the country. The activists came from the Korean Protestant community, from the Religion of the Heavenly Way (Ch'ondogyo 天道教) with its commitment to modernization and nonviolence, and from among the students.

The Chinese reporting of the Korean events in fact provided the students in China with specific guidelines on how to act in a "movement," what to expect in terms of popular participation, and how to elicit such participation. The Korean events were called forth by the frustration over the failure of the Paris Peace Conference to enact Wilsonian principles and return Korea to independence (*Shenbao*, Mar. 9, 1919). The same could be said of the Chinese events. The Korean events were marked by a clear commitment to Western values visible not only in the declaration of independence and the later provisional constitution (*Dagongbao*, April 30, 1919), but also in the ambivalence of, for example, the Ch'ondogyo with regard to the modernizing input of Japan in Korea, which earlier had led this organization "with over a million members throughout the country" to side with the Japanese (Jansen 1975: 243–44; for the number of members, see *Shenbao*, Mar. 5, 1919, quoting a dispatch from Osaka).

The rally on March 1, 1919 (and activities on some later days), in the capital took place—all modernism notwithstanding—in front of the palace of the emperor (*Shenbao*, Mar. 9, 1919), who had just died amid rumors that he had been assassinated by the Japanese. This was obviously a place symbolizing the heart of the nation. The Chinese students held their rally in front of Tian'anmen, the main entrance to the former imperial palace.

The Korean demonstration did not address the official (Japanese) authorities, whose legitimacy in running the country was denied, but the public, and it went directly to the missions of the United States and France to ask their governments for international support. Similarly, the May Fourth demonstration was addressed not to the government but to the public and foreign legations directly.

Both in language and action, the main thrust of resentment was directed not against the foreign power, in this case Japan, but against the domestic traitors who made Japanese encroachment or domination possible. This transferred the problem to a manageable—domestic—level and also provided targets for attack without the risk of taking on the Japanese military itself. Both in Korea and China, violence was directed against people accused to be such traitors such as Yi Wanyong in Korea or Cao Rulin 曹 汝 林 (1876–1966) and Zhang Zongxiang 章 宗 祥 (1879–1962) in China, both of whom had been involved in negotiating the secret loans from Japan in 1917–18 and were seen as advocates of Japan's interests in China.

The forms of propaganda used in Korea were slogans cried out by one leader and then echoed by the crowd, placards with slogans, leaflets, appeals (*xuanyan* 宣言), especially the declaration of independence, and speeches made by students to pedestrians in all parts of the city (*Shenbao*, Mar. 5, 1919). Exactly the same strategies were used in Beijing on May 4.

The appeal was for all classes of Koreans to unite. In fact, apart from the active involvement of the male and female students and the Protestant and Ch'ondogyo communities, the Korean movement managed to get the railway workers to strike and the shops in the major cities to close (*Shenbao*, Mar. 14, 1919). At the same time, in many other cities and smaller towns across the country demonstrations were held on and after March 1 in support of Korean independence. Furthermore, the communities of Koreans residing abroad were active supporters (and became the main props of the movement for the next decades after it was suppressed by the Japanese). Although this could not be enacted on May 4, it held out at least the promise for the Chinese activists of a regionally and socially broad appeal with the concomitant increased pressure on the government. The boycotts and strikes in many cities in the weeks after May Fourth followed the same pattern as those in Korea.

The Korean movement combined militancy with a basically nonviolent strategy. The anarchist tradition of individual assassination or military uprisings was not followed. Instead, the demonstrators confronted saber- and gun-wielding Japanese militia and troops "with bare hands and empty fists," although they were quite willing to throw stones and set a barrack aflame (*Shenbao*, Mar. 13, 1919, quoting Reuters about events on March 3; see also *Dagongbao*, Apr. 25, 1919). The result of this strategy was a clear definition of the villains in the game and growing popular as well as international support for the underdogs, who were willing to sacrifice their lives for the cause of the nation. The Chinese press did report this effect. The Chinese movement also dissociated itself from the use of arms, while maintaining some level of militancy as can be seen in the burning down of Cao Rulin's house and the beating of Zhang Zongxiang. The ensuing arrests set off a wave of popular support for the students.

In fact, this strategy involved a sizable risk. The "movement"-style collective civic action confronts a government with its judicial, police, and military resources, which should have no difficulty suppressing such disturbances. In order to withstand this pressure from officialdom, the participants have to share a double faith. They have to believe that the other participants will be committed enough not to run away and leave them to the mercy of the forces of order. Second, they have to believe that public opinion will be roused to such an extent by a harsh crackdown that the forces of order will not be able to keep up their pressure for a long time or will not even be willing to use force because they anticipate a strongly averse public reaction. This is an exceedingly "modern" form of political calculus that relies on a force as diffuse and fickle as the public for protection and for the possible enhancement of the impact of its claims. Given the exceedingly low opinion of the Chinese public evinced by most "progressive" student publications and even mainstream publications such as the *Chenbao* prior to the event, it took quite some spirit to take this risk.

Chinese reporting about these Korean events was thus friendly and in some cases enthusiastic. Given the short space of time between the Korean and the Chinese events, reporting was mainly in the newspapers, and there was little in the progressive periodicals. The sympathetic stance taken by the papers with the strong dependence on business shows that the support for what was to become the May Fourth cause extended well beyond student and radical circles. It was not surprising that the successful powers of Europe as well as Japan did have such movements, and that their citizens were awakened to the national interest. The Korean events proved, however, that even a mighty power like Japan could be challenged if it was possible to get a "movement" going. *L'Impartial* reported on May 5, 1919, with some respect that the establishment of a provisional government and of a provisional constitution was a step that none of the colonies like India had ever dared to take.

We can thus make a second assertion. The May Fourth movement saw itself as a part of an international upsurge against the big powers and their local representatives and actively copied forms of action employed by other such "movements," especially the movement in Korea, with which the Chinese activists were familiar through the detailed and enthusiastic reporting of the *Morning Post*.

In fact, the May Fourth events were characterized and in part sparked off by the feeling among the young modern elite that China was about to miss another train and trend. It had missed the first one, which had propelled Japan to become a world power, and now all over Asia, in India, Vietnam, Korea, and even Mongolia (Russia was hardly in the picture at the time), Asian peoples were rising, but nothing was happening in China. Some of the extremely violent language the demonstrators used for their countrymen bears witness to this frustration of youngsters who at least wanted to be in the international lead in terms of rebellion if they could not manage to be in the lead in industrialization. If necessary, they would use guilt and force their countrymen into a properly progressive attitude in order to come up with a respectable mass movement in China. This fairly terrorist elitism comes out clearly in the appeal mentioned above, drafted perhaps before the May 4 demonstrations. After praising the Koreans for their daring, the text continues: "If her [China's] people still cannot unite in indignation in a twelfth-hour effort to save her, they are indeed the worthless race of the twentieth century. They should not be regarded as human beings" (quoted in Chow 1960: 107).

Hidden in this alarmist language is a deep Social-Darwinist anxiety about the survival capacity of the Chinese nation, which at one moment led a man like Chen Duxiu to say in 1915 that a Japanese occupation might under certain conditions be more beneficial for China's modernization than a rule like Yuan Shikai's 袁 世 凱 (1859–1916), which would not improve the people's lot (Chen Duxiu 1915a; quoted in Feigon 1983: 148). The desperation about the capacity of the remaining (after Japan) Asian nations—and especially China—to assert themselves becomes evident in a bombastic editorial that *L'Impartial* of May 1, 1919, devoted to the events in Korea on that day, the day on which it published the new provisional constitution of Korea.

> The Great Korean Republic has made its appearance!
>
> Refusing to tolerate further the sufferings of their state's demise and boiling over with National Self-Determinism, Korea has risen impetuously and has loudly proclaimed its independence, even though it does not control a single strip of land or have a few people in its name! One man cried out in the night, and the entire state responded. With bare hands and empty fists they were struggling under guns and swords, and although they were arrested and massacred by the thousands and tens of thousands, their valorous spirit never diminished. And then today, they simply set up a government and promulgated a constitution, solemnly drawing up the model of the new state. This nation, which deserves sympathy and respect, does not know what treatment Japan is going to mete out to it.
>
> Nonetheless, even if the demise of Korea has come about under the might of Japan, it was also caused by the fact that its lacking that capacity for self-rule enabled Japan to realize its tactics of getting the weak under its control and of attacking the unenlightened.

> But [the Koreans] now have suddenly woken up to an understanding [of their weakness].
>
> Their thinking has shed its fetters, and they are establishing something republican; [but] if by chance Japan would in fact conform to the worldwide righteous opinion and would generously let them have their freedom back, we do not know whether the new citizenry of Korea would have the energy to resist the old ways and to implement self-government so that the Great Korean Republic [the name of the proposed state] would not be the flower of a single morning.
>
> If [they did] not [have this energy], then this would only be the Koreans' own doing. (*Dagongbao*, May 1, 1919; see also the *Chenbao* editorial quoted above).

Although supportive of the Korean movement, the editorial evinces an anxiety about whether the Koreans, or for that matter the Chinese, would be able to manage themselves even if they were allowed to. The Chinese students shared, I believe, this anxiety, and much of their exceedingly harsh language for their countrymen is a sign of it.

We make a third assertion. The May Fourth movement was in substantial part prompted by a kind of "profile neurosis" vis-à-vis such nations as Korea, Vietnam, and India. The papers and many critics such as Chen Duxiu felt ashamed at China's sluggish reaction to its ongoing humiliation. The May Fourth activists handed on this international shame to those of their countrymen who would not join the "movement" by excluding them from the race of "human beings," *ren* 人, and assigning them to the genus of "slaves," *nu* 奴, or "wild beasts," *shou* 獸. With this movement thus comes a claim for China as a big power in the anti-imperialist struggle and at the same time a first assertion that through the massive participation in this "movement" subjective conditions were beginning to change in China so that the Chinese populace was now on the way to becoming a nation able to stand on its own feet.

In addition to the above-mentioned elements, which have been described in detail because they may elucidate some new historical connections, the May Fourth demonstrations operated with other traditional and modern symbolical elements, many of which have been copied by later movements down to our days.

1. By staging the demonstrations in the capital, they replicated the political hierarchy of the official power structure. The Beijing movement headed the national movement, just as the central government was above the local governments.

2. By staging the rally in which "the public" spoke out against the government's handling of the affairs of the nation on the small space outside the Tian'an Gate in front of the imperial palace, they made this place the center of the nation, where on a symbolical level the emperor and the people faced each other.

3. By using this place, which in fact was the entrance used by petitioning officials in imperial times, they arrogated for themselves the role of the remonstrating official who "speaks out for the people." At the same time, they radically changed the system of communication; where formerly the official with his writ would enter the palace in strictly internal communication among the officialdom, the addressee of the vindications on May Fourth was not the emperor or the government but the public and, only through and with it, the powers that be.

4. By using the form of the street lecture, they assumed for themselves the elevated role of the teacher as opposed to their actual situation as students. In this role they claimed the legitimacy to tell the other sectors of society what to do.

Encouraged by the public response from students and other sectors of society, the participants assumed that it was the "correctness" of their vindications that had convinced the "masses." One might in fact argue that the main reason why city people in many walks of life showed sympathy for the Beijing students was not so much the fact that the students articulated demands they all supported, but the fact that some were being arrested and that police had shown themselves inept in handling such a new situation. Or one might argue that the failure of the government to come down with a harsh and unified response to the challenge was due to very complex motives among its members.

During the events in May, negotiations were going on in Shanghai between the two parliaments with a view to unification and the establishment of a unified government. The issue might be considered as important as the Paris negotiations because the possible outcome was a unified Chinese government. The deputies in both north and south, however, were not enthusiastic about the threatening dissolution of the two parliaments prior to new elections. The attacks on the Beijing government undermined its position in the negotiations, and forces like Liang Qichao's Research Clique had more than one reason to provide some cover and protection to the students. The blindness of the movement's single-issue orientation helped it to focus attention but made it liable to the charge of having in fact obfuscated other, more urgent issues, and of having been in fact unwittingly used in a political struggle about which they seemed to know very little (Fung 1993). Similar charges would be made against the student demonstrators in 1989.

The Masses, Superstition, and the Calendar

By declaring themselves a "movement" and pursuing a course of action along these lines, the participants in the May Fourth demonstrations assumed or arrogated the role of national vanguard, spokesman, and teacher for themselves. This elitism gave them the subjective legitimacy to proceed boldly and at the same time encoded certain features into the heritage of May Fourth that would quickly become a burden for those inheriting this tradition.

This elitism rested, and rests, on a series of assumptions, some of which have to do with traditional notions about truth being vested in the educated, others with the new notions and concepts espoused by the students:

1. The Chinese race at large is in a state of stupor and in danger of being overwhelmed in the strife of nations.

2. The only mobile and agile element in this stagnant mass are the young, and not just the young, but the "new youth" heralded by *New Youth* and its editorials. They were thus naturally called upon to awaken the nation and to lead in a self-assertive articulation of the nation that was to be the "movement." This was confirmed as the true international trend by the "youth" movements in such countries as Germany, the United States, and Japan.

3. The distance between the stagnant nation and the lively youth ensured that the Western-oriented "progressive" young could articulate the "objective" interests of the nation but could not be the "representatives" of popular opinion, backwards as the latter was. Their vindication was the logic of their newly imported concepts and the actions in other nations they read about in the papers. In fact, there was no way of verifying whether their vindications represented anything like a national aspiration. If support for them was forthcoming, this could be read as their success in awakening the nation to its true aims; if it was not, the blame was on the nation for still being asleep. Sun Yat-sen inserted this assessment into his own institutional agenda. In his 1924 "Fundamentals of National Reconstruction" ("Jianguo dagang" 建國大綱), the first stage on the road to democracy after the end of military operations to unify the country was to be a period of "political tutelage" (Sun

1924: 751), which the GMD in fact began in 1928. The purpose was to help the people overcome their superstitious and traditionalist fetters and to gradually qualify as "masses" in the modern sense.

This elitism was political in that the activists thus staked a claim to be the legitimate purveyors of the national political orientation and the administrators of the modern state, and it was cultural in claiming that this orientation could be articulated and lived only within a "modern" and essentially Westernized cultural environment.[16] In this view, traditional culture was the main obstacle to a modern orientation. In the eyes of May Fourth activists as well as the political parties, traditional high culture—Confucianism—had the political elite of the country under its bane, while the people at large remained caught up in popular superstitions. The battle against this traditional cultural orientation was thus an integral part of the argumentative structure of May Fourth.

In this argument, traditional culture came in two parts, one elite, one popular. Traditionally the Confucian elite had a basically hostile attitude toward popular beliefs and local culture, and local officials would periodically proceed to raze to the ground hundreds of unregistered temples and persecute a fair array of religious organizations (cf. Hansen 1993). The May Fourth agenda inherited this feature and added another one, namely, to redefine the Confucian elite culture as its own caricature, as a "man-eating" culture of weaklings, in a famous phrase coined by Lu Xun 魯迅 (1881–1936).

During the preceding generation of Kang Youwei and others, a continuation and radicalization of this traditional strategy had been tried. In 1895 Kang had advocated "destroying the depraved sacrifices [i.e., popular cults] by way of elevating Kongzi" 毀淫祠以尊孔子 (1895: 1), which he felt was the only way to spiritually unify China against the foreign onslaught. For this end, he promoted a "modern" and even Sino-Japanese cult of Confucius to take the place of Christianity in Western cultures. The beginning of time was to be with Confucius, and the year was to be structured according to his birthday, which would replace Christmas (Wuya sheng 1899; cf. also "Qingri

16. It is significant that the popular and carefully prepared *Handbook for the New Culture Movement* (*Xin wenhua cishu* 新文化辭書) put out by the Commercial Press in 1923 (edited by Tang Jinggao) contained in fact only Western knowledge, and that the topics were organized according to the Western alphabet beginning with Abelard = Abelardus and ending after 1,099 pages with Yoga.

lianhe chongci Kongzi shengdan qi" 1899). Yuan Shikai pursued a similar agenda as a Qing official.

The anti-Confucian element in the May Fourth agenda has been amply dealt with. The criticism of its fairly radical and blind denunciation of everything associated with elite tradition—which is not entirely innocent in view of the fact that the New Youth based their claim for leadership on their "modern qualifications"—has been articulated since the beginning of the New Culture movement by scholars of other denominations (Lin Shu 林 紓 [1852–1924], Liang Qichao), by politicians (Chiang Kai-shek), and by some modern scholars such as Lin Yu-sheng 林 毓 生 and many others from the Neo-Confucian revival.

Probably because many of the critics of the anti-Confucianism of May Fourth share the traditional officials' and the May Fourth youths' attitude toward popular religion, the treatment meted out by the May Fourth generation to the mental universe of the large majority of the Chinese populace has hardly been touched. It is this aspect, however, that properly highlights the elitism of the theory of "movements of the popular masses."

In the radicalism of its denunciation and destruction of traditional culture, the May Fourth activists followed in the tracks and legitimized as ultimately "modern" and "progressive" the equally radical Westernizing Taiping rebels who also had included Confucianism in the list of things to be destroyed because Confucius was seen as responsible, in Hong Xiuquan's 洪 秀 全 (1812–64) vision, for deluding the Chinese into becoming subservient to the devil. The Taipings must be credited with starting the large-scale cultural desertification of the Chinese countryside that is so shocking to the outside observer and has recently been discovered in its shockingness by the writers of "regional," *xiangtu* 鄉 土, literature. The language developed by the Taipings to mark the difference between the deluded and the enlightened Chinese, namely, "slaves" and even "demons" versus "human beings" and "heroes," is the direct ancestor of the slave/man dichotomy of May Fourth parlance. Under the impact, however, of Dewey and Russell and the Soviet Union's religious policies, the May Fourth agenda went further than that of the Taipings and included all religion among the things to be destroyed. Thus we have altogether three manifestations of the cultural agenda of May Fourth, one coming under the familiar slogan "Down with Confucius and his shop," the second in the anti-Christian movement of the years 1922 through 1926, and the third in the form of the campaign "against religion" and especially popular religion, during the 1920s.

The campaign against Confucianism was mostly a campaign against the rules, regulations, and values organizing the life of the traditional ruling segments of society, from which the students came, and against which they were rebelling. The campaign against Christianity, which led to widespread and very popular persecutions of missionaries and Chinese Christians, came in the name of anti-imperialism. The Christian missionary schools were especially attacked for training Chinese in subservience to imperialism, and this notwithstanding the fact that a sizable part of the modern educated youths who took part in the May Fourth movement in fact came from these schools (Zhang Qinshi 1927).[17] The conceptual conflict that the same people who were demanding a ban on even voluntary religious worship in missionary schools were otherwise advocating the introduction of Western-style constitutions that inevitably included the freedom of religious exercise was completely obfuscated by the moralistic layer of this anti-imperialist agenda.

The campaign against popular religion has received much shorter shrift in the literature. This campaign is usually reduced to the campaign launched in 1928 in the areas under the control of the Nanjing government. Clarence Burton Day's *Chinese Peasant Cults* (1940), which has escaped the attention of the scholars writing on the subject, shows that this campaign started well before 1928; it had a much broader basis than GMD ideology and politics (Day 1940; Mitani 1978; Duara 1991). Day writes:

> Before the Nationalist Revolution of 1926–28, iconoclasm had in fact been going on for two years or more. Almost every daily paper contained some item or other about the destruction of idols and temples in different places. Wang Fu-chien reported all the city-god idols destroyed in his home-village of Hai-yen. The same is true for Ning-po and most of the villages and towns in northern Chekiang. Soldiery, students, and children have been the usual agents in the work of demolition. (Day 1940: 194)

Initially, this "continuous attack upon the common religions of the country" (Keng 1926: 98) was not sponsored by the government. The government, however, that came to power through the Nationalist Revolution counted a

---

16. The *Chinese Recorder* gives a fair number of specific reports about this movement during the period when it went on. It also reveals some of the soul-searching within Protestant circles as a reaction to these attacks; see Yamamoto and Yamamoto 1953; Yip 1970; Lam 1978; Chao 1986; Lutz 1988.

fair number of May Fourth people in its ranks. It proceeded to make the anti-traditionalism of the "New Culture movement," which had previously been a program of a segment of the intelligentsia, into state policy. The new schoolbooks, which were mandatory for schools, were written by May Fourth activists and in the language advocated by them as the "spoken language," *baihua* 白 話. The worship of Confucius was banned by Cabinet order in 1929 and then partially reinstated after many public protests, but in the reinstatement the name of the Confucius temple was changed and the plaques in the temple awarded to famous Confucian scholars of the past were removed. The government published an appeal for a general use of the Western calendar; this numbered the official year starting with the founding of the Republic but had not been in use outside officialdom. As part of the same process, it published an official list of state-recognized memorial days, among which there was not a single traditional holiday. This was in effect to do away—very much in the style of the French Revolution's calendar reform (Baczko 1984)—with the superstitiously polluted old year with its auspicious and inauspicious days, its days of fasting and feasting, its peasant rules and ceremonies, and to replace it with a new, ceremoniously regulated "partified" modern year with its memorial days of the revolution and its heroes and its minutely prescribed ceremonies, which were part of the program of replacing the traditional folk religions with the Three People's Principles (Sanminzhuyi 三 民 主 義) on both the ideological and ritual levels (see *Riyong baike quanshu* 1934: 5787–92).

These measures were taken in the context of the Nationalist Government's Movement to Eradicate Superstition (Pochu mixin yundong 破 除 迷 信 運 動) of the years 1928 and 1929. As far as the Central government was concerned, the movement was restricted to the areas under its control, that is, Jiangsu, Zhejiang, and Anhui (Mitani 1978). On December 19, 1928, the *Zhejiang Provincial Gazette* (no. 483) published instructions ordering the destruction of all but a few temples with the following introduction:

> Superstition is a hindrance to progress. The appeal to the authority of the gods is a policy to keep people ignorant. . . . For lack of education there has been a gulf between the highly educated and the illiterate classes; therefore the poison of superstition has sunk into the human mind and the authority of the gods is unquestioned. . . . In the present time of Renaissance and scientific enlightenment, these bad traditions not only keep people ignorant but make us a laughing stock among the nations. . . . According to Dr. Sun Yat-sen (with whom we have had none to compare before), who lectured on the evolution of sovereignty of the people, before

> the sovereignty of the people came the divine right of kings; before the divine right of kings came the divine right of the gods. At present both the divine right of kings and the divine right of the gods have no place in the world. Our party [the Guomindang], struggling for revolution, has opposed those who hindered the development of the sovereignty of the people. For this reason ambitious warlords, rotten officials, etc., have been eradicated. So also harmful superstitions and temple beliefs must be driven out, otherwise, while opposing the divine right of kings, we still submit to the divine right of the gods. How, then, can we develop the sovereignty of the people by seemingly pushing the carriage southward while in reality we are pushing it northward. (Quoted in Day 1940: 190)[18]

This introduction is followed by "A Standard for Confiscation and Recognition of Gods and Temples." Gods who were technically or morally progressive and the chief deities of Buddhism, Daoism, Islam, and Christianity could retain their temples; all else was to be destroyed.

In Guangzhou a Custom Reform Committee was set up to "demolish idols, destroy temples, confiscate their properties, and eradicate superstitious practices among the people" (*Fengsu gaige congkan* 風俗改革叢刊 1930; Hung 1985: 160). As Mitani (1978) has pointed out, the ideological actions against local temples were also attempts to expand the scope of state power into the villages, and the concomitant confiscation of temple property worked in the same direction by decreasing the villages' financial independence and by redirecting village resources for educational purposes, for example, to state coffers.

This is the revolutionary context in which the next series of extensive measures to desertify China's cultural and moral landscape was taken, to which even such famous sites as Mount Taishan fell victim.

Local surveys from the early 1930s show the transition from independent movement against popular superstition to government policy. The missionary D. S. Dye reported in 1931 from Chengdu that there were 175 temples in the town, not counting the small shrines for the tutelary deities that had already disappeared. Of these temples three were used exclusively for religious purposes, 58 percent had been confiscated for public purposes like schools and barracks, and during the past three years only one new temple had been built (Dye 1931). D. C. Graham reported a year earlier from Suifu that "as this article is being written, the streets of Suifu are being widened and modernized. Four large temples are being transformed into vegetable markets.

18. For the Chinese text, see *Minsu* 民俗 41/42 (1929): 127–29.

Some of the images have been destroyed and others crowded together, sometimes more or less broken, into small rooms. There is talk of making over into a public park several large nearby temples, and of making others into arcades" (Graham 1930). And another report, "Iconoclasm in China," from the same year claims that "China's modern leaders feel that everything superstitious is socially undesirable and root it up, by force if necessary" (*Chinese Recorder*, Feb. 1930, p. 74).

It might seem that the strong emphasis on popular culture among the May Fourth activists since the late 1920s, and even the inclusion of much "popular" material into Lu Xun's *A Brief History of Chinese Fiction* (*Zhongguo xiaoshuo shi lüe* 中國小說史略) of 1923 would indicate the opposite trend, namely, a glorification of the "people" and the "popular." On closer inspection, however, the "people" and "popular" appearing in these works and collections are by and large of a strongly sanitized "healthy" character.[19] The perception is highly selective and cannot in any way be considered representative. In fact, the very same intellectuals who were advocating the collection of popular materials and were publishing some of it in journals like *Folklore Weekly* (*Minsu* 民俗) in Canton or in different book series of the time, seem to have been advocating the destruction of unhealthy and superstitious religious cults. The journal *Folklore Weekly* with contributions by Gu Jiegang 顧頡剛 (1893–1980), Luo Xianglin 羅香林 (1905–78), Chen Lifu 陳立夫 (1900–1993), Rong Zhaozu 容肇祖 (b. 1899), and others, came out with a double issue on "Gods," which in fact reads like a rationalization of this government order, which it prints in the end of this issue (*Minsu* 1929, 41/42: 27). From the beginning of an article in this issue, the tone of some of the contributions can be gauged:

> Those of the age-old Chinese people who were concerned with gods were for the most part women and children. In recent years, some of them have gradually come to understand that a god is just a nothingness, a method used by the powers that be to assist them in areas where their vile power does not reach. On the other hand, we still have stupid men and women with simplistic minds who hold on to their old beliefs and are not easy to change. With people like them, we can only wait until they expire together with the gods; there is nothing one can do. (Shang 1929: 24)

---

19. Still, one should mention a strong uneasiness on the side of the government after the Northern Expedition with the folklorists. This indicates a certain tension between the two, which in turn signals that the government felt that the folklorists were in fact preserving and spreading superstition. See Hung 1985: chaps. 1 and 7.

Among the main protagonists advocating the full use of state power to force the people into compliance with their "May Fourth" modernist agenda are well-known names. In 1928, Cai Yuanpei 蔡元培 (1876–1940) himself, as the chancellor of Peking University, submitted together with Minister of Interior Xue Dubi 薛篤弼 (1892–1973) a proposal to the central government to fundamentally and officially reform the two most important popular ceremonies, marriages and funerals, and to replace them with officially approved reformed ceremonies, which Cai designed down to the details of the format and layout of the invitations for these ceremonies (see *Riyong baike quanshu* 1934: 3.5796–5799). The measure was passed by the government.

The legitimation for such measures is simple. Primary is the goal of strengthening the state; from this follows the necessity of mobilizing the citizenry for the modernization effort; this in turn justifies the use of state power for the forced re-education of the populace and justifies the extension of the reach of the state into the local community. The pattern follows directly from the May Fourth political agenda, and its descendants are not only the measures of the Nationalist Government but also those of the Chinese Communists down to the Cultural Revolution as the highest realization of the core May Fourth ideals.

The Canonization of May Fourth

Anniversaries are mental constructs. They result from a definition of the event marking its relevance within a hierarchy of values, from a comparison with competing events within the same discourse, and from a struggle with other agendas that advance other dates as important. In addition, there is a great variety of anniversaries. They might be private or family-related events like birthdays or the anniversaries of marriages or deaths; they might be religious and denominational; they might be important to a social segment and its organizations, as May 1 is for European labor unions; they might be state determined and approved, such as the national days of many countries. But there is a constant flux between them: Sun Yat-sen's birthday might become a national holiday, but October 10 might be transformed from a national day to a regional celebration in Taiwan; May 1 might become a state holiday as it is in Germany, or governments might decide on a competing day to honor labor to recraft the memory and refuse memorial status to May 1, as is the case in the United States. The establishment or abolition of official memorial days often is a long and drawn-out battle. The present contention in the

PRC concerning June 4, 1989, is an example; on June 4, the government blocks Tian'anmen Square, bans the sale of flowers, surrounds campuses with police in order to prevent commemorative activities, while at the same time trying to resanctify the square through joyous popular activities like the dance organized in June 1994 by the Women's Federation under the motto "We Love Beijing's Tian'anmen."

This appropriation of important dates results in the existence of a fair number of different, simultaneous, overlapping, and/or competing memorial calendars and, as a consequence, histories. During the French Revolution, the anti-revolutionary region in the west of France, the Vendée, refused to accept the new calendar with its revolutionary commemorative days. It printed its own version of a commemorative calendar that retained not only many religious holidays but also some of the revolutionary holidays like the anniversary of the king's glorious decapitation, which—in the Vendée—became a day of mourning.

The calendrical structure of the Chinese Republic was exceedingly complex. The complexity existed on three levels: the standard for the time of the day, the internal organization of the year, and the historical denomination of the year. The first issue remained unresolved, although the Customs Offices switched to standard time in 1903. As for the two other issues, it had to be determined whether the months would be those used in the lunar calendar or those of the calendar used in the West, and whether the year would be year X of the Republic or year Y after Confucius, Jesus, Buddha, or some other historical figure or event.

The internal structure of the year was more important because the lunar calendar provided the basis for the calculations of lucky and unlucky days, annual festivals, and a large array of religious practices such fast and feast days. The founding matrix of the Republic eliminated the lunar calendar as a step toward outlawing superstition. The government declared October 10 National Day, and January 1 Founding Day. With this new calendar, it staked a claim to determine the measurement of time and to control its memorial content. It distanced itself from earlier imperial calendrical reforms by joining the calendrical world community built around the solar year. Initially, however, this new calendar was observed only for government timing; the countryside proceeded by and large as before according to the lunar calendar. In fact, most of Shanghai had been operating on the solar year for decades, and its newspapers introduced multiple simultaneous dating within both, lunar and solar, calendars. Only in the late 1920s were efforts made to enforce the use of the new calendar year and to superimpose the memorial days inscribed there over the traditional memories. The extreme confusion that spread in the countryside as a consequence of this effort can be extrapolated from many missionary writings at the time. Since missionaries were seen as specialists in this new calendar, they would be asked for advice on when to plant, when to celebrate, and how to find out what day it was. Upon the urgent appeal of missionaries in the field, the Presbyterian Press in Shanghai printed a cheap calendrical broadsheet for cross-calculations, and even the big household *Encyclopedia for Daily Use* (*Riyong baike quanshu* 日用百科全書) included a full set of parallel tables for both the days and the months, as well as for the years, in its 1934 edition, to help its exclusively Chinese readers to figure out and be able to communicate what day and year it was. May Fourth as a date is registered in this programmatically modern solar year. It inscribes itself into a calendar marked by its statutory hostility to the calendar used by the average Chinese with all its particular implications. This date did not operate in the same time frame as the birthday of Yuhuang shangdi 玉皇上帝, the supreme deity of Daoism.

As to the historical location of a year, many proposals had been floated since the end of the preceding century. As a beginning date competing with Christ's birth, Kang Youwei simultaneously dated the first issue of his *Journal of Self-strengthening Studies* (*Qiangxue bao* 強學報) the year 2373 after Confucius' death and year 21 of Guangxu's reign (1895); the documents promoting the 1911 Revolution, including Sun Yat-sen's *The Minpao Magazine* (*Minbao* 民報), were dated on the basis of the legendary ancestor of the Chinese race, the Yellow Emperor (Huangdi 黃帝), to avoid calendrical recognition of the Manchu dynasty; others suggested returning to the Duke of Zhou (Zhou gong 周公), adhering to the celestial stems, using the Western model, or marking the watershed of the end of imperial China by the double transition to the solar year and the first year of the Republic. This last option won out until the founding of the People's Republic of China in 1949, although in early Republican sources there was a constant side noise of datings in articles, journals, diaries, and newspapers using the "Christian" counting, and there was a continuous discussion about the necessity to switch to this calendar (cf. Qian 1919).

The importance attached to the political issues underlying calendar reform was such that a novel published in 1908, *The New Age* (*Xin jiyuan* 新紀

元), capitalized on the theme. It describes how, in 1999, a China that has grown strong orders all states of the yellow race to switch to the Chinese calendar from next year, which will be year 4709 after Huangdi. Under the pressure to stay with the white-race calendar, Hungary, in which the yellow race has a strong presence, turns to China for help and calendrical orientation. A world war ensues during which the combined Western fleets are sunk by a Chinese armada (Biheguan zhuren 1908).[20]

In terms of a "new beginning" with appropriate calendrical rank, the status of the Xinhai (1911) revolution, implied in its marking the new beginning of the calendar as "Year One of the Republic" (*minguo* 民 國 1), was quickly being questioned. The attempts to restore the monarchy, the acceptance of the Twenty-one Demands in 1915, and the general lethargy of the public regarding political affairs signaled that little had changed—no "new beginning" had been made. Apart from the united hostility toward the superstitious old calendar and the feudal dynastic year counting, there were quite a few competing "modern" claims. May Fourth activists were quick to assert that in fact their movement had been the first self-assertive political articulation of the "masses" and thus was in fact the watershed separating the old from the new. A week after the event, Luo Jialun claimed in his famous "The Spirits of the May Fourth Movement" that this movement was an "unprecedented undertaking (創 舉) of the Chinese students, an unprecedented undertaking of Chinese educational circles, and an unprecedented undertaking of the Chinese citizens," and that already one of its three spirits, that of students' sacrificing themselves, could be "the basic element (元 素) for the remaking (再 造) of China" (1919: 2). Shortly before, *New Youth* had floated a proposal to make October 10 into the birthday of the new human being, but the events of May Fourth apparently overshadowed this proposal.

In an influential critical review of the movement a year later, which was reprinted from *New Tide* in the *Shanghai News*, Luo proclaimed: "No matter whether one approves of it or not, one still must admit that the 'May Fourth movement' was the first great event since the founding of the Republic of China. This event adds to China's political history a new reform, for the history of Chinese society it opens a new era (紀 元), and in the intellectual history of China it marks a new change." "I fervently believe," wrote Luo in this article, "that the principle of the universe is motion (動)" and in this sense the May Fourth movement with all its weaknesses in fact "had one single

---

20. I am indebted to David Der-wei Wang for alerting me to this piece.

achievement, namely, its being able to get China 'moving'" (1920: 846). The goal and historical contribution of the May Fourth thus were to free China from its cosmic anomaly of immobility and stagnation and to insert it into the constantly changing stream of universal motion and change.

Luo's is still a rather moderate assessment.[21] Later, May Fourth ideologues retained mainly the notion that May Fourth had heralded a "new era," because the intelligentsia felt they had made a modern dent and were determined not to let anyone forget. For example, in 1935 Chen Duanzhi 陳端志 called the movement an "epoch-making turning point" 劃時期轉變 (1935: 207). History was thus divided into two parts: the part before 1919 and the part after, with everything before leading up to it and everything after resulting from it. The PRC chronology, which refers to 1949 as the "founding of the state," *jianguo* 建國, claims its own success to be a similar turning point.

Even in the year 1919, establishing May Fourth on the calendar was not easy. There was an official calendar with a prominent date of October 10—the anniversary of the Wuchang upheaval—as its commemorative day. However, very little was done by the government with this potentially important day. In 1918, for example, the Beijing government offices merely erected an arch (*pailou* 牌樓) and ordered the shops to put up flags. The controversy about commemorative days, however, was already on. In January 1919, Chen Daqi 陳大齊 (1886–1983) in an article in *New Youth* argued that October 10 should become the "day that should be most cherished and remembered" and should in fact be made into the beginning of the calendar year in China to mark the end of slavish mentality of blindly following all that was Western. All should celebrate and think "this is the day when our citizens for the first time became human beings" by drinking "wine to celebrate the Republic" (1919: 5–9).

In the mood of the time, the citizens were now taking into their own hands the organization of their modern year with its commemorative days and celebrations. The year 1919 in fact is characterized by numerous com-

21. The article contains a very sober assessment of the movement. It argues that due to the lack of organization and overall concept endemic to a "mass movement," this could not be the only form of action and warns that the movement might just have acted like a morphine shot, which will bring someone back to life who is already fading away. Once back in life, however, he needs drugs that "stabilize the basis and strengthen the fundamentals"; otherwise, this sudden stimulus (衝動) will end up in a counter-reaction (反動) like Yuan Shikai's instead of a healthy liveliness (活動) (Luo 1920: 861).

memorative activities in which groups of citizens vied with the state and with each other for hegemony in determining memorial dates and defining their content. From this resulted an enormous memorial turbulence in China that lasts to the present day and that reflects the deep divisions within the country.

In 1919, the Research Clique of Liang Qichao had scheduled a big meeting for May 7, the day when the Twenty-one Demands had been signed in 1915, to mark "a commemorative day of national shame" 國恥紀念日. Since this was organized by one of the political parties and basically constituted not assertive action but complaints directed at the government, the students decided to move their own activities ahead and have their rally on May 4. October 10 is another example. In 1919 the state proceeded as in the previous year. The students decided to appropriate the event and to make themselves the true inheritors and commemorators of the "end of slavish mentality." They distributed bread dumplings on which they had baked slogans against the traitors in the government, national shame, and the unfulfilled promises of the nationalist revolution (Onu 1989). The government actively but unsuccessfully tried to prevent these commemorative activities by ordering the bakers not to accept orders from the students. We have here the first open appropriation of an official holiday by private citizens for purposes of political remonstrance. The day was used not to commemorate the glorious achievements of the revolution but to remind the government of the revolution's unfulfilled promises.

A year later, more unofficial memorial days crowded into the calendar. May First was for the first time celebrated as a workers' day in Shanghai, and the May Fourth activists began agitating to have this day recognized officially as the day of their glory and as the day of public criticism of corrupt and traitorous government officials. Public mass meetings, all banned, and demonstrations marked the day.

Famous activists or supporters of the movement such as Hu Shi and Jiang Menglin 蔣夢麟 (1886–1964), Fu Sinian 傅斯年 (1896–1950), and Luo Jialun would use the occasion to contribute their evaluations, suggestions, memories, and definitions of the essence of this movement. In 1923, the National Students Association decided to make May Fourth its national holiday and celebrate it each year with an emphasis directed against national traitors and oppressive neighbors (*Shenbao*, May 4, 1923, "Xueshenghui wei wusi jinian zhi tongdian" 學生會為五四紀念之通電). They would call for the meetings in advertisements in major papers like the *Shanghai News* (*Shenbao*, May 4, 1924; May 4, 1925; May 3, 1926; May 2, 3, 4, 1927).

In 1920, Sun Yat-sen had rather reluctantly given his seal of approval to the movement while reserving his judgment on its iconoclasm. A cursory glance, however, at the reports in the *Records of the Important Historical Events in the Chinese Republic* (*Zhonghua minguo shishi jiyao* 中華民國史事紀要) shows to what degree the GMD government by 1927 had tried to gain control over the commemoration of May Fourth (1977: vol. 1927, p. 873). From 1927 to 1935, the day was a school holiday, and mass meetings with rallies were organized. Hu Hanmin 胡漢民 (1879–1936) set the tone in 1927 in his keynote address in which he bluntly instrumentalized the spirit of the movement for the ten purposes of the day, among which "the partification of education" figured as much as the abrogation of the unequal treaties, the arrest of the Communist leaders, and the dissolution of the Wuhan assembly. Similar activities were launched in Shanghai (*Shenbao*, May 6, 1927; May 3, 1929; May 1, 1930). After 1928, the Nanjing government formally assumed administrative and ritual control over the calendar and sent out orders about the particular forms May Fourth celebrations should take and what the contents were to be (*Shenbao*, May 3, 1928). In 1934, the commemorative activities were integrated with the New Life movement.

The Nationalist government did not include May 4 in its official memorial calendar in 1928, and many of the commemorative meetings during the early 1930s, for example, those in 1934, were characterized by struggles between GMD and suspected Communists. Because of the volatility of May with its many commemorative days, the government declared martial law for the entire month (*Shenbao*, May 1, 1934). The Guomindang as a party in power had troubles with the "movement" element of the May Fourth heritage, which constantly threatened independent action. Eventually, in March 1939, both parties (the GMD and CCP) agreed to muster the young for the war against Japan. For the purpose, they formed a united youth organization (Zhongguo qingnian lianhehui 中國青年聯合會) and made May Fourth "Youth Day."

By now youth had become a fixed category, encompassing people between the ages of 16/17 and 23/24 in the Communist world, and 14/15 and 23/24 in the GMD world. As opposed to the glorious definitions of youth in Chen Duxiu's writings in the late 1910s, it was now the age when young people were expected to form their worldview and character according to modern PRC dictionaries, or their worldview, religion, and character according to modern Taiwan dictionaries. The young were not the avant-garde and the educators in this discourse, but those who had to be instructed and were valued for their willingness to follow party orders obediently and sacrifice their lives for what the respective party leaderships defined as the nation's top priorities. Controlling and ritualizing May Fourth activities and keeping the historiography in check were important devices for influencing the formulation of model values. The public sphere was monopolized, it seems, by these two organizations, and there were few options for independent articulations.

With the consolidation of Chiang Kai-shek's power, his own assessment of the events became more and more important. As mentioned above, Sun Yat-sen had been ambivalent about the movement, praising its patriotism but taking issue with many of its iconoclastic features. When Chiang Kai-shek, in March 1943, finally came out with his own blueprint for China's revolution (which was to supplement and replace Sun Yat-sen's "Three People's Principles" and reflected the rapidly deteriorating relationships with the Communists), he presented a chronology of China's modern history in which the May Fourth movement was assigned a completely marginal position. In a speech on April 12, 1943, at the first congress of his own youth organization, he gave the following outline of this history.

The first high point spanned the period from the founding of the Xingzhong hui (興 中 會) in 1894 and Tongmeng hui (同 盟 會) in 1905 to the Xinhai revolution in 1911. The result was the abolition of the Qing imperial autocracy. The second high tide was from Sun Yat-sen's reform of the Guomindang in 1924 and the founding of the Huangpu Military Academy to the Northern Expedition of 1926–28. The results were the elimination of warlords, the establishment of a unified China, and the establishment of the basis for defending the nation and building the state, as well as for abrogating the unequal treaties. The third high tide was the War of Resistance going on at the time of the speech. According to Chiang Kai-shek, in each of these eras, youth had played a pivotal role, and they should be cherished for it. In fact all these high tides went on under the direct guidance of the GMD leadership, and young people acquired merit by sacrificing their lives for the goals set by GMD leaders. The values implied in this chronology were the direct opposite from the values encoded into the May Fourth legend. The May Fourth movement was not even mentioned in this chronology (Chiang

1943a: 1463a). And in his *China's Destiny* (*Zhongguo zhi mingyun* 中國之命運) a month earlier, he had set about demolishing the May Fourth claims quite explicitly, accusing activists of being "slaves of foreign culture," shallow and ignorant with regard to both their own and foreign culture, and destructive of the ethical values and social cohesion of China (Chiang 1943b: 1.135b).

As noted, the talk was given at the end of the first congress of the Sanminzhuyi Youth Organization, which had just been formed to replace earlier GMD youth organizations with Chiang Kai-shek himself assuming the role of chairman. This congress then proceeded to implement what logically followed from the relative unimportance of May Fourth and its espousal of momentary but not eternal values by transferring Youth Day from May 4 to March 29. March 29, the day when this congress actually had started, had been the Day of Commemoration for the Heroes of Huanghuagang (Jinian Huanghuagang lieshi jie 紀念黃花剛烈士節), to commemorate the Huanghuagang martyrs who in 1911 had unsuccessfully stormed the Canton governor's palace and been killed in the process. The transfer signaled that the heroes, from whom youths were to learn, were these youths who had sacrificed their lives for a really important goal, the setting up of the republic, under the direct orders of Sun Yat-sen. The new youth organization optically made its break with the May Fourth clear by posting a banner over the speakers' rostrum inscribed: "Loyalty, filial piety, humaneness, love, confidence, peace." Chiang Kai-shek derided the iconoclasm of May Fourth and claimed that besides a destructive bent it had not given a positive ethic to youths. This new creed should be, as he said: "Replace ruthlessness with humaneness and love, replace self-service with benefiting others, replace passivism by activism, replace destruction by construction, replace disjointed rattle by concrete action, replace empty babble by vigorous action." He furthermore came out with five rules that should govern the organization's propaganda of values: participating in labor, honoring the elders, honoring women, honoring workers and peasants, and following leaders' orders. In 1943, May Fourth was thus abolished in GMD-held areas in favor of Youth Day. In 1945, in a meek attempt to keep the day on the calendar in some form, literary circles petitioned the GMD government to reinstate it as a "Day for Literature and the Arts" (Wenyi jie 文藝節). This request was granted. Yet, it was implied that there would be no day off in school and that the commemoration would focus on the cultural aspects instead of the political. The first ceremonies in 1945 were again disrupted by suspected Communist sympathizers who clamored against this diffusion of the May Fourth heritage. The heritage proved unmanageable, and the GMD conceded defeat in the struggle for the hegemony over this event against the Communists. During the next years, the activities on Youth Day were hygiene contests, contests in scientific experiments, and the awarding of emoluments to model youths in the various realms of economic construction and scientific experiment. In the Civil War period, various more or less independent attempts were made to rekindle the spirit of May Fourth and to mobilize the intellectuals for a more independent action. The stalwarts of May Fourth could not counter the basic line of this new orthodoxy, as Chiang's *China's Destiny* became the basis for the examinations of all future officials, but in commemorative articles during the subsequent years they tried to insert, without much success, the contribution of May Fourth into this chronology.

The memory was not dead, however. Luo Jialun, who himself was under attack within the GMD, claimed in 1950 that in fact the GMD had led this movement. Since Cai Yuanpei had been a GMD member in 1919, it had in fact been this party that had provided spiritual guidance to the movement, and it could justifiably be inscribed into the GMD heritage. Although formally directed against the Communist claim to the leadership of the movement, this article was actually an indirect rebuttal of the GMD dissociation from this heritage (Luo 1950). Still, Luo Jialun himself in a way wrote the final demise of the appreciation of the movement within the GMD framework himself, when he did not mention the movement by name in his very official *The Guomindang and China During the Past Sixty Years* (*Liushinian lai zhi Zhongguo Guomindang yu Zhongguo* 六十年來之中國國民黨與中國) and only marginally alluded to it (Luo 1954). The articles on May Fourth appearing in controversial papers such as the *Free China* (*Ziyou Zhongguo* 自由中國) during the late 1950s and early 1960s again presented a challenge to the authoritarian government style of Chiang Kai-shek (Liang 1957; Ziyou Zhongguo 1958, 1960; Xie Wensun 1960).

Thus, the Guomindang had a threefold trouble with the heritage of the May Fourth movement. First, it threatened the leeway of the political leadership in deciding political priorities through its potential to mobilize a highly volatile and at the same time prestigious and sympathy-evoking group. Second, the tradition of independent action inscribed into its notion of a "movement" was a constant challenge to a government to prove to a constituency operating outside established channels that it was patriotic and had not sold out the national interests. Third, it presented a constant generational challenge to an aging leadership associating, as it did, age with immobility and stagnation and youth with liveliness and progressiveness. The GMD handling of the burden of May Fourth was first, to take over the memorial activities; second, to diffuse and "partify" its content; and third, to redefine the features of its protagonists, and eventually to do away with it altogether as an extremist movement damaging the cultural and value continuity of China. As a political icon, an abbreviation for an entire set of experiences and attitudes, the movement remained present in the argumentative arsenal of those intent on mounting a challenge to conservative forces within the GMD from inside or out.

The Chinese Communist Party had similar problems but pursued a slightly different strategy. In his assessment of 1919 mentioned above, Mao Zedong himself had suggested that the movement was a part of a worldwide social reform movement that, with Russia as its pioneer, would bring changes in many countries as great as those ushered in by the French Revolution. He stressed that in the wake of this movement many new social organizations had sprung up, which eventually could cooperate to confront the highly organized but quantitatively small "nobility and capitalists." When the Red Army reached Yan'an, it celebrated Youth Day as a formal, United Front tribute to the spirit of youthful patriotism manifested in the May Fourth movement. By now, however, the CCP was in a position of power, and it, too, had to come to grips with the burden this movement posed for any political party in power. In 1939, on the occasion of the twentieth anniversary of May Fourth, Mao gave a first assessment, fleshed out shortly thereafter in his "On New Democracy" ("Lun xin minzhuzhuyi" 論 新 民 主 主 義), in which he repeated that the movement had been part of a worldwide current, the driving force of which had been the world war and the 1917 October Revolution in Russia. And in fact intellectuals with Marxist leanings had been present in the movement and had shortly thereafter done the really important thing by founding the CCP; they had learned that only by linking up with the workers could the intellectuals achieve anything. In this manner, the spirit of independent action and organization was depicted as the movement's liberal and essentially bourgeois weakness. The movement had come into its own and into its strength only with the integration with the working class by way of the intellectuals' subordination to the CCP. The movement had played its historical role, and what was seen as its key virtue was just the immature reflection of young students' ambitions. Like Chiang Kai-shek a few years later, Mao felt the movement's iconoclasm had left it without a clear moral guideline, and he developed the concept of "serving the people" as the core virtue for intellectuals and cadres. In practical terms, and this was emphasized through the eulogies for people who were said to do this, this meant complete subordination of young intelligentsia to the directives of the Communist Party leadership because the party represented the best interests of the people. Mao's slogan was taken from Hu Shi, who in 1920 had suggested a moral core for the movement, in which the slogan "Life in the Service of Society," *shehui fuwu de shenghuo* 社會服務的生活, figured prominently (Hu Shi and Jiang Menglin 1920). The concepts were both similar and different. Hu Shi listed a series of social activities such as night classes against illiteracy that the students could undertake, activities that also were on the agenda in Yan'an as serving the people; the concepts were different in that Hu Shi did not envisage a hierarchy ordering the students around in this process, while this was clearly implied in Mao's assessment.

In the CCP chronology and calendar, May Fourth remains the dividing line between the old society and the new because the founding of the party is described as the crowning achievement of the movement; this undermined the GMD's claim for the Xinhai revolution as the turning point. The development of Tian'anmen Square as the national place during the 1950s geographically took up this historical allusion, because the May 4 demonstration had taken place in this very location, to my knowledge the first such public rally at this place in China.

At the same time, the CCP began in Yan'an a series of practical measures to make clear what was meant by truly following the May Fourth spirit, the most important of which was to give prizes to model youths who in agriculture, industry, warfare, or science had excelled in serving the people. This routine remains, with some interruptions, in force to this very day. As a matter of fact, on May 4, 1989, Zhao Ziyang 趙紫陽 spent many hours in a nationally televised ceremony praising and giving flowers to hundreds of such model workers, students, and policemen from all over the country, while outside students were having their own party and making their own history on Tian'anmen with a non-party-organized celebration.

Editorials on May Fourth since the early 1940s have consequently stressed the need for young people and especially intellectuals to learn the great lesson of May Fourth and have themselves re-educated. The triumph of the CCP in 1949 was immediately hailed as the victory of that part of the May Fourth heritage that had placed at its center not liberalism with its predictable end among the running dogs of imperialism but subordination to the party. Chen Boda 陳伯達 (1904–88) added a nice touch by claiming that in fact Mao Zedong was the finest sprout of May Fourth as an individual, as much as the CCP was such a fine sprout in terms of organization (Chen Boda 1949). Different policies toward the intelligentsia within this general framework were negotiated and proclaimed in the editorials on this day in the subsequent years.

It turns out that May Fourth was a burden for all governing forces in China, and they used similar methods to co-opt, supplement, and trivialize this heritage or to abolish it altogether. In this process of reshaping May Fourth, a very particular selection of the acceptable aspects of it was made, especially in the PRC. This was formed into a canon of things literary, intellectual, and youthful that, in its relentless selectiveness and narrowness, shows the constant strain and stress of having to define this movement in the face of a quite different interpretation. Although this selection co-opted elements present within the broad spectrum of May Fourth options, it would seem that these elements from their own heritage became in turn a burden for the intellectual world mostly because of their fusion of a selective interpretation with administrative rules at the hands of the Communist government.

The May Fourth intellectuals' assessment of China's history and of their own role in it was not the only one around, and in fact it presented a challenge to modern assessments already present. One of these assessments marked the Xinhai revolution and the establishment of the Republic as the turning point and therewith credited the Tongmenghui and Sun Yat-sen with inaugurating modern China. A second chronology would claim that the founding of the Communist Party was in fact the decisive event, because it provided ideological and organizational leadership to the diffuse current for reform and revolution. Both of these chronologies were linked to governing bodies that had to determine which values and virtues they would consider most appropriate for young people to imbibe during their education. The official handling of May Fourth by both the CCP and GMD was dependent on their overall policies and would change with their changes. For both, the May Fourth presented a burden and a challenge. A burden, because they had to deal with this movement on which the self-perception of the intelligentsia rested if they were to win over this intelligentsia; a challenge because it assigned crucial importance and leadership claims to neither party, since the first had played no direct role, and the second had not yet come into existence. The status of the day as a day of model behavior was marked again by independent and organized annual activities on May 4 in the decades to follow. These activities always implied that the underlying issues that had prompted the May Fourth outburst were still around and unresolved.

The strategies applied by both governing parties were as similar as the problems they faced. To integrate a set of values stressing independent thought, organization, and action was difficult since both governing parties ran on authoritarian principles. At the same time, both parties had prominent May Fourth participants in their ranks, although they held less important positions in the Guomindang.

As the developments in 1989 showed, however, an alternative interpretation of these events was still around. Many of the claims of the students in that year to both represent and guide the people independently of a government again seen and defined as corrupt and repressive are from the heritage of a May Fourth interpretation surreptitiously kept alive by older intellectuals.

While the various governing parties evince the stress of an essentially hostile bid for the heritage of May Fourth, the protagonists of the movement confronted similar strains. The potential of continuing and deepening a diversified and rich cultural and political movement was undercut by the overblown self-perception of its activists. Since they claimed to have brought about the turning point of history, there was nothing in the land for which they did not have to have an analysis and a solution. This burden stunted the growth of the movement and prevented it from maturing. The early iconoclasm that was a polemical reaction to a society seen as decrepit and corrupt turned into a liability once the movement's perception had in fact become the dominant discourse in the intellectual world and had made the Chinese intelligentsia a partner, and all too often an active participant, in the desertification of the lands they themselves were called upon to till.

Works Cited

Baczko, Bronislaw. 1984. "Le calendrier républicain: décréter l'éternité." In Pierre Nora, ed., *Les lieux de mémoire*, vol. 1, *La République*, pp. 37–83. Paris: Gallimard.

Biheguan zhuren 碧荷館主人. [1908] 1990. *Xin jiyuan* 新紀元 (The New Age). Reprinted in *Zhongguo jindai xiaoshuo daxi* 中國近代小說大系 (A compendium of premodern Chinese fiction). Shanghai: Shanghai shudian.

Cai Yuanpei 蔡元培. 1919. "Gao Beida xuesheng ji quanguo xuesheng shu" 告北大學生暨全國學生書 (Letter addressed to the students of Peking University and the students of the entire country). *Beijing daxue rikan* 北京大學日刊 421, July 23.

Chao, Jonathan T'ien-en. 1986. "The Chinese Indigenous Church Movement 1919–1927: A Protestant Response to the Anti-Christian Movements in Modern China." Ph.D. diss. University of Pennsylvania.

Chen Boda 陳伯達. 1949. "Wusi yundong yu zhishifenzi de daolu" 五四運動與知識分子的道路 (The May Fourth movement and the path of the intellectuals). *Renmin ribao* 人民日報 May 4.

Chen Daqi 陳大齊. 1919. "Gonghe xinxi" 恭賀新禧 (Celebrating the new auspicious event). *Xin qingnian* 新青年 6, no. 1 (Jan.): 5–9.

Chen Duanzhi 陳端志. 1935. *Wusi yundong zhi shi de pingjia* 五四運動之史的評價 (A historical evaluation of the May Fourth movement). Shanghai: Shenghuo.

Chen Duxiu 陳獨秀. [1915a] 1983. Reply to Li Dazhao's "Pessimism and Self-consciousness." *Jiayin zazhi* 甲寅雜誌 1, no. 8 (Aug. 10).

———. [1915b] 1962. "Dikang li" 牴抗力 (Resistance power). *Qingnian* 青年 1, no. 3 (Nov.): 1–5. Reprinted—Tokyo: Taian, pp. 199–203.

———. [1916a] 1962. "1916." *Qingnian* 青年 1, no. 5 (Jan.): 1–4. Reprinted—Tokyo: Taian, pp. 371–74.

———. [1916b] 1962. "Wuren zuihou zhi juewu" 吾人最後之覺悟 (Our ultimate consciousness). *Qingnian* 青年 1, no. 6 (Feb.): 1–4. Reprinted—Tokyo: Taian, pp. 457–60.

Chiang Kai-shek 蔣介石. [1943a] 1963. "Haozhao quanguo qingnian disanci da jiehe" 號召全國青年第三次大結合 (An appeal for the third great unification of the youth of the entire nation). In Jiang zongtong ji bianji weiyuanhui, ed., *Jiang zongtong ji* 蔣總統集 (The works of President Jiang), 2: 1461–63. Taibei: Guofang yanjiuyuan.

———. [1943b] 1963. *Zhongguo zhi mingyun* 中國之命運 (China's destiny). Reprinted in Jiang zongtong ji bianji weiyuanhui, ed., *Jiang zongtong ji* 蔣總統集 (The works of President Jiang), 1: 118–70. Taibei: Guofang yanjiuyuan.

Chow, Tse-tsung. 1960. *The May Fourth Movement*. Cambridge, Mass.: Harvard University Press.

Day, Clarence Burton. 1940. *Chinese Peasant Cults, Being a Study of Chinese Paper Gods*. Shanghai: Kelly and Walsh.

Deltgen, F. 1969a. "'Bewegung' als historischer und soziologischer Begriff. Versuch einer theoretischen Praezisierung." Ph.D. diss., University of Cologne.

———. 1969b. "Was kann unter einer 'Bewegung' verstanden werden." In R. Koenig, ed., *Aspekte der Entwicklungssoziologie*, pp. 411–29. Cologne: Westdeutscher Verlag.

Dewey, John, and Alice Dewey. 1920. *Letters from China and Japan*. New York: E. P. Dutton.

Duara, P. 1991. "Knowledge and Power in the Discourse of Modernity: The Campaigns Against Popular Religion in Early Twentieth Century China." *Journal of Asian Studies* 50, no. 1 (Feb.): 75–81.

Dye, D. S. 1931. "Study of Temples in Chengtu." *West China Missionary News*, May.

Esherick, Joseph, and Jeffrey Wasserstrom. 1990. "Acting Out Democracy: Political Theater in Modern China." *Journal of Asian Studies* 49, no. 4: 835–66.

Feigon, Lee. 1983. *Chen Duxiu, Founder of the Chinese Communist Party*. Princeton: Princeton University Press.

Fung, Allen. 1993. "Reinterpreting the Events of May Fourth: Power and Politics in Mid-1919." *Papers on Chinese History* 2 (Spring): 54–77.

Graham, D. C. 1930. "The Temples of Suifu." *Chinese Recorder*, Feb., pp. 108–20.

Hansen, V. 1993. "Gods on Walls: A Case of Indian Influence on Chinese Lay Religion?" In P. Ebrey and P. Gregory, eds., *Religion and Society in T'ang and Sung China*, pp. 75–113. Hawaii: University of Hawaii Press.

Hanyu wailaici cidian 漢語外來詞詞典 (A dictionary of Chinese foreign-loan words). 1984. Shanghai: Cishu.

Heberle, R. 1951. *Social Movements: An Introduction to Political Sociology*. New York: Appleton-Century-Crofts.

Hu Shi 胡適 and Jiang Menglin 將夢麟. 1920. "Women duiyu xuesheng de xiwang" 我們對於學生的希望 (What we expect from the students). *Dongfang zazhi* 東方雜誌 17, no. 11 (June 10): 117–22.

Hung, Chang-tai. 1985. *Going to the People: Chinese Intellectuals and Folk Literature, 1918–1937*. Cambridge, Mass.: Harvard University, Council on East Asian Studies.

"Iconoclasm in China." 1930. *Chinese Recorder*, Feb., p. 74.

Jansen, Marius. 1975. *Japan and China from War to Peace, 1894–1972*. Chicago: Rand McNally.

Kang Youwei 康有為. [1895] 1991. *Qiangxue bao* 強學報 2, no. 1. Reprinted—Beijing: Zhonghua shuju.

Keng, Lim Boom. 1926. "The Religious Revolution in China." *Chinese Recorder*, Feb., pp. 95–102.

Lam, Wing-Hung. 1978. "The Emergence of Protestant Christian Apologetics in the Christian Church During the Anti-Christian Movements in China During the 1920s." Ph.D. diss., Princeton University.

Liang Shiqiu 梁實秋. 1957. "'Wusi' yu wenyi" 五四與文藝 (May Fourth and literature and the arts). *Ziyou Zhongguo* 自由中國 16, no. 9 (May): 298–99.

Luo Jialun 羅家倫. [1919] 1976. " 'Wusi yundong' de jingshen" 五四運動的精神 (The spirits of the May Fourth movement). *Meizhou pinglun* 每週評論 23 (May 26): 1. Reprinted in *Luo Jialun xiansheng wencun* 羅家倫先生的文存 (Collected works of Mr. Luo Jialun), 1: 2–3. Taibei: Guoshi guan.

———. [1920] 1986. "Yinianlai women xuesheng yundongdi chenggong shibai he jianglai yingqu de fangzhen" 一年來我們學生運動底成功失敗和將來應取的方針 (The successes and failures of our student movement during the past year and the course to be taken in the future). *Xin chao* 新潮 2, no. 4 (May): 847. Reprinted—Shanghai: Shanghai shudian, 846–61.

———. [1943] 1976. Note added to his "Wusi yundong xuanyan" 五四運動宣言 (An appeal for the May Fourth movement). In idem, *Heiyun baoyu dao mingxia* 黑雲暴雨到明霞 (From dark-cloud storms to splendid glory). Chongqing: Shangwu. Reprinted in *Luo Jialun xiansheng wencun* 羅家倫先生文存 (Collected works of Mr. Luo Jialun), 1: 2. Taibei: Guoshi guan.

———. [1950] 1976. "Wusi de zhen jingshen" 五四的真精神 (The true spirits of May Fourth). *Zhongyang ribao* 中央日報 4: 5. Reprinted in *Luo Jialun xiansheng wencun* 羅家倫先生文存 (Collected works of Mr. Luo Jialun), 1: 311–21.

———. 1954. *Liushinian lai zhi Zhongguo Guomindang yu Zhongguo* 六十年來之中國國民黨與中國 (The Guomindang and China during the past sixty years). Taibei: Zhongguo Guomindang zhongyang weiyuanhui disici dang shi shiliao bianxuan weiyuanhui.

———. 1976. *Luo Jialun xiansheng wencun* 羅家倫先生文存. 11 vols. Taibei: Guoshi guan.

Lutz, Jessie G. 1988. *Chinese Politics and Christian Missions: The Anti-Christian Movements of 1920–1928*. Notre Dame, Ind.: Cross Cultural Publishers.

Mao Zedong 毛澤東. [1919] 1990. "Minzhong de dalianhe" 民衆的大聯合 3 (Great unity of the masses) 3. *Xiangjiang pinglun* 湘江評論 4 (Aug. 4). Reprinted in *Mao Zedong zaoqi wen'gao* 毛澤東早期文稿 (Mao Zedong's early manuscripts) 1912.6–1920.11, pp. 389–95. Changsha: Hunan Press.

Masini, F. 1993. *The Formation of the Modern Chinese Lexicon and Its Evolution Toward a National Language: The Period from 1840 to 1898*. Journal of Chinese Linguistics Monograph Series, no. 6. Berkeley: University of California Press.

Meng Zhen 孟真. 1919. "Chaoxian duli yundongzhong zhi xin jiaoxun" 朝鮮獨立運動中之新教訓 (New lessons from the Korean Independence Movement). *Chenbao* 晨報, Mar. 20, p. 2.

Mitani Takashi 三谷孝. 1978. "Nankin seiken to 'meishin daha undō' (1928–1929)" 南京政權と '迷信打破運動' (1828–1929). (The Nanjing government and the "Movement to Eradicate Superstition," 1828–1929). *Rekishigaku kenkyū* 歷史學研究 455 (Apr.): 1–14.

Nihon kokugo daijiten 日本國語大辭典 (A comprehensive dictionary of the Japanese national language). 1972–76. Tokyo: Shogakukan.

Onu Nobushika 小野信而. 1989. "Shensheng mianbao: Minguo 8 nian qiuji Beijing de sixiangjie" 神聖麵包：民國8年秋季北京的思想界 (Holy bread:

the Beijing intellectual circles in the fall of 1919). In Zhongguo shehui kexueyuan, ed., *Wusi yundong yu Zhongguo wenhua jianshe* 五四運動與中國文化建設 (The May Fourth movement and the construction of Chinese culture), 2: 755–83. Beijing: Shehui kexueyuan wenxian.

Qian Xuantong 錢玄同. [1919] 1963. "Lun Zhongguo dangyong shijie gongli jinian" 中國當用世界公曆紀年 (China should adopt the worldwide Gregorian calendar). *Xin qingnian* 新青年 6, no. 6 (Nov.). Reprinted—Tokyo: Taian, 703–8.

"Qing Ri lianhe chongci Kongzi shengtan qi" 清日聯合崇祠孔子聖誕啓 (Appeal to start the Qing and Japanese calendars by honoring Confucius' birthday). [1899] 1990. *Qingyibao* 清議報 12: 3. Reprinted—Beijing: Zhonghua, 1: 765–66.

Riyong baike quanshu 日用百科全書 (Encyclopedia for daily use). 1934. Shanghai: Shangwu.

Shang Chengzuo 商承祚. [1929] 1983. "Guangzhou shi renjia de shen" 廣州市人家的神 (The gods of the people of Guangzhou city). *Minsu* 民俗 41/42: 24–27. Reprinted—Shanghai: Shanghai shudian, 2: 24–27.

Shen Zhongjiu 沈中究 (Zhongjiu 仲九, pseud.). [1919] 1980. "Wusi yundong de huigu" 五四運動的回顧 (May Fourth movement in retrospect). *Jianshe* 建設 1, no. 3 (Oct.): 1–14. Reprinted—Beijing: Renmin, 1: 599–612.

Soeda Tomomichi 添田知道. 1963. *Enka no Meiji Taishō shi* 演歌の明治大正史 (A history of performing songs in the Meiji and Taishō periods). Tokyo: Iwanami shoten.

Stein, Lorenz vom. [1850]. 1921. *Geschichte der sozialen Bewegung in Frankreich von 1789 bis auf unsere Tage*. Leipzig: Wigand. Reprinted—Munich: Drei Masken.

Sun Wen 孫文. [1924] 1973. "Jianguo dagang" 建國大綱 (Fundamentals of national reconstruction). In Zhongguo Guomindang zhongyang weiyuanhui dangshi weiyuanhui, ed., *Guofu quanji* 國父全集 (Complete works of the founder of the nation), 1: 751–54. Taibei: Zhongguo Guomindang zhongyang weiyuanhui dangshi weiyuanhui.

Tang Jinggao 唐敬杲, ed. 1923. *Xin wenhua cishu* 新文化辭書 (Encyclopedia of new culture). Shanghai: Shangwu.

Wagner, R. 1982. *Reenacting the Heavenly Vision: The Role of Religion in the Taiping Rebellion*. Berkeley: Center for Chinese Studies.

———. 1991. "Political Institutions, Discourse and Imagination at Tiananmen." In J. Manor, ed., *Rethinking Third World Politics*, 121–44. London: Longman.

———. 1992. "Reading the Chairman Mao Memorial Hall in Beijing: The Tribulations of the Implied Pilgrim." In S. Naquin and Yu Junfang, eds., *Pilgrims and Sacred Sites in China*, pp. 378–423. Berkeley: University of California Press.

Wuya sheng 無涯生. [1899] 1990. "Quan gedi li ci Kongzi hui qi" 勸各地立祠孔子會啓 (An appeal to the different localities to establish societies in honor of Confucius). *Qingyi bao* 清議報 11: 1–5. Reprinted—Beijing: Zhonghua, 1: 643–52.

Xie Hong 謝鴻. [1915] 1962. "Deguo qingniantuan" 德國青年團 (German youth association). *Qingnian* 青年 1, no. 3 (Nov.). Reprinted—Tokyo: Taian, 243–45.

Xie Wensun 謝文孫. 1960. "Zhuohai 'wusi jingshen' de youling—xiandai Zhongguo shehui xinli de fenxi" 斲害'五四精神'的幽靈—現代中國社會心理的分析 (Smashing the ghost of the "May Fourth spirit"—an analysis of the psychology of contemporary Chinese society). *Ziyou Zhongguo* 自由中國 20, no. 9 (May): 278–81.

Xing Mu 辛木. 1919. "Can" 慚 ([Our] shame). *Chenbao* 晨報, Mar. 14.

Yamamoto, T., and S. Yamamoto. 1953. "The Anti-Christian Movement in China, 1922–1927." *Far Eastern Quarterly* 12, no. 2 (Feb.): 133–49.

Yip, Kam-che. 1970. "The Anti-Christian Movements in China, 1922–1927." Ph.D. diss., Columbia University.

Zhang Guotao 張國濤. 1971. *Wo de huiyi* 我的回憶 (My reminiscences). Hong Kong: Mingbao.

Zhang Qinshi 張欽士. 1927. *Guonei jin shinian lai zhi zongjiao sichao* 國內近十年來宗教思潮 (Religious trends in China during the recent ten years). Beijing: Yanjing Huawen xuexiao.

Zhonghua minguo shishi jiyao 中華民國史世紀要 (Records of the important historical events in the Chinese Republic). 1977. Ed. Zhonghua minguo shishi jiyao bianweihui. Taibei: Zhonghua minguo shiliao yanjiu zhongxin.

Zhongmi 仲密. [1919] 1963. "Sixiang geming" 思想革命 (Ideological revolution). *Meizhou pinglun* 每週評論 11. Reprinted in *Xin qingnian* 新青年 6, no. 4 (Apr.). Reprinted—Tokyo: Taian, pp. 445–46.

Zhu Chengjia 朱成甲. 1989. "Wusi shiqi Chen Duxiu guomin yundong de sixiang yu xin wenhua yundong—jian lun liuxing de duiyu xin wenhua yundong tifa de yizhong pianmianxing" 五四時期陳獨秀國民運動的思想與新文化運動—兼論流行的對于新文化運動提法的一種片面惺 (Duxiu's reflections on citizen movements during the May Fourth period and the New Culture Movement—being at the same time an essay on the one-sidedness of current arguments about the New Culture Movement). In Zhongguo shehui kexueyuan, ed., *Wusi yundong yu Zhongguo wenhua jianshe* 五四運動與中國文化建設 (The May Fourth movement and the construction of Chinese culture), 2: 934–60. Beijing: Shekui kexue wenxian.

Zhu Ruyi 朱如一. [1917] 1962. "Huodong yu rensheng" 活動與人生 (Activity and human life). *Xin qingnian* 新青年 3, no. 2 (Apr.): 1–2. Reprinted—Tokyo: Taian, pp. 193–94.

Ziyou Zhongguo 自由中國. 1958. "Genzhe wusi de jiaobu qianjin" 跟著五四得腳步前進 (Forward in the steps of May Fourth). *Ziyou Zhongguo* 自由中國 18, no. 9 (May): 271–72.

———. 1960. "'Wusi' shi women dengta" 五四是我們的燈塔 ("May Fourth" is our beacon). *Ziyou Zhongguo* 自由中國 20, no. 9 (May): 271–73.

PART II

The Rewriting of China's Literary History

CHAPTER THREE

Literary Historiography in Early Twentieth-Century China (1904–1928): Constructions of Cultural Memory

Milena Doleželová-Velingerová

No histories of literature were written in China before the twentieth century, because Chinese scholars of the past preferred to convey their judgments on historical change in literature in forms other than a single narrative. They chose to collect and preserve literary works of previous periods in voluminous compendia. They engaged in exegetical discourses, in which scholars communicated their views on the literary texts as well as on commentaries by their predecessors. And in casual jottings or more formal essays the literati offered their observations on deviations from or transformations of literary forms and the emergence of new literary genres.

Thus, when Lin Chuanjia 林 傳 甲 (1877–1921) published his *A History of Chinese Literature* (*Zhongguo wenxue shi* 中 國 文 學 史) in 1904 and Huang Ren 黃 人 (1866–1913) his independently written work of the same title in 1905, what reasons motivated the two scholars to change the ways and means of recording literary history? Was it the Darwinian concept of evolution imported to China via T. H. Huxley's *Evolution and Ethics* in Yan Fu's 嚴 復 (1853–1921) translation of 1898? Or were the histories of Chinese literature written by Japanese scholars, such as that published by Sasagawa Rinpū 笹 川 種 郎 (1870–1949) in 1898, impressive enough to change the traditional Chinese views on literature? And how did the Chinese literati cope with the task of establishing an entirely new discipline in literary studies?

In 1911, Huang Ren, a well-known literary critic in his day, addressed some of these problems in the entry "Literature" ("Wenxue" 文 學), pub-

I am much indebted to Dr. Henri M. Day for his pertinent comments, which enhanced the clarity of this essay.

lished in his *New General Encyclopedic Dictionary* (*Putong baike xin da cidian* 普通百科新大詞典). One of the critic's primary concerns was to convey to the public how literature was conceived and studied in China and the West during his time. And since Chinese men of letters generally understood the notion of "literature" as all written texts, Huang Ren emphasized the difference between artistic and non-artistic works:

> Now let me present for your reference how literature is defined in European and American countries. In a wider sense, all texts verbally expressing thoughts and sentiments belong to the realm of literature. Literature proper, on the other hand, emphasizes the reader's emotional response and an accessibility to a common reader. But if this literature strives to move the reader's feeling, its text must possess aesthetic quality. Although literature is related to man's knowledge and will, its principal aspect rests in beauty. As a result, *belles-lettres* (美文學) form a part of fine arts (美術). (Huang Moxi 1911: 106)[1]

Later in the same entry, Huang Ren initiated a discussion of no less challenging a topic—a comparison between the goals and methods of Western literary historiography and the Chinese approach to literary study:

> What is meant by literary history is to examine the sources and the development of literature. This research can be accomplished in many various ways, all beneficial to literature, such as the study of a race, a nation's customs, temporal environment, and the like. Yet, in China these studies have been limited merely to writing literary treatises, critical exegeses, and biographies of famous writers [in official histories]. (Huang Moxi 1911: 107)

Huang Ren's trenchant comments about the differences between literary concepts and research in China and the West clarified that the differentiation of artistic from non-artistic texts and the development of new research strategies were essential for the modernization of literary studies in China. These tasks, however, were not to be carried out easily. To appreciate the difficulties that obstructed ready acceptance of new aesthetic concepts, it will be useful to compare the different solutions to the problem of delineating artistic and non-artistic texts at the beginning of European and Chinese literary historiography. Furthermore, a survey of new trends in Chinese historiography at the beginning of this century will elucidate how literary historiography in China was established as a new scholarly discipline struggling to introduce new research methods.

---

1. Unless otherwise indicated, all translations of Chinese text are mine.

At first sight, it appears that the task of differentiating artistic from nonartistic texts was a common feature of both European and Chinese literary historiographies at the time of their origin. As Ernst Behler writes, "The habitual *Literärgeschichte* prevailing in Europe during the previous centuries . . . had the character of a compendium and presented its material in the form of incoherent aggregates of information, mostly in chronological sequence. . . . The realm of literature often extended to everything written, and the temporal beginning for these presentations was usually at the creation of the world" (1991: 11). The transformation from these *historia litteraria* to modern literary historiography took place only when authors such as Friedrich Schlegel (1772–1829) set aside the vast amount of works not all known to them firsthand, and replaced the literary canon with works that they had personally read (Behler 1991: 12). The result was that the "history" of literature was reshaped by the personal, subjective point of view of the historiographer according to his scholarly knowledge and aesthetic taste.

In China, the reshaping of the notion of "literature" and the concept of "history" took an entirely different course: the historiographer aimed to reformulate "literature" and "history" in directions that he believed would benefit the country. This utilitarian and pragmatic approach toward the making of literary history was facilitated by cultural and political circumstances. The traditional concept of literature as a medium of moral guidance remained deeply ingrained in Chinese culture well into the twentieth century. And the timing of the rise of Chinese literary historiography coincided with the period of China's bitter wars and conflicts with the West and Japan.

To elucidate the origins of the didactic role of Chinese literature, it is useful to remember that in premodern China it was not meaningful to posit the question "What is literature?" To the Chinese, literature was a large body of writings identified not only by aesthetically pleasing verbal patterns, but also by an edifying mission. This mission can be best clarified by the etymology of the Chinese word for "writings," *wen* 文, which can be traced back to the same word and character *wen* 文, with the meaning of "pattern" or "marking" and embracing not only artifacts but also configurations of natural and cosmic phenomena. As James J. Y. Liu so lucidly puts it, it was by linking literature (*wen*) with the configurations (*wen*) of phenomena of the cosmos that Liu Xie 劉勰 (d. ca. 523) was able, in his monumental theoretical work on Chinese literature, *The Literary Mind and Carving of Dragons* (*Wenxin diaolong* 文心雕龍), "to trace the origin of literature to the beginning of the universe, and to elevate literature to a status of cosmic significance. Drawing his ideas from the *Book of Changes* (*Yijing* 易 經) and other ancient works, he evolves the theory of multiple correspondences between cosmic order and the human mind, between mind and language, and between language and literature" (1975: 22).

The linking of literature with the configurations of phenomena of the cosmos—in the Chinese mind essentially moral—obviously fostered a didactic mission for writing and permitted the inclusion of philosophical texts, historiographies, didactic prose, and correspondence, among other forms, within the category of "literature." That it was a foreigner—the Jesuit missionary Guilio Aleni—who in 1623 introduced the compound *wenxue* 文 學 into the Chinese language in order to convey the concept of European belles-lettres to the Chinese imperial court succinctly elucidates the whole problem (Masini 1993: 204).

Given the concept of literature as aesthetically pleasing verbal patterns and morally edifying texts, any attempt to compile an account of all that was written during the millennia-long history of China would be a nonsensical and unnecessary act. Thus, before the twentieth century Chinese scholars preferred to convey their judgments on historical change in literature by self-contained observations of particular phenomena or particular literary works. A single, unified narrative that would explain literary changes over a long period of time by linking them in causal relations was, as far as we know, never written in traditional China.

To explain the sudden arrival of literary histories in China at the very beginning of the twentieth century, it is necessary to consider the deep transformation in Chinese historiography going on at about the same time. As Ying-Shih Yü points out, "The concept of 'national history' in its current Western usage was wholly unfamiliar to Chinese historians before the twentieth century" (1994: 155). It was only thanks to the impact of modernized Japanese historiography that several remarkable Chinese scholars extricated their views from the traditional Chinese perception of a sinocentric world order, which exerted a formative influence on Chinese dynastic historiography until the close of the nineteenth century (Yü 1994: 156). Around 1900, a significant number of Chinese historians involved in anti-Manchu activities who took refuge in Japan—among them Liang Qichao 梁 启 超 (1873–1929), Zhang Binglin 章 炳 麟 (1868–1936), and Liu Shipei 劉 師 培 (1884–1919)—set up entirely new parameters for Chinese historiography. To them, "history" was to be understood not as the genealogy of the ruling house but as a general "history of the nation," which consisted of a wide variety of specialized histories, such as a "history of economics," a "history of arts and crafts," and a "history of diplomacy." Consequently, the widened concept of historical research and writing promoted Chinese national consciousness. Although historians initially attempted to redefine Chinese history from the perspective of world history, in the wake of the bitter conflicts with the West they gradually shifted their interest toward a search for "spirit" in Chinese history from a national point of view. Western ideas and values were then introduced in terms of the Chinese tradition rather than the other way round. Still, Liang Qichao, Zhang Binglin, and Liu Shipei always acknowledged in their writings their indebtedness to many Japanese sinologists who had already published a number of Western-style textbooks on Chinese history (Yü 1994: 161).

This trend in Chinese historiography had one particularly heavy impact on the emerging Chinese literary historiography. As all authors of the early Chinese literary histories readily acknowledged in their prefaces, their aim was to raise Chinese national consciousness. The didactic nature of their works was predestined by the format of the majority of early Chinese literary histories: they were designed to serve as textbooks in the newly founded national universities. Modern Chinese historiographies thus emerged as repositories of intentionally shaped "cultural memory," which was frequently constructed and reconstructed according to a constantly changing understanding of the notions of "literature" and "history."

Despite the potentially highly rewarding nature of the topic, the study of early Chinese literary histories has remained, until very recently, at the very periphery of research on modern intellectual history in China. This rather surprising lack of interest can be explained by the inaccessibility of the sources and ignorance of their very existence. In 1967 Liang Rongruo 梁容若 offered in his *Researches into Histories of Chinese Literature* (*Zhongguo wenxue shi yanjiu* 中國文學史研究) the first descriptions of some of these early histories. But it was only in 1986 that Chen Yutang's 陳玉堂 *Annotated Catalog of Chinese Literary Histories* (*Zhongguo wenxue shi shumu tiyao* 中國文學史書目提要) brought to light no less than 124 general histories of literature produced in China during the first half of this century. In 1993 a leading literary historian and theoretician, Huang Lin 黃霖, wrote the best study to date on premodern Chinese literary historiography, the chapter

"Chinese Literary Historiography" ("Zhongguo wenxue shixue" 中國文學史學) in his *History of Premodern [Chinese] Literary Criticism* (*Jindai wenxue piping shi* 近代文學批評史). Huang Lin's essay comprises exceptionally insightful treatments of various views of Chinese literati on historical change in literature during the second half of the nineteenth century as well as detailed descriptions of Lin Chuanjia and Huang Ren's literary histories of 1904 and 1905.[2]

Despite the considerable advances made in the study of premodern literary histories in recent years, the political concept of periodization in Chinese literary criticism (which sets the end of the premodern era in 1911, the year of the demise of imperial order in China) has hindered a closer observation of literary historiography during the 1910s—the important transitional period from the *ancien régime* to more modern times. Little is thus known about literary histories written in China before the May Fourth era; this makes it difficult to judge whether this period was indeed of such negligible cultural importance as to merit its dismissal from most historical accounts of Chinese literature. Similarly, we find it difficult to determine whether there are links between May Fourth literary histories and their predecessors or whether their relation was one of clean disjunction.

As an initial effort to clarify this situation, this chapter investigates the various manners and forms in which literature of the past was presented in the following four literary histories written between 1904 and 1928: the histories by Lin Chuangjia and Huang Ren mentioned above; *History of Chinese literature* (*Zhongguo wenxue shi* 中國文學史) by Zeng Yi 曾毅, published in 1915; and Hu Shi's 胡適 (1891–1962) *History of [Chinese] Vernacular Literature* (*Baihua wenxue shi* 白話文學史), of 1928.

These histories have been selected to exemplify the change in the concepts of "literature" and "history" in China during the period in question and to elucidate how the rhetoric of literary historiography contributed to the

2. In 1996, Dai Yan 戴燕, a member of the younger generation of Chinese scholars, published an article that offers valuable descriptions but raises issues different from the ones I address here. My sincere thanks to Dietrich Tschanz of Princeton University for bringing this article to my attention. Also in 1996, Huang Wenji 黃文吉 and his team of coauthors from Dong Wu University prepared for publication the impressive *Annotated Catalog of Chinese Literary Histories Published in Taiwan, 1949–1994* (*Taiwan chuban Zhongguo wenxue shi shumu tiyao* 台灣出版中國文學史書目提要, 1949–1994), which features, as an appendix, a most useful catalog of Chinese literary histories from the period 1880–1994, including histories of Chinese literature written by Chinese, Japanese, and Western sinologists.

functioning of literature as cultural memory. During the pre–May Fourth period, between 1904 and 1917, a total of eleven histories of Chinese literature written by Chinese scholars are known to have been published. However, some of these texts are no longer extant or remain only in fragments; others did not meet accepted scholarly standards (Chen Yutang 1986: 1–11). The works by Lin Chuanjia, Huang Ren, and Zeng Yi have been selected for discussion because they exemplify most clearly both the shortcomings and the achievements of this new scholarly field during the pre–May Fourth period.

Following an account of these pre–May Fourth histories, I survey literary histories from the 1920s, in order to indicate the wide spectrum of scholarly approaches to the study of Chinese literature during the decade and thus dispel the myth that histories by May Fourth scholars occupied a dominant position at that time. From the production of the May Fourth reformers, Hu Shi's history of vernacular literature has been singled out for closer examination because it exemplifies how the rhetoric of literary historiography contributed to the rewriting of Chinese literary history.

"History of Chinese Literature" by Lin Chuanjia: The Multiple Meanings of "Wenxue"

In 1904, the year Lin Chuanjia's work was published, propitious circumstances existed for the founding of an entirely new field in Chinese scholarship: the writing of literary histories. During the profound transformation that took place in Chinese higher education at the beginning of the twentieth century in accordance with a model imported from Japan, seven new fields of study—political science 政治, humanities 文學, natural sciences 格致, agronomy 農 學, industrial studies 工 藝, business 商 務, and medicine 醫學—had been introduced into the curriculum at the newly reformed Peking University 京 師 大 學 堂 as well as at the newly founded private universities in some coastal cities, such as Dong Wu University 東吳大學 in Hangzhou. The curriculum for the field referred to above as "humanities"—denoted in Chinese by the term *wenxue* 文學—embraced such subjects as economics, historiography, Neo-Confucian philosophy, early Chinese philosophy, archival studies, stylistics, and the study of Chinese language and literature as well as foreign languages and literatures (Dai 1996: 6).

Lin Chuanjia was only twenty-seven when he arrived in Beijing during the summer of 1904 to direct the Department of Chinese Language and Literature at Peking University. And because his petition to introduce the history of Chinese literature into the school's curriculum was granted, writing a textbook for this new subject became one of his primary tasks. By happy coincidence, in 1903 a Chinese translation of the Japanese *History of Chinese Literature* (*Shina bungaku shi* 支 那 文 學 史) published in 1898 by Sasagawa Rinpū had just been brought out by the Translation Publishing House of Chinese and Western Works in Shanghai (Chen Yutang 1986: 125). In his brief recollections about the genesis of his work, Lin Chuanjia noted that "my book was inspired by *History of Chinese Literature* by the Japanese Sasagawa Rinpū" (1904a: 1).

The book was, indeed, a worthy model to follow. Sasagawa's work was, in fact, one of the earliest histories of Chinese literature[3] and its author was at the time of its publication already a renowned scholar of Japanese and Chinese literature, as well as the future writer of the first history of Chinese fiction. Sasagawa was familiar with the European literary histories of his time, and he imprinted a thoroughly modern outlook on his *History*. He opened his book with a clearly written introduction in which he discussed Chinese culture and civilization, the various nationalities who had lived or were still living in China, the difference between the Northerners and Southerners in China, the Chinese reverence for nature, the Chinese penchant for self-aggrandizement, specific traits of Chinese literature, the Chinese script, and the periodization of Chinese history. Sasagawa divided the development of Chinese literature into nine dynastic periods, beginning with literature from the pre-Chunqiu 春 秋 era (around the fifth century B.C.) to the Qing dynasty (1644–1911), and in each chapter devoted to a specific period he summarized the overall cultural atmosphere of the time, highlighted the dominant literary genres, and indicated the outstanding writers of the era. For his time, the most radical breakthrough in his literary history consisted of inclusions of Chinese drama and the novel among his critical discourses and his specific discussions

3. Evidently unaware of the earliest histories of Chinese literature by a Russian and two Japanese scholars, Herbert G. Giles claims in the preface to his *History of Chinese Literature*, first published in 1901, that the book "is the first attempt made in any language, including Chinese, to produce a history of Chinese literature" (1901: xvii). According to Huang Wenji's *Catalog* (1996: 343), the very first history of Chinese literature was published by V. P. Vasil'ev in 1880 under the title *Ocherk istorii kitajskoj literatury* (History of Chinese literature: an outline) and among the Japanese histories of Chinese literature the earliest one was published in Tokyo in 1897 by Koji Teikichi 古 城 貞 吉 (1866–1949) under the title *History of Chinese Literature* (*Shina bungaku shi* 支那 文 學 史).

(in chapters 7–9) of the novels *Water Margin* (*Shuihu zhuan* 水 滸 傳), *Romance of the Three Kingdoms* (*Sanguo yanyi* 三 國 演 義), *The Journey to the West* (*Xiyou ji* 西 遊 記), and *The Plum in the Golden Vase* (*Jin Ping Mei* 金 瓶 梅), as well as of the dramas *The Story of the Western Chamber* (*Xixiang ji* 西 廂 記) and *The Story of the Lute* (*Pipa ji* 琵 琶 記). A clear sign of this scholar's independent mind, uninhibited by conservative views of some Chinese scholars, emerges in the section of Chapter 9 on the Qing era, devoted to the playwright and fiction writer Li Yu 李 漁 (1611–80), the prominent dramatist Tang Xianzu 湯 顯 祖 (1550–1617), and the founder of Chinese fiction theory, Jin Shengtan 金 聖 歎 (1608–61). As is well known, Li Yu's and Jin Shengtan's works, which were seen as undermining the established literary canon and public morality, were prohibited in China from the eighteenth century well into modern times and earned their authors lasting contempt.

Although Sasagawa's work had inspired Lin Chuanjia to write a history of Chinese literature, Lin eventually rejected the idea of using the Japanese scholar's *History* as a model for his own enterprise. To Lin, Sasagawa's inclusion of fiction and drama into the Chinese literary canon was sacrilegious, and Lin unceremoniously vented his indignation in his own *History*. He attacked all those "vulgar, uneducated, and ignorant scholars who spread around fiction," heaped contempt on Tang Xianzu and Jin Shengtan, and accused the Japanese scholar *ad hominem* of treating in his *History* "obscene and proscribed works from Chinese literature of the past" (1904a: 203–5).

With Sasagawa's model repudiated and with no Chinese precedents for writing literary history, Lin turned to traditional Chinese historiography for guidance regarding the compositional and temporal arrangement of his work. As he noted in a brief comment appended to his table of contents, it was *jishi benmo* 紀 事 本 末—a form of Chinese historical writing that covers a single subject or period from beginning to end—that offered Lin the concept of chapters devoted to specific topics. The example of Sima Guang's 司 馬 光 (1019–86) celebrated *Complete Mirror for Aid in Government* (*Zizhi tongjian* 資 治 通 鑑) gave Lin the idea of organizing the subject matter in chronological order (1904a: *muci* 目 次, 25).

As a result, Lin's work is a peculiar hybrid. His book is divided into sixteen chapters, the first ten of which cover various aspects of Chinese writing in the broad sense of the word, such as Chinese script, prosody, grammar, and rules of composition, as well as the "stylistic features," *ti* 體, of Confucian Classics, dynastic biographies, histories, and early philosophical works.

Only in the twelfth chapter does Lin turn his attention to "classical prose," *guwen* 古文, and "parallel prose," *pianwen* 駢文. But none of the genres that by modern standards represent literature proper, such as poetry, drama, and fiction, is discussed in Lin's *History*. Entirely neglected also are accounts of writers' biographies, not to mention the relationships between authors' lives and their oeuvres. To convey historical change, Lin Chuanjia subdivided each of the sixteen chapters into eighteen brief sections that describe the status quo of a particular cultural phenomenon in a particular dynastic period, from mythical times to the Qing dynasty. Lin demonstrated his aptitude for fine research in the last chapter, which yielded valuable delineation of differences between the past and present stages of *pianwen*. However, in the other chapters, "transformation," *bianqian* 變遷, is to Lin coterminous with the paratactic arrangement of separate facts describing a specific cultural category, with no attempt to explain the causes or nature of the evolutionary transformation. Charles S. Gardner's perceptive observation that "[Chinese] historical writing ordinarily involves, not original composition of any considerable length, but compilation of choice selections from earlier works" (1938: 70) is also true for Lin's *History*.

The contemporary reader can hardly suppress a deep disappointment that a rare historical opportunity to establish a truly modern Chinese literary historiography was so badly missed. It is difficult to comprehend that at a time when Chinese men of letters were striving to introduce the concept of the history of the nation to replace dynastic genealogies Lin Chuanjia was doing exactly the opposite. He distorted the whole spectrum of Chinese literature by misrepresenting a particular part as the whole.

Although Lin's friend Jiang Shaoquan 江紹銓 (fl. 1904) praised—as he was expected to do—the author of the *History* as an unusually talented man and a famous poet of the day (Lin 1904a: preface), Lin's intellectual stature was hardly comparable to Liang Qichao's, Zhang Binglin's, or Liu Shipei's. His search for methodology in traditional Chinese histories suggests that he was probably not well, if at all, acquainted with the new trends in Chinese historiography. Moreover, his categorical rejection of Sasagawa's account of Chinese literature, solely on the grounds of the alleged immorality of fiction and drama, confirms Lin Chuanjia's adherence to the age-old Confucian tenet that the mission of literature rests in moral guidance (*wen yi zai dao* 文以載道). Thus we must ask how Lin Chuanjia understood the meaning of the compound *wenxue* 文學 that figures so prominently in the title of his book.

In contemporary Chinese the compound means "belles-lettres." According to Federico Masini, it was, as already noted, coined in the seventeenth century to convey the concept of European literary texts. Later, during the nineteenth century, it was used by Protestant missionaries to translate the modern English term "literature." The compound became widespread in China via the round-trip diffusion of the Japanese *bungaku* 文 學 by the turn of the century (Masini 1993: 204–5). However, during this particular period, the term denoted a wider semantic area than that of "literature." Thus, the Japanese scholar Sanetō Keishū 實 籐 惠 秀 (1896–1985) maintains that at the turn of the twentieth century the compound *wenxue* 文 學 was understood as a contraction of *wen zhang bo xue* 文 章 博 學 "erudition acquired through patterned texts," a definition of the two self-standing words *wen* 文 and *xue* 學 that appears in the Confucian *Analects* (*Lunyu* 論 語 xi.2; Masini 1993: 205). This is the reason that, as noted above, the term *wenxue* could be used with the wide meaning "humanities," a field that embraces various subjects of study. What exactly these subjects were at the time Lin compiled his book is best clarified by the Imperial Edict of January 4, 1904, regulating university curricula. Whereas it eliminated Neo-Confucianism and economics from the curriculum of *wenxue* ("humanities"), at the same time it stipulated in detail the subjects to be included in the study of Chinese literature, such as "exegesis of script and prosody" 文 字 音 韻 訓 故, "stylistics and creative writing" 文 章 的 修 辭 寫 作, "literary style and grammar" 文 體 文 法, "moral mission of literature" 文 章 中 德, and "propaedeutics" 學 的 養 成 (Qu and Tang 1991: 236–339). A comparison of these subjects with the content of Lin's *History* shows that Lin compiled his *History* by strictly adhering to the instructions of the Imperial Edict.

A historical understanding of the higher-education system prevailing in China at the beginning of the twentieth century, together with an awareness of the multiple meanings of the neologism *wenxue* at that time, thus places Lin Chuanjia's *Zhongguo wenxue shi* in a different light. Today, his title is readily understood as *History of Chinese Literature*, but to Lin the word *wenxue* meant what might be rendered as "humanities." The title of the volume thus accurately describes what it, in fact, was: a well-organized textbook providing a historical perspective on subjects prescribed by the Imperial Edict.

As plausible as this explanation of the title and nature of Lin's *History* appears to be, it nevertheless fails to explain why, from the 1930s on, Lin Chuanjia has been hailed as the founder of modern Chinese literary historiography. Why was such a textbook elevated by some of the foremost May Fourth scholars to the important position of the first Chinese literary history?

As paradoxical as it may seem, this "upward transformation" of the book by the adherents of May Fourth was necessary because Lin's *History* had secured a wide readership and fame for its author. Whether because of its novelty or its practical usefulness, Lin's *History* was reprinted in 1906, and in April 1910 serial publication of the work began in the journal *Prosperity* (*Guangyi* 廣益). In June of the same year, it was reissued by Wulin Mouxinshi 吳林謀新室 for distribution in Shanghai and Guangzhou (Chen Yutang 1986: 3). In February 1914, the book was reprinted by Guangzhou cunzhenge 廣州存珍閣 and by the Commercial Press in Shanghai. The success and popularity of the book in the 1920s posed a potentially dangerous challenge to the efforts of adherents of May Fourth to present themselves as the founders of modern Chinese literary historiography. With the arrival of new cultural policies in the 1920s, Lin's *History* was found ideologically untenable, and the book was entirely rewritten. In conformity with the May Fourth cultural project, Lin's original work was replaced by a version substantially revised by a certain Wang Jianyu 汪劍餘 (fl. 1925), who acknowledged his indebtedness to Lin's work in the preface but excised two chapters and added chapters on fiction and drama. The re-edited and rewritten book was published in 1925 under Wang's name and entitled *History of Literature in Our Country* (*Benguo wenxue shi* 本國文學史).

The rewriting of Lin Chuanjia's textbook was, however, only the first step in the process of its ideological transformation and cultural appropriation. The title of the textbook, *Zhongguo wenxue shi*, which in the 1930s was understood solely to mean *History of Chinese Literature*, facilitated the elevation of Lin's volume to the position of the first history of Chinese literature and conveniently created an early predecessor of May Fourth literary historiography. In 1932, when this important historical role was bestowed on Lin Chuanjia's *History* by Zheng Zhenduo 鄭振鐸 (1898–1958) in his *Illustrated History of Chinese Literature* (*Chatuben Zhongguo wenxue shi* 插圖本中國文學史), it sufficed that Zheng merely proclaimed the work, without further explanation, to be "the earliest Chinese literary history written by a Chinese scholar" (1932: vol. 1, Introduction,p. 2).

"History of Chinese Literature" by Huang Ren: New Perimeters for Literature

The historical role of Huang Ren's *History* as the first Chinese literary historiography has been acknowledged only very recently, in 1986. For reasons that only now become more clear, the whole arresting work of Huang Ren—a formidable turn-of-the-century journalist, literary critic, encyclopedist, and translator, in his time better known as Huang Moxi 黃摩西—was entirely effaced from modern Chinese cultural history soon after Huang's untimely death in 1913. He was given credit for writing his *History* only in Chen Yutang's *Catalog* (1986: 1–2) and the *Great Encyclopedia of China* (*Zhongguo da baike quanshu* 1: 280) of the same year. Because the full text of Huang's *History* has still not been republished and sporadic quotations in histories of Chinese literary historiographies can hardly give an accurate and comprehensive picture of the importance of Huang's oeuvre, the volume *Huang Ren: A Critical Biography and a Selection of His Works*, published in 1998, is a welcome endeavor by its editors Tang Zhesheng 湯哲聲 and Tu Xiaoma 塗小馬. The volume includes substantial parts of Huang's extant scholarly work and poetry, the editors' critical biography of the thinker, and essays in which Huang's friends and contemporaries vividly recall Huang's audacious eccentricity and determination to break through the confines of cultural conventions. My present account of Huang's views on Chinese literature and his new research methods has been largely facilitated by the accessibility of the three introductory chapters to Huang's *History* published in this volume.

Huang Ren wrote his literary history at about the same time and under similar circumstances as Lin Chuanjia. In 1901 he assumed a teaching position offered to him by an American missionary who had only recently established Dong Wu University in Suzhou and who is identified in Huang's volume only by his Chinese name, Sun Yuewen 孫樂文 (Tang and Tu 1998: 4). It was in this connection that Huang, who earned his *xiucai* degree when he was sixteen but was essentially a self-taught scholar, began to write his book to serve as a textbook for his course on Chinese literature.[4] Around 1905 the Society for the Preservation of National Learning (Guoxue fulun

---

4. Although most sources indicate the year 1905 as the time of Huang's conception of the project, the *Comprehensive Dictionary of Chinese Literature* (*Zhongguo wenxue da cidian* 中國文學大辭典), published in 1997, provides the year 1904 for the same event; see p. 1891.

she 國學扶輪社), which was founded in the same year by Huang and Wang Wenru 王文濡 (fl. 1905), printed the volume, but the book remained little known because it was used only as a teaching material (the word "textbook," *keben* 課本, is printed on the title page) and was not distributed in bookstores (Tang and Tu 1998: 8). According to the editors' postscript, the original of Huang Ren's *History*, stored presently at Suzhou University (formerly Dong Wu University), is reportedly the only extant copy of this precious work (Tang and Tu 1998: 324).

Despite the similar circumstances that led to the composition of Lin and Huang's *Histories*, their textbooks turned out to be opposites. Various reasons could be found for this difference—Huang Ren's personality, prodigious talents, wide knowledge of Chinese culture, interest in things foreign, and his experience in professional journalism—but nothing was more decisive than their approaches to the sources of their works and their ability to formulate their own judgments.

Huang Ren, in his late thirties when he began to work on his project on Chinese literary history, was actively engaged in the political and cultural scene of China at the turn of the century. In Suzhou he befriended Zhang Taiyan 章太炎 (1869–1936), a philologist par excellence, as well as two renowned late Qing writers, Zeng Pu 曾樸 (1872–1935) and Xu Nianci 徐念慈 (1875–1908), with whom he founded in 1905 the prominent late Qing literary society Forest of Fiction (Xiaoshuo lin 小說林). In *Forest of Fiction* (*Xiaoshuo lin* 小說林), the influential literary journal of the day published by this society, Huang Ren formulated in his article "Announcement of Publication of *Forest of Fiction*" ("*Xiaoshuo lin* fakanci" 小說林發刊詞, no. 1, 1907) a rarely seen view among his contemporaries that it is the aesthetic aspect which is the "essence of the novel" (*xiaoshuo zhi shizhi* 小說之實質). Huang's least known, but perhaps most impressive, oeuvre is the aforementioned voluminous *New General Encyclopedic Dictionary*. It was single-handedly prepared by Huang Ren and published by the Society for the Preservation of National Learning in 1911, and it provided the Chinese reading public with in-depth and accurate information on Chinese and Western culture, sciences, and society.[5] The admirable ability to fuse his concern for his nation and race with a deep interest in Western culture is perhaps best

5. Huang Ren's *Encyclopedic Dictionary* is highly appraised in Zhong Shaohua 1996, a pioneering work on the little-known encyclopaedic activities of Chinese scholars at the turn of the century.

expressed by two of Huang Ren's many adopted names. Born in Changshu, Zhejiang province, as Zhenyuan 振元, he adopted his pseudonym Huang Ren 黃人, "Yellow Man," only in middle age; as his literary name (*hao* 號) he chose Huang Moxi 黃摩西, "Huang, who is in touch with the West" (*Zhongguo gudai xiaoshuo baike quanshu* 1993: 188).[6] A patriotic liberal, Huang Ren reportedly suffered from severe depression after the collapse of the 1911 Revolution, and mental disorders eventually caused his premature death in 1913 (Huang Lin 1993: 613).[7]

Huang Ren's *History* has an unusual format. According to Chen Yutang's detailed description (1986: 1), Huang Ren's work consists of 29 *ce* 冊, whose content is unevenly distributed. A relatively small section of three *ce* represents the core of the book, embracing three chapters. Chapter 1 ("Zonglun" 總論) is devoted to theoretical problems of general nature, such as "the aim of literature," "historical literature and literary history," and the "use of literature" (Tang and Tu 1998: 37–45). Chapter 2 includes "Outlines" (*lüelun* 略論) on various topics, such as the "origins of literature," "various kinds of literature," and, most important, Huang's innovative periodization of Chinese literature (Tang and Tu 1998: 45–65). Chapter 3 is analytical (*fenlun* 分論) and includes the intriguing "Definition of Literature" ("Wenxue dingyi" 文學定義), in which Huang disclosed the foreign model for his *magnum opus* (Tang and Tu 1998: 66–72). The other section embraces the remaining 26 *ce*, including numerous texts of a documentary character that Huang Ren evidently investigated and transcribed from the originals prior to writing the narrative chapters. These materials dating from early Qin to late Ming periods cover a rather broad scope of topics, including inscriptions on bamboo tablets and bronze vessels, historical discourses, imperial mandates, poetry of various forms, novelistic and dramatic texts, parallel prose (*pianwen* 駢文), eight-legged essays (*bagu wen* 八股文), rhyme handbooks, women's literature (*guixiu* 閨秀), prefaces, and records. This material is organized in sections by historical period and literary genre. Each set of collected texts is

---

6. The same name "Moxi" written in the same characters 摩西 was widely used for the biblical Moses. Whether or not Huang Ren chose the name because of its potential polysemy is difficult to ascertain, but a possibility that he entertained the idea of comparison with the learned leader of the nation under duress should not be discounted. I am very grateful to my colleague Dr. Hua Laura Wu for this suggestion.

7. For more information on Huang's life and work, see the reminiscences of his contemporaries in Tang and Tu 1998: 87–108.

preceded by a short introduction on the topic and biographies of the authors of the sources presented.

Returning now to the three pivotal chapters at the beginning of Huang's *History*, a first look at their formal division into brief discourses gives the impression of a fragmented treatment of various topics organized hierarchically from a general to a more detailed approach. A deeper look into the subjects of the discourses reveals, however, that Huang Ren introduced in these three chapters a radically new strategy with regard to some essential issues of Chinese literary historiography: a treatment of literature in relation to (rather than in separation from) other constituents of Chinese culture, a new understanding of the concepts *wen* and *wenxue* (writings and literature) on the basis of aesthetic aspects, and an innovative concept of periodization of Chinese literature, related to the power of political despotism in China. As we shall see, this new type of strategy was frequently employed by Huang as a reaction to what he saw as harmful adherence to outdated conventions in Chinese culture.

Thus, Huang's new approach toward a more accurate understanding of literature was triggered by his observation in his essay "Historical Writing and Literary History" ("Lishi wenxue yu wenxue shi" 歷史文學與文學史) that the traditional bibliographers' division of Chinese writing into a mere four categories—Confucian Classics (*jing* 經), historiography (*shi* 史), philosophical writing (*zi* 子), and literary collections (*ji* 集)—obscured the mutual interaction between individual categories or historical development within an individual category (Tang and Tu 1998: 38–39). He therefore suggested that Chinese literature should be treated instead *in relation* to such subjects as script or historiography and that the development of individual literary genres and forms should be studied in relation to the development of other literary genres and forms.

As for the narrative part, it does not take long to recognize why some of Huang's contemporaries at the beginning of the twentieth century viewed him as an "eccentric" whereas at the other end of the same century he was prized for doing exactly what made him outlandish—writing his *History* only after he had absorbed Western aesthetic criteria for literature and after he had become acquainted with evolutionary thought and political history (*Zhongguo wenxue da cidian* 1997: 1891). Indeed, what made Huang Ren look outside Chinese culture was the vagueness of literary concepts and terminology in classical Chinese poetics, as he wrote in Chapter 3 in the section

"Definition of Literature" (Tang and Tu 1998: 67–68). When he did not find a much better situation among the Roman rhetoricians, such as Tacitus, Quintilianus, or Cicero, his proficiency of English led him finally to contemporary, late nineteenth-century British literary criticism. When we, after some struggle, identified the English names transcribed by Huang in Chinese characters arbitrarily chosen for their sound, his discourse yielded a myriad of illustrious British literary scholars, such as Matthew Arnold, Walter Pater, Thomas De Quincey, Thomas Macauley, Hutcheson Macaulay Posnett, John Morley, Charles Kingsley, and Edmund Gosse.[8] The names indicated that despite the variety of approaches that appeared during the revival of British literary criticism in the late nineteenth century (Wellek 1965: 141), Huang focused on those two streams in British scholarship that were pertinent to the Chinese situation of the day: a new aestheticism, which opposed the pervading Victorian atmosphere of didacticism and moralism, and a new historicism.

Although apparently overwhelmed by the British critics' matter-of-fact statements about the inherent superiority of imaginative and emotive literature and the need for aesthetic beauty in a literary work as well as the deep coherence of their cultural theories, Huang was obviously disappointed that the critics focused mostly on poetry and that they rarely touched on the problem that he himself considered crucial: those criteria that identify literature (Tang and Tu 1998: 68).

Eventually, Huang found what he called a "brand new" and "most lucid explanation of literature" while reading *A Short History of Modern English Literature* (1897) by Edmund Gosse. The new British literary historiography developed out of the turn-of-the-century aesthetic movement in England (Wellek 1965: 141), and Gosse's work was the first English literary history whose author intended to report more than dry facts. His *History* is an account of English literature from the age of Chaucer (1350–1400) to the early Victorian era (1840–70) and encompassed various literary genres, such as poetry, drama, and fiction, as well as critical and theoretical essays, literary historiography, discussions on the Bible, and diary notes, among other subjects.

Gosse's *History* apparently greatly assisted Huang in delineating the concept of literature on his own, although he presented his ideas as an "abstract," *dalüe* 大略, of Gosse's book. Huang arrived at a recognition that the

8. I wish to express my sincere thanks to Professor Wang Jingxian 王靖獻 of National Donghua University in Taiwan for his generous assistance in identifying the English names.

English term "literature" should be understood in two meanings, broad and narrow. As Huang put it, the term encompasses in its broad meaning all writings (including belles-lettres, historical records, manuscripts) produced by a nation, so that "it could be called national literature" (國民文學). In its narrow sense, Huang comprehended "literature," designated by the Chinese term *wenxue*, as special works that exhibit special qualities, including "literature's own creative act" (作物). "Although it is said," wrote Huang, "that literature transmits moral teaching, it awakens in the process one's thoughts, feelings, and imagination, even to the point that instilling delight in one's thoughts, feelings, and imagination becomes its main goal. . . . Thus, *wenxue* is an indivisible part of fine arts (美術), which, together with painting, music, and sculpture, is engaged in the description of emotions" (Tang and Tu 1998: 68).

Huang does not, however, delineate belles-lettres as a special category, because to him, "it is not the form, but the specific qualities that define literature" 蓋不以體制定文學，而以特質定文學者 (Tang and Tu 1998: 69). Like Gosse, Huang then considers Shakespeare's historical plays, Kailei's(?)[9] *History of the French Revolution*, and Kingsley's and Macauley's essays "to be on equal footing, because they all fulfill the conditions of literature" (Tang and Tu 1998: 69). To clarify what these conditions are, Huang concludes by enumerating the six specific properties that define "literature":

1. Literature transmits doctrine, but its main aim rests in aesthetic delight;
2. Literature should be accessible to the reader;
3. Literature should exhibit artistic skills;
4. Literature is the model of writing expressing feelings;
5. Literature is related to reality by embracing history and science; and
6. The mission of literature is to diffuse healthy beauty.

A final difference between Huang Ren's views and those of previous as well as contemporary scholars is his concept of periodization. It is indeed not surprising that Huang did not accept the traditional periodization of Chinese literature, which divided various evolutionary epochs of literature along particular dynastic eras. What is, however, arresting is that Huang did not adopt the evolutionary model formulated at the turn of the century by

9. I was unable to identify the French counterpart of the name transcribed as Kailei 楷雷.

Liang Qichao in his 1901 *Prolegomena to Chinese History* (*Zhongguo shi xulun* 中國史敘論), in which Liang presents historical development as coterminous with progress. In contrast, Huang devised his own historical periodization of literature, in which the prosperity and the decline of cultural and literary development are closely linked to the power of the autocratic political order. As maintained by Huang Ren in his discussion on periodization of Chinese literature, this autocracy of the imperial court, manifested by oppression and suppression of Chinese intelligentsia, increased continuously throughout history. Accordingly, Huang saw the general picture of literary evolution in China in a rather pessimistic light. Among the four periods into which Huang divided the literary development of Chinese literature, only one is designated as "the period of general prosperity" 文學全盛期, which was allocated to the ancient times of the reign of the Duke of Zhou (ca. ninth c. B.C.; Tang and Tu 1998: 50–54). In Huang's view, the second evolutionary period, designated as "a departure from prosperity" 文學華離期, begins during the reign of the Qin and Han dynasties, because these two periods are associated with the infamous burning of books and physical elimination of nonconformist scholars (Tang and Tu 1998: 54–60). Finally, the Ming and Qing dynasties are described by Huang as two "periods of darkness" 文學暧期, because the despotic rule of the Ming imperial court affected all areas of Chinese culture for 300 years and because the Qing period is the era of stagnation of Chinese culture (Tang and Tu 1998: 60–65).

Within this general framework of continuous decline, Huang, however, recognized the vitality of those specific literary genres or forms that arose in particular periods. Among those vigorous genres, Huang listed for instance, *yulu* 語錄, *pianwen* 駢文, and *shiyu* 詩餘 during the Northern and Southern Song, dramatic *qu* 曲 and its predecessor, *yuanben* 元本, of the Jin and Yuan dynasties, and particularly Ming *xiaoshuo* 小說 (understood as the novel in the late Qing period). Huang's choice of vibrant and vigorous genres from the Qing period is particularly arresting, because he listed not only the dramatic *chuanqi* 傳奇 but also the "eight-legged essay" *bagu wen* 八股文. As is well known, during the late Qing and especially during the May Fourth period, the eight-legged essay, which was dominant in the Qing period, was considered the epitome of artistic sterility, but Huang highly praised its artistic inventiveness and dynamism during its three hundred years of flourishing (Tang and Tu 1998: 56–65). In conclusion, it is appropriate to quote in full a particular passage, which Huang himself put in quotes, probably because he intended to underline his authorship of this highly perspicacious interpretation of cultural development:

> The evolution of a cultural system does not proceed along a straight line, but rather it assumes the shape of an irregular spiral. This is because the line of development encounters obstacles and consequently retreats and submerges, turns sideways and branches out, or still follows its original track. As a result, historical evolution seems to consist of moves forward and backward, as well as of interruptions and circuitous returns. A careful examination also reveals that each [cultural] sphere necessarily expands to a higher level. All these are manifestations of one and the same phenomenon: transformative evolution (*jinhua* 進化). (Tang and Tu 1998: 54–55)

Understandably, contemporary researchers have been mostly attracted by the arresting ideas expressed in the narrative part of Huang Ren's *History*. Yet I would suggest that the more extensive but chaotic part of his work in which he collected his reference sources deserves equally close attention. For it is exactly this part that may well indicate Huang Ren's search for new methods of literary study, methods that, in turn, enabled him to arrive at entirely new perspectives on Chinese literature.

As is well known, in traditional Chinese scholarship there was no need to quote sources because the scholarly community shared a knowledge of a certain corpus of texts learned by rote during childhood. The sources that Huang Ren assembled in his *History* are, however, an entirely new set of reference works, which he selected and read himself. He included a wide range of texts, some of which—like the texts of the novels and dramas—were not necessarily acknowledged by literati as a legitimate part of Chinese culture.

This move by Huang Ren is a major but not yet fully recognized advance in Chinese scholarship, comparable to Friedrich Schlegel's act mentioned above when he replaced the literary canon with works that he had read himself. Huang Ren's strategy of assembling and selecting sources himself was, too, a deed that liberated him from the repetitious copying of facts or arguments from previously written works and prepared the ground for a discourse of his own. Despite the inaccessibility of the original text of Huang Ren's *History*, it is possible to sense the congeniality between Huang Ren's work and the works by the towering figures of Chinese historiography at the beginning of the twentieth century. Instead of presenting the history of Chinese literature by taking one selected part for the whole, Huang Ren attempted to reconstruct Chinese literature in its full range and with no prejudices for this or that constituent of the Chinese literary heritage. It was this balanced perception of a large variety of Chinese texts of a different origin and nature that enabled Huang Ren to write his *History* with a distinctively modern outlook.

"History of Chinese Literature" by Zeng Yi: The Rise of the Historian's Authority

Zeng Yi's *History* was written under circumstances substantially different from those of his two predecessors. As Zeng Yi wrote in the preface to his *History* (1915: 2), he was in charge of economics in the Chinese government administration when the publishing house Taidong shuju approached him with an offer to write a history of Chinese literature. Too busy with his job, he first turned the offer down. But the large number of Japanese histories of Chinese literature written in the first decade of the twentieth century convinced him that he should write what he believed to be the first, pioneering history of Chinese literature by a Chinese.

Zeng Yi's perception of himself as the first author not to write his *History* as a textbook with an explicit educational aim seems to have been an instrumental aspect of his new conception of the history of Chinese literature. Not unlike the Chinese historians who formulated their new ideas along Japanese models at the beginning of the twentieth century, Zeng Yi, too, acknowledged his debt to Japanese literary historiography. It was exactly this willingness to transfer some foreign scholarly methods to China that enabled Zeng Yi to introduce new compositional and editorial principles to his *History* and to write his work with surprisingly novel concepts of literary evolution.

In the "Editorial Guidelines" ("Fanli" 凡例), Zeng Yi wrote that, by following the format of contemporary Japanese histories of literature, he furnished his book with a general introduction and conclusion and covered the history of Chinese literature via the framework of four historical periods: the age of high antiquity (from mythological times to the Qin dynasty); middle antiquity (from the Han dynasty to the Sui dynasty); near antiquity (from the Tang dynasty to the late Ming dynasty); and modern times (the Qing dynasty). The aim, wrote Zeng Yi, is to offer the general public a reference book that would elucidate the evolutionary transformation of Chinese literature in relation to Chinese learning, thought, and politics. Among the subjects discussed in the book, Zeng Yi said that poetry and prose had his foremost attention, followed by the Confucian Classics, drama, and the novel, but he also included in his narrative relevant references to critical discourses and encyclopedias. Recognizing the impact of outstanding writers on the transformation of the general literary climate, Zeng Yi incorporated discourses on individual writers or groups of writers influential during a particular period. Zeng Yi concluded his "Guidelines" by admitting that the most difficult part of his endeavor had been the judicious selection of texts from the rich literary heritage of China, as well as their coherent organization. However, Zeng Yi asserted, his account was always informed by an examination of historical facts and by the elimination of fabricated ideas. He frequently quoted from secondary sources, but Zeng Yi informed the reader that some of them had to be left out so that the narrative of his *History* would not be exceedingly cluttered with references. Zeng Yi assured the reader that his intention was not to plagiarize other people's thoughts—a very new perception of literary history as an oeuvre that requires the author's command over the design and ideas expressed in the work.

Zeng Yi understood "literature" in its broad as well as in its narrow, belles-lettristic sense (1915: 16–17) and he acknowledged, in the chapter "Periodization of literary history" ("Wenxue shi shang zhi shidai quhua" 文學史上之時代區劃), that every change of dynasty had led to political and cultural transformations that imprinted a specific spirit on the literature of the time. At the same time, argued Zeng Yi, the periodization of literature does not necessarily correspond with the succession of dynasties, because rhymed and unrhymed genres of Chinese literature developed according to different laws. Zeng Yi therefore introduced into his *History* the four large periods described above (1915: 18–20). These divisions proved especially beneficial for Zeng Yi's explanation of evolutionary changes in literature. Although he acknowledged that the political situation is the "nourishing tonic," *zibu pin* 滋補品, of literature ("Fanli": 2), new advances in thought and science, as well as the coalescence of previously incompatible elements, are to him the dominant reasons for breakthroughs in literary evolution.

In the chapter on Buddhist intellectual trends during the Six Dynasties period, Zeng Yi therefore maintained that "the gradual spread of Buddhism toward the East initiated a great restructuring (革命) of Chinese literature and art. The construction of Buddhist temples led to innovations in the art of architecture, and the creation of Buddhist paintings and sculpture led to developments in painting and sculpture" (1915: 105). In the realm of literature, continued Zeng Yi, poets became interested in reading Buddhist scriptures and literati liked using Buddhist ideas, and scholars were introduced to the concept of *hetupratyaya*, *yinguo baoying* 因 果 報 應, which offered a new explanation of the causal relations between things and phenomena. All these new developments had a significant impact on the development of literature, because they brought about changes in intellectual thought, the use of a new poetic idiom, and the discovery of the tonal system in prosody (1915: 105). Similarly, Zeng Yi underscored the importance of the interaction between scholars and Buddhists for the efflorescence of Tang literature and "its transformation through its merger with Buddhism" (1915: 174).

Zeng Yi developed this advocacy of the foreign element (Buddhism) as the catalyst for the restructuring and rejuvenation of Chinese culture even further, when he proclaimed that the Yuan period under the rule of the non-Chinese, Mongolian rulers "would have carved a new era in the history of Chinese literature if their reign had not been so short" (1915: 234). He ascribed the dynamism of Yuan literature to several factors: "The *shi* 詩 poetry did not go in the footsteps of Song poets' mediocrity and rose [to glory] by its mystical beauty. As for *ci* 詞 poetry, *qu* 曲 songs, and vernacular fiction *xiaoshuo* 小 說, they happily interacted with each other giving rise to popular literature (通 俗 文 學). In the history of Chinese literature this is indeed a phenomenon that deserves a special and lengthy discussion" (1915: 235). In the chapter devoted to the rise of Yuan drama and fiction (1915: 238–43), Zeng Yi offered an insightful observation about the evaluation of popular literature:

> The literature of the Yuan period was lagging behind the literature of the previous periods, but it should be pointed out that it was marked by one particular characteristic. This was popular literature represented by vernacular fiction and drama. The [Confucian] doctrine that "Literature should convey the Way" (文 以 載 道) was, in principle, disseminating education. But the scholars of the past kept themselves busy merely by paying attention to esoteric matters, so that the development (發 達) of popular literature moved slowly ahead on its own. When vernacular fiction and drama began to be written in the Yuan era, people were likely to look down on them, maintaining that they had no place in literature illuminating the Way. Little did they know that their powerful communicability was incomparably more diffusible and infusible than the works of those who studied the Classics and dynastic histories. (1915: 238)

Recalling the high status of drama in ancient Greek culture and the ideological power of Voltaire's dramas and fiction during the French Revolution, Zeng Yi advocated that Yuan drama and fiction should be held in equally high esteem. He associated the emergence of Yuan drama and fiction with the more frequent use of "vernacular language," *su yu* 俗 語, in Buddhist sermons during the Song and Jin dynasties, resulting in written "analecta," *yulu* 語 錄, and showed a particularly good understanding of how long novels written in the Yuan, such as *The Romance of the Three Kingdoms* and *Water Margin*, developed from short oral or written narratives as these episodes were strung together into full-fledged novels. Moreover, in this, as well as in the chapter on Qing drama and the novel (1915: 327–30), Zeng Yi displayed an intimate acquaintance with early Qing critical discourses on the art of the novel and drama by Jin Shengtan, Mao Zonggang 毛 宗 崗 (fl. 1660), and Li Yu. Zeng Yi's deep interest in vernacular fiction and drama notwithstanding, he devoted equal attention to the rise and development of another new and highly important literary genre, the "prose of our time," *shi wen* 時 文, better known as *bagu wen*.

Finally, in the Conclusion (1915: 330–35), Zeng Yi expressed some disappointments, highly unusual for his time, with two serious defects of Chinese literature and some of his hopes about the future of Chinese literature. According to Zeng Yi, the first deficiency rests in the "deliberate imitation of previous models" 用 以 摹 倣, which leads, in turn, to the high esteem of normative rules and automatization, and ultimately prevents any evolutionary transformation. The other shortcoming lies in the "excessive use of classical allusions" 濫 用 典 故, whose misuse leads to semantic obscurity in the text and confuses the reader. When a literary text reaches this point, argued Zeng, it is possible to call it a "disaster" (1915: 332).

Despite these defects, Zeng Yi complained, Chinese scholarship of the past four millennia had expressed nothing but sighs of admiration for the perfection of Chinese culture. The literati merely brag about themselves, as if they had no predecessors. In fact if Western learning had not reached the East, argued Zeng, it is likely that the Chinese would have closed the door and swept out foreign culture, for some Chinese scholars maintain that the nation could be awakened by returning to the well-worn patterns of the ancients. To support the argument that China's culture had reached the point of exhaustion and was ready to move on, Zeng Yi quoted the famous philologist Gu Yanwu 顧 炎 武 (1613–82), who said that poetry and prose change by periods and when literature of a certain era holds on to the same pattern for a long time, it must be altered. Here is Zeng Yi's rather accurate assessment about the state of Chinese culture and literature in the mid-1910s:

> Today the motion in literature (文 運) matches the times of coalescence during the Tang and Ming. Yet it is not the time for a synthesis. For we Chinese living at this crossroads, it is neither desirable to be inclined toward the West, nor it is possible to turn away from China. Our task is thus to streamline the best of the West and China for the practical needs of the present. One day, these two properties will happily blend and give birth to an extraordinary splendor. (1915: 335)

In 1925 Zheng Zhenduo included Zeng Yi's *History* among the four better-written histories of Chinese literature in his "Survey of the Literary History of Various Countries" ("Ge guo wenxue shi jieshao" 各 國 文 學 史 介 紹). In 1931, Hu Yunyi 胡 雲 翼 accused Zeng Yi of plagiarizing the work of the Japanese scholar Kojima Kenkichiro 兒 島 獻 吉 郎 (1866–1931) (Hu Yunyi 1931: 3). More recently, in 1967, the Taiwanese scholar Liang Rongruo 梁 容 若 described the work as "a forerunner of [May Fourth] discourses on literary reform" (1967: 127).

These three distinctively different evaluations of Zeng Yi's work signal a substantial breakthrough in Chinese literary historiography. That the critics refer to *how* Zeng Yi wrote his work rather than to its content is a clear sign of the changing authority of the historiographer. Although Zeng Yi's *History* is still written in an objective, detached style, the author's individuality is not effaced, as it used to be in traditional historiographies. Although nothing more is known about Zeng Yi's background than that he studied in Japan (Liang 1967: 124), Zeng Yi imprinted his personality on the general concept of the book and in his principal ideas as well as in the organization of the work. Without being aware of Huang Ren's *History*, he continued the writing of his predecessor by adopting the new historical periodization of Chinese literature and by depicting Chinese literature as an entity consisting of various, equally valid elements. But he went further than his predecessor through a stronger emphasis on the creative role of the authors, as much as through his innovative concept of literary evolution. As we have seen, he understood this evolution as an outcome of the fusion of incompatible elements among which the foreign was, to him, especially beneficial for the restructuring of Chinese culture and literature.

The emergence of the new authority of the individual historian presiding over the concept of literary history resulted in a great variety of constructions of the Chinese cultural past as well as of the present. Suffice it to recall that Zeng Yi's *History* appeared in the same year that Chen Duxiu 陳獨秀 (1879–1942) founded his influential journal *Youth* (*Qingnian zazhi* 青年雜誌) and close to the year 1917, when Hu Shi and Chen Duxiu entered into correspondence to contemplate the reform of Chinese writing and a fundamental re-evaluation of Chinese literature of the past.

In principle, there is no disagreement between Zeng Yi and the two future May Fourth reformers about the inevitability of change. Moreover, the three men shared a vivid interest in vernacular fiction and drama. There is, however, a basic difference in the means and ways by which Zeng Yi and the two May Fourth proponents-to-be assessed the cultural situation of the past and proposed a new way out of the dead end. This difference in the methods of writing literary histories culminated in the literary histories produced during the subsequent two decades.

Literary Histories of the 1920s and Early 1930s: Two Incompatible Currents

More than twenty literary histories were written in China from the year 1918 to the early 1930s, but few of them were greeted with applause. A curious rivalry among scholars emanates from the reviews of the day as well as from the prefaces, in which the author of each new history has only critical words for the works of his predecessors. Zheng Zhenduo, for example, complained about the new periodization of Chinese literature, in his view ill-devised by Japanese scholars and later inappropriately adopted in Chinese literary historiography. Moreover, he was irked by the incompleteness of the literary histories, whose authors did not, in his view, pay sufficient attention to storyteller literature (Zheng Zhenduo 1932: vol. 1: Introduction, pp. 1–2). Another prominent literary scholar, Wu Shichang 吳世昌 (1908–86), ascribed the poor quality of literary historiography to its commercialization and proclaimed the just published second volume of Zheng Zhenduo's *Illustrated History*[10] to be entirely unreliable because of its severe confusion of historical facts and lack of thorough research (1932). In the late 1940s, the modern Chinese writer Zhu Ziqing 朱自清 (1898–1948) summarized the situation

---

10. The second volume of Zheng Zhenduo's four-volume *Illustrated History* was published first, because it was the wish of the author not to delay his introduction of information about the newly discovered materials from the storyteller literature of the Six Dynasties to the Song.

in the most acerbic terms, when he wrote that Chinese literary historiography was, after forty years of existence, still at the stage of infancy due to the lack of modern theories and proper research methods (1947: 1).

From the more distant perspective of the late 1990s, the literary histories written during the 1920s and early 1930s appear in a different light. For all their inadequacies, they are an invaluable historical record of the emancipation of Chinese literary historiography from traditional historiography and the contribution of an unprecedented rhetoric and emplotment of historical facts to an entirely new construction of cultural memory.

The emancipation from traditional views and methods of Chinese scholarship was manifested in three new phenomena. First, the authors of the histories of Chinese literature arrived at a clear distinction between literary and nonliterary texts, in which "literature," *wenxue*, began to be understood in the modern sense of belles-lettres. Second, it appears that at least the authors of the prominent histories wrote their works on the basis of firsthand knowledge of the texts they discussed. Such attitudes strengthened, in turn, the authority of the author and enhanced the possibilities of shaping anew the frontiers and functions of literature. Third, another breakthrough was facilitated by the introduction of an entirely novel register of language. As is well known, traditional Chinese historiography was exclusively written in the so-called "literary language," in modern times termed *wenyan* 文言, because this was the language register assigned by convention to scholarly discourse. All three *Histories of Chinese Literature* discussed above adhered to this convention, and in 1918 a voluminous compendium, *A Comprehensive History of Chinese Literature* (*Zhongguo da wenxue shi* 中國大文學史) by Xie Wuliang 謝無量 (fl. 1918), still tended to favor *wenyan*. But following Hu Shi and Chen Duxiu's urgent calls to replace *wenyan* with *baihua* 白話, literary histories began to be written mostly in this register. Owing to the fact that *baihua* had been cultivated for centuries in fiction and drama, this shift in linguistic register may have contributed to the rise of a new and important stylistic feature of Chinese literary historiography, namely, narrativity and conceptual strategies by which historical data were linked together and explained. This imprinted the distinctive stamp of a particular theoretical or ideological concept.

Two major and ideologically different streams in Chinese literary historiography thus evolved in the 1920s. One consisted of scholars who kept their distance from the current political and cultural movements and managed to write histories according to their own concepts of literary evolution. The other current included radical-minded intellectuals who programmatically endorsed the new cultural project launched by Hu Shi, Chen Duxiu, and a handful of other intellectuals in a series of published articles as well as in their correspondence in the late 1910s.

The histories by independent scholars are much less well known than those by their May Fourth counterparts. This is not because they do not offer interesting and original ideas and concepts, but because their works were not in line with the emerging "politically correct" interpretation of the history of Chinese literature and were not republished until the 1990s, if at all. From this group at least two works must be mentioned, both issued in 1928: *Draft Lectures on the History of Chinese Literature* (*Zhongguo wenxue shi jiang gao* 中國文學史講稿) by Hu Xiaoshi 胡小石 (1888–1962) and the especially engaging but entirely neglected book by Zhang Shilu 張世祿 (fl. 1928) titled *On the Transformation of Chinese Literature and Arts* (*Zhongguo wenyi bianqian lun* 中國文藝變遷論).

Hu Xiaoshi's work was compiled on the basis of notes taken by one of Hu's students who attended his lectures on the history of Chinese literature. The original edition of 1928 consisted of eleven chapters and covered the history of Chinese literature up to the Tang era. The 1991 reissue of the work was enhanced by the addition of a chapter on Song literature based on notes by another of Hu's students and by a collection of Hu's previously unpublished theoretical discourses on Chinese literature. The dominant idea in Hu Xiaoshi's works is his belief that only those artistic texts that were created as expressions of sentiment should be included in the realm of literature. He also vehemently advocated that historical studies of literature should aim at the objective study of the transformation of literature throughout the ages.

Zhang Shilu's work is particularly interesting for its new outlook on literary development. The author entirely abandoned dynastic or other kinds of temporal division and instead organized his work around seminal but rarely elaborated issues in Chinese literary scholarship. Among these new topics Zhang included, for instance, a discussion of the puzzling absence of epic poetry in Chinese literature, the relation between the literature of a certain era and the geographical locality of its origin, the impact of regional dialects and local music on the development of prosody, the connections between vernacular fiction and drama, and the topic most taboo in May Fourth discourses on literature: relations between premodern Chinese vernacular literature and texts in classical Chinese, particularly the eight-legged essay. Zhang wrote in the preface that his study was meant as a reaction to the "massification" 群 of current research in Chinese literature (1928: Preface, p. 1). In the last part of his book, he strongly advocated the integration of Chinese literature of the past with present and future trends in Chinese literature. Even today the work has lost none of its striking originality, which is supported by copious and carefully researched material and demonstrates an educated judgment of Western literary theories of the day. But despite its obvious merits, Zhang's book has not yet been republished.

With the arrival of the May Fourth interpretation of Chinese literary history, a drastic change in the scholarly investigation of literature took place. As we have seen, starting with Huang Ren's *History*, the construction of the literary past was drawn from and affirmed by historical material newly assembled by the literary historian. But our observations have led us to the conclusion that the procedures of May Fourth scholarly investigation brought a radical reversal of this trend. First a hypothesis was formulated, with the assertive claim that vernacular literature represents the dominant part of Chinese literature. Only later was this preconceived concept verified by the selective citation of data that were frequently modified to uphold the May Fourth cultural program.

Obviously, this statement controverts the widespread but not well-documented view that May Fourth scholarship adopted Western methods of objective scrutiny of historical facts and detachment from traditional dogmas. Hu Shi himself addressed the issue of research strategies in a lecture delivered on June 12, 1925, before the North China Union Language School. In this speech, he firmly denounced what he called a "propagandist attitude" applied by "the person who, through his research, is trying to find arguments for a pre-accepted position" (1925: 1). In contrast, continued Hu Shi, the "scientific" or "objective attitude" warrants that "the objective study of facts is the primary interest," and he affirmed that to him "the second attitude is the only one which a serious scholar can hold. I am interested in the study of Chinese culture in order to find out what it really is" (1925: 2).

It is especially in view of this convincing proclamation by Hu Shi that my own challenge requires strongly supported arguments. I therefore begin by recapitulating, in chronological order, the changes in Hu Shi's presentation of his thesis about the central position of vernacular literature in Chinese literature. I will pay attention to Hu Shi's rhetoric in his *History of Vernacular Literature*.

January 1917. Hu Shi's tenet about the dominant position of vernacular literature was, as is well known, initially introduced to the Chinese reading public in his article "Some Modest Proposals for the Reform of Literature" ("Wenxue gailiang chuyi" 文學改良芻議), written during his studies at Cornell University and first published in the January 1917 issue of *New Youth* (*Xin Qingnian* 新青年, 2: 5). The article establishes the scholarly credibility of the author's statements through an impressive number of citations from and references to Chinese literature as well as to European culture. In addition, the writer's scholarly authority might have been enhanced in China by his prestigious position as an exchange student at an American university. Finally, Hu Shi's proposal, though of a programmatic nature, is written with a scholarly modesty and clarity that strengthens his arguments. Thus, his statement that "literature in vernacular language represents the mainstream of Chinese literature" gives the impression that this conclusion was the outcome of long-term research. Indeed, the author himself affirmed that although he has at the moment only a few supporters for his claim, "from today's perspective of historical evolution, we can say with complete certainty that vernacular literature is the mainstream of Chinese literature and will be a useful tool for developing future literature" 然以今世歷史進化的眼觀之，則白話文學之中國文學之正宗，又為將來文學之必用之利器，可斷言也 (1917a: 17).

April 9, 1917. Hu Shi toned down his previous claim of "complete certainty" when he wrote in a letter to Chen Duxiu that the correctness of his own proposals "cannot be determined overnight, nor by only one or two men. I wish that my fellow countrymen would join forces with us to calmly investigate this question and that through the heat of debate, the judgment will be clarified on its own" (1917a: 29).

May 1917. Hu Shi admitted that his precept about the central position of vernacular literature is "a hypothetical premise" 假設之前提 whose validity must be confirmed by future generations of writers (1917b: 34).

April/May (?) 1917. In an undated letter Chen Duxiu replied to Hu Shi in a rather militant tone that "no room can be left for a discussion with the opponents. We must uphold our opinion as absolutely right and not allow others to change it" (1917: 32).

Hu Shi's retreat from the "complete certainty" to a "hypothetical premise" suggests his attempt to adhere to scholarly integrity. But in the climate of heated debates that forecast the upcoming power struggle over the hegemony of the cultural scene in China, the difference between a hypothesis and a historical fact was of minor importance. What mattered was that the idea enforcing the dominant position of vernacular literature instilled much needed energy in the intellectual circles. The belief that history moves in the direction of progress and that progress will bring new, democratic culture to China was electrifying. Suddenly, history was endowed with modern philosophy.

The response by young and later well-known scholars and writers was immediate. Feng Yuanjun 馮 沅 君 (1900–1974), Tan Zhengbi 譚 正 璧 (1901–?), and Zhao Jingshen 趙 景 深 (1902–85) as well as many others started to write histories of Chinese literature in which they devoted large parts of their discourse to Chinese storyteller literature, drama, and the novel to demonstrate their enthusiastic endorsement of Hu Shi's radically new and hopeful interpretation of Chinese literature (Feng 1920, Tan 1925, Zhao 1926). This new trend culminated in the publication of literary histories by two leading figures of the May Fourth movement. Hu Shi's *History of Vernacular Literature* appeared in 1928, and in 1932 Zheng Zhenduo published his celebrated *Illustrated History of Chinese Literature.*

Because the scholarly methods and the impact of Zheng Zhenduo's *Illustrated History* and his other historical studies on Chinese literature are addressed elsewhere in this volume, my attention is directed toward Hu Shi's *History of Vernacular Literature.*

"History of Vernacular Literature" by Hu Shi: The Historical Imagination

Despite many profound changes in the Chinese cultural scene during the first quarter of the twentieth century, the motivation for writing Hu Shi's *History* remained the same as it was for the earliest written Chinese literary histories: its primary task lay in edifying a wide audience of readers. As Hu Shi wrote in his preface 自 序 to the *History,* he had been invited in 1921 by the Ministry of Education to give a series of lectures on the history of Chinese literature in "national language," *guoyu* 國 語, and in eight weeks he produced a preliminary draft of fifteen lectures (1928: Preface, p. 1). This draft was published in 1927 by Wenhua xueshe 文 化 學 社 in Beijing under the title *History of [Chinese] Literature in the National Language* (*Guoyu wenxue shi* 國 語 文 學 史). But Hu Shi was not pleased with this publication, because it was made without his consent, and the draft had become outdated due to recent discoveries in the field of vernacular fiction. Therefore he took the first opportunity to substantially rewrite the old version, and this work appeared in 1928, put out by Xinyue 新 月 publishing house in Shanghai (Hu Shi 1928: Preface, pp. 7–12). In order to accommodate a new interpretation of the evolution of Chinese literature, Hu Shi gave the work a brand new title—*History of Vernacular Literature*. Judging from the indication of the book as "Part One" 上, Hu originally planned at least two volumes.

The first, and in fact only, volume of Hu Shi's *History* spans the development of Chinese literature from the Han to the Tang era. The choice of a period extending from the second century B.C. to the tenth century A.D. appears rather awkward. By the time Hu Shi rewrote his *History* in 1928, many Chinese texts written in the vernacular had been discovered in Japanese and European libraries, but none of them dated earlier than the Tang period (Zheng Zhenduo 1934: 964–82). In this light, the temporal frame of Hu Shi's discourse seems to be particularly ill-chosen because of the evident scarcity of documents to support the author's claims about the early origins of literature written in the vernacular. Eyebrows were also raised at the choice of literary genres included in the sphere of vernacular literature. Somewhat belatedly, in 1958, Hu Shi's former staunch supporter Zheng Zhenduo expressed strong dissatisfaction that Hu Shi had misrepresented the development of Chinese literature by the inclusion in his *History* works of some minor importance that were clearly not written in the vernacular (1958: 70).

To explain the boldness of Hu Shi's endeavor, it is worthwhile to recall what Hayden White elucidates in his brilliant study *Metahistory: The Historical Imagination in Nineteenth-Century Europe*: namely, that a historical work is a mixture of science and art. White therefore urged historians to pay more attention to the artistic components of historiography in order to disclose the *poetic* and linguistic grounds by which its theoretical concepts were tacitly sanctioned. "It is no accident," White reminds us, "that the principal philosophers of history were also (or have lately been discovered to have been) quintessentially philosophers of language" (1973: xi). Hayden White explains the methodology of his analysis of the historical imagination in the following way:

> In this theory I treat the historical work as what it most manifestly is: a verbal structure in the form of a narrative prose discourse. Histories (and philosophies of his-

tory as well) combine a certain amount of "data," theoretical concepts for "explaining" these data, and a narrative structure for their presentation as an icon of sets of events presumed to have occurred in times past. In addition, I maintain, they contain a deep structural content which is generally poetic, and specifically linguistic, in nature, and which serves as the precritically accepted paradigm of what a distinctively "historical" explanation should be. This paradigm functions as the "metahistorical" element in all historical works that are more comprehensive in scope than the monograph or archival report. (1973: ix)

Returning now to Hu Shi's *History of Vernacular Literature*, I maintain, in agreement with Hayden White's study, that it is worthwhile to investigate the *poetic* elements of Hu Shi's work in order to disclose its position in modern Chinese literary historiography. Three aspects of Hu Shi's work are of particular importance in this regard: (1) Hu Shi's explanation of historical events by emplotment (the sequence of events fashioned into a plot with a particular message); (2) the presentation of his arguments; and (3) the effectiveness of his verbal communication.

As is generally known, linguistic development is a gradual process, and it is particularly difficult to pinpoint the single factor that most decisively contributes to the transformation of the language. It was, however, exactly this haziness in the past evolution of the Chinese language that served Hu Shi in good stead, for he was at liberty to arrange some rather dubious historical "data" into a narrative with an attractive plot. Since any such narrative must have a beginning, a main exposition of the story, and an end, Hu Shi chose to present linguistic development in organic terms, as manifested by the eternal struggle of birth and death. Thus, the first chapter of Hu Shi's *History* opens with the dramatic question: "When did classical language die" 古文是何時死的? (1928: 1). When Hu Shi determined, by questionable inferences, that the event took place during the reign of Emperor Wudi 漢武帝 (r. 140–87 B.C.) of the Han dynasty, the narrative of Hu Shi's *History* acquires its necessary starting point by mythologizing the birth of the vernacular language.

Although declared dead, the classical language does not, however, disappear from the dramatic stage of the plot. Hu Shi well knew that the language had stayed on to be cultivated by scholars throughout the ages until modern times, and from the point of view of the narrative, the "dead" language could be employed as a useful foil for the vernacular language. The two languages are thus transformed into a pair of actants designated by persuasive epithets. Obviously inspired by Yan Fu's translation of Huxley's *Evolution and Ethics* and the Darwinist concept of the survival of the fittest (see Grieder 1970: 26–27), Hu Shi calls the classical language "dead" and the vernacular language "living" to present them, in Hayden White's words, "as an icon of sets of events presumed to have occurred in the past." Indeed, in the second chapter of his *History* Hu Shi wrote: "From then on [i.e., from the Han era], Chinese literature went by two different roads: one was the road of the imitative, immobile, and lifeless literature in classical language, the other was the road of the spontaneous, vivacious, and full-of-life literature in vernacular language" (1928: 16).

Hu Shi's emplotment of questionable historical data had, however, more serious implications than the simple presentation of history as an attractive narrative. To portray history as a chain of coherent events empowered the historian to claim the correctness of certain theoretical ideas and, eventually, to defend the cultural policies of the present. That the birth of the vernacular language is presented in Hu Shi's *History* as an instance of biological evolution, in which one constituent is replaced by another, could further serve to justify an understanding of the May Fourth language reform as a replacement of an outworn language by a superior one. The desire to defend the present by means of the past was most explicitly articulated by Hu Shi when he explained the motivations for his lectures on literature in the vernacular.

> First, I want everybody to know that vernacular literature is not a castle in the air (憑空捏造) constructed over the past three or four years by a handful of people; I want everybody to know that vernacular literature has a history, a history that is very long and exceptionally brilliant. I want all people to know that literature in the national language (國語) is the product of more than one thousand years of evolution. (1928: Introduction, p. 1)

And further:

> Second, I want everybody to know what position is occupied by vernacular literature in the history of Chinese literature. To tell you the truth, I want everybody to know that the history of vernacular literature is the central part of the history of Chinese literature. (1928: Introduction, p. 3)

The argument as presented in the *History* is semantically identical with Hu Shi's initial manifesto saying that "from today's perspective of historical evolution, we can say with complete certainty that vernacular literature is the mainstream of Chinese literature and will be a useful tool for developing future literature" (1917a: 17). Still, Hu Shi presented new evidence to support his claim about the millennia-long history of vernacular literature when he explained that he had greatly expanded the sphere of vernacular literature to be able to accommodate all works written in clear and distinct language. To him, the term "vernacular language," *baihua*, has three connotations: (1) it can be spoken and is aurally understandable, as with unrhymed speech 白 in traditional Chinese drama; (2) it is plain 白, because it has no embellishment; and (3) it is lucid and perspicuous 白 (1928: Preface, p. 13). These criteria, asserted Hu Shi, allow him to include as "vernacular literature" some passages from the third century B.C. *Historical Records* (*Shiji* 史 記) and the first century A.D. *Dynastic History of the Western Han* (*Han shu* 漢 書), as well as some translations of Buddhist sutras and a great number of Han and Tang poems and songs, particularly those in the form of *yuefu* 樂府 and *jueju* 絕句.

What Hu Shi's discourse so obviously lacks in insight into linguistic matters is richly compensated by the justly admired mastery of his own language—the language of an "enlightener" (Yü 1993: 62). In fact, his language corresponds exactly to his own definition of *baihua*. It is simple, it is lucid, and it is readily comprehensible both to the reader and to the listener. The two excerpts quoted above moreover serve to illustrate how Hu Shi saturated his discourse with effective rhetorical devices, such as the parallel configuration of his sentences and the ubiquitous repetition of the same argument.

The history of vernacular literature presented in Hu Shi's extremely clear language and in his logically arranged narrative thus greatly contributed to the persuasiveness of Hu Shi's story of vernacular literature. In the "Author's Preface," Hu Shi went so far as to proclaim that despite the title, the *History of Vernacular Literature* is "in fact a history of all Chinese literature" (1928: Preface, p. 12). To justify this argument, Hu Shi quoted a passage from his own introduction to the *History*, in which he reiterated that "literature in the vernacular forms the core of the history of Chinese literature, . . . the liveliest component in the history of Chinese literature, and because it is also most productive, it is in the position to represent the history of [Chinese] literature in its entire development."

Hu Shi's "invention" of narrativity in literary history, as well as his rhetoric of persuasion performed in *baihua*, undoubtedly marked a turning point in the development of modern Chinese historiography. Whereas earlier Chinese literary histories followed the norms of traditional historiography and were written in classical Chinese, Hu Shi boldly wrote in the vernacular. And whereas the earlier literary histories, like the traditional historiographies, merely registered concrete events and basic facts without the projection of the personality of the registrar (Gardner 1938: 69), the literary historiographer of the late 1920s turned into a foregrounded persona who arranged historical data with such persuasive logic and clarity of language that his imagination created the impression of historical truth.

Not all Chinese scholars and professors were impressed, however. Already in the year 1919 and especially in the 1920s and 1930s a group of Western-educated professors gathered around the magazine *Critical Review* (*Xue heng* 學衡) in Nanjing and raised strong objections against Hu Shi's concept of language and literary evolution (Chow 1969: 282; Sun and Guo 1995).[11] Still, the notions that history moved in the direction of progress and that progress would bring a new, democratic culture to China were electrifying and instilled much needed energy into the cultural scene. As a result, the May Fourth concept of Chinese literature, based on the notion that vernacular literature had already been dominant in the past, was generally accepted among both Chinese and Western scholars in the 1930s.

In the long run, Hu Shi's ahistorical construction of China's cultural past, later disseminated as historical truth in countless histories of Chinese literature, contributed to the impoverishment of twentieth-century Chinese culture. Compared with the old Confucian dogma that divided Chinese literature (also without historical evidence) into two separate streams, of which only one—literature written in the classical language—represented the true body of Chinese writing, Hu Shi's tenet of the dominant role of vernacular literature eventually emerges as nothing more than this Confucian dogma read in reverse. If we ask why only a few masterworks were written in twentieth-century China, it is worth remembering that Chinese literature was cut off from the vital energy arising from the confluence of its diverse components.

A Retrospective

Looking back at the first twenty-five years of Chinese literary historiography from 1904 to 1928, the sheer number of histories produced in this period (more than thirty) is astounding, especially if we consider that in the West

11. See Sun and Guo 1995 for a collection of articles and lectures by the members of the Xueheng group.

the publication of a literary history has always been a rare event. Even more unexpected is their textbook format and their course of development.

The format of textbook written at the invitation of the Ministry of Education to become a part of curriculum—as was the case with three out of four histories under examination—is an important sign of the purpose of the literary histories. Obviously, these histories were meant to disseminate the "official" version of literary history, not to search for new, unknown territories to produce a new picture of China's literary heritage. In this way, the writing of literary histories was in fact institutionalized, leaving little room for the author to establish his own methods of research and writing. Among the four literary historiographers examined here, Huang Ren was perhaps the only one whose status was comparable with that of a private scholar, because he had access to primary sources and was ready to write a literary history based on his research as an individual scholar. Zeng Yi could also afford to express his own views because his *History* was a commercial enterprise.

Keeping in mind the purpose of these four literary histories, it is not difficult to predict the course of their development. Lin Chuanjia's work was grounded in the age-old speculative theory of traditional aesthetics, because his *History* was written under the directives of an imperial edict on education. By contrast, Huang Ren's work greatly advanced the field through the study of first-hand documents, because the author was a professional journalist independent of the state educational system. Similarly, Zeng Yi arrived at conclusions close to views of our own time because he was entirely free from the bondage of the state. This promising advancement of modern Chinese literary historiography was interrupted, however, when Hu Shi's work became a medium of May Fourth doctrine. Once again, the conception of China's literary past was anchored in a hypothetical presumption about two incompatible currents in Chinese literature, but this time the old model was inverted to claim the dominance of vernacular literature to fit the political agenda of the day. Although efforts had been made in the 1920s to write literary histories with an independent outlook, the persuasive rhetoric of the May Fourth rewriting of Chinese literary history was instrumental in the acceptance of its hypothetical premise as historical truth and assured its general acceptance in the scholarly community for a good part of the twentieth century.

The peculiar, circuitous line of development of early Chinese literary historiography, starting from an ideological interpretation of literature and returning to it in a new attractive garb, prompted our reflection about the difficulties met by a new scholarly discipline in a culture with a millennia-long tradition. Was it indeed possible to escape the firm grip of old aesthetic norms and tenets so deeply ingrained in Chinese culture?

A relatively smooth acceptance of the differentiation of artistic and non-artistic texts suggests that such an escape was possible. By the 1920s, the term *wenxue* was understood for the most part to refer to artistic texts, and the authors of the literary histories did not even raise the issue of the content of the word in their prefaces, as most of the authors of the 1910s had done. It is perhaps because of this easy acceptance of the Western notion of literature, facilitated by the vague differentiation between "serviceable prose," *bi* 筆, and "more prestigious *wen*" 文 in traditional poetics (see Owen 1992: 272–73), that the substantial significance of this event has been rather overlooked. It is necessary, however, to stress that the abandonment of the concept of writing as a link between human creativity and the powers of heaven could be considered a major move toward modernization, because it means emancipation from traditional aesthetics and the "secularization" of the notion of human creativity. The author was elevated to the level of an authority solely responsible for his writing, thus clearing the ground to explore new possibilities.

If this expansion of creative freedom worked well for literary production, the task of modernizing literary historiography was much harder. It could well be that some of the exceptionally gifted young intellectuals disregarded the strength of the power of culture and presumed that the course of the history could be reversed solely by the power of their own intellect. Yet, it was the model of traditional historiography that exerted a strong force over the outlook and goals of the new literary historiography. Judging from the writing methods and the dominant edifying mission of the literary histories alone, these forces were not auspicious. Appearing now in the new garb of literary history, the old and persistent cultural patterns transferred from traditional historiography were, however, barely noticeable. Consider first the process of writing.

It was my presupposition at the beginning of this study of early Chinese literary histories that publishing a history of literature, no matter the culture, is a rare event because the process of researching and writing such a work must necessarily be a long-term project. It therefore struck me as surprising that in the prefaces to both Lin Chuanjia's and Hu Shi's *Histories* it is noted, with a positive sense of accomplishment, that the authors carried out the preparation of their histories over a mere two months or so.

Such uncanny speed cannot be explained other than by the conclusion that the two histories did not arise from the independent pursuit of sources but were the result of the assemblage of a large number of well-known texts edited, excised, and modified according to a preconceived paradigm. This "cut and paste" method had been the usual method of writing historiographies in the past (Gardner 1938: 71). One well known example is by Li Zhi 李 贄 (1527–1602), the astounding nonconformist philosopher, who was able to present in his *Books for Burning* (*Fen shu* 焚 書) an entirely new portrait of Chinese history by reassembling, excising, and displacing the usual order of the historical materials in dynastic histories (Billeter 1979: 14–15). This process of compiling traditional histories naturally served to sanction this same method as entirely legitimate when transferred to the process of compiling new literary histories.

This approach to "writing" literary histories proved, however, to be detrimental to the development of literary historiography in China and eventually to the development of modern literature. Because this inherited methodology discouraged original research in primary sources and encouraged the repetition of previously recorded "facts," literature itself was portrayed as static, with no significant transformation over the centuries. This fictitious picture, mistaken for historical reality, naturally inspired projects aspiring to its reform. It is no wonder that these reforms or revolutions did not work in the long run: they lacked accurate knowledge of historical data. Neither did it help that literature continued to be seen as a savior of the nation long after the age-old Neo-Confucian tenet *wen yi zai Dao*, which claimed that literature is the vehicle of moral enlightenment, had been dislodged from its privileged position.

That this tenet sustained its dominant role can be convincingly verified by the claim of each of the four authors examined here, namely, that the primary goal of their history was the education of the nation. During a period of considerable national insecurity for China at the beginning of the twentieth century, the edifying role of literary histories could perhaps be understood as a positive albeit ultra-conservative feature because it boosted the readers' national consciousness through an awareness of the long and glorious history of Chinese literature.

But the edifying role of these literary histories also had a darker side, for it legitimized the questionable role of the literary historian as censor in selecting, editing, or excising information. Thus, paradoxically, the very channel of education meant for enlightenment could, as it did, potentially become the power to control access to information, construct cultural memories, and disseminate manipulated historical data. Suffice it to recall that it was precisely this power that effaced the achievements of the early literary histories by Huang Ren and Zeng Yi and constructed the notion that literary history was the invention of the May Fourth intellectuals.

Works Cited

Behler, Ernst. 1991. "Problems of Origin in Modern Literary History." In David Perkins, ed., *Theoretical Issues in Literary History*, pp. 9–34. Cambridge, Mass.: Harvard University Press.

Billeter, Jean-François. 1979. *Li Zhi, philosophe maudit (1527–1602)*. Geneva: Librairie Droz.

Chen Duxiu 陳獨秀. [1917] 1953. "Ji Hu Shi" 寄胡適 (A letter to Hu Shi). In *Hu Shi wencun* 胡適文存 (Collected works of Hu Shi), 1: 31–32. Taibei: Yuandong.

Chen Yutang 陳玉堂. 1986. *Zhongguo wenxue shi shumu tiyao* 中國文學史書目提要 (Annotated catalog of Chinese literary histories). Hefei: Huangshan.

Chow Tse-tsung. 1969. *The May Fourth Movement: Intellectual Revolution in Modern China*. Stanford: Stanford University Press.

Dai Yan 戴燕. 1996. "Wenxue, wenxue shi, Zhongguo wenxue shi—lun ben shiji chu 'Zhongguo wenxue shi' de faren" 文學，文學史，中國文學史—論本世紀初"中國文學史"學的發軔 (Literature, history of literature, a history of Chinese literature—on launching the study of the *Histories of Chinese Literature* from the beginning of this century). *Wenxue yichan* 6: 4–15.

Feng Yuanjun 馮沅君. 1920. *Zhongguo wenxue shi* 中國文學史 (A history of Chinese literature). Shanghai: Wenhua.

Gardner, C. S. 1938. *Chinese Traditional Historiography*. Cambridge, Mass.: Harvard University Press.

Giles, Herbert G. [1901] 1977. *History of Chinese literature*. Reprinted—Taibei: Dunhuang.

Gosse, Edmund. [1897] 1898. *A Short History of Modern English Literature*. New York: D. Appleton.

Grieder, Jerome B. 1970. *Hu Shih and the Chinese Renaissance: Liberalism in the Chinese Revolution, 1917–1937*. Cambridge, Mass.: Harvard University Press.

Hu Shi 胡適. [1917a] 1953. "Wenxue gailiang chuyi" 文學改良芻議 (Some modest proposals for the reform of literature). In *Hu Shi wencun* 胡適文存 (Collected works of Hu Shi), 1: 5–21. Taibei: Yuandong.

———. [1917b] 1953. "Lishi de wenxue guannian lun" 歷史的文學觀念論 (On the genetic concept of literature). In *Hu Shi wencun* 胡適文存 (Collected works of Hu Shi), 1: 33–6. Taibei: Yuandong.

———. 1925. *Sinological Research at the Present Time. Lecture Before the North China Language School*. June 12, 1925. Peking: Peking Leader Press.

———. 1927. *Guoyu wenxue shi* 國語文學史 (History of literature in the national language). Beijing: Wenhua xueshe.

———. 1928. *Baihua wenxue shi* 白話文學史 (History of vernacular literature). Shanghai: Xinyue.

Hu Xiaoshi 胡小石. [1928] 1991. "Zhongguo wenxue shi jiang gao" 中國文學史講稿 (Draft lectures on the history of Chinese literature). In *Hu Xiaoshi lunwen ji xubian* 胡小石論文集續編 (Supplements to Hu Xiaoshi's collected works). Shanghai: Guji.

Hu Yunyi 胡雲翼. 1931. *Zhongguo wenxue shi* 中國文學史 (History of Chinese literature). Shanghai: Jiaoyun.

Huang Lin 黃霖. 1993. "Zhongguo wenxue shixue" 中國文學史學 (Historiography of Chinese literature). In idem, *Jindai wenxue piping shi* 近代文學批評史 (History of [Chinese] premodern literary criticism), pp. 754–808. Shanghai: Guji.

Huang Moxi 黃摩西 [Huang Ren 黃人], ed. 1911. *Putong baike xin da cidian* 普通百科新大辭典 (A new general encyclopedic dictionary). Shanghai: Zhongguo cidian.

Huang Ren 黃人. [1905]. *Zhongguo wenxue shi* 中國文學史 (History of Chinese literature). Cited from Tang Zhesheng 湯哲聲 and Tu Xiaoma 塗小馬, eds., 1998, *Huang Ren: pingzhaun, zuopin zuan* 黃人: 評傳, 作品選 (Huang Ren: a critical biography and a selection of his work). Beijing: Zhongguo wen shi chubanshe.

Huang Wenji 黃文吉. 1996. *Taiwan chuban Zhongguo wenxue shi shumu tiyao* 台灣出版中國文學史書目提要, 1949–1994 (Annotated Catalog of Chinese Literary Histories Published in Taiwan, 1949–94). Taibei: Xinwenju.

Liang Rongruo 梁容若. 1967. *Zhongguo wenxue shi yanjiu* 中國文學史研究 (Researches into histories of Chinese literature). Taibei: Sanmin.

Lin Chuanjia 林傳甲. [1904a] 1914. *Zhongguo wenxue shi* 中國文學史 (History of Chinese literature). 8th ed. Shanghai: Shangwu yinshuguan.

———. [1904b] 1981. *Zhongguo wenxue shi* 中國文學史 (History of Chinese literature). Reprinted—Taibei: Xuehai.

Liu, James J. Y. 1975. *Chinese Theories of Literature*. Chicago: University of Chicago Press.

Masini, Federico. 1993. *The Formation of Modern Chinese Lexicon and Its Evolution Toward a National Language: The Period from 1840 to 1898. Journal of Chinese Linguistics* Monograph Series, no. 6. Berkeley: University of California.

Owen, Stephen. 1992. *Readings in Chinese Literary Thought*. Cambridge, Mass.: Harvard University Council on East Asian Studies.

Qu Xingui 璩鑫圭 and Tang Liangyan 唐良炎, eds. 1991. *Zhongguo jindai jiaoyu shi ziliao huibian* 中國近代教育資料匯編 (Collection of materials on the early modern history of education in China). Shanghai: Shanghai jiaoyu chubanshe.

Sasagawa Rinpū. 笹川種郎. 1898. *Shina bungaku shi* 支那文學史 (History of Chinese literature). Tokyo: Hakubunkan.

Sun Shangyang 孫尚揚 and Guo Lanfang 郭蘭芳, eds. 1995. *Guogu xin zhi lun—Xueheng pai wenhua lunzhu jiyao* 國故新知論—學衡派文化論著輯要 (New knowledge and China's literary heritage—a sourcebook of discourse on culture by the *Critical Review* school). Beijing: Zhongguo guangbo dianshi.

Tan Zhengbi 譚正璧. 1925. *Zhongguo wenxue shi da gang* 中國文學史大綱 (A comprehensive outline of the history of Chinese literature). Shanghai: Guanghua.

Tang Zhesheng 湯哲聲 and Tu Xiaoma 塗小馬, eds. 1998. *Huang Ren: pingzhaun, zuopin zuan* 黃人: 評傳, 作品選 (Huang Ren: a critical biography and a selection of his work). Beijing: Zhongguo wen shi chubanshe.

Wang Jianyu 汪劍餘. 1925. *Benguo wenxue shi* 本國文學史 (History of literature in our country). Shanghai: Shanghai lishi yanjiu she.

Wellek, René [1965]. 1983. *A History of Modern Criticism, 1750–1950*, vol. 4, *The Later Nineteenth Century*. Cambridge, Eng.: Cambridge University Press.

White, Hayden. [1973] 1993. *Metahistory: The Historical Imagination in Nineteenth-Century Europe*. Baltimore: The Johns Hopkins University Press.

Wu Shichang 吳世昌. 1932. "*Chatuben Zhongguo wenxue shi*" 插圖本中國文學史，第二冊 ([Review of the] *Illustrated History of Chinese Literature* [by Zheng Zhenduo], vol. 2). *Xin yue yuekan* 4, no. 6: 1–14.

Xie Wuliang 謝無量. [1918] 1967. *Zhongguo da wenxue shi* 中國大文學史 (A comprehensive history of Chinese literature). Reprinted—Taibei: Zhonghua.

Yü, Ying-shih 余英時. 1993. *Zhongguo jindai sixiangshi shang de Hu Shi* 中國近代思想史上的胡適 (Hu Shi in modern Chinese intellectual history). Taibei: Lianjing.

———. 1994. "Changing Conceptions of National History in Twentieth-Century China." In Erik Lönnroth, Karl Molin, Ragnar Björk, eds., *Conceptions of National History: Proceedings of Nobel Symposium 78*, pp. 155–74. Berlin: Walter de Gruyter.

Zeng Yi 曾毅. 1915. *Zhongguo wenxue shi* 中國文學史 (History of Chinese literature). Shanghai: Taidong.

Zhang Shilu 張世祿. 1928. *Zhongguo wenyi bianqian lun* 中國文藝變遷論 (On the transformation of Chinese literature and arts). Shanghai: Shangwu.

Zhao Jingshen 趙景深. [1926] 1961. *Zhongguo wenxue xiao shi* 中國文學小史 (A brief history of Chinese literature). 19th ed. Hong Kong: Da fang.

Zheng Zhenduo 鄭振鐸. 1925. "Ge guo wenxue shi jieshao" 各國文學史介紹 (Survey of the literary history of various countries). *Xiaoshuo yuebao* 16, no. 1 (Jan.): n.p.

———. 1932. *Chatuben Zhongguo wenxue shi* 插圖本中國文學史 (Illustrated history of Chinese literature). 4 vols. Beiping: Pushe.

———. 1934. "Sanshi nianlai Zhongguo wenxue xin ziliao de faxian shilüe" 三十年來中國文學新資料的發現史略 (A brief history of discoveries of new materials on Chinese literature made during the past thirty years). *Wenxue* 2, no.

6 (June 1): 964–82. Reprinted in idem, 1988, *Zheng Zhenduo wenji* 鄭振鐸文集 (Zheng Zhenduo's collected works), 6: 467–500. Beijing: Renmin wenxue.

———. [1958] 1988. "Zhongguo wenxue shi de fenqi wenti" 中國文學史的分期問題 (Problems with the periodization of the history of Chinese literature). *Wenxue yanjiu* 1958, no. 1. Reprinted in idem, 1988, *Zheng Zhenduo wenji* 鄭振鐸文集 (Zheng Zhenduo's collected works), 7: 68–81. Beijing: Renmin wenxue.

Zhong Shaohua 鐘少華. 1996. *Renlei zhishi de xin gongju: Zhong Ri jindai baike quanshu yanjiu* 人類知識的新工具：中日近代百科全書研究 (New tools of human knowledge: a study of Japanese and Chinese encyclopedias in the early modern period). Beijing: Beijing tushuguan chubanshe.

Zhongguo da baike quanshu 中國大百科全書 (Great encyclopaedia of China). 1986. 2 vols. Shanghai: Zhongguo da baike quanshu chubanshe (s.v. "Huang Moxi" 黃摩西).

Zhongguo gudai xiaoshuo baike quanshu 中國古代小說百科全書 (Comprehensive encyclopaedia of the classic Chinese novel). 1993. Beijing: Zhongguo da baike quanshu chubanshe (s.v. "Huang Moxi" 黃摩西).

Zhongguo wenxue da cidian 中國文學大辭典 (Comprehensive dictionary of Chinese literature). 1997. Shanghai: Shanghai cishu chubanshe.

Zhu Ziqing 朱自清. 1947. "Zhu Peixian xiansheng xu" 朱佩弦先生序 (Preface by Mr. Zhu Peixian). In Lin Geng 林庚, *Zhongguo wenxue shi* 中國文學史 (History of Chinese literature), n.p. Xiamen: Guoli Xiamen daxue.

CHAPTER FOUR

The End of the Past: Rewriting Chinese Literary History in the Early Republic

Stephen Owen

The argument presented in this chapter is a tentative venture into a large area, the proper treatment of which lies beyond both the scope of an essay such as this and my competence. To be done properly, it would require a large enterprise of literary sociology, including a study of how literature came to be instituted as a discipline within the Republican and later the PRC school systems. We have ample access to debates carried on by May Fourth scholars regarding literary education, but the practical process by which new generations of teachers were educated and the May Fourth reinterpretation of the literary past became the standard curriculum lies at the heart of the larger questions I raise here.

Although I offer some particular cases, each period, genre, and author entered the Republican period with its own prior history of criticism and anthologizing. In each case Republican anthologists and literary historians had to negotiate with the historical inertia of each component of the literary past. A sociologist of literature would find here a rich field in the publication of anthologies, their composition, critical allegiances, and size of print runs. Generalization about the new "story" of literature cannot be separated from a vast number of particular cases.

The larger issue at stake here is the Republican reification of "traditional China." The increasing homogeneity of anthology selections as we move closer to the present, a homogeneity supported by a standard account of literary history, permits a remarkable agreement about the general outlines of the literary past. This is often strongest precisely in those who feel that they are preserving "tradition," as if it were some unchanging consensus through the ages. Major re-evaluations have occurred in many areas of premodern Chinese culture, but classical literature, meaning the literature written in literary Chinese, seems to have become the icon of reified "traditional" culture.

Good scholars and students know better; they know that the premodern period was a history of disagreement and changing points of view. But when it comes to classical literature, there is a remarkable faith in the unchanging nature of canon. "Why aren't we reading the famous poems (*mingpian* 名篇)?" I have been often asked by students. I may point out that the poems we were reading were considered important at some earlier time and that the pieces they are identifying as *mingpian* were first anthologized and praised only in the Republican period (or sometimes, especially in the case of Tang poems, in the Qing). These *mingpian*, however, have come almost magically to embody "tradition," and it is hard to question or historicize their status. To some degree, the attachment to and faith in these poems derive from childhood studies, but they also embalm the past. And that embalmed version of the past was constructed by May Fourth scholars.[1]

Declaring the Revolution

May Fourth was the second Date in the history of Chinese culture; the first was the founding of the Republic. These were close enough in time to blur together into something we can simply call the Date. The Date was a way to divide time into pre's and post's. The Hebrews had a Date (although one without a "pre"); the Romans had a Date; the Christians and Moslems each had their own Date. Among other cultural imports, China assimilated the idea of a Date. By the Date was created "premodern China," or "imperial China," or "traditional China." Just a short time earlier, people had believed they were living in the Qing dynasty; after the Date, they discovered they had formerly been inhabiting premodern China. Practices continued across the Date suddenly became "out of date." One might seek to reform and to change China, or one might seek to preserve "tradition"; however important the differences between those two might seem, both are consequences of the Date.

---

1. For the record, I am not attacking the May Fourth critics and attempting to praise premodern views of literature at their expense. A certain irony is necessary to historicize them and those aspects of their critical judgments that are still taken for granted.

By the brilliant fiction of the Date, May Fourth, young intellectuals had a device around which cultural and literary history could be reinterpreted. If the Chinese cultural past was a burden, this was the means to declare that the past was over. Standing on the "modern" side of the boundary, one could claim to understand the past in an entirely new light. Those who continued older modes of writing on this side of the boundary became "holdovers," strangely out of place, their work no longer valid because it happened at the wrong time. Lu Xun's 魯 迅 (1881–1936) classical poetry is treated more as an adjunct to his "real" literary writing than as part of it. Classical literature, in its various genres, continued to be written extensively and enjoyed in the 1920s and 1930s, but it was no longer relevant. To a smaller degree, it is still being written and it is still irrelevant.

The May Fourth literary scholars were every bit as erudite as the scholars of the preceding generation, but in their eyes they were first true scholars, the first to "study" the past as an object. Zheng Zhenduo 鄭 振 鐸 (1898–1958) begins his *New Course for the Study of Chinese Literature* (*Yanjiu Zhongguo wenxue de xin tujing* 研 究 中 國 文 學 的 新 途 徑) of 1927 with a series of portraits of traditional scholars engaging in traditional literary pursuits. The portraits verge on satire. This is the first:

> Underneath the thick green shade there has been set a rattan chair, a literary man [文 人] sits casually dressed in the chair, in a soft voice intoning a collection of poems—maybe it's *The Collected Poems of Li Bai*, or maybe it's *The Collected Poems of Wang Wei*—and he looks as though he has become immersed in the poetry's realm of beauty. Over him the small golden rays of the sun peer flickering down through the cracks in the small leaves, a gentle breeze lightly slips past his side calling out, but he is aware of nothing. He has been moved, and the perfectly natural process that has moved him gives rise to an inexpressible inspiration, a kind of inspiration above which there is nothing higher. From his heart he heaves a sigh ever so lightly saying, "This is really good—this poem of Li Bai's!" Then he chants it over again. Can something like this be counted as studying (研 究) Li Bai or Wang Wei? No—this is appreciation, it is not study. (Zheng 1927: 1)

Zheng Zhenduo is correct: in the premodern world literature and literary history had never been an object of "study" in the way Zheng means it.

Zheng Zhenduo writes here in the novelistic vernacular. The revolution that created a displaced past was also a revolution in language, by which some kinds of language could be recognized as belonging to the past. "Literary language," *wenyan* 文 言, was supposed to belong to the past; "vernacular language," first as *guoyu* 國語, then as *baihua* 白話, was supposed to belong to the present. Thus the premodern history of writing in the vernacular became part of a literary historical narrative that led to the present.

The "vernacular" was supposed to be the living, spoken language, as opposed to the dead, artificial literary language, imposed from the past and force-fed to young children in school. If, however, we look at this passage by Zheng Zhenduo, the primary link to the spoken language is that it could be understood aurally—certainly no one ever spoke that way except in a public lecture. Indeed, the only true representation of "spoken language" is the line held up for mockery: "This is really good—this poem of Li Bai's!" (真好呀，太白的這首詩). We are much closer to a sketch in the *Unofficial History of the Literati* (*Rulin waishi* 儒林外史) than to the language people speak. Thus, from another point of view, this was no revolution in language, no victory of the present over the past; rather, the written novelistic vernacular, already with a long history, was laying claim to new genres—poetry, drama, and above all, the discursive prose of the essay. This generic expansion of an established linguistic register was significant, but hardly revolutionary enough to sustain a Date. The revolutionary Date was a performative utterance, and a successful one.

The expansion of the novelistic vernacular into genres from which it had been previously excluded may indeed have had profound consequences, but those consequences were not necessarily the same as the stated aims of the cultural revolutionaries. The novelistic vernacular was not a neutral linguistic medium but the means to tell a vivid story, rich with sketches and incidents. It should come, then, as no surprise that critical prose in the vernacular tended to discover meaning as part of a story, an ongoing narrative. This is in striking contrast to the complex but essentially non-narrative balances of judgment and comparison in premodern criticism, written in literary Chinese.

Revolutions and phases of radical change are compelled to tell a story, to rewrite their past to produce the present as something inevitable. But what may have seemed a self-evident representation of the past to a revolutionary can appear as an intensely motivated construct to someone well outside the revolutionary phase. Such motivations seem particularly clear now at the beginning of a new century. In their literary histories, in their critical essays, and above all in their anthologies, the May Fourth intellectuals effectively rewrote the history of premodern Chinese literature to serve their purposes.

Because of the sheer weight of canon, this was more difficult with classical literature than with literature in the vernacular. They succeeded—probably beyond their wildest expectations. Their daring judgments have in many cases become today's commonplaces. Such success was due in large measure to the mass publishing houses that disseminated their work and to the use of their anthologies within the school system. It was also because they told a good story.

In their histories of literature they needed to tell a story that at last came to the conclusion that classical literature was over. This end governed the construction of historical narrative.

Here it is worth recalling some simple and basic contrasts that came into being through this performative declaration of modernity. The first of these was "literature" itself. Literature in the Qing was essentially a large group of distinct genres. The elite genres of classical prose and poetry still retained something of their exclusive privilege, but there was a broad range of other kinds of writing that had grown in status.[2] Between *The Literary Mind and the Carving of Dragons* (*Wenxin diaolong* 文心雕龍) at the turn of the sixth century and the earliest literary histories at the end of the Qing, there was not, to my knowledge, a single work that conceived of itself as treating literature as a whole.[3] Likewise the Chinese written language consisted of a large number of registers loosely located on a gradation between the "popular," *su* 俗,

2. By the Qing, literary drama, both *chuanqi* 傳奇 and *zaju* 雜劇, although generally excluded from *sibu* 四部 classification, had clearly acquired the status of a high genre. Large claims had been made about the seriousness of vernacular fiction in the seventeenth century, and by the time of the *Dream of the Red Chamber* (*Honglou meng* 紅樓夢) cult of the nineteenth century it was exceedingly difficult to argue that fiction could not be serious. Informal letter collections and anthologies enjoyed vogues. Numerous collections of classical tales followed the great popularity of *Strange Stories from the Leisure Studio* (*Liaozhai zhiyi* 聊齋志異).

3. Needless to say, no treatment of "literature" included the vernacular genres, but there was nothing that treated the various classical genres as a unity. One might except the *Introduction to the Arts* (*Yigai* 藝概) of Liu Xizai 劉熙載 (1813–81), which did include critical comments on prose, poetry, *fu* 賦, *ci* 詞, and *qu* 曲, calligraphy, and the Classics, each category divided into its own section. There was, however, no attempt to integrate these rubrics in relations that constituted a whole of the "arts." A *guwen* 古文 anthology would exclude parallel prose, and vice versa. *Ci* might be included in someone's collected works, but anthologies would generally not mix *shi* 詩 and *ci*—much less *qu*. The earliest history of Chinese literature in Chinese was *A History of Chinese Literature* (*Zhongguo wenxue shi* 中國文學史, 1905), authored by Huang Ren 黃人 (1866–1913).

and a variety of "elevated" registers suggesting erudition.[4] Different registers were associated with different genres and values, and each had its proponents. There was, however, as yet no "classical Chinese" and "vernacular Chinese" as a basic distinction within the language; that distinction was a creation of the May Fourth intellectuals.

Although late Ming and early Qing intellectuals praised the "vitality" of literary forms using "popular" linguistic registers and Tongcheng 桐 城 masters valued the purity of their *guwen* 古 文, these different linguistic registers were *never* in direct competition: they occupied different generic niches. Written language was tied directly to genre. One would never write a tomb inscription in the language of "dramatic dialogue," *binbai* 賓 白, any more than one would use the diction of parallel prose for a personal diary. Together these genres and their associated registers were a constellation that defined a range of possibilities. Unlike Latin and the European vernaculars, to which May Fourth intellectuals sometimes compared "classical Chinese" and "vernacular Chinese," there was no clear dividing line; rather, written Chinese was conceived as one language with complex gradations of registers (see Hu 1928a: 5–6).[5]

I sketch this outline to call attention to the profound differences between the situation in the mid-Qing and the way we now conceive of Chinese literary history. First and foremost, we now have histories and anthologies of Chinese "literature": there are books and courses that conjoin, under one rubric, texts that had never been mixed before. An anthology of Six Dynasties literature will include poems, *zhiguai* 志 怪, anecdotes from *New Account of Tales of the World* (*Shishuo xinyu* 世 說 新 語), and parallel-prose letters.[6]

---

4. An archaic style, a euphuistic parallel prose style, and a pure *guwen* style were all "elevated" registers and quite distinct from one another. The simple antithesis between "literary" and "vernacular" collapses significant distinctions in written vernaculars and in registers signifying "erudition."

5. The situation does bear some similarities to classical Latin and vulgar Latin in the late empire and Dark Ages; however by the time of Dante's *De vulgari eloquentia* there was a clear distinction drawn between Latin and the vernacular. When the two were mixed, as sometimes occurred in the Renaissance writing known as macaronic, it was a distinct form, somewhat comic, that foregrounded the idea of mixing things that were distinct.

6. In his preface to *An Illustrated History of Chinese Literature* (*Chatuben Zhongguo wenxue shi* 插 圖 本 中 國 文 學 史, 1932), Zheng Zhenduo takes earlier attempts at writing Chinese literary history to task for not being comprehensive, precisely for leaving out the vernacular tradition, from *bianwen* 變 文 to *zhugongdiao* 諸 宮 調 to *tanci* 彈 詞 and *baojuan* 寶 卷. At the same time, he accuses his predecessors of just "giving an account of some representative au-

Such a construction of literary history permits a story of continuous struggle, in which the "low" genres and registers are competing with, overcoming, or being overcome by "elevated" forms.[7] The revolution had created an "us" and "them"; it created "modern" and "premodern"; and in rewriting the literary past, the real diversity of the tradition became no less binary and oppositional. The crowning achievement of the May Fourth anthologists and literary historians was to construct a line of development in which a literature in the vernacular was continually struggling against an eternally moribund "classical" literature; the vernacular was perpetually emergent. Such a version of Chinese literary history fulfills the necessary conclusion mentioned above: it places the May Fourth writers themselves at the culmination of literary history.

Zheng Zhenduo's *An Illustrated History of Chinese Literature* (*Chatuben Zhongguo wenxue shi* 插圖本中國文學史) of 1932 contains a set of "bird's-eye views" of the three periods into which Zheng divides Chinese literary history. The first period, covering the time up to the introduction of Buddhism in the Jin Dynasty, had little that would have been surprising from the point of view of a Qing reader, apart from the conjunction of forms. The second period, covering twelve hundred years up to 1522, mentions poetry and the *guwen* movements, but is concerned largely with *bianwen* 變文, *ci* 詞, and the rise of vernacular fiction and performance genres. Remarkably, Zheng sees many of these as coming from outside influence. In the final "bird's-eye view," from 1522 to May Fourth, Zheng dismisses classical literature altogether and focuses entirely on a vernacular literature that, he says, leads directly to the May Fourth movement, when, in a characteristically purple passage, he has sleeping China waking up and rubbing its eyes. In a large sweep, he tells a story of classical literature being overcome by "living" literature and then, in the final period, becoming irrelevant.[8]

---

thors and works." The inclusion of the vernacular tradition makes possible a story of "progress," *jinzhan* 進展.

7. In premodern criticism, proximate genres that we now see in competition were conceived as supplements. Thus *ci* is *shiyu* 詩餘. The May Fourth account of literary history has *zaju* superseded by *chuanqi* and ignores the continuous production of literary *zaju* through the Ming into the Qing. There was, occasionally, comment on interaction between proximate genres, but this was not part of a narrative of the whole.

8. In the actual chapters of the literary history, Zheng Zhenduo pays more attention to classical forms, although he does have a large number of chapters on vernacular literature in

Although not all of Zheng Zhenduo's broad account of literary historical importance has been sustained—*bianwen* and *zhugongdiao* 諸宮調 have not made the contemporary anthology canon—his "overviews" are remarkably consistent with what is now studied. This is all the more remarkable because his account of literary history is largely his own creation and in many areas militantly ignores the history of taste. After Song *shi* 詩 and Northern Song *guwen*, classical literature survives only as a ghostly opponent of the vernacular literary revolution.

Following Western and sometimes indigenous Chinese historicism, May Fourth scholars often rewrote the literary past as a history of generic supersession. One form was appropriate in one period; a new form was appropriate in the next period. Once a form's time was past, it was over and done with. The past was no longer a repertoire of possibilities for the present, as it had been in the Qing; it was a lineage of dead things. As many May Fourth scholars recognized, this particular way of understanding the past was itself a choice from the repertoire of Chinese literary thought, a radicalized version of ideas current in the late Ming.[9]

Hu Shi's 胡適 (1891–1962) *History of Vernacular Literature* (*Baihua wenxue shi* 白話文學史), first published in 1928 but based on lectures first given in 1921 at the request of the Department of Education, offers a delightful account of this issue of historicism and the role this newly invented "vernacular literature" played in it:

> Yesterday a student came and asked me, "In the West every age has its own literature. And the literature of an age represents overall the spirit of that age. Why is it that our literature in China cannot represent its age? Why is it that Yao Nai's essays and Han Yu's don't have any period distinction?" I answered, "You are in error about literary history—that's why you feel that Chinese literature doesn't represent an age. In fact what you're seeing as 'literary history' is just the 'history of the *guwen* tradition.' In that 'history of the *guwen* tradition' writers of prose can only imitate Han Yu, Liu Zongyuan, Ouyang Xiu, and Su Shi; writers of poems can only imitate Li Bai, Du Fu, Su Shi, and Huang Tingjian. One age imitates another, people

---

the middle period and only a few chapters on classical literature, treating it in terms of literary theory, in the final period.

9. I do not want to underestimate the degree to which this drew on one account of literary history in the late Ming, in which "vigorous" vernacular forms replaced classical forms in sequence. This was only one current in late Ming writing on literature, and it was singled out by May Fourth writers themselves, whose essays and publishing efforts raised those late Ming advocates of vernacular literature to the esteem they currently hold.

just want to be 'good little boys and good little grandchildren'; naturally they can't represent the changes of an age." (Hu 1928a: Preface 3)[10]

As one might expect, Hu Shi recommends the reading of fiction in place of Tongcheng prose.

Several points should be observed here. Classical literature is treated as essentially ahistorical or in stasis due to imitation. The Qing model of accretive change, with literature growing by the addition of new forms, is replaced by a model of linear change, whose alternative is stasis or repetition. According to the model presented, to have literary history and a link between literature and history in the larger sense one needs vernacular literature, standing for change and innovation against classical literary stasis. Premodern Chinese criticism had, of course, always discussed the way in which literature represented its age and was acutely aware of historical differences. But rather than engage that indigenous tradition, Hu Shi has his student appeal to the example of the "West," *xiyang* 西洋, and ask: "Why don't we have it here?" This permits Hu Shi to say, "We do!" and to uncover that "living" history from beneath the deceptive veil of the "*guwen* tradition." The modern literary historian is thus placed in a privileged position to know the past, whereas those in the past are considered generally incapable of seeing what is important. This privileged position is roughly the same as Zheng Zhenduo's "study," set in contrast to the traditional scholar's restriction to "appreciation." Finally, Hu Shi understands this as a revolutionary act within a household: the bad writers are "good little boys," *xiaozi* 肖子; by implication he and his May Fourth friends will be the Confucian father's worst nightmare.

Hu Shi is smart enough to see the gaping hole in his argument; and after railing against "good little boys" in his preface, he introduces another interlocutor who points out that if there indeed have been two millennia of vital vernacular literature, changing with its age and representing its age, why do we need a "vernacular literature movement," *guoyu wenxue de yundong* 國語文學的運動? Why not just let things follow their natural course? To answer this, Hu Shi distinguishes between natural evolution and evolution helped on by human agency, which he calls "revolution." Natural evolution is slow, inconsistent, sometimes overcome by conservatism. Revolution, which

10. It is hard not to observe that in making this crucial point, Hu Shi adopts one of the oldest and most authoritative of literary forms, the dialogue between master and disciple.

is after all simply following the natural course of things, gets the job done quickly. Perhaps the most significant objection is that not everyone recognizes what the real literature of the time is—in fact, very few may.

> . . . in the more than one thousand years of history of this vernacular literature, there has only been natural evolution and there has been no conscious revolution; there has been no one to shout out quite clearly, "Look! This is a living literature; that is a dead literature; this is a genuine literature; that is a false literature"—because there has never been this kind of conscious advocacy. (Hu 1928a: Preface, 6)

We may set aside the striking historical inaccuracy of this claim: the long-awaited shout is precisely what Li Zhi 李贄 (1527–1602) wrote in "On the Child-like Mind" ("Tongxin shuo" 童心說). In another sense, however, Hu Shi is correct: Li Zhi may have said much the same thing, but he did not write it in *baihua*. What is significant here is that Hu Shi is leaving no room for a variety of opinions about literature and literary history. The Qing literary world was open to multiple specialties: some were drawn to fiction; some preferred *chuanqi* 傳奇 drama, and others liked *zaju* 雜劇; some adored parallel prose, whereas others were devotees of *biji* 筆記. Hu Shi is telling us that just as there is one general category of "literature," so there is *one* literary history, in which values are self-evident if one only looks. The good texts are the ones that show the vernacular; the bad texts are the ones that are "classical." Hu Shi is, in short, claiming an orthodoxy of judgment on a scale to which no doddering Tongcheng critic would ever have aspired. The Tongcheng critic, after all, made authoritative judgments only on what constituted good *guwen* prose. Hu Shi is making judgments for all literature.

This comes back to my earlier observation on the remarkable consistency of choices in modern anthologies and the consistency of the judgments offered. I hope it will not seem too perverse to suggest that, within the larger course of Chinese culture, the May Fourth critics, in their treatment of the past, represent the reassertion of an orthodoxy, and it was an orthodoxy on a scale hitherto unimagined. This orthodoxy was closely related to the closure and reification of tradition, which would now be the "possession" of Chinese culture, rather than its medium. "Literature" in the large sense, rather than a few selected elite genres, would be taught in the school system, and the teacher would tell you what was good and progressive, as well as what was bad and reactionary. And since the students would be "good little boys"—and girls now as well—a new orthodox canon would be erected on this revolution.

My interest here is not in the creation of literary history per se, but in the ways in which the diverse histories of different genres intersected with the new enterprise of literary history and early Republican anthology-making. This is not easy because each genre in each period brought with it not only a very different history but also a different weight of history. With Yuan *sanqu* 散曲 the Republican anthologists could invent a canon; with Tang poetry they had to deal with an immense inertia of canon formation. When Hu Shi speaks of "imitative" poetry composition, he says "Li, Du, Su, Huang"—Li Bai 李白 (701–62), Du Fu 杜甫 (712–70), Su Shi 蘇軾 (1037–1101), and Huang Tingjian 黃庭堅 (1045–1105). Within that set of names, Li Bai and Du Fu were so deeply rooted in the tradition that they could not be easily dislodged. This was true canon. But the inclusion of Su Shi and Huang Tingjian as models for imitation was very much part of an ongoing debate in the study of poetry and by no means as unchanging a value as Hu Shi's passage suggests. The task was to integrate diverse histories, which previously had rarely impinged on one another, into one orthodox history.

Cases

The general imperatives and consequent outline of the new story of the literary past required a large-scale re-evaluation of numerous particular writers and works. It required new heroes, polemics, and complex negotiations with the inertia of earlier judgments. It required new anthologies with guiding headnotes to make these new judgments "self-evident" (like their predecessors, the May Fourth critics depended heavily on the claim that their judgments were ahistorically self-evident—in their case, once the blinders of lingering prejudice were removed). This enterprise, to make the past the story behind the present, is interesting less in terms of theory than in terms of the pervasive changes that took place in the literary stock market. Since I cannot describe all these, I will take up just a few exemplary cases: the account of origins, the re-evaluation of a single writer, the radical revision of the most important figures in a particular period, and the creation of a new period genre. Each of these topics merits a separate study in its own right, and what follows are only the briefest of sketches.

Insofar as the literary past tells a story of the rise of vernacular literature and its victory over classical literature, some point must be identified as the beginning of the struggle. Both Hu Shi's lectures, first published as *A History of Literature in the National Language* (*Guoyu wenxue shi* 國語文學史, 1927),

and the revised *A History of Vernacular Literature* of 1928 begin with a chapter entitled "When Did *Guwen* Die?" ("Guwen shi heshi si de" 古文是何時死的). The argument that Hu Shi offers can be summarized as follows: as a consequence of imperial unification, the polity needed a common language to unify regional linguistic differences as well as a corps of officers trained in that language.[11] Hu Shi cites a memorial by Gongsun Hong 公孫弘 (200–121 B.C.) to Han Wudi 漢武帝 (r. 140–87 B.C.) toward the end of the second century B.C. complaining that local officials could not understand the elegance of imperial communications to the populace, and for Hu Shi this is taken as a sign that *guwen*, being incomprehensible, was already dead. The dubious inferences and accuracy of this account are less important than its foundational role in a narrative. Once there is a dead *guwen*, the vernacular is born: in the "Chu songs," *Chuge* 楚歌, of the imperial house, in village ditties, and above all in *yuefu* 樂府. Elements of this account of Han poetry have deep roots in earlier criticism and values of vitalism that are to be traced back not just to the late Ming but to the mid-Ming Archaists. But Hu Shi adds an agonistic structure in which the role of the opponent is taken by the officer corps, later transformed into the mandarinate, shaped by the needs of the imperial state.

Hu Shi's was, of course, not the only new story of beginnings. As pointed out earlier, Zheng Zhenduo located the beginning of the vernacular impulse with the introduction of Buddhism and foreign influence in the Jin dynasty. Zheng's account is less agonistic than Hu Shi's, permitting classical poetry and *guwen* to be innovative in the Tang, alongside the vernacular genres. Zheng is often remarkably tolerant of some work in classical forms, even in the post-1522 "recent period"; in devoting most of his attention to the vernacular genres, however, he allows classical literature to be gradually overshadowed, overwhelmed, and reduced to irrelevance. And throughout, he introduces the language of sickliness, death, and darkness to foreground the vitality and light that shine steadily from his description of vernacular forms.

Although Han song and *yuefu* have retained their inaugural importance in recent literary histories and anthologies, neither Hu Shi's tendentious dating of the death of *guwen* nor the introduction of Buddhism's epochal importance for literature have been sustained. More recent literary history gives vernacular literature a subsidiary place in the Tang and Song and a

---

11. I have not encountered any awareness on Hu Shi's part that *guoyu* is also just such a unifying language.

predominant role only in the Yuan, Ming, and Qing. Indeed this has been so thoroughly taken for granted that we should recall its historicity, that this began in *An Illustrated History of Chinese Literature*.

In other areas the canonical accounts of ancient literature were also being revised. Wen Yiduo 聞一多 (1899–1946) never wrote the history of literature he planned to write, but his essays, gathered in his collected works (and later published separately) under the rubric "Myth and Poetry" ("Shenhua yu shi" 神話與詩), pointed toward a background of mythic and religious origins of ancient literature that completely contradicted the traditional Confucian account. Such work also left its traces in modern literary study. In the textbook reader of ancient literature put out by the Chinese Department of Beijing University, *Source Materials for the History of Pre-Qin Literature* (*Xian-Qin wenxue shi cankao ziliao* 先秦文學史參考資料), published by Zhonghua shuju in 1962, the first section that students encounter is now "Myth" (based entirely on sources from the end of the ancient period). Wen Yiduo and other Republican mythographers produced an account of Chinese literary origins more in keeping with concepts of cultural origin elsewhere.

The canon of Han and Six Dynasties poetry was one of the most stable—far more stable, indeed, than that of Tang poetry. This stability was due not only to its age but also to the fact that the survival of texts already showed the traces of the early anthologist's hand. The major era of re-evaluation had occurred at the hands of the Archaists in the mid-Ming, who, for virtually the first time, called attention to Cao Cao's 曹操 (155–220) poetry and cultivated the taste for the roughness of early *yuefu* and Han poetry. As we have seen, anonymous *yuefu* were obviously important to the May Fourth account of literary history, and there was a boom in the study of *yuefu*, most notably perhaps in *Notes on Yuefu Poetry* (*Yuefu shi jian* 樂府詩箋) of Wen Yiduo. With the exception of culture heroes like Tao Qian 陶潛 (365–427), re-evaluation became possible according to the degree to which literary writers showed the influence of *yuefu*.

This brings us to the case of Bao Zhao 鮑照 (ca. 414–66). Bao (like Tao Qian) had been ranked only in the middle grade by Zhong Rong 鍾嶸 (ca. 465–518) in *An Evaluation of Poetry* (*Shipin* 詩品) early in the sixth century. He fared reasonably well in the *Anthology of Literature* (*Wen xuan* 文選), from the same period, which selected eight of his *yuefu* (but none of the now-famous *Ni xinglu nan* 擬行路難). There is no doubt that Bao's *yuefu* were a major influence on Li Bai, and Du Fu described Bao as exhibiting *junyi* 俊逸, something like "magnificent insouciance." In the Tang, however, Bao's denser landscape poems, modeled on Xie Lingyun 謝靈運 (385–433), were also much read and influential. As an example of Qing judgment, let us consider *Selected Old-style Poetry* (*Gushi xuan* 古詩選) by Wang Shizhen 王士禎 (1634–1711), an anthology that retained some influence in the eighteenth and nineteenth centuries, having been reissued with extensive critical comments by the prominent Tongcheng scholar Fang Dongshu 方東樹 (1772–1851). That anthology has 39 of Bao Zhao's poems, of which only four are *yuefu*; the *yuefu* chosen do not include any of the *Ni xinglu nan*.[12] Zhu Ziqing's 朱自清 (1898–1948) *Selected Poems of Fourteen Poets* (*Shisijia shichao* 十四家詩鈔) (compiled from Zhu's lecture notes) has ten Bao Zhao poems, of which seven are *yuefu*, including five *Ni xinglu nan*. To offer some filiation into the modern pedagogic tradition, in Yu Guanying's 余冠英 influential *Selected Poems of the Han, Wei and Six Dynasties* (*Han Wei liuchao shixuan* 漢魏六朝詩選, 1958) there are seventeen Bao Zhao poems, of which eleven are *yuefu*, omitting only one of the *yuefu* selected by Zhu Ziqing. Beijing University's *Source Materials for the History of Wei, Jin, and Northern and Southern Dynasties Literature* (*Wei Jin Nanbeichao wenxue shi cankao ziliao* 魏晉南北朝文學史參考資料), published by Zhonghua shuju in 1962, includes twenty poems by Bao Zhao, of which thirteen are *yuefu*; six of the other seven are imitations of third-century styles; only one is in the contemporary mode. In Lin Geng 林庚 and Feng Yuanjun's 馮沅君 *A Chronological Selection of Chinese Poems and Songs* (*Zhongguo lidai shige xuan* 中國歷代詩歌選), issued in 1981 by Renmin wenxue chubanshe, we have eleven poems by Bao Zhao, of which only two are not *yuefu*. In Cheng Qianfan's 程千帆 and Shen Zufen's 沈祖棻 *Modern Selection of Old-style Poetry* (*Gushi jinxuan* 古詩今選), published by Shanghai guji chubanshe in 1983, there are eight Bao Zhao poems, all of which are *yuefu*. Five of those eight are the *Ni xinglu nan*. Xie Lingyun, the great master of the generation preceding Bao Zhao and considered Bao's superior by Zhong Rong, is allowed only four poems in Cheng and Shen's anthology. I choose these

12. *Origins of Old-style Poetry* (*Gushi yuan* 古詩源) by Shen Deqian 沈德潛 (1673–1769) includes a much better representation of the *yuefu*, including eight of the *Ni xinglu nan*. One often *can* find precedents for modern selections; in premodern anthologies, in contrast to modern anthologies, there was a great diversity of judgment.

recent examples of anthologies because all were done by eminent scholars, published by major presses in large print runs; this is now the "canon."

One could continue to multiply the statistics, both in the case of Bao Zhao and many other writers. We might ask what literary-historical ideology informed this change. It is hard to resist quoting Hu Shi again:

> The greatest poet of the time was not Xie [Lingyun] or Yan [Yanzhi]—it was, in fact, Bao Zhao. Bao Zhao was someone who had the highest degree of natural talent. When he wrote the *Ni xinglu nan* at the age of twenty, his energy moved freely as it pleased; no ancients were before him, and he paved the way for a hundred generations to come. His achievements should have been very great. Unfortunately he was born into a decadent age, and in that crowd of dwarves, a tall man was not permitted to raise his head; and in the end he had no choice but to suppress his natural talent; he had no choice but to bow to the current tastes of the literary world of the time. (1928a: 115)

Hu Shi continues in this vein at some length, pointing out how the "popular" (*su*) quality of Bao Zhao's poetry earned the contempt of some of his contemporaries and how he was influenced by popular song. It is a familiar story in Hu Shi's literary history, one of natural talent and energy, allied with the "popular," suppressed by the forces of elite taste. A large proportion of Bao Zhao's oeuvre consists of densely ornamented descriptive poems showing the strong influence of Xie Lingyun. Hu Shi accounts for this by a narrative of youthful vitality driven to conformity by the social pressures of a decadent and repressive age. Needless to say, this narrative cannot be sustained by a scholarly examination of Bao Zhao's poems. Hu Shi provides his own examples, including many of the modern anthology pieces. If a young reader had only Wang Shizhen's anthology, he would have no idea what Hu Shi was talking about. This new literary history required anthologies to confirm judgments made.

In *An Illustrated History of Chinese Literature* Zheng Zhenduo provides a less polemical and more comprehensive version of literary history than Hu Shi's; but the main outlines of re-evaluation remain clear. Xie Lingyun is not dismissed, but Zheng quotes some of his least ornamented passages approvingly—to show that the traditional valuation of Xie Lingyun can be sustained because he is not always as "literary" as earlier critics have suggested. As is the case for Hu Shi, to Zheng Zhenduo Bao Zhao is "a writer with truly natural talents," who was far more favored by later ages than Xie Lingyun and Yan Yanzhi 顏延之 (384–456) (1927: 185; this is true of Yan Yanzhi, but not of Xie Lingyun). Zheng next gives Zhong Rong's judgment of Bao, including a comment on his "daring obliquity," *weize* 危仄 (suggesting rhetorical obscurity). He then cites a series of passages from the *yuefu*, especially from the *Ni xinglu nan*, asking rhetorically where, indeed, was such "daring obliquity" to be found. We should note what Zheng Zhenduo has done here; he has eliminated from consideration a large portion of Bao Zhao's poetry—the kind of poems to which Zhong Rong's judgment applied and which continued to be anthologized in the Qing *Selected Old-style Poetry*. Instead he cites passages from the *yuefu*, and later from a few selected *shi*, to sustain the image of Bao Zhao as fresh and direct. The modern critic claims to be the superior judge by controlling the evidence.

The enemy is an elite, rhetorical, ornamental writing. To make Bao Zhao a hero of the natural, both Hu Shi and Zheng Zhenduo suppress the larger part of Bao Zhao's poetry. In the case of Xie Lingyun, Hu Shi downgrades him, and Zheng Zhenduo preserves his canonical stature by choosing passages that can be reconciled with the new values. Both are telling a larger story about *yuefu* and popular taste, in which Bao Zhao is a brief moment of brightness. The general outline of Hu Shi's and Zheng Zhenduo's judgments are uniformly restated in the headnotes of anthologies published over the past four decades, anthologies that, we may recall, place inordinate weight on Bao's *yuefu*, thus confirming the judgments. Bao's poor background and resistance to elite culture are mentioned; the superiority of his *yuefu* is reaffirmed; critics praise the popular and natural quality of his language; they speak of his energy and "romanticism."

Fang Dongshu gives a long section of critical discussion before the Bao Zhao selection in *Selected Old-style Poetry*. The contrasts between Fang Dongshu's critical procedures and those of the May Fourth critics are striking. Fang begins with an observation with which Hu Shi and Zheng Zhenduo would have agreed: Bao's poetry has an "energy," *qi* 氣, that overwhelmed the "flaccidity," *miruo* 靡弱, of the Western Jin poets. Fang then quotes Wang Shizhen's judgment that Bao was superior to Yan Yanzhi and the equal of Xie Lingyun. But he then goes on to say that the virtue of Bao Zhao's poetry lay in the craftsmanship of diction and lines that was animated by his "insouciant energy," *yiqi* 逸氣, by which he avoided the plodding quality of such craftsmanship as practiced by others. Bao Zhao's originality is acknowledged, but it is seen as deriving not from "natural talent," but from "extreme seriousness regarding the rule of getting rid of worn-out diction" (去陳言之法尤嚴). Fang continues for pages, making extensive comment on Bao Zhao's relation to his predecessors and his influence on later poets.

Fang Dongshu was intensely aware of Bao Zhao's place in a history of poetry—contemporary, past, and future—but his work was not part of a linear "literary historical" narrative, much less a narrative of struggle. Fang understood Bao Zhao's work in the context of a family of writers who found their own identity and practiced their craft in relation to one another. In contrast to Hu Shi's narrative of a natural young talent crushed by social pressure, Fang Dongshu's Bao Zhao was someone who consciously controlled his skill in various forms. This comparison between Fang Dongshu and the May Fourth critics is not to favor one approach over another, but to show the intensely narrative, often agonistic quality of the May Fourth critics' account.

Song *ci* offers an interesting case of a complete change in the image of a period—the Southern Song. In the Qing, various schools of *ci* advocated different values and very different canons. Some, such as Wang Guowei 王國維 (1877–1927), strongly supported Northern Song *xiaoling* 小令, but probably the majority of Qing *ci* readers preferred Zhou Bangyan 周邦彥 (1056–1121) and the Southern Song. Thus in 1873 Zhou Ji's 周濟 (1781–1839) influential *Selected Lyrics from the Four Masters of the Song* (*Song sijia ci xuan* 宋四家詞選) was published. The "four masters" of Song *ci* were Zhou Bangyan, Xin Qiji 辛棄疾 (1140–1207), Wang Yisun 王沂孫 (1240–90), and Wu Wenying 吳文英 (ca. 1200–1260). This is not a canon any modern student would recognize. To offer some statistics, we may compare three Republican anthologies. Zhu Xiaozang's 朱孝臧 (1857–1931) *Three Hundred Lyrics of the Song* (*Song ci sanbaishou* 宋詞三百首) of 1924 represented the tradition of *ci* specialists (it was this anthology that Tang Guizhang 唐圭璋 chose to annotate in 1947). Hu Shi's *Selected Lyrics* (*Ci xuan* 詞選) of 1927 is squarely in the May Fourth tradition. Hu Yunyi's 胡雲翼 *Selected Lyrics of the Song* (*Song ci xuan* 宋詞選) of 1962 is based on the *Selected Celebrated Lyrics of the Song* (*Song mingjia ci xuan* 宋名家詞選) of 1937 and represents the elaboration of the May Fourth model. The proportions of representation and selected texts of more recent anthologies in the PRC closely follow Hu Yunyi.

In terms of proportions, the representation of Northern Song *ci* is similar in the three anthologies.[13] But when we move into the Southern Song, we get a very different picture (see Table 1). The Hu Shi and Hu Yunyi anthologies do offer examples of the Southern Song *wanyue* 婉約 *ci* tradition but reduce it to relative unimportance in terms of the proportions of selection. Furthermore, as with the modern anthologist's treatment of Bao Zhao, the particular selections can redirect the image presented by a given writer. In anthologizing primarily Bao Zhao's *yuefu*, the modern anthologists took one aspect of Bao Zhao's work that had always been appreciated and made it Bao Zhao's sole defining quality. In his Wu Wenying selection Hu Shi spends most of his long headnote attacking Wu Wenying. In the headnote he quotes and holds up for scorn one of Wu's characteristically dense *manci* 慢詞; for the selection proper, however, he then chooses a relatively straightforward *xiaoling*. Hu Yunyi also criticizes Wu in the headnote, then in the selection offers one *manci* and three lighter *xiaoling*.

To fill in the literary-historical hole created by downgrading the Southern Song *wanyue* tradition, a group of lyricists, hitherto little read and valued, were promoted to constitute a family around Xin Qiji and confirm his sole pre-eminence in the tradition: Zhu Dunru 朱敦儒 (1081–1159), Lu You 陸游 (1125–1210), Liu Guo 劉過 (1154–1206), and Liu Kezhuang 劉克莊 (1187–1269).

The politics of value among Qing *ci* critics and anthologists had been intense. Zhou Ji may have included both *haofang* 豪放 and *wanyue* lineages by combining Xin Qiji with Zhou Bangyan, Wu Wenying, and Wang Yisun as his "four masters," but the exclusion of the much admired Jiang Kui 姜夔 (ca. 1155–1221) from this group was a willful act in *ci* debates. Given such fluidity of evaluation, the May Fourth critics were staking their claim on Southern Song *ci* as several centuries of critics before them had done. Their claim, however, was supported not simply by a debate within the *ci* tradition

13. The case of Liu Yong 柳永 (ca. 971–1053) is very revealing. Liu Yong was, without a doubt, the most vernacular lyricist in the Song. His work was also genuinely popular, and he should have been the favorite of anyone interested in the growth of vernacular literature. Unfortunately his lyrics are mostly about feasting and the liaisons of the entertainment quarter—not the seriousness that the May Fourth writers wanted. In *A History of Literature in the National Language*, Hu Shi quotes a number, praising them for their use of the vernacular, but in his *Selected Lyrics* he comments, "His style is not elevated (風格不高)," a comment that precisely echoes the disdain of traditional critics.

Table 1
Southern Song *ci* in Three Anthologies

Lyricist	Zhu Xiaozang	Hu Shi	Hu Yunyi
Zhang Xiaoxiang 張孝祥	2	0	8
Zhu Dunru 朱敦儒	0	30	9
Lu You 陸游	1	21	11
Xin Qiji 辛棄疾	12	46	40
Liu Guo 劉過	1	6	7
Jiang Kui 姜夔	16	9	10
Shi Dazu 史達祖	9	7	2
Liu Kezhuang 劉克莊	4	16	12
Wu Wenying 吳文英	25	1	4
Wang Yisun 王沂孫	6	3	3

itself but by a sense of value in literary history as a whole. And their sense of values, demonstrated in anthology headnotes and the proportions of selection, continues to dominate textbook anthologies.[14]

In *A History of Literature in the National Language* of 1927, the publication of Hu Shi's lectures that led him to write *A History of Vernacular Literature*, Wu Wenying, whom many *ci* lovers had considered the "culmination," *jida chengzhe* 集大成者, of the *ci*, came in for special denunciation, as he did in Hu Shi's anthology (1928b: 183–85).[15] Zheng Zhenduo offered a more measured (and more subtly contemptuous) judgment. Wu Wenying, Zheng says, is all right if you do not read the obscure bits and do not expect too much from him, "but he's not someone who had very much poetic talent" (1932: 590). Zheng passes over Wang Yisun, one of Zhou Ji's "four masters," in one in-

14. The mid- and late twentieth century world of *ci* scholarship shows less orthodoxy than almost any other field of premodern literature. This is due to the presence of great *ci* scholars who represent a more or less continuous tradition from the Qing. In the schools where they teach and among their students, the representation of Southern Song *ci* would be less unfamiliar to a premodern reader. Scholars like Xia Chengtao 夏承燾 and Tang Guizhang, the compiler of the *Complete Lyrics of the Song* (*Quan Song ci* 全宋詞), represent a significant counterbalance to the version of Southern Song *ci* that follows from the May Fourth critics. It should be pointed out that *ci* composition also continued to be considered "serious" longer than any other classical literary genre: "Qing" or "recent" *ci* anthologies often represent lyricists active from the late Ming down to the end of the 1930s.

15. Hu Shi published only the first volume of *A History of Vernacular Literature*, covering the period through the Tang. Although less full, the lectures of *A History of Literature in the National Language* go through the Song.

dented line and a half, most of which is taken up with his names, his place of origin, and the name of his *ci* collection. One lyric is quoted. Characteristically, Zheng Zhenduo teaches the new structure of values by the amount of attention he gives to a form or a writer. Proportions of representation were perhaps an even more powerful tool than particular selections in changing the reader's sense of importance.

One of the most striking transformations of premodern judgments of literary history was the virtual invention of the genre we now know as "Yuan *sanqu*." Although this was a vernacular genre, it differed from drama and fiction by finding itself placed in a direct lineage that passed from *shi* to *ci* to *sanqu*.[16] *Sanqu* has now been fully "instituted" in anthologies, literary histories, and the curriculum that follows from the two preceding critical genres. The numerous *sanqu* anthologies of the past two decades show a remarkable homogeneity both in the proportions of representation of individual lyricists and in the particular pieces selected.[17] This "canon" cannot be dated earlier than the 1930s.

Throughout the Qing, *sanqu* had been very much a form for a few specialists (excluding popular aria collections, which probably reached a much wider audience). Although it is difficult to know with certainty, it appears from the number of works published that Yuan *shi* were more widely read than *sanqu*.[18] Furthermore, although the commonplace period designation "Yuan *qu* 曲" was already in use (primarily suggesting drama),

16. When the term *qu* had been used in earlier sequences that went "Tang *shi*, Song *ci*, Yuan *qu*," *qu* usually meant drama. The radical differentiation of the category of "drama" from "lyric poetry" was part of the Western generic system rather than the Chinese. Once drama had been set in a radically different literary category, a lyric successor to *ci* was needed. As Zheng Zhenduo describes it, it belongs to the "field of poetry," *shitan* 詩壇.

17. Because these are often intended as textbooks, such anthologies also show a remarkable homogeneity in their exclusion of the erotic, sometimes obscene lyrics that figure so prominently in the extant *sanqu* corpus.

18. Considering the strict division of genres in the premodern period, comparison is difficult. Yuan classical poetry was widely known and frequently commented on in *shihua* 詩話. *Sanqu* are occasionally mentioned in *quhua* 曲話, but with nothing comparable to the frequency of comment on *shi*. Needless to say, the extant corpus of Yuan poetry exceeds by many times the surviving Yuan *sanqu*. The Zhonghua shuju edition of the standard Qing anthology of Yuan poetry, *Selected Yuan Poetry* (*Yuan shi xuan* 元詩選), runs to more than 4,500 pages. The complete Yuan *sanqu*, also published by Zhonghua shuju in larger print, is less than 1,900 pages. Volume is, of course, no index of quality, but it does suggest the quantity of production and the evaluation that supports preservation.

"detached arias," *sanqu*, were not linked specifically to the Yuan, but to the Yuan *and* Ming. Anyone interested in *sanqu* was more likely to read Kang Hai 康海 (1475–1540), Li Kaixian 李開先 (1502–68), or Feng Weimin 馮惟敏 (1511–ca. 1580) than Guan Hanqing 關漢卿 (ca. 1220–1300), whose detached arias had never been published independently. The May Fourth generation transformed *sanqu* into *the* poetic form of the Yuan dynasty, the "vigorous vernacular" form that supplanted Song *ci* after it became decadent. In most anthologies the far richer world of Ming *sanqu* was omitted or included in far smaller proportions.

When Wang Yi 王易, a traditional scholar, wrote his *A History of Lyrics and Drama* (*Ci qu shi* 詞曲史) (preface 1927), *qu* meant drama; he passed over detached arias (*sanqu*) lightly in a few pages (he gave Yuan *ci* a far more thorough treatment). Despite some earlier scholarly work, Yuan *sanqu* reappeared (or appeared) in history with the publication of Ren Zhongmin's 任中敏 *Collected Reprints of Sanqu* (*Sanqu congkan* 散曲叢刊) by Zhonghua shuju in 1930. In this collection the Yuan and Ming anthologies, from which the corpus of *sanqu* has now been reconstructed, were republished and made widely available. In that same year, Ren Zhongmin published *Three Hundred Yuan Sanqu* (*Yuanqu sanbai shou* 元曲三百首), one of the first anthologies of the genre intended to be representative (with all the implications of the *sanbai shou* as an anthology title; cf. Zhu Xiaozang 1924). The first history of the form was Liang Yizhen's 梁乙真 *A Short History of Yuan and Ming Sanqu* (*Yuan Ming sanqu xiaoshi* 元明散曲小史) of 1934.

The early Republican period saw a flurry of interest in the rediscovery and republication of earlier vernacular literature. Zheng Zhenduo's *An Illustrated History of Chinese Literature* (1932) was remarkable for the ease and speed with which Zheng imported such newly republished works into his history—not for mere mention but as the most important literature of various periods. Works that had been, only a few decades earlier, either undiscovered or known only to a handful of scholars, were elevated to represent the mainstream of Chinese literature. The following is the opening of Zheng Zhenduo's chapter on *sanqu*:

> During the Jin and Yuan a strange bloom suddenly appeared in the field of our poetry, once again infusing renewed vitality into the movement of the sickly and lifeless field of "poetry" (*shi*).[19] It made it shoot forth beams of light for thousands of yards, as if, af-

19. Classical literature maintained a strict generic distinction between *shi*, *ci*, and *qu*. Zheng uses *shi* as "poetry" in the Western sense, meaning verse centered on lyric poetry. The first use

ter being sunk in foggy gloom for a long time, golden sunbeams suddenly shot down in several threads through the clouds; it was as if, after passing through harsh winter, the very first gust of the spring breeze blew a faint green upon the plants and the willow buds were about to open. Its fresh and cheerful manner can be immediately sensed by the reader. This strange bloom is what is known as *sanqu*. (1932: 729)[20]

I cite this purple passage to call attention to the kind of literary historical claims that Zheng Zhenduo makes. In contrast to the "famous poems," *mingpian*, of Tang poetry, in which the literary historian had to contend with the history of taste, here he claims the model of nature, the appearance of light, warmth, and vitality that should be self-evident. The fact that hardly anyone read Yuan *sanqu* between the early Ming and 1930 is immaterial: all we need do is look and *we* can see immediately how fresh and lively it is. From this outburst praising renewed life in the "field of poetry," Zheng immediately goes on to filiate Yuan *sanqu* to the tradition of Song vernacular literature; it had "secretly been nurtured for a long time."

What is remarkable is the degree to which this literary-historical judgment is a pure act of ideological will. Except by the criterion of "vitality," which is one stylistically coded value within a tradition that had many values, it is very hard to maintain that Yuan *sanqu* has much to offer the reader of poetry. It is fun, lightweight; its pleasures, though undeniable, are immediate and on the surface. By Chinese standards, there isn't very much of it. Most important, to sustain his literary historical narrative, Zheng Zhenduo is compelled to exclude a large proportion of surviving Yuan *sanqu*. Here it is important to keep in mind that Zheng did not have a received canon; he had the "raw" corpus, the early anthologies reprinted by Ren Zhongmin. Zheng had to exclude the large body of erotic and sometimes obscene verse in those anthologies. He also had to exclude the densely ornamented songs that were the staple of the entertainment quarters, as well as the large number of lyrics that were pastiches of poetic lines or rewritings of earlier songs and songs created out of play titles. Much of Yuan *sanqu* represented precisely the kind of "literary games" that Zheng detested and for which he condemned many writers. Out of the "raw" material in Ren Zhongmin's *Collected Reprints of Sanqu*, Zheng Zhenduo "constructed" Yuan *sanqu*, with Guan Hanqing as its "great poet," *da shiren* 大詩人.

---

of "poetry" in this sentence is in the extended Western sense; the second use is placed in quotation marks, referring the reader to what Zheng saw as the moribund *shi* tradition.

20. Zheng's dependence on Ren Zhongmin is apparent in Zheng's notes.

A *sanqu* canon, created by suppressing a large number of kinds of existing *sanqu*, came into being through this historicist law of supersession: a new form *must* arise and supplant an old form. In its appearance, the new form must always be better than the old form, which is "sickly and lacking vitality" (懨懨無生氣的).[21]

Coda

The degree to which the May Fourth reinterpretation of the history of classical literature has become an unquestioned standard tells us that the past is indeed over. A few traditionalist scholars remain, but their work rarely possesses the popular authority of critics who follow the May Fourth line. Recent publications have begun to explore areas that were excluded from consideration in May Fourth literary history, but such topics tend to be done apologetically or as pure scholarship, without a claim to significant intrinsic merit that would conflict with the judgments of the May Fourth critics. Often these are areas in which the academic demand to do something new and recently untouched overwhelms the scholar's desire to do something significant.

Although the judgments and the new orthodoxy of the May Fourth critics of classical literature have remained remarkably consistent to the present (Marxist modifications essentially took them for granted, with fine-tuning), I would argue that their positions had a different meaning now than they had then. In the 1920s and 1930s, the views that they articulated existed in a tense relation to a classical literature that was still a powerful force. When Hu Yunyi's *ci* anthology first came out, someone interested in *ci* could still easily find competing Qing anthologies, and even contemporary anthologies representing Qing taste, in the bookstores. The polemical aspect of many of his comments was quite clear. The present reader can still go into a bookstore and buy a Zhonghua shuju reprint of Hu Yunyi's anthology, as well as dozens of other anthologies representing minor variations on Hu Yunyi's selections. The case of *ci* is particularly interesting. Qing anthologies and twentieth-century anthologies representing a taste in *ci* that differs from

---

21. Zheng was less successful in extending the *sanqu* tradition into the Ming. He devoted a long chapter to Ming *sanqu* in *An Illustrated History of Chinese Literature*, giving *sanqu* a full life cycle like that of *shi* and *ci*; but without the inertia of received canon, there was little interest in anything but the ideologically favored moment of origin and first flowering.

May Fourth judgments are still available. Simply by looking at bibliographies one might think that here, uniquely, is a viable challenge to May Fourth orthodoxy. But when we look at this alternative tradition, we find that the books are usually published in small print runs, use traditional characters, and have either no commentary or a brief classical commentary. The restriction of most students and the general reading public to books published in simplified characters and the increasing dependence on vernacular annotation and translation give the academic scholarly establishment the power to shape and control access to the Chinese past. In the classroom and for interested readers who have not studied in a Zhongwenxi 中 文 系, the past is radically mediated by May Fourth taste.

In the 1920s and 1930s the reinterpretation of the past was an ongoing event; it existed in relation to the still powerful classical tradition. Now the enemy is dead, and it has supplanted that tradition. But since the values of the May Fourth critics and scholars were so deeply tied to their narrative of struggle, we must wonder what remains when the Antagonist is dead.

Works Cited

Beijing daxue Zhongguo wenxue shi jiaoyan shi 北京大學中國文學史教研室, ed. 1962a. *Xian-Qin wenxue shi cankao ziliao* 先秦文學史參考資料 (Source materials for the history of pre-Qin literature). Beijing: Zhonghua.

———. 1962b. *Wei Jin Nanbeichao wenxue shi cankao ziliao* 魏晉南北朝文學史參考資料 (Source materials for the history of Wei, Jin, and Northern and Southern Dynasties literature). Beijing: Zhonghua.

Cheng Qianfan 程千帆 and Shen Zufen 沈祖棻, eds. 1983. *Gushi jinxuan* 古詩今選 (Modern selection of old-style poetry). Shanghai: Shanghai guji.

Gu Sili 顧嗣立, ed. [1694] 1987. *Yuan shi xuan* 元詩選 (Selected Yuan poetry). Beijing: Zhonghua.

Hu Shi 胡適. [1928] 1959. *Baihua wenxue shi* 白話文學史 (A history of vernacular literature). Hong Kong: Yingzhong.

———. 1927. *Guoyu wenxue shi* 國語文學史 (A history of literature in the national language). Beijing: Wenhua xueshe.

Hu Shi 胡適, ed. 1927. *Ci xuan* 詞選 (Selected lyrics). Shanghai: Shangwu.

Hu Yunyi 胡雲翼, ed. [1962] 1970. *Song ci xuan* 宋詞選 (Selected lyrics of the Song). Hong Kong: Zhonghua.

Liang Yizhen 梁乙真. [1934] 1935. *Yuan Ming sanqu xiaoshi* 元明散曲小史 (A short history of Yuan and Ming *sanqu*). Shanghai: Shangwu.

Lin Geng 林庚 and Feng Yuanjun 馮沅君, eds. 1981. *Zhongguo lidai shige xuan* 中國歷代詩歌選 (A chronological selection of Chinese poems and songs). 2 vols. in 3. Beijing: Renmin wenxue.

Ren Zhongmin 任中敏, ed. 1930. *Sanqu congkan* 散曲叢刊 (Collected reprints of *sanqu*). Shanghai: Zhonghua.

———. [1930] 1992. *Yuanqu sanbai shou* 元曲三百首 (Three hundred Yuan *sanqu*). Changsha: Yuelu.

Shen Deqian 沈德潛, ed. 1891. *Gushi yuan* 古詩源 (Origins of old-style poetry). Hunan: Sixian.

Tang Guizhang 唐圭璋, ed. 1965. *Quan Song ci* 全宋詞 (Complete lyrics of the Song). Beijing: Zhonghua.

Wang Shizhen 王士貞, ed. 1866. *Gushi xuan* 古詩選 (Selected old-style poetry). Annotated by Fang Dongshu 方東樹. Jinling: Jinling shuju.

Wang Yi 王易. [1927] 1960. *Ci qu shi* 詞曲史 (A history of lyrics and drama). Taibei: Guangwen.

Wen Yiduo 聞一多. [1938] 1982. *Shenhua yu shi* 神話與詩 (Myth and poetry). In *Wen Yiduo quanji* 聞一多全集 (Collected works of Wen Yiduo), vol. 1. Beijing: Sanlian.

———. [1940] 1982. *Yuefu shi jian* 樂府詩箋 (Notes on *yuefu* poetry). In *Wen Yiduo quanji* 聞一多全集 (Collected works of Wen Yiduo), 4: 95–137. Beijing: Sanlian.

Yu Guanying 余冠英, ed. [1958] 1978. *Han Wei Liuchao shixuan* 漢魏六朝詩選 (Selected poetry of the Han, Wei, and Six Dynasties). Beijing: Renmin wenxue.

Zheng Zhenduo 鄭振鐸. [1927] 1969. *Yanjiu Zhongguo wenxue de xin tujing* 研究中國文學的新途徑 (New course for the study of Chinese literature). Hong Kong: Longmen.

———. [1932] 1961. *Chatuben Zhongguo wenxue shi* 插圖本中國文學史 (An illustrated history of Chinese literature). Hong Kong: Shangwu.

Zhou Ji 周濟, ed. [1873] 1940. *Song sijia ci xuan* 宋四家詞選 (Selected lyrics from the four masters of the Song). Changsha: Shangwu.

Zhu Xiaozang 朱孝臧, ed. [1924] 1958. *Song ci sanbaishou* 宋詞三百首 (Three hundred lyrics of the Song). Annot. Tang Guizhang 唐圭璋. Beijing: Zhonghua.

Zhu Ziqing 朱自清, ed. 1981. *Shisijia shichao* 十四家詩鈔 (Selected poems of fourteen poets). Shanghai: Guji.

CHAPTER FIVE

The Rhetoric of Retrospection: May Fourth Literary History and the Ming-Qing Woman Writer

Ellen Widmer

One of the more striking trends in sinology of late has been its increasing engagement with a large residue of writings left by women writers of the Ming and Qing. Educated in the May Fourth belief that, with few significant exceptions, Chinese women were not writers until the May Fourth era, contemporary sinology has by turns been disoriented and delighted to learn how much writing Ming-Qing women left behind.[1] Because scholarship on these works is relatively new, I begin by giving a brief overview of this archive and of certain findings to which it has already given rise. I then turn to my central argument, which is about the process that obscured this literature for decades and the dynamics of its resuscitation in recent years.

As for the size of the archive, Hu Wenkai's 胡文楷 (fl. 1934) *Research on Chinese Women's Writings Through the Ages* (*Lidai funü zhuzuo kao* 歷代婦女著作考, 1957) lists at least 300 women who published their poems during the Ming dynasty and over 4,000 for the Qing. Most of these women published individually, although they sometimes co-published in "composite collections," *heke* 合刻, with friends and relatives, and their writings were often anthologized. This output is significant not only in its own right but also as evidence of the patterns and processes by which women fell into association

I am grateful to the Committee on Scholarly Exchange with China and to the United States Information Agency for sponsoring much of this research.

1. For example, Chow Tse-tsung states: "Although there were a number of women poets and painters in Chinese history, the traditional view of Chinese ethics was that 'lack of learning is a credit to a woman's virtue'" (1960: 257). This statement is entirely accurate, but it does not call attention to the materials with which I am concerned.

with one another. As scholars such as Paul Ropp (1976, 1994), Marsha Weidner (1988), Maureen Robertson (1992), and Dorothy Ko (1994) have begun to tell us, they reveal, in broad outline, that women who wrote during the Ming and Qing came mostly from the upper classes, that for the most part they were educated at home, that they were painters as well as poets, and that they got together in literary societies, named and unnamed, that linked family members and friends.[2] Today the most famous of the named societies are the Banana Garden Poetry Club (Jiaoyuan shishe 蕉園詩社) of the late seventeenth century and two rather differently organized groups from about a hundred years later: the Ten Women Poets of Wu (Wuzhong shizi 吳中十子), who published collectively in 1789; and a looser assembly known as "Suiyuan nü dizi" 隨園女弟子 (i.e., Yuan Mei's 袁枚 [1716–98] disciples), many of whom continued to stay in touch after the death of this mentor, either directly or as fellow mentors of Yuan's younger colleague Chen Wenshu 陳文述 (1775–1845).

Following a strong surge of activity that began in the late Ming and continued until about 1700, women's poetry networks appear to have weakened. Although women went on writing during the eighteenth century, published collections of some of the most productive reveal that their output was directed mostly at family members, not at the wider world of writing women (see, e.g., Cao Xishu 曹錫淑 in Hu Wenkai 1957: 539). Thanks to Yuan Mei and others, the late eighteenth century spells the beginning of a second period of momentum, set in motion at the end of the Qianlong reign (1736–95) (see Widmer 1997). These data further reveal that, especially during the two periods of greatest activity, women were able to establish literary reputations that transcended the bounds of family and friendship. Despite the noncommercial nature of much of this publishing, printed versions of their poetry circulated within the cloisters that separated living women from one another and reached out both to audiences who did not write back and to those who were moved to respond in kind.

Not surprisingly, given that so much of this work originated in the upper classes, Ming-Qing women's writings tended to promote rather than ques-

2. Dorothy Ko (1994) summarizes many of the findings in the field to date, especially as they pertain to the seventeenth century. Her bibliography is a good index of new scholarship as of the time of her writing. See also Paul Ropp (1994), who provides digests and critiques of a number of books and articles. For a much earlier, well-researched review of some of the same material, see Gálik 1979.

tion traditional feminine virtues, although they might do so disingenuously. By entitling a collection *Poems Saved from Burning* (variously rendered as *Fen yu cao* 焚餘草, *Fen yu ji* 焚餘集, *Fen yu shi cun* 焚餘詩存), a woman could both present her work and show her modesty about publishing it. Yet the vast majority of Ming-Qing women's poetry is devoid of political content. Because so many works reached print on the strength of gentry families' financial assets, it was unusual for them to refer to domestic turmoil in any but the most oblique of ways. Still more protective of family interests were the major anthologies edited by women, such as Wang Duanshu's (1621–ca. 1706) 王端淑 *Classics of Poetry by Famous Women* (*Mingyuan shiwei* 名媛詩緯) of 1667 and Yun Zhu's 惲珠 (1771–1833) *Collected Correct Beginnings of Gentlewomen of This Dynasty* (*Guochao guixiu zhengshi ji* 國朝閨秀正始集) of 1831. As detailed below, these anthologies follow somewhat different agendas, but they are alike in their attention to the virtue of the poet, with women of less than stellar background omitted altogether or relegated to the back pages. The type of poem that survived this sorting process was often particularly uncritical of the status quo, which is to say, particularly easy to satirize as a literature "without content" once May Fourth modernizers came along (Tan 1930: 19–21).

Boosted by Hu Wenkai's revised anthology, as well as by a growing body of analysis based on the sources he catalogued, scholars are beginning to unearth a far more complex picture from this material. Partly thanks to Hu's own orientation, which led him to select the more striking prefaces for full quotation, his bibliography is more than just a bibliography. Texts such as the following lend new insight into the dynamics through which the writing women of the Ming and Qing developed and sustained their creativity against a mentality that would have preferred to shut it down.

Luo Qilan's 駱綺蘭 preface to her collection *Gentlewoman Friends of Tingqiu Studio* (*Tingqiu guan guizhong tongren ji* 聽秋館閨中同人集) dates from 1797. Luo, a disciple of Yuan Mei, was born around 1756 and lived until at least 1808.[3] This preface reads:

> It is harder for a woman to be good at poetry than for a man. It is also harder for a gentlewoman's name to be transmitted than for a talented man's. Why is this? When one lives in complete seclusion, one hears and sees very little; moreover, one has no friends with whom to talk things over and stir the spirits, nor are there mountains and rivers

3. Luo's date of birth is established within her preface. That she was alive in 1808 is documented in Wang Qiong 1808b.

to explore as a means of stimulating one's talent. Unless she has a worthy father or elder brother to help her trace things back to their sources and distinguish truth from falsehood, there is no way she can accomplish anything. And once she marries, she must take care of the household, serve her husband's family, and tend to the details of providing food. She never has any free time. The man of talent, on the other hand, takes up official training and takes the examinations, competing for rank and reputation in the world of letters; he travels ever more broadly; the celebrities of the age follow his doings and praise them, so that his name is increasingly well known. As for the woman, only if she is lucky enough to find a companionate husband with whom she can exchange poems will her poems be cherished and transmitted, not destroyed. And if she ends up with a dolt, he will not understand what poetry is, and she might as well use her poems to cover the pickle jar.

The transmission of a woman's writings is also unbelievably difficult, although the reasons vary. In my case, I studied poetry with my father and in my youth knew the basics of prosody. When I grew up, I married Mr. Gong. Along the way we fell on hard times and stopped chanting poetry, concentrating instead on making ends meet. Next I became a widow and kept house for myself: from Yangzhou I moved to the west of Dantu, where I had an old cottage with a few rooms. By the light of an autumn lamp, I conducted classes for women, substituting my literary skills for weaving [as a way of supporting myself]. Naturally I was often short of food. Eventually, more and more people began to seek out my prefaces and paintings, but some people were suspicious, saying that the poems that came out under my studio name were all ghostwritten.

My temperament is straightforward. When they said my poems were no good, I was sincerely regretful, and I felt ashamed of myself. But when they said I was not capable of writing poems, I was rather angry and did not accept their criticism. At this point I started going here and there in the vicinity of the Yangzi River, meeting various teachers and lodging and exchanging poems with them, in order to dispel the slander about ghostwriters and block the mouths of irresponsible chatterers. My teachers were Yuan Mei, Wang Wenzhi 王文治 [1730–1802], and Zeng Ao 曾燠 [1760–1831], to whom I presented my old drafts with a request for their suggestions and corrections, which the three of them agreed to give. Those who listen rather than look might not believe me, but they would not dare disbelieve these three men. Then the doubters gave up, but discussion of me arose on a new front, to the effect that it was not proper for a married woman to write poetry, and that for me to carry on literary relationships with three gentlemen was especially immoral.

I myself believe that the *Classic of Poetry* was largely written by women [she gives examples of specific poems to prove the point]. If the great sages had followed the repressive idea that discussions within the family should not circulate outside it, then these poems would have been suppressed and forgotten. Yet the poems themselves are still preserved in the *Classic*. Why is this? Yuan Mei, Wang Wenzhi, and Zeng Ao have hoary faces and white hair. Their reputations are glorious, equal to those of the [legendary] Luo Society; thus, the talented men of this age collectively look up to them, as if they were Mount Tai or the Big Dipper. A hundred generations from now, posterity will not lack for people who have heard of their reputation and personal virtue. I deeply appreciate my chance to bask in their glory and receive their instruction. It is one of the great good fortunes of my life. To say I was wrong to have dealings with them is tantamount to saying that it is wrong for a woman to behold Mount Tai or look up at the Big Dipper. When I hear this kind of talk, I ought to laugh out loud.

Those who doubt someone's ability without knowing about it are prejudiced; those who know a person's ability and denigrate it are heartless. Prejudiced and heartless people lack the even temper appropriate to a gentleman. I am now forty-two years old. Today I read for pleasure in the Buddhist classics and enjoyed myself pursuing vacuity; then just for fun I wrote a guide to pursuing the Dao. When slanderers come my way, I believe I can keep cool. I deeply regret that I was so worried about my good name in the days that I was attracting slander. But habits are hard to change.

Whenever the light of a bright moon penetrates my curtain, I light incense and meditate, thinking about the various women far and near that I have entered into close friendship with, women I can never forget. I read their works aloud and am overwhelmed with a deep feeling that transcends the meaning of their words. It is as if I were in the company of these people. So I have put their works together, edited them, and found a publisher, in the hope that the ignorant will realize that not all women are untalented. It is just so hard for them to show it.

Superficial people should not undervalue what they see and overemphasize what they regard as strange. I edit this book both because of all that I have suffered in comparison to these others and because I would like to extend to them my good fortune of today by making their work known. (Hu Wenkai 1957: 939–40)[4]

Obviously, Luo is not seeking to overturn the rules on female chastity as May Fourth leaders would later do, yet her lament for women who chose to write and her praise for Yuan Mei give some indication of the struggle over female literacy that was taking place in her day. This passage belies the prevailing May Fourth impression that Ming-Qing woman were anesthetized into complete passivity by discriminatory Confucian norms. Although the five-plus centuries of Ming-Qing history offer peaks and valleys of feminine

4. As this chapter was going to press, I had occasion to consult the translation of Luo's preface by Irving Yucheng Lo in Chang and Saussy 1999: 703–6.

self-expression, not to mention variations by class, region, and family circumstance, Luo Qilan's passage is hardly an isolated exception that proves the rule. It aligns Luo's *Gentlewomen Friends* with the anthologies of women's poetry by women mentioned above, inasmuch as these anthologies also sought to encourage women writers by publishing their writings. On the other hand, it lacks the emphasis on correctness of behavior found in Yun Zhu's introduction to *Correct Collected Beginnings*, which implies a limit on the extent of free expression appropriate to a woman. In this rhetorical posture, Yun outdoes even Wang Duanshu, whose *Classics of Poetry by Famous Women*, while attentive to class and other nonliterary valences, was less prescriptive.[5]

Commercial publishing adds another dimension to this picture. Although most published collections were family-sponsored, it appears that publishing houses circulated women's writings for a time in the mid-seventeenth century and again during the early nineteenth century. Probably not coincidentally, both of these were also periods during which impoverished women sold their writings and paintings or hired themselves out as teachers, in contrast to the eighteenth century, when this may have happened much less frequently, if at all. One index of these periods' greater commercialization lies in the appearance of printed editions of *tanci* 彈 詞, or novel-length narrative poems, during the early Qing and the Jiaqing reign period (1796–1820), despite evidence of their availability in oral and hand-copied versions at other times (see Widmer 1997; Hu Wenkai 1957: 411–12; T. Chen 1974). Hu Siao-chen's (1994) recent doctoral dissertation on *tanci* by women writers details the light these writings shed on the stresses and strains of family living even when their manifest rhetoric is strongly in favor of domestic control.

---

5. Yun's preface is reprinted in Hu Wenkai 1957: 630–34. The difference between them is encapsulated by the difference in the way they designate their subjects: *mingyuan* 名 媛, "famous woman," could include courtesans, while the term *guixiu* 閨 秀 was confined to "gentlewoman" alone. For her emphasis on the *guixiu*, as opposed to the *mingyuan*, and the virtue she makes of "sincerity and gentleness," *dunhou wenrou* 敦 厚 溫 柔, see p. 631. Both anthologies have sections of various categories of "others" in the back pages. In Wang Duanshu's case, her end sections include courtesans, prostitutes, nuns, ghosts, Koreans, and other foreigners; in Yun's case there are no nuns or ghosts, just a few courtesans and prostitutes, and a notice carefully advises the reader that these writers are not, properly speaking, *guixiu*. After this comes a final section on Korean *guixiu*. Susan Mann's *Precious Records* (1997) is significantly about Yun Zhu.

It is not clear when women began writing *tanci*, but the dates of Hou Zhi 侯芝, the first female editor of this type of writing, are approximately 1764 to 1829.[6] Hou was the woman most responsible for bringing *tanci* to press during the Jiaqing reign. She is one of the friends to whom Luo Qilan's preface refers and can also be linked to other Yuan Mei disciples as well as the Ten Women Poets of Wu. Drama was another genre authored by women during the Ming and Qing (Tan 1930: 308–67; Xu Fuming 1986: 270–80; Hua 1998), and the era produced at least one work of fiction by a woman, a historical novel about the late Yuan entitled *Lost History of the Yuan and Ming* (*Yuan Ming yishi* 元明遺史), by the celebrated poet and critic Wang Duan 王端 (1793–1839), Chen Wenshu's daughter-in-law (Hummel 1943: 839–40). Wang Duan burned this work before it reached print.

The full import of this material is only now beginning to be recognized. At the very least, it suggests several ways in which premodern China was capable of internally generated evolution, as opposed to change brought about in response to Western imperialistic encroachment. The movement generated by Yuan Mei and his disciples in particular, although it faced considerable resistance, appears to have stimulated women to write in several genres, and its influence continued until the end of the Qing.

The Problem of the Past in Traditional Women's Literature

The problem posed by depictions of traditional women's writings in the twentieth century lies not in the perception that they were passé. Few would deny that premodern women's writings were too closely linked to traditional Chinese family culture to be able to serve modern ends. The problem is that many of the signs of proto-feminism in China's literary past—signs to which Hu's work gives access but which were also accessible before it—do not seem to have impressed May Fourth literary historians, feminist though many of them were. Rather, these historians constructed narratives that, if they mentioned Ming-Qing women's writings at all, emphasized certain

6. Hou's date of birth is established in Hou Zhi 1811, a preface to writings by Jiang Zhu 江珠, one of the Ten Women Poets of Wu. Her date of death is documented by her son, Mei Cengliang (see Zhang 1981: 1434). Hou can also be connected with Wang Qiong 王瓊 (fl. 1808), another disciple of Yuan Mei. Wang's poems to Hou are found in her *Selected Poems of Ailan Studio* (*Ailan xuan shixuan* 愛蘭軒詩選). My "The Trouble with Talent" (1999) gives more detail. On Wang's status as a disciple of Yuan Mei, see Goyama 1985: 131. I am indebted to Dorothy Ko for supplying me with a copy of this source.

features over others, cannibalizing the old tradition even as they recast it in new terms. At the same time, men and women schooled in the old order continued a process of preservation that can be traced as far back as Chen Wenshu. This tradition can be represented by the career of Xu Naichang 徐乃昌 (1862–1936), a late Qing collector and publisher of traditional writings whose *Transcribed Lyrics of Gentlewomen* (*Guixiu cichao* 閨秀詞鈔) of 1909 is one of several classical anthologies in the field (Hu Wenkai 1957: 856–61, 924–25). It is from this and similar efforts that much of Hu Wenkai's work derives.[7]

Chronologically, if not ideologically, these more conservative voices were a part of the May Fourth era. As I describe below, many such scholars remained active in the first several decades of the twentieth century, and some worked into the 1940s. Yet, from the perspective of May Fourth, theirs was a retrograde motion, conserving rather than supplanting, which worked against the prevailing mood of erasure to which May Fourth imperatives had given rise. This act of erasure constitutes one of the more intriguing features of May Fourth reactions to Ming-Qing women writers. It is not only that May Fourth leaders disregarded evidence that might have made their own feminism look less pathbreaking. It is that the "burden" of their break with feudalism was so total as to submerge evidence of this old system's own efforts at self-reform, knowledge of which is only now re-entering the scholarly mainstream.

What follows is a look at three approaches by leading May Fourth literary historians to women writers of the Ming and Qing. Together, these approaches provide complementary lines of insight into the question of what role "the past" played for May Fourth modernizers, what about it struck them as worth preserving, and why, in this past, much of traditional women's writing tended to fade from view. After that I offer three examples of more conservative interpretations of this same subject matter, interpretations appearing more or less contemporaneously with the other three, but outside the framework of "enlightenment" (Schwarz 1986), to which the first three belong. Ultimately, these contrasting approaches are used as background to a concluding section on Hu Wenkai's *Research on Chinese Women's*

---

7. Xu was a descendant of Liang Desheng 梁德繩, a well-known woman writer. Liang was the second author (after Chen Duansheng 陳端生) of the most outstanding *tanci*, *Love Destiny Reborn* (*Zaisheng yuan* 再生緣). On Xu's relationship to Liang, see Hu Wenkai 1957: 565.

Writings Through the Ages, a work indebted to both schools of thought as well as to late Qing scholars like Xu Naichang.

Three Approaches to Women in May Fourth Literary History

In his "Zheng Zhenduo and the Invention of Chinese Literary History," Marston Anderson (1991) identifies some of the imperatives that lay behind Zheng Zhenduo's 鄭 振 鐸 (1898–1958) *Illustrated History of Chinese Literature* (*Chatuben Zhongguo wenxue shi* 插 圖 本 中 國 文 學 史, 1932), his *History of Chinese Popular Literature* (*Zhongguo su wenxue shi*, 中 國 俗 文 學 史, 1938), and other works. Crucial to Zheng's enterprise, in Anderson's opinion, was the notion of a literature that evolves and, thus, that expresses the evolving concerns of the masses. Radically iconoclastic toward China's "high literature," which he regarded as blocking or preventing true literary expression, Zheng singled out popular literature (*su wenxue* 俗 文 學), as the place to look for the expressive potential that lies at the heart of his definition of what literature should be. Although the main point of the *History of Chinese Popular Literature* is to single out dynamic moments in China's literary history, not to celebrate women writers, it does touch on their work incidentally, especially in the discussion of *tanci*, which it puts forward as an important category of popular literature.

Zheng's book advances in time by identifying the genre or genres that lay at the heart of each dynasty's accomplishment. With the Ming and Qing, these include fiction and drama, which Zheng sets aside for treatment in another book, as well as the more popular genres that are the main subject of discussion here. Zheng regards the division between high and popular cultures as particularly acute, to the point of great antagonism, during the Qing. In this construction, Qing poetry, by now moribund and repressive, contributes nothing of value to, indeed actually impedes, literature's forward march (Zheng 1938: 17).

Tanci and other popular genres, by contrast, become the site of positive value in Qing literature. Zheng's treatment stresses the anonymity of the authors of all forms of popular literature and the tendency of this literature to be composed in oral, performance-related ways. The specifics of his definition make for some dissonance when it comes to "women's *tanci*," which he distinguishes from *tanci* of other kinds. Unlike these others, women's *tanci* are usually by identifiable authors, and their most prominent early editor, Hou Zhi, is a woman whose name is also known. Moreover, "women's *tanci*" fit much less securely under the rubric of oral and performative literature than other types of *tanci* and other popular genres. They challenge the notion of authorial anonymity by expressing the concerns of specific authors, a point borne out in Zheng's discussion of *Love Destiny Reborn* (*Zai sheng yuan* 再生緣), authored by poets Chen Duansheng 陳端生 (1751–96?) and Liang Desheng 梁德繩 (1771–1847). Zheng made a distinction between the initial part of the work by Chen Duansheng, which he sees as fresh and iconoclastic, and Liang's concluding chapters, which make visible compromises with prevailing norms. Working his way around these minor problems, Zheng makes it clear that what he really cares about in this literature are the fresh and sincere feelings that define these works as popular. Unlike poetry, which women regarded as the province of male writers, *tanci* offered them the opportunity to speak their minds. Zheng went on to talk about the comparative ignorance of history on the part of the women who enjoyed this medium. However, except to mention that the women who wrote them lived in "the inner chamber," he says nothing about the class background from which they came. Class, it would seem, is essentially irrelevant when a woman is a popular writer. Because all women knew little, all might as well have been déclassé. Indeed, their expressions of frustration were enhanced by their freedom from class-based learning and moribund literary forms (Zheng 1938: 370–81, 21, 348).

Zheng's emphasis on the fresh, the spontaneous, and the expressive becomes still more obvious when one looks more closely into the data from which his survey was drawn, data Zheng certainly was aware of, although he may not have studied them in detail. Had Zheng not been writing in such broad outline, his distinction between poetry and popular forms of writing would have been more difficult to sustain. Not only were all the women who wrote *tanci* also poets; their *tanci* were produced in a context reminiscent of the more elevated literary levels on which they normally functioned. Thus, the prefaces and identifiable editors of *tanci* by women that appeared during the Jiaqing era reflect the well-established traditions of women's poetry with which their authors were quite familiar, since they left behind works in those genres as well. Familiar, too, is the habit of endorsement by the editor's friends. Luo Qilan is among those known to have written a poem on a *tanci* edited by Hou Zhi, *Blossoms on Brocade* (*Jinshang hua* 錦上花); and a poem commemorating what must be Liang's version of *Love Destiny Reborn* is found in the poetry of Gui Maoyi 歸懋儀, Yuan Mei's disciple before she made her way to Chen Wenshu (Hu Wenkai 1957: 411–12).[8] In this way, the social background of women *tanci* writers is actually more relevant to the form of this type of writing than Zheng makes it out to be.

As with other writing women, those who can be identified as *tanci* writers came from families in which the male members expected to have official careers. This meant that their husbands, fathers, and brothers were cultivated people, who could see to the education of family women and very often helped them to publish their writings. That Chen Duansheng was related to Chen Wenshu, Hou Zhi was the mother of the well-known literatus Mei Cengliang 梅曾亮 (1786–1856), and Liang Desheng was raised in and married into a household of respected scholars was clearly important in the kind of education they had and the confidence with which they approached their role as writers.[9] A full assessment of the lives of these literate women suggests that certain of Zheng's starkest oppositions—between poetry and *tanci* in particular—should be recast in softer terms.

Conversely, the impression one gains from Zheng's work that all the expressiveness in traditional literature is found in popular genres is not completely true of traditional women. Earlier, Luo Qilan's preface was invoked to show the benefits of Yuan Mei's protection; it could also be cited as a sign of women's ability to use traditional genres for contentious ends. Similarly, the poetry of women linked to *tanci*, though often highly conservative, is capable of raising questions about women's roles. For instance, the first stanza of a poem by Wang Qiong 王瓊 (fl. 1808), a friend of both Hou Zhi and Luo Qilan, describes the late Ming female general Qin Liangyu 秦良玉, in the following terms:

The Female General Qin Liangyu 女總兵秦良玉

Commanding in Shizhu [Sichuan], her troops were broadly arrayed.	指揮石砫陣雲橫
For this woman is remembered as a general.	環佩能傳大將名
Could it have been her husband who truly saved the dynasty?	豈有丈夫真報國

8. "Peixiang" 佩香, who endorsed *Blossoms on Brocade*, is Luo Qilan. See also Gui 1823: 4.9b–10a. Gui's poem is entitled "On the *Chuanqi Love Destiny Reborn*" ("Ti *Zai sheng yuan chuanqi*" 題再生緣傳奇). It refers to the heroine's marriage in the final stanza. This is how one knows it applies to Liang's revised version of the text.

9. On Chen Duansheng's connection to Chen Wenshu, see Tan 1930: 388–9. On Liang's relationships, see Hummel 1943: 324. On Hou Zhi's relationship to Mei, see Hu Wenkai 1957: 411.

No, it was the woman who best
understood war. 由來女子最知兵

—Wang Qiong 1808a: 5b, stanza 1 of 2

In its celebration of unusual feminine accomplishment, this poem echoes emphases in such women's *tanci* as *Love Destiny Reborn*, whose heroine disguised herself as a male, attained the highest rank in the civil service examination, and became a prime minister. This poem is not radically different in spirit from the following stanza of a juvenile work by the celebrated woman-revolutionary Qiu Jin 秋 瑾 (?1879–1907), also about Qin Liangyu (and another woman warrior), that was written on the eve of the May Fourth era:

Endorsing *Zhikanji* 提芝龕記

Do not overvalue men and undervalue women.	莫重男兒薄女兒
Granting [Qin Liangyu] an audience, the emperor favored her with poems.	平臺詩句賜蛾眉
When we heard of her, women like me took heart.	吾儕得此添生色
We began to believe that we, too, could be heroes.	始信英雄亦有雌

—Qiu 1982: 55–56, stanza 3 of 8

Neither Wang nor Qiu are quite feminist by modern standards, but Qiu, at least, was taken seriously by the May Fourth movement, whereas poems of earlier Qing women like Wang Qiong were consigned to oblivion, along with prefaces like Luo Qilan's.

Similarly, Zheng Zhenduo's blanket assertion that women associated with *tanci* knew little history needs qualification. Liang Desheng's surviving work, in particular, establishes that she had an excellent education, and she served for a time as tutor to her niece Wang Duan, one of the best female historians and literary critics of the Qing (Hummel 1943: 839). Here, however, Zheng may be right in principle, for the women poets who wrote *tanci* do not emphasize their learning in this genre. Zheng's categorization may have merit in another respect as well. As Chen Yinke 陳 寅 恪 (1890–1969) would later argue (1975), Chen Duansheng's life was hard despite her elevated origins. Without her long periods of living alone and her husband's troubles with the law, she might never have experienced the frustration that sets her work apart from other *tanci* and makes her contribution particularly evocative for the modern world. Conceivably, there is a relationship between the fact that she thought and wrote so much more uncompromisingly than Hou Zhi, Liang Desheng, and the others and the scarcity of biographical data about her, for unlike her sister Chen Changsheng 陳長生, she cannot be traced in the writings of Yuan Mei and others. In the near anonymity of its principal author as well as in its popularity, *Love Destiny Reborn* may be closer to Zheng's definition of popular literature than many writings by upper-class women of its time.

The point, obviously, is not to find fault with Zheng's treatment, which can be defended on many grounds, but rather to understand the imperatives that led him to emphasize one side of the picture over others. Driven by a definition of literature that put a premium on expressive and evolutionary potential, Zheng took the occasion to look past traditionally esteemed genres and to disconnect popular literature from the literati, even when the facts only partly justified these moves. Had his agenda been otherwise, he might have recast some of his generalities, accommodating them more closely to the realities represented by Chen Duansheng, Liang Desheng, Hou Zhi, Luo Qilan, Wang Qiong, and their friends.

Tan Zhengbi's (b. 1901) 譚正璧 *Historical Discussion of Chinese Women's Literature* (*Zhongguo nüxing wenxue shihua* 中國女性文學史話, 1930) shares many key assumptions with Zheng Zhenduo, in particular that literature is most effective when it evolves along with society and thus gives voice to "the feelings of the times" (21). Tan, like Zheng, endorsed a model of literary development that highlights leading genres for each dynasty. Marston Anderson discusses this model in connection with Zheng's work, arguing that "most [May Fourth literary historians] accepted the traditional notion that there was a natural correspondence between dynastic alternations and literary change; they continued mechanically to assign particular genres to particular dynasties in which they were thought to have flourished" (1991). In fact, Tan was more serious about this model than Zheng, who saw several popular genres as dynamic, perhaps as dynamic as fiction and drama, during the Ming and Qing. Tan's work also differs in its emphasis, for he took literature by women as his principal subject, not as something that arose only secondarily, when women turned to popular genres.

Tan's application of the leading-genre-per-dynasty model to the history of women's literature means, of course, that he concentrated primarily on women who wrote *fu* 賦 during the Han, *yuefu* 樂府 during the Six Dynasties, and so forth. Yet he often retreated from this evolutionary emphasis in his discussion of particular dynasties. With Zheng's work, too, the emergence of new popular forms appears to be mainly spontaneous; indeed spontaneity is one of their chief virtues, for they can thus escape the more mechanical correspondences between established literature and historical change. In Tan's case, the weakness of the generic/dynastic model of evolution is evident in the discussion of Ming and Qing fiction and drama. Although these are the dominant genres of the era, he cannot spend much time discussing them, since women wrote so little in these forms. Rather, he simply notes that women did contribute in these categories, even when he cannot say what their work was about or when it was written. But he provides no reassurance that women's several dramas or the two novels he cited as being by women (Wang Duan's *Lost History of the Yuan and Ming* among them) move beyond the "contentless" birds and flowers of traditional women's poetry, of which he did not approve (Tan 1930: 21, 330–78).

Like Zheng Zhengduo, Tan Zhengbi has much to say about "women's *tanci*." One of his goals was to emphasize this genre's more or less continuous development throughout the Qing. Thus he has almost nothing to say about the very long interval between the first example of this form, *Heaven Rains Flowers* (*Tian yu hua* 天 雨 花) in 1651, and a new edition in 1804 (see Xiong Deji 1979), around the time Hou Zhi's edited *tanci* began to be widely known. The dampening effect on women's literature of censorship in the meantime, for example, or the uplift when men like Yuan Mei took up the women writers' cause—all may be crucial to a full understanding of how *tanci* evolved. But Tan's net was set too loosely to address these patterns of change.

Tan's professedly feminist agenda may be one reason for a related tendency in his writing to downplay the support extended to women writers by sympathetic males, such as Yuan Mei. This, too, might be set forth as a contrast to Zheng's work. Although Zheng does not mention Yuan, the omission is not striking, since his emphasis throughout was on the fate of "popular" literature, not the contributions of individuals. But when Tan mentions Yuan, it is only to suggest that improprieties in his conduct made it harder for later males to support women writers as Yuan had done (1930: 18). Not only does this mean that Yuan's vast support for women is significantly underreported, Tan also makes little or no mention of Yuan's several contemporaries and successors, such as the poet and calligrapher Wang Wenzhi and Chen Wenshu, who likewise braved negative public opinion when they taught women and published their poems. And, of course, it does not raise questions about the allegations of improper conduct, which could have been trumped up or at least exaggerated by Yuan's enemies, because of his help to women like Luo Qilan.

Tan's feminism leads, further, to a slightly recast version of Zheng's progressive and regressive literary forces. In contrast to Zheng, in whose writings such oppositions are primarily generic—progressive *tanci* versus regressive poetry during the Qing, for example—Tan tends to view the achievements of his leading women writers as a triumph over the oppressive force of patriarchy. This makes for at least one specific point of disagreement between them. To Zheng it is not particularly worrisome—in fact it is rather plausible—that the first important women's *tanci*, Tao Zhenhuai's 陶真懷 *Heaven Rains Flowers*, may have been written by a man (Zheng 1938: 371–72). Since authorship is always hard to pin down in popular literature, this uncertainty about *Heaven Rains Flowers'* origins makes it more, not less, true to form. For Tan, on the other hand, although he mentions this possibility as a rumor, it undermines his affirmation of women's accomplishments, and he dismisses it out of hand (1930: 382).

Another difference is Tan's greater willingness to turn to poetry as a source of biographical information about his woman *tanci* authors. Although admitting that much poetry by women committed the error (from a May Fourth standpoint) of crying when there was nothing wrong, he is much more receptive than Zheng to the possibility that this poetry could, upon occasion, express true feelings. Yet even on this point, Tan was somewhat under the thrall of the leading-genre-per-dynasty model. I take this to be the reason that he does not explore Ming and Qing poetry by women for its own sake or in detail. Thus he misses many ways in which women's literature outside *tanci* proved responsive to historical developments, as in poetry tinged with loyalism during the late Ming and early Qing (see Widmer 1997) or in nineteenth-century poems about war and foreign invasion (see Qian 1869).

Moreover, Tan, like Zheng, paid no attention to criticism and to editing, whole new areas for women writers beginning in the late Ming. Although men had worked in such capacities for centuries by the time women took them up, the change for women writers after women gained editorial prominence was not insignificant, for with this change they began to have a role in establishing the canon. For the most part, the object of their editorial and critical writings was the work of other women, but this was not always so.[10]

---

10. For example, Wang Duan 1822 is wholly about male writers. Xiong Lian 1845 (written several decades before publication) discusses the work of both women and men. Information

As previously mentioned, women's editorial work could suppress as well as celebrate female talent, and it tended to emphasize virtue among other evaluative categories; yet there is no doubt that many women writers sought to place their works in the new anthologies of women's works by women editors (see Chang 1997). Tan's discussion of *tanci* does mention the work of Hou Zhi, this genre's most distinguished editor, yet his best analogy for her editorial exertions are Feng Menglong's 馮 夢 龍 (ca. 1574–ca. 1646) and Ling Mengchu's 凌 濛 初 (1580–1644) volumes of Ming short stories, not Wang Duanshu's *Classics of Poetry by Famous Women* and other collections with women editors, of which he makes no mention at all (Tan 1930: 398).

Had he taken poetry and criticism more seriously, Tan might have had reason to tone down another of his points, that women enjoyed *tanci* more than fiction, although he may be correct on balance. Women certainly took a new interest in fiction after *The Dream of the Red Chamber* (*Honglou meng* 紅 樓 夢) appeared in print, for the writings of a number of late eighteenth- and early nineteenth-century women give their responses to this masterpiece. Moreover, certain publishers appear to have catered to this interest—Wang Xilian's 王 希 廉 1832 edition of *The Dream of the Red Chamber* publishes poems by his wife Zhou Qi 周 綺 among the prefatory materials; and the 1828 edition of Li Ruzhen's 李汝珍 (ca. 1763–1830) *Flowers in the Mirror* (*Jing hua yuan* 鏡 花 緣) publishes congratulatory poems by readers, including four by women (see Widmer 1997). This latter point, in conjunction with evidence linking several of Li Ruzhen's friends with women's poetry and poetry societies, may ultimately show that *Flowers in the Mirror*'s satire of foot-binding derives, at least in part, from the new thinking about women associated with Yuan Mei. Poetry provides better insight than *tanci* into fiction's growing currency among women readers in the wake of *The Dream of the Red Chamber*, although *tanci* too bear evidence of this change. Yet such nuances slip through the net of the leading-genre-per-dynasty model, which in any case is geared to production not reception, as Anderson observes (1991).

Let me emphasize, once again, that to make such observations is not to take issue with a leading scholar's basic project, which has had the effect of advancing *tanci* study to a whole new stage. The point, as with Zheng, is to identify certain parts of his agenda that help to account for emphases and omissions. I would attribute many of the idiosyncrasies in Tan's work to the

---

on Xiong's work is found in Shen Shanbao's 沈 善 寶 preface to her *Mingyuan shihua* 名 媛 詩話 (Remarks on poetry by famous women), on which see Hu Wenkai 1957: 367.

leading-genre-per-dynasty model, but it is certainly further colored by his wish to set forth women's literary accomplishment in staunchly feminist terms. This accounts, at least in part, for his de-emphasis of male mentoring, as well as for his celebration of *tanci*, where a diminished debt to masculine models can be claimed. It also accounts for a slight defensiveness when it comes to women's performance as writers in the fields of fiction and drama. Commenting on their lateness in entering these areas of literary development, he explains that their cloistered existence cut them off from the more rambunctious genres (Tan 1930: 21). Had he known about their responsiveness to these forms as readers—to *The Dream of the Red Chamber* and *Flowers in the Mirror* in particular—he might have accounted for this lateness in other ways.

Liang Yizhen's 梁乙真 (b. 1900) work offers a third perspective on what motivated May Fourth scholars when they sought to write women into the literary tradition. Focusing exclusively on poetry, Liang escapes some of the problems of the leading-genre-per-dynasty model, although he, too, uses dynasty as a primary organizing concept. Within dynastic boundaries, both his *History of Qing Dynasty Women's Literature* (*Qingdai funü wenxue shi* 清代婦女文學史, 1925) and his *Historical Outline of Chinese Women's Literature* (*Zhongguo funü wenxue shigang* 中國婦女文學史綱, 1930) proceed more or less chronologically. Liang's treatment is centrally concerned with individual women poets, whom he groups according to such divergent categories as political affiliation (Ming loyalist women), mentors (Yuan Mei's disciples), geographical location (Fujian writers), and social category (courtesans).

Like Zheng's and Tan's, Liang's affirmation of women writers is a rewriting of more orthodox constructions, but his attitude is less Manichaean and his overhaul less extensive than theirs. Unlike Zheng, Liang was well aware of poetry's expressive powers, even during the Ming and Qing. His treatment, although it mentions *tanci*, does so only incidentally; he finds no special virtue in women's popular writing (Liang 1925: 131). And unlike Tan, Liang accords full honors to male mentors, organizing several sections around men like Yuan Mei, Chen Wenshu, and Zeng Guofan 曾國藩 (1811–72). Judging only from his work on the Ming and Qing, Liang's treatment seems closer than Zheng's or Tan's to the picture that emerges in women's writings of those periods, in which *tanci* operated somewhere on the margins and male family members and teachers occupied prominent roles.

This is not to say that Liang's studies answer all the questions I have raised in conjunction with Zheng and Tan. Quite vague about historical dating within dynastic categories, he tends to lose sight of the links between literary and historical change. Liang's argument that a leading mentor of the Banana Garden Poetry Club, Gu Ruopu 顧若璞, the club itself, and Yuan Mei are evolutionarily connected, for example, completely sidesteps the point that Gu and the Banana Garden women were contemporaries and personally acquainted, and that the relationship between the first two and Yuan, both in terms of lapsed time and artistic indebtedness, is so distant as to suggest rupture rather than continuity (Liang 1930: 404). Needless to say, his vagueness about time means that he did not comment on other manifestations of discontinuity, as when Chen Wenshu and his female associates sought to reintroduce late Ming women poets like Feng Xiaoqing 馮小青 and Liu Rushi 柳如是 (1618–1664) into the consciousness of contemporary women during the early nineteenth century (see Hummel 1943: 103–4). And because he was unconcerned about narrative or editing, he did no better than Zheng or Tan at showing how women's literature operated across a range of genres. Moreover, Liang's division of writers into groupings obscures cross-group relationships. For example, he does not discuss important connections between courtesans and gentry women at the end of the Ming, and he has little to say about the significant number of women who migrated to Chen Wenshu's orbit after the death of Yuan Mei. Yet such silences and divisions seem to me to be attributable to the introductory nature of his studies rather than to a hidden agenda or to revisionist concerns.

This is not to say that Liang's studies are completely agenda-free. Given Liang's detailed reading of the poetic record, it is striking that he spends so little time on one of the most outstanding features of Qing poetry, its production by Manchus as well as Chinese. For, beginning as early as the early eighteenth century, one finds examples of important Manchu woman poets, and new Manchu women writers continue to appear throughout the Qing. Often their collected poems came out in unusually fine editions, and their social level appears to have been particularly high (Hu Wenkai 1957: 608, 776, 813). Additionally, male Manchus and their friends in bannermen circles were prominently involved in supporting the publication of poems by Chinese women, as well as by Manchu and Mongol women writing in Chinese. One of the most important bannermen of the mid-Qing, the Mongol Fa-shi-shan 法式善 (1753–1813; Hummel 1943: 227), for example, wrote several prefaces to collections of women's poems (see Sun 1959: 504; Hu Wenkai 1957: 699, 762, 776). His mother, a consort of Heshun 和順, the overseer of the Imperial Army, is said to have played an important role in his education, and he was interested in women writers throughout his lifetime.

Yun Zhu, whose editorial project is mentioned above, is another example of the ethnic blurring that took place at this time (Hu Wenkai 1957: 630–36). Yun was married to a Manchu. Her son, Linqing 麟慶 (1791–1846), was a prominent Manchu intellectual (Hummel 1943: 506–7; Mann 1997), and she herself had many friends in the Manchu and Chinese banner communities, among them *The Dream of the Red Chamber*'s second author, Gao E 高鶚 (ca. 1740–ca. 1815), who wrote a preface to one of her poetry collections in 1814 (Hu Wenkai 1957: 630–36). Here again, fiction and poetry show points of intersection, despite their treatment in May Fourth literary history, whose tendency to relegate them to antithetical, progressive and regressive, categories of literature helped obscure such ties. Manchu rule may have dampened Han energies in many areas of endeavor, but the indications are that it was supportive of women poets, who flourished under Manchu control.

Liang's *History of Qing Dynasty Women's Literature* does have a short section on the leading Manchu woman writer Gu Taiqing 顧太清 (1799–ca. 1875), but this separate treatment de-emphasizes her close connections with Chen Wenshu's household; and in his discussion of Yun Zhu, Liang fails to mention her Manchu husband, emphasizing rather her own Chinese genealogy, which includes the famous painter Yun Shouping 惲壽平 (1633–90). Moreover, in the slightly later *Historical Outline of Chinese Women's Literature*, Liang Yizhen completely sidesteps this issue, referring to the many apolitical poems that were written during the late Qing and then turning his attention in his final pages to the patriotic, anti-Manchu writings of Qiu Jin (1930: 419–28). It would appear that uneasiness about this subject may have caused him to blur certain ties between Manchus and Chinese.

Had he addressed this issue more directly, Liang would have found ample evidence to support the view that "collaboration" was not a simple matter for either side. Even among banner people, it must have been quite complicated, as evidenced by several examples of their antiquarian interest in Chinese figures of the Ming and Qing.[11] On the Chinese side, Chen Wenshu's household both honored the memories of Ming loyalists and maintained

11. For example, Fa-shi-shan once undertook a study of Ming Grand Secretary Li Dongyang 李東陽 and Linqing was proud to own land that had previously belonged to Li Yu 李漁; see Hummel 1943: 227, 507.

friendships with Manchus. It may have been in response to this apparent contradiction that so much of Wang Duan's written work is about loyalists to the Yuan, another dynasty in which Chinese and "barbarians" coexisted. Yet such complexities are invisible in *Historical Outline of Chinese Women's Literature*. Whether this simplification stemmed from Liang's personal convictions, or whether the times themselves militated against frank discussion of the Manchu issue, he was not interested in calling attention to cooperation between Manchus and Chinese.

Liang's rewriting of the past provides important insight into the questions posed at the beginning of the chapter. His defensiveness about the Manchu issue points to yet another role the past could play as far as the present was concerned. For nationalistic Chinese of the May Fourth era who happened to be interested in traditional women, it was reassuring to be able to defend their subject of study as consistent with modern goals. Women of the late Ming and early Qing were unproblematic because all the famous women writers of that era—courtesans as well as gentry—were Ming loyalists; and Ming loyalism called for a China ruled by Chinese. In contrast, a second "problem of the past" arose in the second half of the Qing, when "women's literature" began to include more writings by Manchus and when male mentors included more Mongols, Manchus, and their friends. The taint of collaboration that could have been read into the networks supportive of women by the end of the Qianlong era appears to have worried Liang Yizhen; by extension, it would have raised suspicions about Liang's project among his fellow patriots in modern times.

Ying-shih Yü has suggested that Liang's scholarly activity, his writing style, and the way he approached his subject align him more closely with late Qing currents than with May Fourth scholarship, despite the fact that his works were published in the 1920s.[12] It is on the strength of his comment that I turn, now, to three examples of what might comfortably be called a late Qing style of scholarship, although they came out after the end of the Qing. These were not literary histories but rather anthologies and bibliographies, often put together by women scholars who were themselves close to the *guixiu* 閨秀 tradition. Together, these scholars provide a basis for deciding whether Liang's work can or cannot be categorized as truly "May Fourth" in style.

12. Remarks prompted by the first draft of this paper, delivered at the Prague Conference, August 1994.

Anthologizing Ming-Qing Women's Writings in Republican China

Ambiguously dated, Shan Shili's 單士釐 *Sequel to Continued Collected Correct Beginnings of Qing Gentlewomen* (*Qing guixiu zhengshi zaixuji* 清閨秀正始再續集) came out in installments, with all but the final section in print by 1918. If one accepts the date 1918 for the entire collection, this would make it the first to appear of the three more conservative examples. In contrast to some of Shan's other works, this date is figured in the old stem-branch system, suggesting that she approached the poetry of gentlewomen in a conservative mode.[13] This work is also traditional in its classical language, its organization by individual biography, its address to women readers, and the style and method of printing—in imitation Song font by family press, family publication being the main venue for upper-class women poets of the Ming and Qing. The title and prefaces, further, identify this collection as a sequel to Yun Zhu's work, which it seeks to update with new data collected since Yun's time. Not surprisingly, this collection also inherits all of Yun Zhu's emphases. Its orientation toward the *guixiu* reader means that it pays no heed to courtesans, as well as to non-courtesan women such as Qiu Jin, whose behavior as a wife left something to be desired.

The circles in which Shan traveled and her periods of residence in Japan make it inconceivable that she had not heard of Qiu by 1918. She must also have been aware of Qiu's poetry, which was widely quoted, although Qiu's *tanci* might have escaped her notice. Thus, it is reasonable to infer meaning in the fact that Qiu's name does not appear in *Sequel to Continued Collected Correct Beginnings*. More exclusively than Yun Zhu, whose appendix on "non-*guixiu*" includes courtesans, Shan concentrates on women whose lives and writings could be taken as models for other wives. Qiu's masculine dress and military activity would have placed her beyond the pale of acceptability in Shan's eyes, even had Qiu held fast to family ties. Unlike celebrated courtesans and palace ladies of the late Ming, who posed no problems for anthologists since their patriotism did not come at the expense of family, Qiu's

---

13. Her travel diary (Shan 1904) gives all dates in both Chinese and Western calendars. Her collection of poetry (Shan 1900) also pays close attention to the question of dating. See Shan 1900: 25 for an example of a poem about the turn of the (Western) century.

combination of identities—as patriot and as married woman—tested categorizations of the old style.

Also following Yun Zhu, Shan accorded equal honor to Manchu *guixiu* and Chinese. Shan's other writings establish that she was moved by modern nationalism, but this was expressed as resentment at Western imperialism, not primarily as embarrassment at the long collaboration between Manchus and Chinese under the Qing.[14] However, in the context of the May Fourth movement, Shan's inclusion of Manchu writers could be viewed as a reactionary gesture, quite different from Yun Zhu's simultaneous embrace of Chinese and Manchus in 1831. Shan is like Yun, finally, in her neglect of *tanci*. Thus, Shan's update on Liang Desheng is silent about Liang's work on *Love Destiny Reborn*, as Yun herself had been. However, this omission has less political resonance than Shan's other editorial choices. She may not have known of May Fourth interest in *tanci* and hence may not have been writing against that interest when she refrained from commenting on this form.

Published in 1922, the pseudonymous (but presumably female) Hong Meige Zhuren's 紅梅閣主人 *Transcribed Poems of Qing Dynasty Gentlewomen* (*Qingdai guixiu shichao* 清代閨秀詩鈔) offers another glimpse into how Ming-Qing women were set forth at this time. At first glance, the dual dating of 1922 for this text—both *minguo* 民國 11 and *renxu* 壬戌—suggests a slightly less conservative posture than Shan Shili's in *Sequel to Continued Collected Correct Beginnings*. However, the format and the language imply a range of identifications similar to Shan's. Moreover, this work makes a more explicit point of emphasizing wifely virtue, deemed no less important than poetic talent as a criterion of selections, according to the prefatory materials. In contrast, Shan's invocation of Yun Zhu's title alone suffices to announce her identification with this pair of goals. Naturally, names of husbands and mentors are an inevitable feature of every biography, as was normal in this style; nor is it surprising, given the title, that poetry is the main focus. Thus, women who wrote only *tanci* do not appear. The only real point of contrast between this work and Shan's is that *Transcribed Poems of Qing Dynasty Gentlewomen* pays almost no attention to Manchu women poets.[15] This time,

14. Examples of her patriotism are sprinkled throughout Shan 1904. For a summary, see the introduction by Zhong Shuhe 鍾叔河 (Shan 1904: 12–16).

15. She does mention Wanyan Dui 完顏兌 in section 4, but the names of most other prominent Manchus are not included.

because the author is anonymous, one cannot turn to other materials to establish whether a particular omission is deliberate; moreover, the collection is less comprehensive and systematic than other works in the same vein. However, Qiu Jin's absence is consistent with this work's prescriptive view of female virtue and its identification with Yun Zhu's goals. *Transcribed Poems of Qing Dynasty Gentlewomen*'s relative lack of attention to Manchus, in contrast to the works on which it draws, may imply a deliberate departure from earlier works in this style.

Published in the same year, Shi Shuyi's 施淑儀 *Anthology of Qing Dynasty Gentlewomen Poets* (*Qingdai guige shiren zhenglüe* 清代閨閣詩人徵略) stands at a certain remove from its two intellectual neighbors. Introductory materials affirm its debt to Yun Zhu, among other traditional anthologies, and the classical biographical style is again familiar, but the *Anthology of Qing Dynasty Gentlewomen Poets* quietly abandons Yun's privileging of wifely virtue as a standard of good poetry. Thus, virtue simply fails to be mentioned as a criterion of selection in the prefatory section. This important omission may explain, in part, the long and enthusiastic entry on Qiu Jin on the concluding page. Yet, unlike Liang Yizhen, Shi Shuyi is not so nationalistic that she obscures Manchus and Mongols altogether. Rather, she relegates them to an appendix, along with nuns and other women whose family names are not known. In all other respects, this anthology is typical of older works—in its focus on poetry, its omission of *tanci* writers, and its references to husbands and mentors in the biographical materials. And here again, as in the other conservative anthologies of the May Fourth era, non-*guixiu* like Liu Rushi do not appear. However, Shi's willingness to celebrate Qiu Jin's accomplishments and her diminished emphasis on virtue mark an important change. Her receptivity to the times is only modest, yet it heralds the turn from prescription for *guixiu* to a less judgmental affirmation of female talent that would pave the way for Hu Wenkai.

Together, these three anthologies provide a basis on which to evaluate Liang Yizhen's position as a May Fourth writer. The integrated, narrative character of Liang's analysis alone would distinguish it from all three of these more conservative anthologies. Liang's reluctance to discuss Chinese and Manchu relations can be taken as another sign of modernity, albeit a defensive one, which is foreshadowed in Shu Shiyi's *Anthology of Qing Dynasty Gentlewomen Poets*. Like Shi Shuyi, too, he is willing to acknowledge Qiu Jin's contributions. Whether we count him as a late Qing holdover or a relatively conservative literary historian of the May Fourth era, he and Shi were flexible in bending old categories of analysis to serve modern needs.

Liang's willingness to discuss *tanci* and other popular genres is a second sign of his distance from Yun Zhu's way of thinking. This feature distinguishes him from the three late Qing holdovers, all three of whom concentrate on poetry, as had Yun Zhu. Liang's attention to literate women outside the upper classes makes a third point of contrast between him and the three more conservative anthologists, who may have been inhibited against such a broadening of horizons by their female gender, as well as by traditional *guixiu* ambivalence toward talented courtesans like Liu Rushi.

The Evolution of Hu Wenkai's "Chinese Women's Writings Through the Ages"

Born in 1900 (Hu Wenkai 1957: 974), Hu was old enough to have corresponded with some important female bibliographers, yet at the same time was friends with leading May Fourth scholars, such as Zheng Zhenduo.[16] This is made clear in his bibliography, which draws on both sets of scholarly writing under discussion here. The most obvious link to the former is found in his prefaces, *fanli*, and colophons, in which he cites writers like Yun Zhu, Shan Shili, and Shu Shiyi, either discussing his debt to their work or suggesting ways in which his list of titles supplements theirs (Hu 1957: 3, 8, 972–73). And elsewhere in Hu's bibliography Wang Duanshu, Yun Zhu, Shen Shanbao, and other prominent female anthologists of the Qing are regularly cited.

A second link to this stream of writings lies in the way Hu reached his interest in the subject—via his wife, Wang Xiuqin 王 秀 琴, who died in 1934 (Wang Xiuqin 1947: 1). Wang is credited with two published collections, *Letters of Famous Women Through the Ages* (*Lidai mingyuan shujian* 歷 代 名 媛 書 簡, 1931) and *A Garden of Prose Writings by Famous Women, Concise Edition* (*Lidai mingyuan wenyuan jianbian* 歷 代 名 媛 文 苑 簡 編, 1947), although the latter was finished long after Wang's death by Hu. Both were meant to address an important oddity in the transmission of women's writings from the dynastic period: the relatively poor survival rate of prose. It was only in the course of working on these collections that Hu decided to turn his hand

16. For example, Xian Yuqing 冼 玉 清, an important early bibliographer of Cantonese women's poetry, endorsed Hu's bibliography. For information on Zheng, see below.

to the entire spectrum of writings by women. These early projects, in particular, project an air of nostalgia for old times and a sense that the beauties of traditional women's literary culture are irrevocably lost.[17] Yet they refrain from any attempt to impose old values on modern women and, in that sense, are typical of May Fourth views.

In addition, despite Hu's affinity for old-style collections of women's writings, he clearly benefited from the revisionist thinking of scholars like Zheng Zhenduo and Tan Zhengbi. Indeed, Zheng was one of several scholars to whom Hu turned for assistance in gathering titles (Hu Wenkai 1957: 5). In addition, Hu's approach inherits some of the liberalizing effects of the May Fourth cultural project. Not only does he quote men like Zheng and Tan upon occasion, he benefits from the breadth of their interests: in women as distinct from men; in *tanci*, drama, and novels as distinct from poetry; and in courtesans, concubines, nuns, and prostitutes, along with *guixiu* wives. As the quotation from Luo Qilan at the beginning of this essay demonstrates, Hu was adept at using old materials subversively, bringing out patterns of nonconformity—even as he set down names, publishers, and prefaces in precisely the original terms. Whereas he does not privilege the nonconformist, he does not suppress her either, and he refrains from elevating the folkish above the classical, as was natural for Zheng and Tan. In all these senses, Hu combines May Fourth openness to popular forms of literature and non-*guixiu* authors with a sensibility and a set of purposes that harks back to a much earlier time.

This is not to say that Hu is without idiosyncrasies. His ties to May Fourth ways of thinking may account for one peculiarity of his work, his handling of Manchu and Mongol women. Rather than following Yun Zhu's and Shan Shili's practice of interfiling them with Chinese, like Shi Shuiyi and Liang Shizhen he cordons them off in a final section devoted to Manchus and Mongols, as well as Buddhist and Daoist nuns. Here the guiding principle may simply be linguistic, for the surnames of Manchus and Mongols are, after all, different from Chinese surnames, and nuns have no surnames at all. This might further explain why he interfiles Korean women—whose names fit Chinese patterns—alongside Chinese. It is just as likely, however, that his reasons derive in part from the anti-Manchu sentiments of

17. See, e.g., Gu Tinglong's 顧廷龍 preface to *A Garden of Prose Writings by Famous Women, Concise Edition.*

the early twentieth century, even when his work provides evidence of literary links between Manchus and Chinese.[18]

Another way of approaching Hu's contribution is in terms of its impact on the national and international sinological scenes. Collected over twenty years of war and revolution, the first edition of *Research on Chinese Women's Writings Through the Ages* came out in 1957, just before the Great Leap Forward. This was a year in which scholarly volumes could still be published, as witnessed by the republication of Zheng Zhenduo's *History of Chinese Popular Literature* that year.

Understandably, the initial impact of Hu's work's publication on the Chinese scholarly community was modest. Between 1957 and the publication of the second edition in 1985, the type of scholarly labor that would benefit from Hu's work—or any scholarly work, for that matter—was not easy to conduct in mainland China. And, whereas the first edition was available in certain foreign libraries, interest in unearthing texts written by women was not great outside China. Meanwhile, Hu labored on, collecting approximately 200 more titles in the twenty-odd years between the two editions, but also witnessing the destruction during the Cultural Revolution of many of the works he had previously catalogued.

Coming after the Cultural Revolution, 1985 was like 1957, in that scholarly books could again find an audience in China. The republication of *Research on Chinese Women's Writings Through the Ages* may have owed something to Gu Tinglong 顧 廷 龍, then director of the Shanghai Library, whose calligraphy graces the second edition's title page.[19] A longtime friend of Hu's, Gu had been instrumental in collecting materials in this and other volumes edited by Hu (see Gu's preface to Wang Xiuqin 1947). Compared to the several thousand entries in the original edition, the 200 new listings were but a drop in the bucket. Although it was typeset anew and had a few fresh prefaces, the revised edition is not significantly different from that of 1957.[20]

18. For example, the famous Manchu poet Gu Taiqing 顧 太 青 appears on p. 800 with Chinese poets. Her sister, Xilin Xu 西 林 旭, appears on p. 814 with other Manchus, but a note points out that she is Gu's sister.

19. For another example of a scholarly publication from this era, see Wang Chongmin 1983, which also bear calligraphy by Gu Tinglong.

20. Interestingly, the old edition's author index has been dropped in the new edition. Apart from the 200 new entries, a preface by Pan Jingzhen 潘 景 鄭 and a colophon by Hu are the only new additions to the 1985 text.

Nevertheless, the impact of this bibliography on Chinese and international scholarship began in earnest with the second edition. This is not to say that one cannot find scholars who used the book in its first incarnation (Sharon Hou 1986), but its republication met a rising tide of interest in archival work on woman writers, to which it soon became the indispensable guide. Distribution or marketing might account for part of the contrast between these two receptions, but the crux of the matter lies in the surging importance of research on traditional Chinese women in the China field.[21] This surge, in turn, owed much to the newly feminist cast of literary and historical scholarship outside Chinese studies. This combination of factors meant that in contrast to the first edition, which emerged in a rather indifferent climate, the second edition has become a bible in the field. Buoyed by Hu's efforts, feminism thus adds its voice to a centuries-long conversation about the Ming-Qing woman writer, finding new potential in the vast conservative endeavor that catalogued their writings even as the May Fourth movement paved the way for radical change.

Looked at from a certain angle, Yun Zhu, Shan Shili, Hong Meige Zhuren, and Shi Shuyi make unlikely allies for contemporary feminist scholars in this field. Their strong sense of entitlement and prescription puts them significantly at odds with contemporary goals. What makes them important today, however, is the care and assiduousness with which they chronicled a dying literary form. Thanks to the thoroughness of their research, as well as to Hu Wenkai's four decades of labor, contemporary scholarship has access to a body of traditional women's writings that might otherwise have disappeared from view.

Conclusion

No literary history is agenda-free, and this look at May Fourth approaches to traditional litrature suggests a number of ways in which women's writings of the Ming and Qing were shaped to serve nonliterary goals. Had May Fourth scholarship had other preoccupations, a different "tradition" might have emerged. As I stated at the outset, the May Fourth movement's claim to special enlightenment on the question of women may have been one rea-

21. As a rough index of the change, compare the "Oft-cited Works" section of *The Indiana Companion to Traditional Chinese Literature* of 1986 with that in the second volume of 1998. Only in the latter do studies involving archival work on traditional women appear.

son that it downplayed the originality of women writers of earlier times. Like other areas in which it sought reform, it showed a tendency to exaggerate its own accomplishments. In the tendentiousness of its vision, the May Fourth movement is congruent with other belated "modernizations" around the world (Bhabha 1990: 5). In China such typicalities are compounded, I believe, by the pattern of Manchu colonization that preceded the May Fourth movement. Partly because Qing women's literature thrived under Manchu dominion, but also for other reasons, May Fourth scholarship on this history is significantly skewed. Its depictions of traditional women writers present a past that is highly polarized between goods and bads, with the bads often banished from view. The result, it seems to me, is to obscure the full picture of traditional women's writings that can be drawn from less tendentious sources, like Hu Wenkai's.

A reconceptualized look at traditional women writers can repair some of the artificial breaches of earlier scholarship without abandoning every May Fourth aim. Zheng Zhenduo's singling out of expressive and evolutionary potential, although his work has produced much of value, had the disadvantage of splitting "women's *tanci*" from other literature by women. Had he written about their literature in its entirety, he might have noticed continuities between *tanci* and women's poetry or paid attention to prefaces like Luo Qilan's. Tan Zhengbi's feminist approach, too, led to major contributions, but his marginalization of male mentors overemphasizes the independence of the women he describes. In my view, it does traditional women no disservice to show how much they needed male protection, for their dependence is one index of the extremely negative social climate in which they made their way. Finally, Liang Yizhen's defensiveness on the Manchu question, though completely understandable, obscures one of the most salient features of women's writings from the mid-Qing on. The less such defensiveness shapes literary history, the more scholars can begin to look carefully at how the Manchu question and the question of women writers were intertwined.

Though it came to seem reactionary, Manchu support may well have been crucial to the effort launched by Yuan Mei described above. Well in advance of the full shock of Western colonization in China, Manchu, Mongol, and Chinese men and women developed widespread patterns of sympathy that raised serious questions about the traditional subordination of women. These questions were countered in many quarters, but they were never suppressed altogether. They were probably related to subsequent incursions by women into various kinds of writings, such as *tanci* and editing, and they took shape in new attitudes toward fiction among women readers, most visibly in the wake of *Dream of the Red Chamber*, itself a product of Sino-Manchu ties.

Today's scholarship on Ming and Qing women's literature is seeking to repair some of the breaches imposed on it by the May Fourth legacy—between popular literature and high, between women and men, between new styles and old. Another holdover, the leading-genre-per-dynasty model, is beginning to lose its former power. Finally, as anxiety about the Manchu question gives way to new attitudes, we will be freer to view old configurations in new ways. Zheng, Tan, and Liang were pioneers who achieved impressive results with, by now, outmoded tools. Hu Wenkai's vast catalogue of sources provides a powerful means through which to reconsider their ideas.

Works Cited

Anderson, Marston. 1991. "Zheng Zhenduo and the Invention of Chinese Literary History." Paper presented at the "The Burden of the May Fourth Movement" workshop, John King Fairbank Center for East Asian Research, Cambridge, Mass., May 11.

Bhabha, Homi K., ed. 1990. *Nation and Narration*. London: Routledge.

Chang, Kang-i Sun. 1997. "Ming-Qing Anthologies of Women's Poetry and Their Selection Strategies." In Ellen Widmer and Kang-i Sun Chang, eds., *Writing Women in Late Imperial China*, pp. 147–70. Stanford: Stanford University Press.

Chang, Kang-i Sun, and Haun Saussy, eds. 1999. *Women Writers of Traditional China: An Anthology of Poetry and Criticism*. Stanford: Stanford University Press.

Chen, Toyoko Yoshida. 1974. "Women in Confucian Society: A Study of Three *T'an-tz'u* Narratives." Ph.D. diss., Columbia University.

Chen Yinke 陳寅恪. 1975. "Lun *Zaisheng yuan*" 論再生緣 (On *Love Destiny Reborn*). In Yang Jialuo 楊家駱, ed., *Zaisheng yuan yu Chen Yinke Lun Zaisheng yuan* 再生緣與陳寅恪論再生緣 (*Love Destiny Reborn* and Chen Yinke's "On *Love Destiny Reborn*"), pp. 1–25. Taibei: Dingwen.

Chow Tse-tsung. 1960. *The May Fourth Movement*. Cambridge, Mass.: Harvard University Press.

Gálik, Marián. 1979. "On the Literature Written by Chinese Women Prior to 1917." *Asian and African Studies* (Bratislava) 15: 65–100.

Goyama Kiwamu 合山究. 1985. "En Bai to jodeishi tachi" 袁枚と女弟子たち (Yuan Mei and his female disciples). *Bungaku ronshū* 31: 113–45.

Gui Maoyi 歸懋儀. 1823. *Xiuyu xucao* 繡餘續草 (Continued drafts after embroidery). Original in the Harvard-Yenching Library.

Hong Meige Zhuren 紅梅閣主人. 1922. *Qingdai guixiu shichao* 清代閨秀詩鈔 (Transcribed poems of Qing dynasty gentlewomen). Shanghai: Zhonghua xin jiaoyu.

Hou, Sharon Shih-jiuan. 1986. "Women's Literature." In William H. Nienhauser, Jr., ed., *The Indiana Companion to Traditional Chinese Literature*, pp. 175–94. Bloomington: Indiana University Press.

Hou Zhi 侯芝. 1811. Preface to Jiang Zhu 江珠, *Xiao Weimo shiji* 小維摩詩集 (Collected Poetry of Little Vimalakirti). Original in Beijing Library.

Hu Siao-chen. 1994. "Literary *Tanci*: A Woman's Tradition of Narrative in Verse." Ph.D. dissertation., Harvard University.

Hu Wenkai's 胡文楷. [1957] 1985. *Lidai funü zhuzuo kao* 歷代婦女著作考 (Research on Chinese women's writings through the ages). Rev. ed. Shanghai: Guji.

Hua Wei 華 瑋. 1998. "Ming-Qing funü juzuo zhong zhi 'ni nan' biaoxian yu xingbie wenti" 明清婦女劇作中之擬男表現與性別問題 (Transvestitism and gender in Ming-Qing women's plays). In Hua Wei 華 瑋 and Wang Ayling 王愛玲, eds., *Ming-Qing xiqu guoji yantaohui lunwen ji* 明清戲曲國際研討會論文集 (Collected essays from an international conference on Ming-Qing drama), v. 2, pp. 575–83. Taipei: Institute of Chinese Literature and Philosophy, Academia Sinica.

Hummel, Arthur, ed. [1943] 1967. *Eminent Chinese of the Ch'ing Period.* Reprinted—Taibei: Chengwen.

Ko, Dorothy. 1994. *Teachers of the Inner Chambers: Women and Culture in Seventeenth-Century China.* Stanford: Stanford University Press.

Liang Yizhen 梁乙真. [1925] 1958. *Qingdai funü wenxue shi* 清代婦女文學史 (History of Qing dynasty women's literature). Reprinted—Taibei: Zhonghua.

———. [1930] 1990. *Zhongguo funü wenxue shigang* 中國婦女文學史綱 (Historical outline of Chinese women's literature). Reprinted—Shanghai: Pujiang.

Mann, Susan. 1997. *Precious Records: Women in China's Long Eighteenth Century.* Stanford: Stanford University Press.

Nienhauser, William H., Jr., ed. 1986 (v. 1). 1998 (v. 2). *The Indiana Companion to Traditional Chinese Literature.* Bloomington: Indiana University Press.

Qian Shoupu 錢守璞. 1869. *Xiufo lou shigao* 繡佛樓詩稿 (Draft poems of Xiufo lou). Original in the Harvard-Yenching Library.

Qiu Jin 秋 瑾. 1982. Ed. Guo Yanli 郭延禮. *Qiu Jin shiwen xuan* 秋瑾詩文選 (Selected Poetry and Prose of Qiu Jin). Beijing: Renmin.

Robertson, Maureen. 1992. "Voicing the Feminine: Constructions of the Gendered Subject in Lyric Poetry by Women of Medieval and Late Imperial China." *Late Imperial China* 13, no. 1 (June): 63–110.

Ropp, Paul. 1976. "The Seeds of Change: Reflections on the Condition of Women in the Early and Mid Ch'ing." *Signs* 2: 5–23.

———. 1994. "Women in Late Imperial China: A Review of Recent English Language Scholarship." *Women's History Review* 3, no.3: 347–83.

Schwarcz, Vera. 1986. *The Chinese Enlightenment.* Berkeley: University of California Press.

Shan Shili 單士釐. [1900] 1986. *Shouci shi shigao* 受茲室詩稿 (Transcribed poems of Shouci house). Reprinted—Changsha: Hunan wenyi.

———. [1904] 1981. *Guimao lüxingji* 癸卯旅行記 (An account of 1903 travels). Reprinted—Changsha: Hunan renmin.

———. 1918. *Qing guixiu zhengshi zaixuji* 清閨秀正始再續集 (Sequel to *Continued Collected Correct Beginnings of Qing Gentlewomen*). Gui'an: Qian.

Shi Shuyi 施淑儀. 1922. *Qingdai guige shiren zhenglüe* 清代閨閣詩人徵略 (Anthology of Qing dynasty gentlewomen poets). Shanghai: Shangwu.

Sun Dianqi 孫殿起. 1959. *Fanshu ouji* 販書偶記 (Jottings on books sold). Shanghai: Zhonghua.

Tan Zhengbi 譚正璧. [1930] 1984. *Zhongguo nüxing wenxue shihua* 中國女性文學史話 (Historical discussion of Chinese women's literature). Rev. ed. Tianjin: Baihua.

Wang Chongmin 王重民. 1983. *Zhongguo shanbenshu tiyao* 中國善本書提要 (Annotations on Chinese fine editions). Shanghai: Guji chubanshe.

Wang Duan 王端. 1822. *Ming Sanshi jia shixuan* 明三十家詩選 (Selected poems of thirty Ming poets). In Beijing Library.

———. 1839. *Ziran haoxue zhai ji* 自然好學齋集 (Collected writings of Ziran haoxue studio). In Beijing Library.

Wang Duanshu 王端淑. 1667. *Mingyuan shiwei* 名媛詩緯 (Classics of poetry by famous women). In National Central Library, Taibei.

Wang Qiong 王瓊. 1808a. *Ailan xuan shixuan* 愛蘭軒詩選 (Selected poems of Ailan studio). Naikaku bunko.

———. 1808b. Preface to *Qujiang ting guixiu changhe shi* 曲江亭閨秀唱和詩 (Poems written in harmony by gentlewomen of Qujiang pavilion). Naikaku bunko.

Wang Xiuqin 王秀琴. 1931. *Lidai mingyuan shujian* 歷代名媛書簡 (Letters of famous women through the ages). N.p.

———. 1947. *Lidai mingyuan wenyuan jianbian* 歷代名媛文苑簡編 (A garden of prose writings by famous women, concise edition). Shanghai: Shangwu.

Weidner, Marsha. 1988. "Women in the History of Chinese Painting." In Marsha Weidner et al., eds., *Views from Jade Terrace: Chinese Women Artists, 1300–1929*, pp. 13–29. New York: Rizzoli.

Widmer, Ellen. 1997. "Ming Loyalism and the Woman's Voice in Fiction After *Honglou Meng*." In Ellen Widmer and Kang-i Sun Chang, eds., *Writing Women in Late Imperial China*, pp. 366–96. Stanford: Stanford University Press.

———. 1999. "The Trouble with Talent: Hou Zhi (1764–1829) and her *Tanci Zai Zaotian* of 1828." *CLEAR* v. 21, pp. 131–50.

Widmer, Ellen, and Kang-i Sun Chang, eds. 1997. *Writing Women in Late Imperial China*. Stanford: Stanford University Press.

Xiong Deji 熊德基. 1979. "*Tian yu hua* zuozhe wei Mingmo qinüzi Liu Shuying kao" 天雨花作者為明末奇女子劉淑英考 (Research on the author of *Heaven Rains Flowers*: the extraordinary woman Liu Shuying of the late Ming). *Zhonghua wenshi luncong* 11: 318–28.

Xiong Lian 熊璉. 1845. *Danxian shihua* 澹仙詩話 (Danxian's remarks on poetry). In Beijing Library.

Xu Fuming 徐扶明. 1986. *Yuan Ming Qing xiqu tansuo* 元明清戲曲探索 (Explorations of Yuan, Ming, and Qing drama). Hangzhou: Zhejiang guji.

Xu Naichang 徐乃昌. 1909. *Guixiu cichao* 閨秀詞鈔 (Transcribed lyrics of gentlewomen).

Yun Zhu 惲珠. 1831. *Guochao guixiu zhengshi ji* 國朝閨秀正始集 (Collected correct beginnings of gentlewomen of this dynasty).

Zhang Huijian 張慧劍. 1981. *Ming Qing Jiangsu wenren nianbiao* 明清江蘇文人年表 (Chronology of literati from Jiangsu during the Ming and Qing). Shanghai: Guji.

Zheng Zhenduo 鄭振鐸. [1932] 1957. *Chatuben Zhongguo wenxue shi* 插圖本中國文學史 (Illustrated history of Chinese literature). Reprinted—Beijing: Wenxue guji.

———. [1938] 1957. *Zhongguo suwenxue shi* 中國俗文學史 (History of Chinese popular literature). Reprinted—Beijing: Zuojia.

PART III

The Dialectic of History: May Fourth and Contemporary Chinese Literature

CHAPTER SIX

Root Literature of the 1980s: May Fourth as a Double Burden

Catherine Vance Yeh

The May Fourth Legacy Reconsidered

For the new generation of Chinese writers entering the literary scene after the end of the Cultural Revolution, connecting with the outside world was high on the agenda. Later, this would translate into the slogan "Chinese literature must join the world" (Zheng Wanlong 1986). For these young writers, the essential issue was to break out of the imposed isolation of Chinese literature from world literature and to overcome the internal political constraints regarding subject matter, ideological perspective, and artistic style. With their general skepticism toward the Center (in whatever constellation) heightened by the crushing of the Democracy Wall movement in 1979,[1] they moved away from the mainstream writers of the older generation. After many years of ostracism and persecution, these older writers had been rehabilitated, but they resumed where they had been cut off in 1957 with a literature of critical loyalty to the newly installed Communist Party leadership. For many of the young writers, it was evident that new avenues for Chinese literature could only be found under the stimulus of new Western literary models. By the middle of the 1980s, exposure to recent

1. At the time of the Fourth National Congress of Chinese Writers and Artists in September 1979, when the government pledged to give more freedom to writers, writers like Liu Binyan and Wang Meng had already published many literary attacks on party corruption and social injustice (see Wagner 1992: chaps. 14–19, 22). However, this liberalization was accompanied by the crackdown on the dissident movement and the Democracy Wall, including the arrest of Wei Jingsheng in March 1979.

translations from the West had stimulated broader discussion on culture among them.

The young writers first reacted with enthusiasm to what they found in this newly accessible literature. Within a very short period, they acquainted themselves with the major literary trends that had developed in the West during the previous decades, reading translations of works by Kafka, Borges, Márquez, Joyce, Virginia Woolf, Faulkner, Kawabata Yasunari 川端康成, and Aitmatov. They tried to digest and apply the newly learned literary theories and techniques in their own writings (Lee 1980: 66; Han 1985: 3).

In this relationship with Western literature, Chinese literature was in the receiving position. This provoked the second reaction: self-reproach. There was a strong sense of being inferior. In the context of a broader "cultural self-reflection," *wenhua fansi* 文化反思, which began as the country's intellectuals tried to deal with the origins of the Cultural Revolution and its connection with a "Chinese national character," the young writers asked what had gone wrong with Chinese literature that it was so much behind the times (Lin 1986; Chen Cun 1985; Liu Zhi 1992).

The Chinese translation of Gabriel García Márquez's *One Hundred Years of Solitude* (*Cien años de soledad*) in 1982 marked a watershed in this discussion (Maerkesi 1982). As numerous Chinese writers and critics recalled later, seeing how this Latin American writer used his homeland's traditional myths and regional folklore and blended realism with the "fantastic" was a revelation (Chen Cun 1985). They discovered the loss of their cultural roots as the reason for the dearth of their own creative imagination. In a situation in which they saw themselves "perplexed by their own national tradition and at the same time perplexed by the modern literature of the West," *One Hundred Years of Solitude* both inspired them and showed them the core of their dilemma (Chen Cun 1985: 94). Their search for the possible causes of their loss of roots led many writers to a reconsideration of the May Fourth movement. Being rather ignorant about this historical movement itself and being constantly reminded by the Communist Party that this movement's triumphant success had been the break with tradition, they located the origin of their literary and cultural dilemma explicitly or implicitly in the May Fourth movement, to which they assigned the responsibility for cutting the country off from its cultural heritage.

A Cheng's 阿城 "Culture Is Conditioning Humanity" ("Wenhua zhiyuezhe renlei" 文化製約著人類, 1985) was one of the first articles to define the problem of Chinese literature as being caused by a "cultural rupture," *wenhua duanlie* 文化斷裂, and to argue that this rupture, a major catastrophe for the nation, had been brought about by the May Fourth movement. A Cheng wrote: "Although May Fourth clearly had a positive impact on social change, its rather complete rejection of the nation's culture together with the ongoing turmoil in society led to a rupture with this culture that to this day has not been overcome" (1985: 2–3).

Zheng Yi 鄭義, the author of "Old Well" ("Lao jing" 老井) and "Distant Village" ("Yuan cun" 遠村), also joined the discussion in July 1985 with his "Leaping Over the Cultural Rupture Zone" ("Kuayue wenhua duanliedai" 跨越文化斷裂帶). Traveling along the Yellow River in the area of the ancient state of Jin 晉, he found that of the famous cultural sites still listed in the local gazetteers, "nothing remains. Like a blank void, the land is truly swept clean! It is as if our national culture had been 'cut off from the waist' with one clean stroke" (Zheng Yi 1985: 3). Reflecting on the fact that he and his generation had been denied any understanding of traditional Chinese culture, he evoked a common assumption among his friends that May Fourth was the movement responsible for this cultural rupture:

> Recently, whenever I got into a deeper discussion with friends, we always ended up talking in very unflattering terms about May Fourth. It is true that at one time, the May Fourth movement did inject vitality into our nation. But it is also true that it rejected too much and kept too little and thus is responsible for a rupture with national culture. "Down with Confucius & Co."—and one of the most richly layered intellectual traditions of the national culture, that of Confucius and Mencius, was trampled to the ground. This was not criticism, but demolition, not critical adaptation but wholesale destruction! This was certainly satisfying but culture was from then on cut off. If Confucianism was already wiped out in this summary manner, it goes without saying what happened to Chan [Buddhism] and Daoism. As far as our social life is concerned, we certainly had the wherewithal during these past decades to produce works up to the highest international standards. But the lack of familiarity of an entire generation of writers with their cultural heritage makes it hard for us to conquer the world. (Zheng Yi 1985: 3)

Both A Cheng and Zheng Yi argued that a nation that had been cut off from its own cultural roots could not produce first-class literature even if the talents and life experience of the writers were there. A Cheng wrote:

> I am so pessimistic because to this day Chinese literature has not been firmly established within a broad and rich cultural opening (中國文學尚沒有建立在一

個廣泛厚的文化開掘之中). Without a strong and marked cultural definiteness (文化限製), it will neither have the freedom to reach the highest literary levels nor be able to communicate with world culture. (1985: 2)

The new party leadership used the celebration of the sixtieth anniversary of May Fourth and the Writers Congress during 1979 to promote a reconnection with May Fourth, calling it the cultural foundation of modern Chinese society as opposed to what they described as the "social fascist line" of the "Gang of Four" during the Cultural Revolution. The young generation of writers, who had lived through and participated in the Cultural Revolution, rebelled against this interpretation and defined the Cultural Revolution as the culmination of the iconoclastic rupture with traditional culture proclaimed by this very May Fourth movement. A Cheng explicitly defined the Cultural Revolution as the radical extension of the May Fourth movement: "The Cultural Revolution went a step further [than the May Fourth movement] and, defining national culture as class culture, made a clean slate of it all so that not even a piece of cloth was left to us to hide our shame" (1985: 2).

In the "cultural self-reflection" discussion on national character and its link to the origins of the Cultural Revolution, critics argued that the radical transformation of the cultural into the political had begun with the May Fourth movement. Although there are some national characteristics that prevented China from modernizing quickly (and these had prompted the radical strategies of the May Fourth movement), the movement had done great harm by severing the cohesion of the Chinese cultural heritage. Facing what they saw as the outcome of the May Fourth trajectory, the young writers now argued that without a sense for and an understanding of the national cultural heritage, there could be no truly great national literature. In their eyes, the May Fourth literary heritage consisted in the replacement of cultural and literary considerations by social, moral, ideological, and political considerations based on political and social commitments (Li Qingxi 1995: 402). Against this May Fourth / Cultural Revolution trajectory, which had succeeded in "cutting the nation off from its own cultural roots" and making an entire people lose their spiritual foundation, the new writers saw nothing laudatory in the May Fourth claim of establishing a "new" culture; rather, they advocated a re-examination of the nation from the perspective of its traditional culture. In this context, the "search for cultural roots," *wenhua xungen* 文化尋根, guided their endeavor. Associated with names such as Li Zehou 李澤厚, whose works on Chinese aesthetics (1982; 1984) reassessed traditional Chinese culture shortly after the Cultural Revolution, and movements such as a reviving Neo-Confucianism, the "search for cultural roots" called for a reappraisal of traditional Chinese culture and values. Translated into literary production, it defined both the subject matter and the method of writing. Works attempting to reconnect with the "severed" culture were thus designated "literature seeking for [cultural] roots," *xungen wenxue* 尋根文學, which I will refer to as "root literature."

Where to Find Cultural Roots?

The Latin American writers had not only shown a way to use traditional culture in order to create a distinct and modern literary style but also offered an example and proved to young Chinese writers that economic backwardness did not prevent a nation from producing first-class literature. As Chen Cun 陳村 wrote: "The Latin Americans are not well-to-do, they are on par with our country; except for soccer, it seems they are leading the world in nothing. But the level of a culture is not equivalent to that of its national income, and a television set does not represent culture. . . . *One Hundred Years of Solitude* has brought us this proof" (1985: 94). The Latin American example showed the Chinese writers that a cultural heritage which was once seen as a burden could indeed be the sought-for cultural treasure. The introduction of the "literature of the fantastic," together with Kafka (including the "Metamorphosis"), and of American novels about the Middle and Far West with its "natural and wild culture," created a new climate for Chinese literature (Zhu 1988; Dan 1982). It served to make the young Chinese writers aware of a new possible way to "leap over the cultural rupture zone" and find a solution to the burden of their May Fourth heritage.

The first problem for these writers was to locate this traditional culture. That culture existed only as a concept in their minds but had not been a part of their lives. This complicated their search. The writers had to define what they meant by traditional culture and how they might go about recovering it.

Han Shaogong 韓少功, a writer from Hunan, was the first to articulate the issue in April 1985 with his article "The Root of Literature" ("Wenxue de gen" 文學的根).[2] "Where has the colorful culture of Chu gone?" he asked

2. This essay came out of a pathbreaking meeting in Hangzhou in December 1984 where the question of reassessing traditional culture and its importance for finding new paths for literature dominated the discussion (see Li Qingxi 1995: 401).

as he recalled his experiences when sent to the countryside during the Cultural Revolution. "At that time I was sent down to settle by the Guluo river, where I lived twenty kilometers from Qu Zi's [Qu Yuan 屈 原] ancestral temple. If one examined closely the local customs, of course there were still words that could be linked with the *Songs of Chu* (*Chuci* 楚 辭).[3] . . . Other than this, Chu culture seemed to have left little trace" (1985: 2). He defined the problem as far larger in scope than a simple criticism of May Fourth; rather, he saw an erosion of regional culture in premodern China that was exacerbated first by the May Fourth movement and then by the Cultural Revolution, with the May Fourth marking the most important rupture.

> Since May Fourth, Chinese literature has been learning from foreign countries, from the West (西 洋), from Japan (東 洋), from Russia and then the Soviet Union; there was also a period when our doors were closed [to the outside world], in ignorance and pompousness all "foreign goods" (洋 貨) were "thrown into the fire." The result was the total demise of our national culture, and a low point in national confidence. . . . But in this absolute "clearing of accounts" and criticism [of Chinese culture], in this withering and demise, there is a chance for Chinese culture to be reborn. (Han 1985: 5)

Evidently, Han Shaogong was not too pessimistic, because he felt that the deeper layers of culture are indelible. In the very fabric of life, especially in the countryside outside of canonized tradition, the culture is still alive in the unofficial histories, fables, jokes, folk songs, stories about gods and spirits, local customs, and courtship ceremonies: "All this is like the gigantic, diffused and tumultuously boiling deeper layers of the great earth, and hidden underneath the crust of the surface and supporting this surface is our mainstream culture" (Han 1985: 4).

If traditional culture could be recovered from these deeper layers beneath mainstream life, how were writers to define their own ties with traditional culture? What roots were they searching for?

Han Shaogong wrote: "If literature has a root, this root must be deeply planted in the soil of national traditional culture," and he emphasized the difference between Northern and Southern cultures (1985: 2). Conversely, A Cheng argued that "modern consciousness" should derive from "the overall

3. *Songs of Chu* is an anthology of poetry in the so-called *sao* 騷 form, composed between the third century B.C. and the second century A.D. The work was compiled and provided with its first and most influential commentary by Wang Yi 王 逸 (d. A.D. 158). On Wang Yi, see Schimmelpfennig 2000.

culture of the nation," *minzu de zhengti wenhua* 民族的整體文化, as embodied in the interrelated structures of Confucianism, Daoism, and Buddhism in the national psyche (1985). Against this identification of the national culture with the mainstream elite strands, another root literature writer, Li Hangyu 李杭育, argued in "Putting in Order Our Roots" ("Liyili womende gen" 理一理我們的根, 1985) that the only traditional cultures still alive and worth reviving were minority and regional cultures outside this mainstream. Zheng Wanlong 鄭萬龍 stressed the subjective aspect of this search in "My Roots" ("Wo de gen" 我的根, 1985a), arguing that the search for the lost culture could start within one's self. Recalling his adolescence in China's Northeast, he found that his creativity was sustained by that experience.

Notwithstanding these differences in their views, all the advocates of root literature were determined to overcome the May Fourth rupture with traditional culture. At the same time, they tried to dissociate themselves from the subordination of literature to social and ideological concerns characteristic of Chinese literature from the May Fourth movement through the Cultural Revolution (Lin 1986). In this effort, they stressed the importance of direct experience with what remained of traditional folk culture away from urban centers, rejecting in the process classical elite learning and the reading of official historical texts from the past as a valid way to reconnect with traditional culture. Although writers such as A Cheng suggested Confucianism, Daoism, and Buddhism as the core of traditional culture—which does imply a refamiliarization with the literary heritage of these doctrines—and although in fact Han Shaogong spent—in the words of one critic—"years reading" before writing his most famous works of root literature (Wu 1995: 904), it was their personal experience of spending years in the countryside during the Cultural Revolution and their common stance against the May Fourth cultural project that largely conditioned their understanding of traditional culture.

Ironically, it was one of the most radical policies of the Cultural Revolution, namely, the decision to rusticate young city dwellers, that brought this generation of authors into contact with the remainders of traditional culture. During the late 1960s and early 1970s, almost all of the root literature writers spent years in poor villages, far away from the urban environment in which they had grown up, living close to nature and engaged in a basic and often very real struggle for survival. In the process, they inadvertently discovered what they would, after they returned to the city, describe as China's "primordial culture." This experience in the countryside became the source for their concept of traditional culture, and it was shaped first and foremost by the way in which common folk lived there.

Their view of traditional culture results from a disillusionment with the prevailing political doctrine, which they associated with the Cultural Revolution and the urban environment. Their lack of formal education together with their ignorance of the Classics and of classical Chinese language made them potentially more receptive toward the folk culture of the countryside as it survived in customs, dialects, and oral transmissions.

After their return to the city and under the impact of the challenge of Western literature, they revived the memory of this experience, which was then reinvented and transformed from "the bitter suffering of hardship" into a mythical experience of the living culture. This recrafted experience became the most important source for their literary creativity.[4] Their retrospective idealization of their years of hard labor in the Chinese countryside, combined with their polemical stance against a literature serving the party or, in the new formula, "socialism and the people," led them to romanticize what they considered nature itself and the natural ways of life of the rural folk.

Although the theoretical discussions started as polemics against the features officially heralded as the very essence of the May Fourth cultural project, later the focus came to be the search for alternatives to this project. Hidden in this search was an implied polemics against what they considered the core of May Fourth. With a great sense of being betrayed, they made this movement into a unified dark force, whose thrust extended well into the 1930s. In their need for a point of departure, the May Fourth movement offered an easily identifiable target.

The Literary Experiments of "Root Literature"

The story seen by many root literature writers as the pioneering work inspiring their own was Wang Zengqi's 汪曾祺 "Taking the Vows" ("Shoujie" 受戒). This short story came out in 1981, a few years before the root literature movement took off and before most of the Western translations had appeared; its author belonged in fact to an older generation and was virtually

4. Many root literature writers had in fact begun to write while in the countryside, but they remained stylistically wedded to the prevailing realistic mode (see Liang Yuli 1986).

unknown up to that time (Wang Zengqi 1993, *xiaoshuo* 1: 158–79). By introducing the concept of "culture" as the force underlying literary creativity, "Taking the Vows" opened a new horizon for the young writers who were struggling to free themselves from the highly utilitarian practice of socialist realism. The notion of "culture" had in fact been so ostracized in the PRC that with the exception of a reprint of Liang Shuming's 1923 comparison of Eastern and Western culture, not a single book published between 1950 and 1980 had the term "Chinese culture" in its title. In contrast, a glance at lists of PRC publications since the middle of the 1980s reveals dozens upon dozens of books and articles sporting "culture" and "Chinese culture" in their title.

Wang's story is set sometime before 1949; it tells the story of a love between a young monk and a village girl. With colorful details of actual practices and daily life in a village monastery, the work reintroduces folk culture, folklore, and "local or regional color" as possible literary subjects. Unaware of the early writings of Shen Congwen 沈 從 文 (1902–88) and of Wang Zengqi's lifelong admiration for this author,[5] the young writers found the absence of value judgments in "Taking the Vows" daring and thought-provoking. The narrative seems to follow the "natural terrain" of the lives lived by those ordinary people who belonged to another age and another time, creating, in the minds of the readers of the 1980s, a refreshing distance and possibly triggering memories of their own lives in the countryside. All these aspects and elements would be taken up a few years later by the root literature writers.

When the discussion on "literature seeking for cultural roots" began in 1985, other literary works that were later claimed by this current had already appeared. They include most prominently Jia Pingwa's 賈 平 凹 "First Visit to Shangzhou" ("Shangzhou chutan" 商 州 初 探, 1982), A Cheng's "The

---

5. As to the level of knowledge of the younger generation about May Fourth, David Wang told the following story at the "Burdens of the May Fourth Cultural Movement" conference in Prague in 1994. Jia Pingwa, one of the main root literature writers, told him that at the end of the Cultural Revolution, he happened to read a book that had neither front nor back cover. The book moved him very much, and he used it as a kind of model, only to discover years later that it was a novel by Shen Congwen. Shen was one of the May Fourth writers who had been cut out of the PRC version of the May Fourth legacy and thus was unknown to Jia. Many other writers from the May Fourth era who had been censored by the PRC party authorities were also unknown to generations born after 1949. Shen Congwen was once Wang Zengqi's teacher in Xi'nan Lianda, and Wang has written many short pieces on his former teacher and his writing. See Wang Zengqi 1993, *sanwen*: 127–34.

Chess Master" ("Qi wang" 棋 王, 1984), and Wang Anyi's 王 安 憶 "Bao Village" ("Xiao Bao zhuang" 小 鮑 莊, 1985a). Other works followed in quick succession, such as Zheng Wanlong's "Strange Land, Strange Stories" ("Yixiang yiwen" 異 鄉 異 聞, 1985b), Han Shaogong's "Dad, Dad, Dad" ("Ba Ba Ba" 爸 爸 爸, 1986), and Zhang Chengzhi's 張 成 志 "The Yellow Mud Hut" ("Huangni xiaowu" 黃 泥 小 屋, 1986). To revive "culture" in its richness and diversity, to inject new life into literature, the writers of these works attempted to recover traditional culture from "the rock strata of culture," *wenhua yanceng* 文 化 岩 層 (Zheng Wanlong 1986: 70), and from the "nation's primordial pattern of life," *minzu de yuansheng tai* 民 族 的 原 生 態 (Liu Zhi 1992: 1).

The presence of the May Fourth countertext gave these texts, all their diversity notwithstanding, at least four important shared characteristics. Of course, this was a May Fourth heritage that came to them largely filtered and orchestrated through post-1949 official historiography.

First, root literature moves away from what its authors felt to be the subjective "personal voice" used by May Fourth literature and, with it, from the autobiographical exploration of the individual. Among the different alternatives are adaptations of the traditional objective narrative, especially of the *biji* 筆 記 style of narration. Jia Pingwa's Shangzhou stories, often fragmentary and plotless accounts of one event and one character (cf. Song 1988: 289), provide excellent examples.

When the first of the Shangzhou stories appeared in 1982–83, it attracted little critical attention. However, the later writers of root literature recognized it as an important event signaling a turning point. In 1985 these stories gained acclaim among both readers and writers, and the movement for root literature singled them out as models conveying the meaning of "seeking for roots."

Situating his stories in an imaginary place called Shangzhou 商 州 in Shaanxi province, Jia Pingwa returned to a narrative voice (including point of view and point of reference) that seems as old as the landscape itself. It is a voice that re-establishes a sense of time unchanging. It evokes in the reader's mind an image of another world of a distant past. This narrative voice challenges the very notion of modernity; human action is rooted not in individual consciousness but in a collective culture-bound past. The challenge posed by Jia Pingwa to the May Fourth tradition of a realism, which had been, as Marston Anderson has suggested, frequently put forth in the "subjective mode,"[6] is his telling the story not as the "story of our time" but as the "story of all times" and thus recovering a sense of tradition and continuity.

One of Jia's stories, "How Much Can a Man Bear?" ("Ren ji" 人 極), begins:

> It is an old custom in Shangzhou to call good friends "close relations." When two men become especially friendly and their wives give birth at about the same time—one to a son and the other to a daughter—the children will be married when they grow up. This custom is quite barbarous, particularly nowadays, but, according to the experience of the mountain people, those who grow up to do their own courting are not assured of marital bliss, while those who are betrothed while still in mothers' wombs will not necessarily be unhappy. (1985: 2; translation based on Zhu 1988: 1)

The story, published in 1985, is set during the Cultural Revolution. Yet, this time frame with its familiar connotations is challenged and subverted through the archaic narrative form. It subverts the very notion of "present time" as "naturally identifiable" by presenting it without the aid of established and accepted indicators. The narrative voice is from the outset recognizable as belonging to the highly stylized *biji* tradition. To make his point, Jia Pingwa firmly set his story into contemporary history known to all his readers. But he told the story in a different way. This strategy splits the horizon of the reader's perspective. The reader enters the familiar Cultural Revolution story as it has been kept as a part of a collective memory of the readers and he looks back from the present to this recent past. The story in turn takes the opposite perspective and looks at recent history from the "traditional past," superimposing itself over this collective memory. To obliterate the notion of natural time, for example, Jia, instead of using the familiar "1967," says "in the second year of the Cultural Revolution (文 革 二 年)," treating the Cultural Revolution as a dynastic reign with its traditional "era title," *nianhao* 年 號. In other passages the narrative presents time as universal and unidentifiable, establishing a "natural time" far more significant than "political time." An example is the following passage:

---

6. Marston Anderson (1990: chap. 2) rightly points out that in European Realism subjectivity was supposed to be strictly avoided in narrative, because it was through the objectivity of the narration that the impression of reality was to be created. But he argues that some modern Chinese writers deviated from this European Realist practice because they could not extricate themselves from the subjectivism of classical Chinese aesthetics.

> The next year, Shangzhou was hit by a great drought, the surface of the soil was cracked like the back of a turtle, the crops were poor, and many deserted their homes to go out begging. Guangzi was alone and had only one mouth to feed, his life was easier. Every day when he ate inside, all the children from the neighborhood would sit on his doorsteps and stare as he ate. Guangzi would scold them: "You've been sent by your parents! Rascals!" But he would still scoop up a ladleful of oats for them to share. All of a sudden one day . . . (Jia 1985: 4)

The narrative language allows Jia to present the point of view of Guangzi, a peasant whose outlook on life is not colored by the fashions of the time and who represents a shared traditional cultural norm of his community. As Guangzi steadfastly holds on to what he considers human decency, his life is full of strange and fable-like encounters and love relations couched in the framework of retribution. All these encounters are in one way or the other related to events during the Cultural Revolution. But the readers no longer perceive them in connection with the Cultural Revolution because they are presented as a narrative of Guangzi's life, dislocated from the rhetoric of recent Chinese history and transformed into an age-old fable of fate dominated by retribution.

The retreat from the subjectivity of the narrative voice took different forms. It went as far as appearing to have only the "natural present" without an identifiable narrator. So, for instance, in "Bao Village," Wang Anyi revived the "wedge chapter," setting up a scene of traditional storytelling, and proceeded to tell her story from a point of view that surpasses the limitations of a particular time and viewer (1985b). As Huang Ziping 黃子平 pointed out, "They have, quite in the manner of the *Shiji* and the *biji* tradition on which they are drawing, only recorded a particular event that happened to a particular person at a particular place in a particular time" (1991: 204). With this narrative stance, the root literature writers also abandoned the very core of the modernist May Fourth writing, the short story, and opted for looser forms with a less restricted time frame.

Second, as root literature writers moved away from "modern" narrative techniques, they also moved away from the highly moral stance that "literature should serve the welfare of the nation," a stance developed and firmly defended by most May Fourth writers, especially during the Anti-Japanese War, and later transformed into a prescribed artistic norm in the PRC. The manifest aim of the writers of root literature was to follow artistic callings and was geared toward creating art. Although the call by these writers for an overall cultural renewal of the nation in itself strongly suggested an ideological commitment, they saw culture at this stage very much as the antithesis to the extremes of politicization of the Cultural Revolution. The discussion of this issue can be best seen in A Cheng's first novelette, "The Chess Master." The protagonist focuses on two activities most clearly antagonistic to the May Fourth didacticism: *chi* 喫, "food / to eat," and *qi* 棋, "chess / to play." In the deliberateness and relish with which the narrator describes these two activities in minute detail, one senses the angry rejection of the May Fourth code marked by its complete disregard—in the name of the high and lofty purpose of serving the nation—of the humaneness of human desires and of traditional Chinese culture.

The story depicts Beijing youths sent to the countryside during the Cultural Revolution. For the hero Wang Yisheng 王一生, only two things are of importance, to have enough to eat and to be able to play chess. For him, eating simply fulfills the function of maintaining himself, and although it is connected to higher feelings, the basic sense of survival that he attaches to it humbles all other lofty pursuits. Wang Yisheng's plain name, which translates "Wang One-life," talks back to the grandiose, politicized names of Cultural Revolution fictional heroes as much as to the new sophisticates of the post-1977 period. The writer spends much of his time in the story describing his hero in the preparation and consumption of his meager food.

> When he got his food, he would at first eat very fast, his throat contracting, and the tendons on his face tight. He often stopped suddenly, with care, he would wipe a few grains of rice and the splattered traces of soup and oil from his chin with his index finger. If some grains of rice fell on his clothes, he would immediately press them down and put them into his mouth. If he failed to catch one, and it had rolled off his clothes onto the ground, he would directly hold his feet still and bend over to look for it. (Liu Xiqing 1992: 95)

In A Cheng's depiction, eating replaces the contemplation of the social and political welfare of the nation. In fact the passage evokes its opposite: Lu Xun's 魯迅 (1881–1936) highly politicized description of the old society as "man-eating," *chiren* 喫人, in "Madman's Diary" ("Kuangren riji" 狂人日記). In "The Chess Master," "to eat/ food" becomes a symbol of a re-established humaneness. With the concentration on food, A Cheng brings the contemplation of humanity to its very fundament. As Wang Yisheng comments during the opening of the story: "We will be fed where we are going, what's all this crying and fussing about?" But A Cheng was not satisfied with challenging *chiren* with *chi*; he also reread history as the madman did. His restoration of belief in Chinese traditional philosophy through a depiction of the art of chess playing effectively denounces the inhumanity and cultural rootlessness of the nation's acceptance of the madman version of Chinese history and traditional culture. Root literature's renunciation of the May Fourth agenda of literature in the service of some higher social and moral purpose, and later in the service of "the working class," could not be more unequivocal.

Third, as the movement pondered ways to re-establish the ties with "lost traditional culture," it re-established "culture," *wenhua* 文 化, as a category in itself (unconnected to morality and politics), replacing the once dominant position of "society," *shehui* 社 會, in the modern novel. In direct opposition to the May Fourth's call for "a new culture suitable for those who live in the twentieth century" (Chen Duxiu 1916: 1), the "culture" that the root literature movement sought to establish is based on the acceptance of "the way in which [the Chinese] people have thought and lived throughout time." In practice, this "search for cultural roots" manifests itself in a variety of ways, including the exploration of different kinds of culture, ranging from "traditional" to "regional" to "ethnic," and different styles of literary traditions such as "the Wei/Jin manner," "the Han/Tang grandeur," "the literary spirit of the literati from the Wu/Yue region," and the reintroduction of the notion of "nature," *ziran* 自 然, the natural state of being, as one of the most important links to a lost tradition. The re-exploration takes the form of giving new meaning to natural elements such as "soil," "earth," "land," "field," "river," "ocean," "sky," "man's body," or "woman's body" and discovering a philosophy underlying rural people's way of life. In short, root literature is interested in what Li Qingxi 李 慶 西 calls somewhat vaguely "man's fundamental way of life," *ren de jiben shengcun xingwei* 人 的 基 本 生 存 行 為, and the "liberated form of life," *shengming de ziyou zhuangtai* 生 命 的 自 由 狀 態 (1995: 409). In literary terms, when the root literature writers moved away from "realism" as perceived by the May Fourth cultural project and discovered "the fantastic," *mohuan* 魔 幻, they reintroduced fairy tales, myth, witchcraft, and popular religion.

Among the best-known works embodying the spirit and the complexity of this "search for cultural roots" is Mo Yan's 莫 言 "Red Sorghum" ("Hong gaoliang" 紅 高 粱, 1986). The story is told as an attempt to rediscover family roots and to retell a family history spanning three generations. Its unique combination of narrating—a mixture of realism and the "fantastic"—"revolutionary history" together with the story of a love as the celebration of the natural vitality of life, has a most provocative effect. As in the case of Jia Pingwa, Mo Yan superimposed the "familiar story" (anti-Japanese war) with an unfamiliar story of "natural love," *yehe* 野合. The passions of the heart, which lead to sex, violence, and murder, are defended against moral norms. This combination in effect highlights "the other story," the unorthodox story of humanity, which has always been left out, pushed under, and streamlined into the "story of revolution." The politically "correct" anti-Japanese story is used to subvert the very notion of correctness. By restoring through romantic fantasies the "natural picture" of "how people actually lived," Mo Yan helps to create a new kind of myth in literature bound up with earth and nature.

In "Red Sorghum," the "I" narrator goes back to his ancestral home in Shandong to find out "how it was," "how people lived," a knowledge he no longer possesses. As he finds out the story of his grandmother, grandfather, and father, he not only presents "their story" from their point of view (as seen through their eyes) but defends their "immoral" love and passions. At the center of this romantic version of his family history is the "love making in the red sorghum field" out of which sprang the entire family. He himself is in fact the product of "natural love" and proof of the vitality of a life without the sanctification of social conventions. This is where he comes from, this is his root! This story of roots, "the true state of the natural being," gives the "revolutionary story" its foundation and humanity. One scene shows how the two stories are related to each other.

The scene begins when the narrator's grandmother is hit by Japanese machine-gun fire as she and the grandfather are organizing an ambush against the advancing Japanese army. As she lies dying in the sorghum field with her son by her side, she recalls and reflects on her life. She was forced by her family to marry a much older man infected with leprosy. On the way to her wedding, she falls in love with one of her sedan-chair carriers. Her feelings were understood and reciprocated. A few days later this man waited for her by the red sorghum field. This man thus became the narrator's grandfather.

> Up ahead was a bend in the road, and as the donkey negotiated the turn, Grandma tipped backward, leaving the security of the animal's back. A muscular arm swept her off and carried her into the sorghum field.

Grandma fought halfheartedly. She really didn't feel like struggling. The three days she had just got through were night-marish. Certain individuals become great leaders in an instant; Grandma unlocked the mysteries of life in three days. She even wrapped her arms around his neck to make it easier for him to carry her. Sorghum leaves rustled. Great-Granddad's hoarse voice drifted over on the wind: "Daughter, where the hell are you?"

From near the bridge came the shrill long sound of the bugle, followed by the staccato rhythm of the machine-gun fire. Grandma's blood continues to flow in concert with her breathing. 'Mom,' Father pleads, 'don't let your blood run out. You'll die when it's all gone.' He scoops up a handful of black dirt and smears it over her wound; blood quickly seeps out from under it. He scoops up another handful. Grandma smiles in gratitude, her eyes fixed on the azure sky, deep beyond imagining, and fixed on the warm, forgiving, motherly, nurturing sorghum around her. A glossy green path, bordered by tiny white flowers, appears in her mind. . . .

Grandma and Granddad exchanged their love surrounded by the vitality of the sorghum field: two unbridled souls, refusing to knuckle under to worldly conventions, were fused together more closely than their ecstatic bodies. They ploughed the clouds and scattered rain in the field, adding a patina of lustrous red to the rich and varied history of North-east Gaomi township. My father was conceived with the essence of heaven and earth, the crystallisation of suffering and wild joy. (Mo Yan 1988: 362–63; trans. Goldblatt 1994: 73–75)

In Mo Yan's reinvention of the myth and the romantic vision of the past, it is not important what is "real" and what is not, the emphasis is on creating an alternative understanding of human action untainted by the judgment of modern values.

The return to a natural state of life became the theme of many works of root literature. Writers such as Zheng Wanlong, Zhang Chengzhi, and Ma Yuan 馬 原 focused in their work on the cultures of national minorities. By juxtaposing "natural and primitive values" with "civilized modern values," the subversive effect is even greater. These stories challenge and restore the belief in cultural vitality. Since most readers do not know about this "other story," the contrast is with the values enshrined in the reader's mind, which sometimes are represented by a character, a city dweller, ignorant of other "natural" ways of life. The root literature writers move their stories out of the familiar city into "nature," China's "wild west," the far-off countryside, places where the cultural destruction is believed to be less complete. With their "man's struggle for survival" paradigm and an environment in which life is governed by rituals and beliefs alien to the "civilized" reader, the authors try to recuperate "culture" in its most unfamiliar form. They thus inject new vitality into literature and into their own creative impulses, combining the search for literary roots with that for their own roots.

A fourth shared characteristic of root literature is a frustration with the literary discourse prevailing in most of twentieth-century Chinese fiction. By presenting alternatives to the "politically correct" story or exploring the "unexplored and forgotten side of this story," writers of root literature express their resentment of cultural impoverishment and the domination of modern Chinese literature by political ideology, the cause that prompted them to experiment with new and old possibilities of language. The major tendency is to move away from the Westernized modern Chinese of the May Fourth era and to reconnect with traditional Chinese writing styles. Some reinstated a kind of *wenbai* 文白, a classical vernacular visible already in Jia Pingwa's "Shangzhou Series," with its provocative contrast between this language and the contemporaneousness of events.

A simple change in subject matter would have fallen short of challenging the core of a value system that is stored in the very linguistic structure of what is often referred to as "Mao style," *Mao wenti* 毛文體 (Li Tuo 1991: 38; Wagner 1999). The root literature writers explored and experimented with regional dialects, mystic language used in folklore, oral narratives, and religious ceremonies in an attempt to revive and reinvent the rich narrative traditions of the past. To bring vital vigor back into language, root literature also rediscovered the folk song as a rich source of raw earthiness in language. Unknown to them, "going to the people" as projected by the "folk literature" movement was very much an outgrowth of the May Fourth agenda (Hung 1985). Rather than accepting the hierarchical division into "high" and "low" language claimed by the May Fourth movement, language was for the writers of root literature more a question of power and control. In a collective effort, root literature introduced a polysemic literary language uncontrolled by newly imposed norms, a language ultimately defying a unified system of interpretation. One of the outstanding examples of this effort is Han Shaogong's "Dad, Dad, Dad" with its language drawing on local myth and allegory (1986; see also Li Qingxi 1986).

Parallels Between the May Fourth Cultural Project and the Search for Cultural Roots

As root literature challenged what were seen as the achievements of the May Fourth literary revolution, a question arose: How different were its authors from their forefathers? Were they able to escape their heritage and drop the burden? Or might it be that their rejection of the May Fourth heritage landed them in the same dilemmas that this earlier movement had faced?

The origins of the root literature movement have much in common with those of the May Fourth movement. Like the May Fourth writers, the root literature writers were inspired by translations of foreign literature and took it as the standard by which to judge their own creative efforts. Their works thus mainly fit Western standards, if they were not directly written under the impact of works by Western and Japanese writers. In fact, while they tried to re-establish links with traditional culture, they emphasized that they were in no way "closing the door" to foreign literature. Some even declared that their literary movement should be understood as part of a world literary movement (Zheng Wanlong 1986; Mao 1986: 66), restating in fact Zhou Zuoren's 周 作 人 (1885–1967) opinion on New Literature and the question of local color: "A strong indigenous flavor is positively one of the ingredients of 'world' literature" (Zhou 1926: 11).

Like the works of May Fourth, root literature centered its discussion on culture. As in the case of the May Fourth, "culture" or "traditional culture" could be and was seen from two perspectives. From the political point of view, both movements agree that something fundamentally intransigent in Chinese traditional culture prevents it from changing at the same speed as Western culture, and that this is not necessarily a good thing (Lin 1986: 92). From the point of view of literary development, the opinions of root literature writers seem as diverse as those of May Fourth writers (see Hsia 1961; Lee 1973). Both divided traditional culture into the dominant, mostly Confucian culture (*zhengtong* 正 統) and the marginal popular culture (*fei zhengtong* 非 正 統), which the root literature writers refer to as "the culture beyond the official norm," *guifan zhi wai* 規 範 之 外 (Li Hangyu 1985: 75). In an influential article written at the beginning of the "search for roots" movement, Li Hangyu in fact began with Lu Xun as a point of reference and pointed to his "Old Tales Retold" ("Gushi xinbian" 故 事 新 編) as an example of seeking literary inspiration from unorthodox cultural roots (1985: 77). Some modern writers even accept a May Fourth distinction between "bad roots," *liegen* 劣根, and "good roots," *yougen* 優根 (Gu 1986: 76).

Since both movements placed great emphasis on the need for a new language (and language reform) as fundamental to national cultural transformation, they shared a common assumption about the powers of the written word to transform culture, and from this developed a similar strategy for coping with what both considered as a national crisis. The languages of the future envisaged by the two movements had, of course, little in common with the May Fourth movement favoring the introduction of a newly created vernacular to replace the traditional written language (known as the *baihuawen yundong* 白話文運動; Kaske 1998) and the root literature authors opting for the reintroduction of a traditional language that was in fact as much a new creation as the "vernacular" of their opponents. The impulse governing the perceptions and experimentations of the two camps seems to have come from a very similar, and very ideological, frame of mind.

Similarly, the distinction between orthodox and unorthodox cultural traditions begs the question of the relationship between the 1980s root literature movement and the 1930s "native soil literature," *xiangtu wenxue* 鄉土文學,[7] represented for example in the works of Shen Congwen (see Hsia 1961: 189–211; Kinkley 1987; Wang Dewei 1993; Liu Na 1986: 7; Ding 1986, 1992).

Most root literature writers would agree that Shen Congwen represents a literary tradition that they at least find akin to their own philosophy if they have not directly inherited it. They used, in fact, the same kind of distinction between orthodox and nonorthodox culture with regard to the May Fourth heritage that the May Fourth literati had used for the older tradition. When Shen Congwen was active writing, the League of Leftist Writers was founded and came to dominate the literary mainstream according to the histories written by its members, who occupied leading positions in the cultural bureaucracy after 1949. As a politically uncommitted writer who found inspiration in rural settings, Shen Congwen represents the marginal "minority"

7. The term *xiangtu wenxue* was first used in the 1920s and later established by Lu Xun as a literary category in his preface to the fiction volumes of the *Zhongguo xin wenxue daxi* (Zhao 1935, *xiaoshuo* 2: 9). Ding Fan (1992) argues in his *Zhongguo xiangtu xiaoshuo shilun* that from the very beginning of the May Fourth literary movement, both Lu Xun and Zhuo Zuoren emphasized "local color" as the basis of unique literary character.

in the May Fourth heritage. The rediscovery of Shen Congwen by root literature writers (or of Liang Shuming by the cultural philosophers) is not accidental. To signal their departure from the orthodox May Fourth tradition and express their opposition to what was later defined as the mainstream in modern literature, they used a writer from the period who did not fit this definition to illustrate their cause.

Although it may be argued that in their criticism of the May Fourth tradition, the root writers linked with *xiangtu wenxue* a countercurrent associated with Shen Congwen already present in the early stages of the May Fourth movement, in fact their approach to popular culture was much closer to that of Lu Xun or Zheng Zhenduo 鄭振鐸 (1898–1958). As C. T. Hsia pointed out, Shen Congwen was interested in reinstating the wholeness of life in modern society, and his concern was "to stress, in the teeth of a materialist civilization, the virtues of an ordered existence in rhythmic keeping with nature and the gods, filled with animal grace and pride and yet without cunning and greed" (1961: 190). For the root writers, the indigenous culture is but a literary source; their commitment is not to "reinstall the wholeness in modern life" but to advance the modernist search for a new literary style, which ultimately is the search for the "self." As the critic Li Qingxi pointed out, the movement is essentially a self-searching movement and is, in fact, opposed to a cultural revival (1995: 413–14). The works of these authors demonstrate that their concern with traditional culture goes only as far as it serves as a vehicle for literary exploration, but they are not in any way committed to reflect "the true condition of traditional life." It is not surprising, then, that many of the works that represent the root literary movement are also considered by critics to be in the category of "avant-garde literature" for the same period. For example, as the critic Wu Liang 吳亮 points out in "Looking Back at Avant-garde Literature," Mo Yan's "Red Sorghum" has nothing to do with "tradition" or traditional culture but is a product of his artistic fantasy and imagination; it is invented tradition to its core (Wu Liang 1995: 902–4).

Although the root writers mostly situate their stories in the countryside, these are not intended to be stories about the countryside or about country people. While the root literary movement no doubt is in some degree influenced by writings on village themes by Sun Li 孫犁 (1913–) (1981; see also Ran 1982; Ding 1992: 143–64) and Zhao Shuli 趙樹理 (1906–70) (Gao 1985; see also Ding 1992: 143–64, 253–58) during the 1930s and 1940s, as well as the post-1949 writings by Liu Shaotang 劉 紹 棠 (1981; 1985), the differences predominate. The movement shows no tendency toward a rediscovery and representation of peasant culture, authentic or otherwise. Unlike writers of the literary schools mentioned above, who unreservedly stated their love for and commitment to presenting the life and people of the very countryside where they had been born and where they had grown up, the root writers had mostly grown up in the city, and their relationship to the countryside remained an artificial one. The root literature writers were no more interested in giving a kind of pictorial representation of "local customs," *fengsu hua* 風 俗 畫, or "local scenery," *fengjing hua* 風 景 畫, than they were in "painting a historical picture of the twentieth-century lives of men and women from the countryside" (Liu Shaotang 1990: 3). The root writers were not interested in writing "literature for the people" in the tradition of these schools. The one thing, however, the writers of root literature did have in common with these earlier writers of *xiangtu wenxue* is the choice of the countryside as the locale for their work in their rejection of the city. As Han Shaogong wrote in his essay on "The Root of Literature":

> The countryside is the city's past; it is the museum of our national history. Even if it was only a single roof beam, a ridgepole, an eave, alas, of a farmer's house, all might project the [cultural heritage] from the Han and Wei, Tang and Song dynasties. But, as for cities, except for Shanghai having a corner with the City Temple, and Beijing having the Forbidden City, they are all filled with tall buildings, wide paved roads, and many-hued neon lights, making North and South alike; somehow they seem to lack character. Furthermore, by having such a short history and changing easily, the city seems not to have much for one to discover. (Han 1985: 4)

For the root literature writers, the city symbolized "transience" and the "cultural desert," whereas they saw the countryside as full of hidden cultural treasures for those who care to look. The two settings become two opposite spiritual realms. This myth of the great contributions the countryside, as opposed to the city, can offer to national culture once again echoes a strong sentiment expressed by the May Fourth writers (Hung 1985: 12–14). The root literature writers' attitude toward the city, however, was in part a reaction to the Communists' cultural grip on the cities; the need to escape from this oppressive environment led them to the countryside. There, Han Shaogong believed, the "authentic" Chinese culture may still be found, and this fantasy formed the basis of the movement.

Like the May Fourth generation, the root literature writers wholeheartedly accepted foreign literature as important to their own literary endeavor. And like their predecessors, they argued about how to define the role of foreign literature as a model. Their discussion recapitulated the old debate about "total change" versus "renovation." The critic Li Tuo 李陀 argued that the root literature movement first had to learn from the Western modernists and then try, on that basis, to absorb Chinese traditional culture; otherwise the root literature movement would become a "traditionalist revival" movement. Once Western modernist thought was accepted, it would make such a "revivalist" tendency impossible and as a result create a "hybrid" literature, which for Li Tuo would be the ideal outcome. Only by combining modern concepts and traditional culture can Chinese literature "join the world," *zouxiang shijie* 走向世界 (Lin 1986; Han 1985; Zheng Wanlong 1986). Other critics argued against this prevalence of Western thought and for a "search for cultural roots" in an internally generated renewed understanding of traditional culture, which should be combined with the "modern spirit of our time" (Chen Sihe 1986: 25–26).

Like their May Fourth predecessors, many root literature writers saw themselves as part of a world literary movement. Their "search for cultural roots" was a means of exploring a particular cultural heritage and on this basis contributing to world culture and entering into a dialogue with it. During the initial stage of the movement, when writers were fascinated by the idea of rediscovering cultural roots, their emphasis was on rediscovery and on discarding moral or other nonliterary criteria. But some of them soon realized the danger that their movement would be seen as an attempt to turn back the clock of "progress," and they emphatically claimed that their movement was searching for cultural inspiration from a modernist point of view, as had been done by Márquez and other Latin American writers who used "tradition" as a literary theme. "Chinese literature must join the world," Zheng Wanlong urged (1986). Critics even went as far as to claim that this search for roots could result in "a rebuilding of Chinese culture" and that it was a movement to critically reassess traditional culture: "If you look at the literary works of the root literature movement, there is not one piece that is not critical of traditional culture. But this critique of the spirit of traditional culture is in a contradictory manner combined with the revival of some aspects of traditional aesthetics" (Lin 1986: 96). This point of view, if not shared by all writers of the root literature movement, at least expresses a common sentiment: whether critical of traditional culture or not, the movement was in no way an attempt to abandon the spirit of modernity, which again is a part of the May Fourth heritage.

Like the May Fourth writers, the root literature writers also tried to use the novel as a means to build a new national cultural consciousness. Yet, the latter were badly equipped for such a task. Their understanding of traditional culture was not based on a direct link with tradition as it had been with most May Fourth writers, who had received a traditional education and had grown up in the countryside. The "cultural revival" accordingly was not born out of a living link with this tradition but came from the search for literary inspiration outside the overdefined social realities of contemporary mainland China. As Li Hangyu put it: "If I were not a writer, I would have no contradiction. I would not hesitate to do away with this undesirable 'national consciousness' (民 族 精 神). . . . On the one hand, I know what a terrible 'national consciousness' I have inherited; on the other hand, if I do not defend it, I'm afraid I will be left with nothing [as a writer]" (1986: 52).

This ambiguity and helplessness in the face of what the writer considers the unavoidable world trend of "seeking for cultural roots," an ambiguity that is also evident in the awkwardness with which the "national culture" terminology was used by these writers, shows to what degree the movement is a "response to the West." In fact by placing great emphasis on literary technique and on writing about the "human being," culture and cultural forms often became source materials rather than the inspiration for literature.

To fully understand the relationship of root literature to May Fourth, the impact of the Cultural Revolution on this particular generation must be taken into account. First, to May Fourth writers the traditional literary forms and classical language seemed incompatible with the new spirit of modern times (see Zhao Jiabi 1935: 2.15); similarly, for the root literature writers the orthodox "Mao-style language" since 1949, and especially since the Cultural Revolution, seemed stale and bankrupt, unable to express new ideas. Both groups of writers saw their country in a national and spiritual crisis, be it the late Qing or the Cultural Revolution, which left them without a credible tradition.

Second, the root writers saw the May Fourth heritage through the eyes of survivors of the Cultural Revolution. As they tried to come to terms with the cultural and political radicalism that had landed the country in such turmoil, the "reflection on cultural roots" tried to fathom what made the Cultural

Revolution possible. In this context they accepted an interpretation that saw the Cultural Revolution as nothing but the continuation and radicalization of the May Fourth movement and the cultural destruction of their time as the fruit of the radical anti-traditionalism of the May Fourth movement.

The root literature movement, however, ultimately did not escape the agenda set by May Fourth. The topics of the new movement's discussion—the role of traditional culture, the link with world literature, the social responsibility of literature, and the language and mode suitable to a modern sensibility—remained very much those of May Fourth even if the root literature writers did not go along with the main May Fourth conclusions.

Unperceived by them, the burden of the May Fourth fell on them in double measure. Besides what was understood by them as their burden, the root writers were preconditioned by the May Fourth cultural project to repeat the same search and fall victim to the very cycle begun with the project. Due to the success of this project, the young generation was brought up in an educational system that rejected traditional learning. Thus their understanding of traditional culture and classical language was limited and biased. Although they tried in their own way to break away from the May Fourth notion that the "orthodox tradition" (*zhengtong*) of Chinese literature in the classical language is something undesirable, with the little education they had had before the Cultural Revolution they were not in a position to perceive that the interaction between high and low cultures might have been the vital force in rejuvenating premodern Chinese culture. Due to the May Fourth interpretation, Chinese culture has been presented as naturally monistic, and every new generation of Chinese writers has attempted to bring in the source of rejuvenation from abroad. This, however, has proved unsatisfactory. Having grown up in an environment determined by May Fourth, the young writers were unequipped to finally break free from its legacy.

The inability of the root literature writers to reprocess and reassess the Chinese classical tradition, which no longer was theirs, doomed the "root-seeking" project from the outset. With the belief that there was such a thing as a reified "national cultural essence," *minzu de wenhua jingsui* 民族的文化精髓, with an identifiable shape and color, the "seeking cultural roots" movement created for itself an empty premise that could not sustain a sophisticated handling of the literary and cultural heritage.

Works Cited

A Cheng 阿 城. 1984. "Qi wang" 棋 王 (The Chess Master). *Shanghai wenxue* 7: 15–35. Reprinted in Liu Xiqing 劉 錫 慶, ed., *Xungen xiaoshuo* 尋 根 小 說 (Fiction in search of roots), pp. 89–128. Beijing: Beijing shifan daxue, 1992.

———. 1985. "Wenhua zhiyuezhe renlei" 文 化 製 約 著人 類 (Culture is conditioning humanity). *Wenyi bao* (July 6): 2–3.

Anderson, Marston. 1990. *The Limits of Realism: Chinese Fiction in the Revolutionary Period*. Berkeley: Univ. of California Press.

Chen Cun 陳 村. 1985. "Guanyu 'Xiao Bao zhuang' de duihua: Chen Cun zhi Wang Anyi" 關 於 小 鮑 莊 的 對 話 ： 陳 村 致 王 安 憶 (A conversation regarding "Bao Village": Chen Cun to Wang Anyi). *Shanghai wenxue* 9: 93–94.

Chen Duxiu 陳 獨 秀. 1916. "Yijiuyiliu nian" 一 九 一 六 年 (1916). *Xin qingnian* 5: 1–6.

Chen Sihe 陳 思 和. 1986. "Dangdai wenxue zhong de wenhua xungen yishi" 當 代 文 學 中 的 文 化 尋 根 意 識 (The seeking of cultural roots in contemporary literature). *Wenxue pinglun* 6: 24–33.

Dan Ailun 丹 艾 倫 (Daniel Aaron). 1982. "Zhongxibu de mimi" 中 西 部 的 祕 密 (The midwest mystique). Trans. by Chen Kun 陳 焜. *Shijie wenxue* 2: 261–78.

Ding Fan 丁 帆. 1986. "Xin shiqi xiangtu xiaoshuo de dishan yanjin" 新 時 期 鄉 土 小 說 的 遞 嬗 演 進 (The gradual evolution of the new period of "native soil" fiction). *Wenxue pinglun* 5: 11–18.

———. 1992. *Zhongguo xiangtu xiaoshuo shilun* 中 國 鄉 土 小 說 史 論 (On the history of Chinese "native soil" fiction). Jiangsu: Jiangsu wenyi.

Gao Jie 高 捷, ed. 1985. *Shanyaodan pai zuopin xuan* 山 藥 蛋 派 作 品 選 (Selected works of the "Potato" school). Beijing: Renmin.

Goldblatt, Howard, trans. 1994. *Red Sorghum*. Berkshire, Eng.: Cox & Wyman.

Gu Hua 古 華. 1986. "Cong gulao wenhua dao wenxue de 'gen'" 從 古 老 文 化 到 文 學 的 '根' (From old culture to the "root" of literature). *Zuojia* 2: 74–76.

Han Shaogong 韓 少 功. 1985. "Wenxue de gen" 文 學 的 根 (The root of literature). *Zuojia* 4: 2–5.

———. 1986. "Ba Ba Ba" 爸 爸 爸 (Dad, Dad, Dad). In idem, *Youhuo* 誘 惑 (Temptation), pp. 155–99. Changsha: Hunan wenyi.

Hsia, C. T. 1961. *A History of Modern Chinese Fiction*. New Haven: Yale University Press.

Huang Ziping 黃 子 平. 1991. *Xingcunzhe de wenxue* 倖 存 者 的 文 學. Taibei: Yuanliu.

Hung, Chang-tai. 1985. *Going to the People: Chinese Intellectuals and Folk Literature*. Cambridge, Mass.: Harvard University, Council on East Asian Studies.

Jia Pingwa 賈平凹. [1982] 1993. "Shangzhou chutan" 商州初探 (First visit to Shangzhou). In Li Tuo 李陀, ed., *Zhongguo xungen xiaoshuo xuan* 中國尋根小說選 (An anthology of Chinese fiction in search of roots), pp. 7–47. Hong Kong: Sanlian.

———. 1985. "Renji" 人極 (How much can a man bear?). *Wenhui yuekan* 10: 2–12.

Kaske, Elisabeth, 1998. "Der alte Staat und die Schriftreform. Bildung, Schrift und Sprache am Ende der Qing-Dynastie." Master's thesis, University of Heidelberg.

Kinkley, Jeffrey C. 1987. *The Odyssey of Shen Congwen*. Stanford: Stanford University Press.

Lee, Leo Ou-fan. 1973. *The Romantic Generation of Modern Chinese Writers*. Cambridge, Mass.: Harvard University Press.

———. 1980. "Recent Chinese Literature: A Second Hundred Flowers." In Robert B. Oxnam, ed., *China Briefing*. Boulder: Westview Press.

Li Hangyu 李杭育. 1985. "Liyili women de gen" 理一理我們的根 (Putting in order our roots). *Zuojia* 9: 75–79.

———. 1986. "'Wenhua' de gan'ga" '文化'的尴尬 (The awkwardness of "culture"). *Wenxue pinglun* 2: 50–54.

Li Qingxi 李慶西. 1986. "Shuo 'Ba Ba Ba'" 說爸爸爸 (On "Dad, Dad, Dad"). *Dushu* 3: 49–58.

———. 1995. "Xungen: bashi niandai de wenhua huigui" 尋根：八十年代的文化回歸 (Seeking roots: return to culture during the 1980s). In *Sishinian lai de Zhongguo wenxue* 四十年來的中國文學 (Chinese literature of the last forty years). Taibei: Lianhe wenxue.

Li Tuo 李陀. 1991. "Xiandai hanyu yu dangdai wenxue" 現代漢語與當代文學 (Modern Chinese language and contemporary literature). *Xin de wenxue* 6: 38–49.

Li Tuo 李陀, ed. 1993. *Zhongguo xungen xiaoshuo xuan* 中國尋根小說選 (An anthology of Chinese fiction in search of roots). Hong Kong: Sanlian.

Li Zehou 李澤厚. 1982. *Mei de licheng* 美的歷程 (The path of beauty). Beijing: Wenwu.

———. 1984. *Zhongguo meixue shi* 中國美學史 (A history of Chinese aesthetics). Beijing: Zhongguo shehui kexue.

Liang Shuming 梁淑溟. [1923] 1960. *Dong Xi wenhua ji qi zhexue* 東西文化及其哲學 (Eastern and Western cultures and their philosophies). Hong Kong: Taiping yang.

Liang Yuli 梁預立. 1986. Postscript to Han Shaogong 韓少功, *Youhuo* 誘惑 (Temptation), pp. 259–62. Changsha: Hunan wenyi, 1986.

Lin Weiping 林偉平. 1986. "Xin shiqi wenxue yi xitan: fang zuojia Li Tuo" 新時期文學一席談：訪作家李陀 (Conversation on literature of the new period: an interview with the writer Li Tuo). *Shanghai wenxue* 10: 91–96.

Liu Na 劉 納. 1986. "Zai ni xianxiang zhong jinxing de xin shiqi wenxue" 在逆現象中進行的新時期文學 (Literature of the new period proceeding counterphenomenologically). *Wenxue pinglun* 5: 3–10.

Liu Shaotang 劉紹棠. 1981. *Liu Shaotang zhongpian xiaoshuo ji* 劉紹棠中篇小說集 (Novellas by Liu Shaotang). Changsha: Hunan renmin.

———. 1985. *Puliu renjia* 浦流人家 (Family by the river mouth). Beijing: Renmin.

———. 1990. *Xiangtu wenxue sishi nian* 鄉土文學四十年 (Forty years of "native soil literature"). Beijing: Wenhua yishu.

Liu Xiqing 劉錫慶, ed. 1992. *Xungen xiaoshuo* 尋根小說 (Fiction in search of roots). Beijing: Beijing shifan daxue.

Liu Zhi 劉稚. 1992. "Xungen: minzu de yuanshengtai he wenxue de xiandaigan" 尋根：民族的原生態和文學的現代感 (Seeking for roots: the nation's primordial pattern of life and the modern sensibility of literature). In Liu Xiqing 劉錫慶, ed., *Xungen xiaoshuo* 尋根小說 (Fiction in search of roots), pp. 1–11. Beijing: Beijing shifan daxue.

Lu Xun 魯迅. 1935. "Daoyan" 導言 (Preface). In Zhao Jiabi 趙家璧, ed., *Zhongguo xin wenxue daxi* 中國新文學大系 (A compendium of new Chinese literature), *xiaoshuo* 2, pp. 1–17. Shanghai: Liangyou.

Maerkesi 馬爾克斯 (Gabriel García Márquez). 1982. *Bainian gudu* 百年孤獨 (Cien años de soledad). Trans. Shen Guozheng 沈國正, Huang Jinyan 黃錦炎, and Chen Quan 陳泉. *Shijie wenxue* 6: 33–139.

Mao Shian 毛時安. 1986. "Wenhua de jiazhi he wenxue de xungen" 文化的價值和文學的尋根 (The value of culture and literature's search for roots). *Zuojia* 4: 65–66.

Mo Yan 莫言. [1986] 1988. "Hong gaoliang" 紅高粱 (Red sorghum). In Yan Gang 閻綱, ed., *1986 nian zhongpian xiaoshuo xuan* 1986 年中篇小說選 (Anthology of novellas from the year 1986), pp. 295–375. Beijing: Renmin wenxue.

Ran Zhunzhou 冉準舟. 1982. *Lun Sun Li de wenxue daolu* 論孫犁的文學道路 (On Sun Li's literary journey). Xi'an: Shaanxi renmin.

Schimmelpfennig, Michael. 2000. "Von wahren Menschen zum wirklichen Dichter: Der Kommentar von Wang Yi zum *Li sao* und den Liedern von Chu." Ph.D. diss., University of Heidelberg.

Song Yaoling. 1988. *Shinian wenxue zhuliu* 十年文學主流 (The mainstream of literature of the past ten years). Shanghai: Shanghai wenyi.

Sun Li 孫犁. 1981. *Sun Li wenji* 孫犁文集 (Collected works of Sun Li). Tianjin: Baihua wenyi.

Wagner, Rudolf. 1992. *Inside a Service Trade*. Cambridge, Mass.: Harvard University, Council on East Asian Studies.

——— (Luduofu Wagena 魯多夫瓦各納). 1999. "Zhonggong yijiusiling nian—yijiuwusan nian zhengli zhengyu, zhengwen de zhengce dalüe 中共一九四零

年—一九五三年建立正語，正文的政策大略 (Chinese Communist Party policies to establish correct-speak and correct-writing, 1940–1953)." In Peng Xiaoyan, ed., *Wenyi lilun yu tongsu wenxue* 文藝理論與通俗文化 (Literary theory and popular culture), pp. 11–38. Taipei: Institute of Literature and Philosophy, Academia Sinica.

Wang Anyi 王安憶. 1985a. "Xiao Bao zhuang" 小鮑莊 (Bao Village). *Zhongguo zuojia* 2.

———. 1985b. "Wo xie 'Xiao Bao zhuang'" 我寫小鮑莊 (My writing of "Bao Village"). *Guangming ribao* (Aug. 15): 4.

Wang Dewei. 王德威. 1993. "Yuanxiang shenhua de zhuisuizhe: Shen Congwen, Song Zelai, Mo Yan, Li Yongping" 原鄉神話的追隨者：沈從文、宋澤萊、莫言、李永平 (The followers of the myth of native soil: Shen Congwen, Song Zelai, Mo Yan, Li Yongping). In idem, *Xiaoshuo Zhongguo: wan Qing dao dangdai de Zhongwen xiaoshuo* 小說中國：晚清到當代的中文小說 (Narrating China: Chinese fiction from the late Qing period to the present), pp. 249–78. Taibei: Maitian.

Wang Zengqi 汪曾祺. 1993. *Wang Zengqi wenji* 汪曾祺文集 (Collected works of Wang Zengqi). 5 vols. Nanjing: Jiangsu wenyi.

Wu Liang 吳亮. 1995. "Huigu xianfeng wenxue" 回顧先鋒文學 (Looking back at avant-garde literature). In *Sishinian lai de Zhongguo wenxue* 四十年來的中國文學 (Chinese literature of the past forty years), pp. 901–11. Taibei: Lianhe wenxue.

Zhang Chengzhi 張成志. [1986] 1993. "Huangni xiaowu" 黃泥小屋 (The yellow mud hut). In Li Tuo 李陀, ed., *Zhongguo xungen xiaoshuo xuan* 中國尋根小說選 (An anthology of Chinese fiction in search of roots), pp. 346–423. Hong Kong: Sanlian.

Zhao Jiabi 趙家璧, ed. 1935–36. *Zhongguo xin wenxue daxi* 中國新文學大系 (A compendium of Chinese New Literature). 10 vols. Shanghai: Liangyou.

Zheng Wanlong 鄭萬龍. 1985a. "Wo de gen" 我的根 (My roots). *Shanghai wenxue* 5: 41–44.

———. 1985b. "Yixiang yiwen santi" 異鄉異聞三題 (Strange land, strange stories). *Shanghai wenxue* 5: 26–43.

———. 1986. "Zhongguo wenxue yao zouxiang shijie" 中國文學要走向世界 (Chinese literature must join the world). *Zuojia* 1: 70–74.

Zheng Yi 鄭義. 1985. "Kuayue wenhua duanliedai" 跨越文化斷裂帶 (Leaping over the cultural rupture zone). *Wenyi bao* (July 13): 3.

Zhou Zuoren 周作人. [1926] 1987. *Jiu meng* 舊夢 (Old dreams). Reprinted—Shanghai: Shanghai shudian.

Zhu Hong. 1988. The Chinese Western: Short Story Fiction from Today's China. New York: Ballantine Books.

CHAPTER SEVEN

Return to Go: Fictional Innovation in the Late Qing and the Late Twentieth Century

David Der-wei Wang

Despite incessant political, cultural, and economic upheavals during the 1990s, contemporary fiction from mainland China, Taiwan, and Hong Kong underwent a drastic shakeup in conceptual schemes, stylistic formats, authorial stance, and readership. Chinese fiction from the early 1980s to the early 1990s demonstrates a vitality that underlines, and sometimes even contributes to, the volatile nature of the historical circumstances from which it arose.

In recent studies of contemporary Chinese fiction, two directions come to one's notice. On the one hand, scholars search for a link between writers of the May Fourth generation and writers of the June Fourth generation, with a conviction that the latter have revived the creative vigor and critical spirit that once characterized the former. On the other hand, scholars look for a new theoretical model, or even a new "paradigm," by (again) turning to Western theories. Through the prism of "theoretical interventions and cultural critique" (K. Liu and Tang 1993), these model-oriented scholars hold, contemporary Chinese literature can function as a powerful social and intellectual agency, one that informs the second coming of Chinese modernity. Both approaches have yielded creditable results, as attested by a selection of publications (see K. Liu and Tang 1993; Widmer and Wang 1993). But when looking deeper into the premises of these two approaches, one cannot help but feel that there is much left to be done.

By forcing contemporary works into the parameters first established by writers such as Lu Xun 魯迅 (1881–1936), Ding Ling 丁玲 (1904–86), or Shen Congwen 沈從文 (1902–88), one risks turning a revitalized practice of fictional modernity into a recapitulation of a mythical Modernity. Contemporary Chinese fiction's affinity to its May Fourth precursors can be appreciated at best in negative terms, if one is to believe that the May Fourth tradition indicates an "obsession with China" (Hsia 1971), or perhaps an inherent clash between the "epic" mode and the "lyrical" mode (Průšek 1980). The May Fourth fictional tradition has also been described as comprising a gallery of "Promethean" and "Faustian" heroes or heroines (Lee 1973), as an excessive attachment to "tears and sniveling" (Lau 1980), as a persistent indulgence in a monological "authorial voice" (Huters 1993), and in terms of self-imposed "limits of realism" (Anderson 1990). This critical discourse, as I argue in the following sections, has become increasingly insufficient, especially when it is set against what has been happening in recent Chinese fiction.

A paradox: if contemporary writers were the true inheritors of the radical iconoclasm of their May Fourth antecedents, they would have already overthrown May Fourth iconoclasm in favor of another rigid iconoclasm, since by now the old iconoclasm must have itself become an obsolete tradition. Perhaps one should feel only gratitude that contemporary writers are *not* wholehearted practitioners of the virtues of the May Fourth literature as defined above, after having seen how that literature started out celebrating humanitarian anti-traditionalism and modernism and ended up endorsing ideological fanaticism and total conformism.

One finds no fewer problems with scholars, especially those recently trained in the United States, who use contemporary Chinese fiction to demonstrate their grasp of conventional theories. From liberal Marxism to radical feminism, from post-colonialism to culture critique, a wide range of Western theories has been applied to works by the new generation of writers (see K. Liu and Tang 1993; Lu Tonglin 1992; Chow 1990). There is no doubt that these theories have provided modern Chinese literary studies with a much-needed rigor and led to an extrapolation of familiar paradigms into unfamiliar territories, thereby making possible the present dialogue between "insiders" and "outsiders." But there is a problem. Although a particular, national literature—Chinese fiction from the 1980s and the 1990s—remains the target of their critical endeavor, theory-oriented scholars often produce a discourse so universally palatable that it becomes anything but nationally distinctive or indigenously characteristic. Instead of confronting the puzzle of how China is both modern and different, these scholars seem intent on showing that China is "modern" (or "post-modern") only because it is exactly like the formulaic pattern laid down in the Occident. A theory that produces no new results when applied to new data has not been properly understood.

In addition to these two approaches to contemporary Chinese fiction—a return to a narrowly defined May Fourth tradition or a passive reliance on Western applications of theory rather than the potential inherent in the theories themselves—I would suggest a third approach: constructing a new perspective on late Qing fiction while pushing Western theory in the direction of serving our understanding of Chinese practice. Rather than one "modernity," I find that there were many "modernities" and that not all "modernities" were exhausted in Western practice. This suggestion may sound out of tune with the current critical canon, but it is based both on a historical concern and on a theoretical engagement. A territory seldom explored by scholars of modern Chinese literature, late Qing fiction contains a collection of ecologies far more complex than conventional wisdom has led us to expect; these earlier ecologies have to be understood before we can really hope to grasp the evolution of twentieth-century Chinese literature.

To begin with, for more than seven decades the May Fourth era has been regarded as the harbinger of literary modernization in China. In contrast to the May Fourth era, which is said to promise progress, change, and the rise of modernity, the late Qing is presented as the last stage of decaying China, the final moment in an extended premodern period. Changes and reforms are allowed to have taken place during this period, but they are seen only in abortive or negative terms. For all its volatile cultural politics, late Qing fiction has never won much acclaim among critics of modern literature: there are no masterpieces, no decisive breaks with tradition, no "real" signs of modernity. At best, it is said to have served either as a prelude to or as a transitional moment on the road to the May Fourth modernization movement.

In fact, the experience of modern Chinese literature and politics from the Literary Revolution to the Cultural Revolution should have taught us a bitter lesson, that what was once thought to be modern may turn out to be a cruel replay of convention; and likewise, that what was rejected as non-modern or obsolete may hide unexpected dimensions of novelty. The idea of linear progress and continued forward motion, the quintessential temporal factor in the concept of modernism, has to be carefully examined. The dialectical relations between the May Fourth and the late Qing are much more complicated than those described by literary historians. To differentiate their time from the previous one, to register their sense of historical crisis, the May Fourth intelligentsia had good reason to place the divide between the modern and the premodern between themselves and the late Qing. It does not follow, however, that, more than eight decades after the May Fourth movement, we still need to adopt their views on what is and is not modern.

To talk about contemporary Chinese fiction in connection with late Qing fiction serves as *one* way to critique the view that May Fourth discourse is the sole origin of modern Chinese literature. The May Fourth–oriented critical paradigm can no longer subsume the new diversity of current fictional practices, even if we recognize the genealogical ties between the two periods. The Late Qing is the moment in which fiction was first brought to bear on a wide range of public and private issues of modern times; it is also an era that witnessed a dynamic outburst of imagination on the part of both writers and readers. With its rigid postures—its "obsession with China," for instance—mainstream May Fourth fiction inherited only one aspect, and a rather narrow one at that, of the late Qing tradition. In terms of its far-reaching fantasies, protean styles, and ambivalent politics, late Qing fiction finds less resonance with its immediate successors than with the variety of works from late twentieth-century China.

By "late Qing fiction," I do not mean merely the "new fiction" as propagated by enlightened intelligentsia such as Yan Fu 嚴 復 (1853–1921) and Liang Qichao 梁 啓 超 (1873–1929). The spirit of the "new fiction" was scrupulously recapitulated by Lu Xun's generation, despite their apparent anti-traditionalist pose, and has since been seen as the only modern endeavor of its time. The late Qing fiction I have in mind covers a wider range; it refers to fiction produced from the beginning of the Taiping Rebellion to the fall of the Qing empire, a corpus of narratives that comprises genres as different from each other as depravity romance and science fantasy, chivalric cycles and social exposés. This immense complex of fictional genres underwent radical transformations in the second half of the nineteenth century, and as such, it contributed to the literary imagination of Chinese modernity. Liang Qichao's "new fiction" was one of the strains of the late Qing tradition; this "new fiction," however, eventually came to be the sole, legitimate progenitor of mainstream modern Chinese fiction.

A revisitation of late Qing fiction will help sharpen at least three of the theoretical issues that concern modern Chinese literary studies. First, by relating late twentieth-century Chinese fiction to late Qing fiction, I am aiming at something more than a superficial parallel between the two periods in terms of historical ambiance, political motivation, or formal experiment. It is too tempting not to see contemporary China undergoing a chaotic social-cultural transformation reminiscent of that of the late Qing—a ghostly *déjà vu* of history. My view is much more polemical than this. I am concerned less with how history can be re-enacted, as if responding to a certain prefigured scenario, than with how history can be *retold*, in such a way as to let the past and the present illuminate each other.

By setting late twentieth-century and late Qing Chinese fiction side by side, I have no intention of reinstating the law of historical causality; in sharp contrast to this mechanical notion, I am looking for clues and traces that would enable us to recognize anew the complex voices in the formation of modern Chinese literature. The parallel between the late Qing and the late twentieth century, accordingly, takes on an allegorical dimension. It points to certain questions: if late twentieth-century Chinese literature recapitulated some of the highlights of late Qing literature, does it mean that we have not gotten much beyond the program of the first generation of modern writers? Or does it mean that our modernist endeavor has taken us full circle since May Fourth, back to where we started a century ago?

Second, by constructing a dialogue between late Qing and contemporary Chinese fiction, I have little intention of "overthrowing" the May Fourth paradigm in order to replace it with something new. "Strong" thoughts such as overthrowing, paradigm changes, and revolution—with their utopian connotation of a quick transcendence of the old period, power, or genre to the new—have left enough scars on China already. At issue here is a methodology based not so much on irretrievable laws of conquest and resistance but on a practice of continued trafficking, so to speak, among various periods and genres.

Both C. T. Hsia and Jaroslav Průšek, the two pillars of twentieth-century Chinese literary studies, traced their studies of modern fiction back to the heritage of the late Qing and even earlier periods.[1] For them, the modernity

1. For perceptive genealogical studies of the subjective inclination of modern Chinese prose narrative writers in light of the classical lyrical tradition, see Průšek 1980: "Subjectivism and Individualism in Modern Chinese Literature" (pp. 1–28) and "The Changing Role of the Narrator in Chinese Novels at the Beginning of the Twentieth Century" (pp. 110–20). See also Hsia 1971, in which he traced May Fourth and post–May Fourth writers' political consciousness to late Qing novels such as *The Travels of Lao Can*. Next to Průšek and Hsia, one should also pay homage to Semanov 1980, a seminal work.

of Chinese literature lay not in an ostensible break but in a tortuous negotiation between the new and the old literature. But Průšek's and Hsia's studies have inspired only a handful of followers.[2] By contrast, historians of our time have drawn a more complex picture of the conceptual and political mutations stemming from the late Qing intelligentsia's search for modernity. Works by such scholars as Benjamin Schwartz (1964), Paul Cohen (1984), and Hao Chang (1971; 1989), to name only a few, teach us that the late Qing was not a period of mere preparation for the rise of Chinese modernity but a time that witnessed a most dynamic conflation of ideas and actions.

In view of the recent, vital development of Chinese fiction in mainland China, Taiwan, and Hong Kong, it is now possible to redraw the map of the May Fourth–centered constellation of modern Chinese literature. To read contemporary fiction in the light of late Qing works will help us trace a different genealogy for the debate over modernity and reclaim that which writers and scholars inspired by May Fourth have overlooked. It compels us to open up the orthodox closure of modernity and restore those muffled, but no less modernizing, voices. Genres such as neo-impressionism, critical lyricism, chivalric romance, and Mandarin Ducks and Butterflies fiction have contributed just as much as realist fiction to the discourse of modern Chinese literature.

Third, the comparative and contrastive study of late Qing and contemporary Chinese fiction enables one to re-examine the artificial distinctions between the new and the traditional, the modern and the premodern, in literary periodization. The questions What constitutes Chinese (literary) modernity? and When will modernity finally be realized? have been asked repeatedly since the May Fourth era. In the aftermath of the June Fourth massacre, more pessimistic questions have been added, such as, "Have we missed the magical moment of modernity before it has happened to us or will we yet attain modernity, however belatedly?" With their implied historical urgency, these queries treat modernity both as something innate, inherent in one's foreknowledge of what every country should be like, and as something inaccessible, ever tantalizing to any Chinese effort to acquire it.

---

2. The most prominent one is Milena Doleželová-Velingerová. The book she co-authored and edited in 1980, *The Chinese Novel at the Turn of the Century*, still remains the sole full-length English-language study of the late Qing period informed by historical awareness and methodological rigor.

I argue that Chinese literary modernity does not take place with a single formula, for an elite group of writers and readers, or at a sanctioned historical moment. Modernity indicates not a mythical telos but a historical repositioning, one that enables us to continuously resurrect the new from the old and tease out the conventional from the avant-garde. To examine the "making" of the modern in twentieth-century Chinese literature, therefore, one looks not only into areas whose modernity has been admitted but also into those whose modernity has been denied.[3] Only when one is aware of the various temporal zones played out against each other in the dialectics of modernity can one continuously enact the modern *as well as* undo its spell.

We can redeem the apparently fading modern heritage of the May Fourth only by constantly renaming it. Instead of speculating whether modern Chinese literature has come to its end, I would try to open up its two ends, by calling attention to the hidden dialogue between the pre–May Fourth and the post–June Fourth era. In what follows, I describe four of the fictional discourses that prevailed in the late Qing period: social exposé, chivalric and court-case cycles, depravity romance, and science fantasy. Each of the four headings refers to more than an ill-defined "theme" or a static genre; rather, it points to a *discursive stance* from which the narrative format of "modern China" has been enunciated. I examine how these four narrative tendencies in fictional discourse lent themselves to the dialogue of Chinese modernities, only to be repressed when the May Fourth writers upheld a new master narrative in the light of Western models. I also address how these repressed modernities surfaced in the writers of late twentieth-century China and what this resurfacing implies about the subliminal aspects of modernity in the May Fourth tradition between the late Qing and the late twentieth century.

One fascinating phenomenon in Chinese literature since the late 1980s has been the *carnivalization of realist discourse*, the discourse canonized since the May Fourth era. No longer restricted to either critical or socialist realism, writers in mainland China, as in other Chinese communities, have explored

3. There has been a long debate over the issue of modernity versus pre- and postmodernity in recent Western intellectual circles, involving such major thinkers as Habermas, Foucault, Vatimmo, Jameson, and Lyotard. With respect to the current study, see Calinescu 1987 and Compagnon 1994. See also articles by scholars of China studies, such as Lee 1990 and Metzger 1990.

materials hitherto considered untouchable and rendered them in a wide range of forms: grotesque parade, black farce, eerie fantasy, uncanny romance. Instead of emotive conventions such as the "call to arms" or "tears and sniveling," works in this new vein are punctuated by defiant and cynical laughter. Particularly in mainland China, this rejuvenated creativity has become a powerful critique of Maoist discourse, the formidable literary and political discourse that dominated China for more than three decades and suppressed all possibility of free literary expression. But now, by turning the world into a realm of unrealistic elements or by identifying normalcy with the bizarre and laughable, writers awaken their readers from aesthetic and ideological inertia and initiate them into a different kind of reality.

This grotesque approach to reality, however, is not all the invention of contemporary mainland writers. Comparable examples can be cited from works by such Taiwan writers as Wang Zhenhe 王禎和 (1940–90), Huang Fan 黃凡, and Wang Wenxing 王文興. Mixing laughter and mockery, fantasy and buffoonery, works of fiction by these Taiwan writers from the late 1960s to the early 1980s in turn embarrassed, baffled, and amused a generation of Taiwan readers groping for a new way of defining reality in the midst of social and political change.[4] One can trace this tradition further back, to the post–May Fourth era, and find among writers such as Lu Xun, Lao She 老舍 (1899–1966), Zhang Tianyi 張天翼 (1906–85), Wu Zuxiang 吳組緗 (1908–94), and Qian Zhongshu 錢鍾書 (1910–) an impulse to radicalize mainstream realism with exaggerated figures, outrageous episodes, and diabolic laughter. Their works demonstrate that, besides critical or socialist realism, Chinese writers are capable of developing a different fictional mode, a mode bolstered not by the notion of mimesis but by the notion of mimicry.

The comic and satiric styles practiced by May Fourth writers and their followers, however, are still too benign when compared with the products of contemporary writers. For all their intent to mock and ridicule, writers like Lao She and Zhang Tianyi cannot altogether forgo their mission of rectifying social malaise with curative writing; they are a generation of writers burdened by an "obsession with China." In them, late Qing grotesquery survives on the margin of May Fourth purposefulness. But contemporary Chinese writers, in view of their frivolous attitudes toward "serious subjects," their ambivalent strategies for undoing the bond between nation and narration,

4. For a detailed analysis of the politics of radical laughter as seen in Taiwan fiction from the 1960s to the 1980s, see Wang 1990.

and their willingness to shock and scandalize their audience at whatever expense, are more readily descendants of late Qing exposé writers. It is from novels such as Wu Jianren's 吳趼人 (1867–1910) *Eyewitness Reports of Strange Things from the Past Twenty Years* (*Ershinian mudu zhi guai xianzhuang* 二十年目睹之怪現狀, 1910) and Li Boyuan's 李伯元 (1867–1906), *Exposure of Officialdom* (*Guanchang xianxing ji* 官場現形記, 1906) that these contemporary writers derive their force and inspiration.

As a discursive mode, *grotesque realism* was discussed in detail by Mikhail Bakhtin, particularly in his studies of Rabelais. Bakhtin considered grotesque realism a Renaissance literary and cultural form, characterized by systematic reversal of the social hierarchy, celebration of body, and the emotive effects of collective laughter (1968: 18–58). Grotesque realism functions as a "positive force" which facilitates a society's capacity to regenerate itself (Bakhtin 1968: 19). In the context of modern Chinese fiction, however, this Bakhtinian notion has to be altered. In contrast to the "orthodox" realism sanctioned by May Fourth writers, which vows to represent life so as to reform it, the Chinese brand of grotesque realism defines, or defies, the real—by exaggeration, distortion, and even metamorphosis. But this "carnival" does not necessarily bring about a revitalization of the social body, as Bakhtin would have had it; rather, it produces a new and more virulent mutation of the social malaise. Late Qing writers recognized the "positive" potential in a grotesque re-vision of reality but dwelled on the exuberance of cynical play in itself to the extent that the presentation of grotesqueries becomes an end. In a society in which values have disintegrated and order no longer exists, social evils cannot be done away with and flaunt themselves openly. On the other hand, communist literature from the 1940s to the 1970s, with all its description of plebeian revolt against the authorities, its invocation of voluntary and involuntary bodily resources, and its indulgence in collective euphoria, blatantly subordinates the Bakhtinian ideal to the reinstallation of tyranny. The treacherous tie between the Bakhtinian theory of the carnival and the Marxist theory of history and revolution has been repeatedly remarked (see, e.g., Clark and Holquist 1984: 212–38); the Chinese case indicates again how grotesque realism can be used to serve, rather than subvert, a grotesque reality.

The challenge for contemporary Chinese writers in the vein of grotesque realism, therefore, is threefold: to lay bare the complacent elitism of realism in the May Fourth tradition; to identify the vulgar artifice in the realism of the Communist tradition; and, most important, to renegotiate the cynical allure of the realism of the late Qing tradition. In so doing, they have (unwittingly) obliged themselves to think anew the *figural dialectic* embedded in late Qing grotesque exposés. This dialectic posits social "reality" and social "imagination" as two discursive forces continually engaged in a battle to demolish and appropriate the legitimacy of the other. Whereas grotesquery may be seen as an outrageous simulacrum of the real, the real can prove more unthinkable and terrible than what has already been imagined.

As Wu Jianren describes in *Eyewitness Reports of Strange Things from the Past Twenty Years,* this is a world turned upside down, one that honors "devils, monsters, phantoms, and goblins," *chimei wangliang* 魑魅魍魎, and celebrates violence and irreverence. But perhaps the most desolate aspect of this grotesque exposé is its view of chaos: its clowns' attacks on each other and the surrounding society generate a certain new "order"; the audience's "pleasure" derives both from distancing the embarrassing or uncomfortable circumstances and from becoming imaginatively involved in them. In the name of eyewitness reports and exposés, fiction along this line sensationalizes and fabricates a given subject; *roman à clef,* a narrative mode that reveals truth by concealing the truth, is widely adopted by writers. What ensues is a crisis in the verisimilar law that makes any textual or extra-textual presentation of the real intelligible.

Contemporary Chinese grotesque exposés do not merely recapitulate the farcical strategy inherent in late Qing exposés, however; they particularly invoke a critique of mimesis-centered realism that could not have been conceived by late Qing writers. The Chinese people, who have gone through so many calamities over the past half-century, have had no shortage of grotesquery and disruption in their everyday lives. Reality *is already* as eerie and unthinkable as that which any fiction could conjure. But the horrors and unpredictabilities of ordinary experience are legitimated; the temptation to see these everyday events as uncanny is repressed. If one finds works by contemporary exposé writers too ridiculous to believe, one should first ask if their lived reality was any more believable. Tracing contemporary grotesquery to the late Qing antecedents, therefore, is to explore certain paradoxical questions: Why should such dreadful things ever have been taken as natural in late Qing or in late twentieth-century China? Why could Chinese reality be validated only when disguised as the uncanny and the absurd? How could laughter be permitted where tears are supposed to be shed?

Exposés of bureaucratic abuses and absurdities have been one of the major strands of PRC fiction since the 1980s, but not until recent years have writers started to let their imaginations take flight into worlds where exasperating critique induces fiendish laughter. An example that comes immediately to mind is a series of novellas and novels by Liu Zhenyun 劉震雲, such as *The Bureaucrats* (*Guanren* 官人, 1991), *The Office* (*Danwei* 單位, 1989), *Officialdom* (*Guanchang* 官場, 1989), and "A Groundful of Chicken Feathers" ("Yidi jimao" 一地雞毛, 1991). In these works, petty bureaucrats parade like a circus of clowns, each with his or her own distinct idiosyncrasies. These clowns take turns as allies and enemies engaging in endless games of conspiracies, counter-conspiracies, backbiting, factionalism, bribing and being bribed, and sex scandals. His sarcasm notwithstanding, Liu Zhenyun is clearly fascinated by his characters' unflagging pursuit of their goals. Liu's works may remind one of Lao She's comic fiction, especially *Divorce* (*Lihun* 離婚, 1934), but their ultimate models (like Lao She's) must be late Qing exposés. Tear off the socialist masks of Liu's bureaucrats, and one finds a full range of grotesques and buffoons borrowed from a work like *Exposure of Officialdom*.

A more flagrant example can be found in Zhang Jie's 張潔 novella, *Getting Feverish* (*Shanghuo* 上火, 1992). Taking place in a governmental organization, "Mengma yanjiu xiehui" 猛馬研究協會 or "The Institute for Mengma Research," the novella features a group of clownish officials and scholars who are involved in endless power struggles. The organization was founded to study "mengma," an extinct species from the age of dinosaurs, but it thrives largely due to the cyclical power struggles among the staff. Insofar as the ancient *mengma* suggests "meng" 猛 "ma" 馬, or ferocious Marx, Zhang Jie may have intended a political allegory. But at issue here is not how Zhang Jie has insinuated an ideological criticism, but how she has presented a world in which all values are void and therefore laughable. In so doing, Zhang reproduces the most cynical aspect of a late Qing novel such as *Eyewitness Reports of Strange Things from the Past Twenty Years*.

The "strange things" in Zhang Jie's world take a stranger turn as the members of the institute literally become more and more beastlike in both looks and mentality. While the protagonist of the novella, a veteran bureaucrat of the institute, is running an ugly election campaign for the chairmanship, he is also busy climbing into the bed of his widowed daughter-in-law; the latter is willing to continue the incestuous affair so as to outvie her demanding mother-in-law and, more important, to open a backdoor to her own brother's ambitions. Compared with the new widow in the famous episode in *Eyewitness Reports of Strange Things from the Past Twenty Years* (chap. 64) whose father-in-law persuades her to sleep with his boss in exchange for his own promotion, the daughter-in-law in *Getting Feverish* appears even more motivated and resourceful.

More eerie is the fiction that treats "strange things," however weird or even horrific, as part of Chinese daily routine. Yu Hua's 余 華 novella *A Kind of Reality* (*Xianshi yizhong* 現 實 一 種, 1988) is an example. The novella chronicles the transformation of a chance family squabble into a series of family murders. Few readers will be left undisturbed by the disjunction between the bloody family feud and the matter-of-fact style with which Yu Hua narrates the incident and its horrible consequences. One surely discerns macabre humor when the narrator catalogues the ways the family members humiliate, torture, and mutilate each other—an exhibition of Chinese cruelty *à la mode* Qing, as in *Living Hell* (*Huo diyu* 活 地 獄, 1907), about the spectacle of corporeal tortures. One of the most talented avant-garde writers in mainland China, Yu Hua has been read in terms of many foreign labels, but his avant-gardism may very well be derived from wittingly or unwittingly rewriting a rearguard Chinese convention. Given his desolate view of life, his violent deformation of language, and his penchant for the neurotic, all Yu Hua does is to lay bare the horrors that Chinese are used to in life but would rather judge incredible when encountered in art. Yu Hua purports to record merely a slice of life, a story about "nothing." Can the sadomasochist festivity of the family murders still be seen as uncanny, when the bloody national carnival of the Cultural Revolution or of the Tian'anmen Incident is an unrepressed everyday affair?

Mo Yan's 莫 言 novel *Wine Republic* (*Jiu guo* 酒 國, 1992) is one of the more spectacular Chinese grotesqueries to date. In the novel, a detective is sent to the notorious Wine Republic to investigate a case of baby eating, only to be lured into a vertiginous labyrinth of conspiracies and scandals. There are also several subplots in the novel, including the novelist Mo Yan's correspondence with a mediocre writer, a seemingly inexhaustible introduction to banquets of all kinds (including one in which "babymeat" is served), an uprising organized by a dwarf on behalf of the "babymeat babies," and the detective's romance with a woman who turns out to be the archvillain's mistress.

Wine Republic is a mock epic, or more fittingly, a farce in a Gargantuan scope, that threatens to laugh away every code of the conventional revolutionary romance. Against the ideological stoicism that has suppressed the Chinese body for more than four decades, *Wine Republic* is a novel about excess and in excess, celebrating a theater of corporeality that features ruthless and endless eating, drinking, vomiting, and lovemaking. Amid the remote echoes of Lu Xun's famous call to "save the children," contemporary Chinese as depicted in *Wine Republic* are happily eating children. Nowhere else in modern Chinese fiction can we find such a large-scaled fantasy that mixes the spleen of Swiftian satire, the absurdity of Kafkaesque fable, and the cannibalistic jubilation of late Qing exposés. In a world where the high and the low, the fragrant and the putrid, mingle, nobody has clean hands; the protagonist is fittingly murdered by drowning in a manure pit at the end of the novel. Eschatology and scatology turn out to be two readings of the same reality.

The frivolity and playfulness suggested by contemporary Chinese writers' exposés must be treated with no less caution than the deadly gravity of literature from earlier generations. From one angle, it reflects writers' ironic self-contemplation of literature's position in a post-modern multimedia network, one in which images deconstruct realities and morals boil down to mere manners. But from another angle, these writers' "flirtation with China" informs us of the writers' strategic repositioning vis-à-vis their volatile political surroundings. Through their "light" writings, writers either tantalize the formidable organs of censorship or tease the apparent solemnity of the state and thus redeem their readers as well as themselves, however tentatively, from the old cycle of obsession with China.

Before deploring contemporary writers' pursuit of commercialism or loss of historical sense, one might first reconsider the ambiguous ambiance of late Qing fiction. It was a time when "morally correct fiction" had acquired a ridiculous predictability, a time when fiction represented a means by which writers could teach *and* titillate, indict *and* get rich. Works by two writers, Zhang Dachun 張大春 from Taiwan and Wang Shuo 王朔 from mainland China, can best illustrate my argument.

Zhang's novel *The Great Liar* (*Da shuohuangjia* 大說謊家, 1990), employs a sly, comic strategy that has raised many eyebrows in Taiwan. First serialized in a daily newspaper, each installment appeared in the evening edition as a retelling of a topical event that appeared in the morning edition.

Underneath these apparently discrete episodes/events, the novel reveals a fantastic plotline that involves all the necessary elements of a "bad" detective novel. Turning events in the morning news into events for evening fiction, Zhang subverts the law of authenticity for news reports on the one hand and questions the organic structure of storytelling on the other. Since the actual writing of the novel depended heavily on the accidental happenings of each day, Zhang foregrounded the vulnerability of all attempts to record the present before it is lost and the flimsiness of all efforts to comprehend history while still caught up in it. Just as its generic form—parody of detective fiction and journalistic writing—suggests, the novel is a hilarious critique of the hermeneutic intention: a *con-fusion of horizons*. A critic may very well discuss Zhang Dachun's post-modernist devices as demythifying journalism and fiction, history and fabrication, but I see in them a recapitulation of late Qing exposé writers' shrewd taste for sensationalism coupled with a deep-seated anxiety about the ephemeral quality of any subject, from national crises to private gossip.

A comparable case can be made for Wang Shuo's "humorous" fiction. A self-styled contemporary literatus, Wang Shuo won tremendous popularity by writing about the drifter mentality and nonchalant lifestyle assumed by mainland youth. It has become common wisdom to say that Wang Shuo's comic fiction, together with the movies and television serials based on his works, reflects the despondency of PRC culture after the Tian'anmen Incident, a one-man industry catering to popular taste. But what makes priggish readers uneasy is perhaps not the subject matter that Wang Shuo deals with—small-scale swindlers, shallow social climbers, and petty entrepreneurs—so much as the nonchalant, matter-of-fact attitude he takes, in his subject matter as in his career. Wang Shuo has said again and again that he writes to entertain his audience and therefore to make money.

Wang Shuo's fiction tackles issues "serious" critics should not have shied away from: the market value of literature; middle-brow fiction and its evanescent marketability; and above all, *literary production that really is for the people*. Thus, one cannot help laughing when reading the opening chapter of *Not Serious at All* (*Yidianer zhengjing meiyou* 一點兒正經沒有, 1989), in which four second-rate writers sit around a table playing mahjongg and discussing how they plan to make money by writing "obsession with China" stories. In the midst of calls orchestrated by the post–June Fourth censorship for more "new realism," it is Wang Shuo who shows us what "new" realism means.

The meaning of justice has been one of the most important themes of modern Chinese literature, and the manifestation of justice in fiction one of literature's principal duties. In view of social and political chaos at various levels, writers since the May Fourth have been occupied with the mission of "representing" justice in both narrative and legal terms. Questions have been raised again and again: How can writers articulate the pain of those who are suffering mutely? How can they denominate the source of evils in fiction and see to its eradication in reality? How can they right wrongs and thus restore poetic as well as social justice? More important, if chivalric and court-case fiction can be said to be the classical genre through which a set of concepts about justice, order, and agency was valorized, what is the modern equivalent that renegotiates these concepts?

This persistent concern about the relation between literature and justice took on a new dimension in the 1980s, as the social and political structures on both sides of the Taiwan Straits underwent drastic changes. When the judicial system proved too slow or too perfunctory in response to individual and governmental wrongdoings, some of which had not been even disclosed until recently, Chinese people found in literature an imaginary road to justice. The popularity of "scar literature" (*shanghen wenxue* 傷痕文學) and numerous pieces of reportage at this time testify to the public desire to define and realize justice anew. Writers like Wang Meng 王蒙, Bai Hua 白樺, Liu Binyan 劉賓雁, and Dai Houying 戴厚英, among others, who dared to confront censorship and taboos and speak out for the people, were hailed as modern counterparts of chivalric heroes and investigative judges.[5]

That Chinese writers are honored as spokesmen or even avengers on behalf of "the insulted and the injured," however, has to be subjected to a kind of somber reflection. Granting their willingness to be so, writers are neither imperial investigators nor chivalric law enforcers. When writers take up roles that should appear in fiction, and a rather old-fashioned type of fiction such as the chivalric and court-case novel at that, it means less an overflow of their moral potential than the fundamental shortcircuiting of social and individual agency in implementing justice. Lu Xun's dilemma between answering the call to arms and simply wandering serves as a classic example illus-

5. For his series of investigative reportage on the corruption of the PRC bureaucracy, such as *People or Monsters* (*Renyao zhijian*, 1981), Liu Binyan was nicknamed "The impartial investigative judge Liu," Liu Qingtian 劉青天, by his readers. See afterword to Liu Binyan 1985: 323.

trating modern Chinese writers' painful search for a proper role. That search, as Marston Anderson succinctly argues, would end up with a realization of the "limits of realism," of the impossibility of being a writer and a fighter at the same time (1990: chap. 5).

But Lu Xun's and his followers' syndrome should be traced back even to the late Qing era. In Liu E's 劉 鶚 *The Travels of Lao Can* (*Lao Can youji* 老 殘 遊 記), it will be recalled, Lao Can behaves like a chivalric hero in helping the weak withstand the strong even though he is by profession only a wandering literatus/doctor. Leo Lee points out this mixed identity of Lao Can, calling him a "civilian knight-errant, a *wen-hsia* [*wen xia* 文 俠] who uses his mind and herbal medicines, rather than his sword, to redress social injustice" (1985: 286). The term "civilian knight-errant" contains a paradox: instead of a sword, Lao Can uses a pen to right wrongs; in the battle for social justice, instead of blood, he spills ink. Throughout the novel, Lao Can's integrity drives him again and again to challenge authorities at the expense of personal well-being, but in a society in which the incorruptible judges are described as even more dangerous than the corruptible ones, can a civilian knight-errant like Lao Can really re-enact the old chivalric victories with his pen as his weapon?

Lu Xun did not fully appreciate the dilemma besetting Lao Can, but his skepticism would have kept him from believing in an easy conflation of writing with justice. The majority of writers in the wake of the May Fourth literary revolution failed to understand the lesson of Lao Can. Lacking the type of self-reflection and skepticism inherent in Lu Xun, however, they opted for a very different union of the sword and the pen. In the name of "literature for the sake of revolution," these writers made themselves and their characters alike new-styled "civilian knights-errant," if not militant fighters who forsook their pens altogether. Against social establishments, they wanted to enact justice on an ideal plane of their own.

To be sure, these modern writers denigrated classical chivalric and court-case fiction as feudal literature of the worst kind. But as I have argued elsewhere (Wang 1994b), the traditional notion of "chivalric knight-errantry," *xia* 俠, had already been frequently invoked by late Qing progressive writers as an archetype for modern-day revolutionaries. Liang Qichao's *The Future of New China* (*Xin Zhongguo weilai ji* 新 中 國 未 來 記, 1902), Yuyi nüshi's 羽 衣 女 士 *Heroines of East Europe* (*Dongou nühaojie* 東 歐 女 豪 傑, 1904), Wang Miaoru's 王 妙 如 *A Flower in Woman's Jail* (*Nüyu hua* 女 獄 花, 1904),

and Haitian duxiaozi's 海天獨嘯子 *The Rock of Goddess Nüwa* (*Nüwa shi* 女媧石, 1906) are only the most salient examples. The noble concepts of altruism, rebellion, valor, fraternity, self-sacrifice, and even stoicism that spewed forth from the pens of the young, revolutionary authors of the post–May Fourth era were not all due to foreign influences; they were the familiar tropes of chivalric fiction. These concepts facilitated their rationalizations of the act of writing, if not the writings themselves.

Covertly, however, the post–May Fourth revolutionary writers permitted themselves some secret models, models drawn from such novels as *Three Knights and Five Sworn Brothers* (*Sanxia wuyi* 三俠五義, 1872). These novels carry authorial messages and character alignments that would have been regarded as most reactionary; they celebrate chivalric heroes' dedication, gallantry, and fraternity only insofar as they serve the absolute imperial power. But change the ruling classes to the party, and the villainous rebels to those with antiparty programs, and the old novels could easily be copied into the new. History witnessed the ghostly return of reactionary themes, however, when rebellious "new youth" in modern Chinese fiction and reality traded in their militant individualism for a collective utopia and dedicated their personal talents to a total(itarian) ideology that tolerated no challenge.

Just as the domestication of men- and women-at-arms into imperial watchdogs constitutes the major theme of the late Qing chivalric and court-case novel, so the taming of male and female rebels/revolutionaries into ideological robots became the gist of modern revolutionary novels from the 1920s to the 1960s. Modern variations of the chivalric and court-case novel appear to have been denied entry to the canon of mainstream Chinese fiction but in fact underlie its commonplace forms. So my questions lie in the opposite direction: Were the other traces of the old genre ever written out of the canon? Were the late Qing subversions of the old genre absorbed into the new genre along with the oldest of its conventions?

These questions become all the more pertinent when one views selected fiction of the late twentieth century in the light of late Qing chivalric and court-case fiction. Writings of the early 1980s may have indicated that, after all the chaos and turmoil, limited justice can still be restored, at least at the poetic level. Writings on the eve and in the aftermath of the Tian'anmen Incident teach a new lesson, however, about how even that frail poetic justice has to be undone in order to twice flaunt the injustice of history. When the last group of modern-day "civilian knights-errant" and investigative judges like Liu Binyan and Dai Qing have been driven into exile, can we expect any more chivalric-minded writers to right wrongs for us? The younger generation of writers have cast deep doubts on becoming "civilian knights-errant," and they have been reluctant to create such heroes in their works.

As the title of Ye Zhaoyan's 葉兆言 new novella, *A Hero Who Mourns over the Past* (*Shangshi de yingxiong* 傷逝的英雄, 1993), neatly suggests, aging heroes and decaying heroism have occupied contemporary Chinese writers whenever the subjects of heroes and hero worship arise. The protagonist of the novella fought for both the Nationalist and the Communist parties during his long career. Years of experience in the battlefield, however, have left the retired hero with no pride, with nothing but unfathomable nihilism and frustration. At moments, he wishes he had died young in a certain war for a certain ideology like most of his comrades. But now each of his (involuntary) remembrances of things past brings to light hidden motivations and petty contingencies behind the façade of those wars he has fought. Surviving the memories of the past becomes the gravest challenge of his life.

A similar theme is explored in Wang Anyi's 王安憶 novella *The Story of My Uncle* (*Shushu de gushi* 叔叔的故事, 1991). Like thousands of enlightened youth of his time, the uncle in the novella committed himself to the cause of revolutionary literature, only to realize that, after the ups and downs of a long career as a cadre/writer, he has ended up being a man without a firm belief. He finds solace in endless sexual liaisons, which humiliate his family and scandalize his colleagues. As Wang Anyi notes, the uncle's story is not so much about the loss of his moral bearings as about the eclipse of one kind of heroism. Through losing himself in illicit sexual consummations, the uncle experiences the dissemination of his ideals and sacrifices.

The Taiwan writer Zhang Dachun predates Ye Zhaoyan and Wang Anyi in dealing with aging heroes and aged heroism. Zhang Dachun first won wide acclaim in the late 1970s for his sensitive portraits of aging mainland retired soldiers engaged in a losing war against time. Zhang's work underwent a remarkable change in both style and content in the 1980s as Taiwan's economic and political upheavals signified the arrival of a new age. In "The General's Monument" ("Jiangjun bei" 將軍碑, 1986), a story about an old GMD army general's fantastic visitations of the past through a time tunnel, Zhang questions the myth of total history through an anachronistic plot; in "Sixi Worries About His Country" ("Sixi you guo" 四喜憂國, 1988), a story about a retired GMD soldier's one-man campaign against Chinese Communists waged by writing posters in the style of a presidential address, he ponders the ironic terms of patriotism. At a time when ideological conviction has degenerated into empty slogans, when national alliances have given way to commercial contracts, the sound of offstage laughter is persistent.

In terms of a heroism held at bay, it is never too farfetched to relate works by Ye Zhaoyan, Wang Anyi, and Zhang Dachun to the dark subtexts underlying late Qing chivalric fiction. The "heroes" in these contemporary writers' descriptions are heroes whose valor and wisdom were once validated by huge propaganda machines. They fought for a noble immediate end, in service of some higher ultimate ideology beyond their understanding. When the immediate ends vanish and the ideology loses its mystery, these heroes suffer from a deep sense of loss. In a way, these late twentieth-century heroes live out the unwritten part of the lives of those late Qing chivalric knights-errant. In a novel like *Three Knights-Errant and Five Sworn Brothers*, one recalls, traditional men- and women-at-arms are honored for trading in their individual codes of valor and accepting higher, imperial mandates.

Late Qing writers want to make it seem as if the co-optation of the knights-errant is a happy solution for the conflict between the lawbreakers and the lawgivers, producing a kind of higher synthesis of the modes of justice and injustice. Their actual novels can betray that intention, implicitly showing the disastrous effects of co-optation. Late twentieth-century writers relearn the ugly aspect of the late Qing co-optation scenario: submission may lead to fame and fortune or, just as easily, to purge and liquidation. But in contemporary fiction there is one even more unbearable fate: to survive death and humiliation and to be nothing at all, not even worth remembering.

Writing in an age in which heroes can only "mourn over the past," it is little wonder that contemporary Chinese novelists should hark back to past ages whenever retelling a story with chivalric bearings. Mo Yan's *Red Sorghum Family* (*Hong gaoliang jiazu* 紅高粱家族, 1987), for example, takes us to the rural northeastern Shandong of mid-Republican days. The heroes and heroines introduced here are neither revolutionaries nor warriors but a group of strong, self-reliant peasants. Amid natural disasters, internal wars, and Japanese attacks, these peasants live and even thrive by walking the fine line between banditry and law enforcement. They establish their own legal and moral codes, for which they would willingly sacrifice their own lives. Through his exuberant language and rich symbolism, Mo Yan describes these peasants as larger-than-life figures, their adventures and romances having already become legend. Gone are the days of these last chivalric heroes, and the legendary tone of the narration emphasizes the inaccessible pastness or even mythicality of the heroism. As the narrator, the sole descendent of the red sorghum family, relates his family's legends, he does so as someone too young to have seen or done the deeds, except in imagination.

Another mainland Chinese writer, Zhang Chengzhi 張承志, moves the time of the last spark of chivalric heroism further back, to the turn of the twentieth century. Zhang's "A Study of an Assassination Plan in the West Province" ("Xisheng ansha kao" 西省暗殺考, 1991) is a novella about the capricious terms of revenge against the background of Muslim northwest China. Its protagonist starts out as a teenage member of a Muslim assassination squad, which has vowed to kill Zuo Zongtang, the late Qing general allegedly responsible for thousands of deaths in his crackdown on the Muslim rebellions of the late nineteenth century. The young assassin witnesses numerous abortive assassination attempts, all the while sacrificing his own youth, marriage, family, and everything else for the cause. After Zuo dies from natural causes, Zuo's descendants become the target of the aging assassin. But just as he is about to launch his final attempt, he is struck most unexpectedly by the news that the Qing government has collapsed: the ultimate reason for his vendetta evaporates. Zhang rationalizes his protagonist's lifelong dedication to revenge by making reference to religious fanaticism, although the way he recounts his novella reminds one more of those ancient stories about chivalric assassins. The peculiar kind of heroism that is founded on political and religious conviction bids fair, in the modern world, to leave the hero stranded, the quest emptied of all meaning.

As if corresponding to Mo Yan's and Zhang Chengzhi's nostalgic mood, Zhang Dachun sets his collection of chivalric stories, *Happy Thieves* (*Huanxi zei* 歡喜賊, 1990), in the 1860s and 1870s. By the time his stories take place, according to Zhang, some provincial Qing governments have already reached a peace agreement with local thieves and bandits. The deal was reached, however, not by having the lawbreakers serve investigative judges, as old chivalric and court-case fiction would have had it, but by granting them the right to commit crimes in areas only outside their home provinces! The thieves and bandits in Zhang's stories faithfully carry out the deal; a new collaboration between the outlaws and the (local) government is formed, creating a network of mutual victimizations.

Zhang Dachun thus radically mocks late Qing chivalric and court-case novels such as *Three Knights-Errant and Five Sworn Brothers.* These novels became popular in the second half of the nineteenth century, just about the same time Zhang's thieves and bandits allegedly enjoyed their prosperity. *Happy Thieves* seems to suggest that, even in the golden days of the chivalric and court-case novel, the codes of chivalry and justice had already degenerated. Perhaps the genre of the chivalric and court-case novel can thrive only by basing its verisimilitude on a regressive temporal agenda. After all, *Three Knights-Errant and Five Sworn Brothers* supposedly takes place not in the late nineteenth century (late Qing) but in the mid-eleventh century (early Northern Song).

Chinese fiction since the late 1980s is the ironic intrusion of the writer into a dream world of romance and sophistication. Often set against a luxurious urban backdrop, dangerous liaisons and libertine romances are depicted in such a way as to implicate a society deeply devoted to the twin sports of desiring and being desired. Eroticism is an important ingredient in works along this line, but it is not necessarily generated by sensual episodes or sexually explicit descriptions, at least no more than by the "grammar" of eros in a given ambiance. For all their protestations of lives dedicated to nonchalant prurience, these works demonstrate something else: frenzy in quest of bodily satisfaction; fatigue with quotidian existence, however glamorous it may appear; and unfathomable desire for anomalies, for transgressions of the bounds of ordinary sensuality.

I would describe fiction of this tendency as the "new depravity fiction." By saying "new" depravity fiction, I have in mind late Qing depravity fiction as the immediate antecedent to contemporary writers' turn to the decadent aspects of the Chinese imagination. The term "depravity fiction," *xiaxie xiaoshuo* 狹 邪 小 說, was coined by Lu Xun in his study of late Qing fictionalized lives of courtesans (1976: 319–35). In his usage, Lu Xun indicated that *xiaxie* meant not only the decadent subject matter but also the air of prurience and even self-congratulation that pervaded the narratorial closure. "Depravity fiction" therefore means a writing that is wayward both in content and in narrative attitude. Following in Lu Xun's steps, critics of the May Fourth tradition have usually complained that late Qing depravity novels are crudely written, full of clichéd descriptions and formulaic actions. But these are themselves conventional observations. To be "wayward," one must disobey conventions; truly "wayward" fictions may therefore disguise their disobedience of convention by an exaggerated observation of certain obvious conventions.

Elsewhere I have discussed that a closer reading of novels such as *Precious Mirror for Judging Flowers* (*Pinhua baojian* 品花寶鑒, 1849), *Singsong Girls of Shanghai* (*Haishang hua liezhuan* 海上花列傳, 1892), and *A Flower in the Sea of Sins* (*Niehai hua* 孽海花, 1905) may lead one to some unexpected discoveries, to traits that inform a Chinese modernist consciousness already at the turn of the twentieth century (Wang 1994a). At its best, late Qing depravity fiction redefines conventions of romantic and erotic fiction and creates three things: a social space—the courtesan house—in which supposedly incomparable intellectual, ethical, and ideological worlds mingle and conflate, thereby bringing into question all boundaries; a body politic, which derives its liberating force from the circulation of "en-gendered" flesh and dissemination of desire; and an economy of excess, through which the traditional modes of communication and consumption (sexual, economic, and literary), productivity and expenditure, are reconfigured.

By invoking the term *xiaxie* or "depravity" to describe a trend in contemporary Chinese fiction, I do not mean that these works are consciously reviving the theme of prostitution or courtesan life against the background of late twentieth-century China or Taiwan; rather, I am suggesting that contemporary writers' penchant for eroticizing social/historical dynamics, together with their fascination with a stylistics of expenditure and ornamentation, constitutes a discourse reminiscent of that of the late Qing. Late Qing depravity fiction makes the prostitute house a chronotope wherein games of money and desire, love and lust, are played out; the new depravity fiction breaks that symbolic/geographical closure, seeing society itself as the promiscuous space in which the mingling of classes, trades, ideologies, and bodies is carried on.

The rise of new depravity fiction also sheds light on a modern Chinese literary trend, one that was driven to the margin as mainstream May Fourth discourse thrived. This marginalized writing can be evinced in the Mandarin Ducks and Butterflies writings, by the sexual aesthetics of the notorious Dr. Sex, Zhang Jingsheng (see Peng 1992), by neo-impressionists such as Mu Shiying 穆時英 (1912–40), Liu Na'ou 劉吶鷗 (1900–1940), and Shi Zhecun 施蟄存, by romantic literati from Yu Dafu 郁達夫 (1896–1945) and Shao Xunmei 邵洵美 (1906–68) (see Lee 1993) to Wu Mingshi 無名

氏, and by Eileen Chang 張愛玲 (1921–95). Despite their play with the new, Western sexual politics, these writers demonstrated a range of sensibilities already cultivated in late Qing *xiaxie* fiction. Their writings reconstructed the old locus in which desire is legitimated and transgression systematized in newly established public and private spaces, exhibiting depravity in a gallery of modern *flaneurs* and *femmes fatales* consumed by a perennial desire. Instead of obsession with China, these writers looked into aspects of modern Chinese people rarely touched on by literary histories: their insatiable curiosity to probe the labyrinth of desire, their indulgence in the aesthetic as well as erotic spectacles of the decadent, and their postures of indifference, compelled by the premature anxiety of a fin-de-siècle epoch.

Recent works by two women writers from Taiwan, Zhu Tianwen 朱天文 and Li Ang 李昂, can illustrate my argument. In Zhu Tianwen's acclaimed *Fin-de-siècle Splendor* (*Shijimo de huali* 世紀末的華麗, 1990), a collection of seven stories about the new, self-styled "Taibei people," Taibei is seen as a city that is masquerading on the way to its eternal downfall in a most dazzling, spectacular manner, an East Asian "Sodom decorated with flowers and perfumes" (Zhan 1990: 11). The "new people" of Taibei—gay yuppies, models/mistresses, moviemakers, elite intellectuals—thrive and fail in the hustle and bustle of the cosmopolitan city, desperately searching in vain for love. Amid a sense of eschatological melancholy and the urge to seize the day, Zhu Tianwen's characters abandon themselves to their fin-de-siècle syndromes.

But might not this fin-de-siècle self-abandon already be stale repetition: a decadent posture borrowed from the post-Victorian West as well as from late Qing China? It is not difficult to discern Zhu Tianwen's indebtedness to Western fin-de-siècle aesthetics, as I have done elsewhere (Wang 1992b). It is more challenging to ponder the possibility that Zhu may have inherited the moral anxiety and decadent poetics of late Qing depravity fiction. Zhu is a diligent follower of Eileen Chang, the spokeswoman of the Chinese decadent of the 1940s. Chang, it will be remembered, was an enthusiastic consumer of late Qing depravity fiction; she translated *Singsong Girls from Shanghai* from the Wu dialect into Mandarin Chinese as late as the early 1980s (Zhang Ailing [Eileen Chang] 1983).[6] For all their pursuit of fun and games, characters in Zhu's stories amplify themes already inherent in works of late

---

6. The original version of the novel has 64 chapters; Chang shortened the original and produced a 60-chapter edition.

Qing depravity fiction such as *Traces of Flowers and Moon* (*Huayue hen* 花月痕, 1858) and *Singsong Girls from Shanghai*: a fear that the good time the courtesans and their patrons are having will soon run out, or, worse, that the good times they thought they were having may never have come and never will come.

Whereas Zhu Tianwen creates a hollow spectacle for people of Taibei who cannot love, Li Ang's *Labyrinthine Garden* (*Miyuan* 迷園, 1991) presents a sensual *and* bleak view of people of Taibei who do love. *Labyrinthine Garden* deals with the painful process through which its heroine comes to terms with her own body and sexuality. But this woman's education in femininity cannot be complete without her being initiated into other realms of Taiwan politics, such as Taiwan's colonial experience under Japanese occupation, the rule of the GMD after 1949, and the burgeoning Taiwan dissident movement of the 1990s. Sex does not stand alone, defining sensuality; political action mingles with it, also defining sensuality. The result is a dazzling portrait of a politicized eros and an eroticized politics. As such, *Labyrinthine Garden* partakes of one of the themes of the late Qing novel, *A Flower in the Sea of Sins*: that of the legendary courtesan and socialite Sai Jinhua (1884–1936), who allegedly changed late Qing history through her sexual adventures.

In terms of reiterating the kind of sexual politics first expressed in *A Flower in the Sea of Sins*, Shi Shuqing 施叔青, a Taiwan woman writer who has lived in Hong Kong since the late 1970s, perhaps accomplishes even more than Li Ang. In her most recent novels, *Victoria Club* (*Weiduoliya julebu* 維多利亞聚樂部, 1993) and *Her Name Is Butterfly* (*Ta ming jiao hudie* 他名叫蝴蝶, 1993), the rise and fall of Hong Kong is literally paralleled with the ups and downs of a prostitute. The legend of Sai Jinhua has found its late twentieth-century counterpart. Hong Kong is the place where everything can be bought or sold, a place where people can come and go in a promiscuous mingling. Promiscuity indeed becomes the emblem of Shi's fictional Hong Kong for the intercourse of the no-longer-different worlds of commerce, politics, literature, theater: it spreads metaphorically throughout the text in the way in which it spreads throughout the city. Bankers, merchants, politicians, socialites, call girls, compradores, and intellectuals find themselves mixed together, all engaged in promoting the circularity of money, financial tips, sex, fashions, ideas, social critiques. In the shadow of the impending crises of 1997 and 1999, men and women in Hong Kong are willing victims of an eschatological masquerade.

Another woman writer from Hong Kong, Li Bihua 李 碧 華, replaces the anxiety or indignation that occurs in Shi Shuqing's and Li Ang's works with a display of unsurprised narratorial tranquility. Witness her ingenious rewriting of the old stories about *femmes fatales*, such as *Green Snake* (*Qing she* 青 蛇, 1990). The novel is a testimonial to desire as the magical force that reproduces itself, forever, against all adversity. But the desire thus conceived points to a closed system of the desired object and its displacements. Each time White Snake and Green Snake, her servant/lover/rival, wake up from their slumber in search of a new liaison, they re-enact their libidinous wish to overcome the lapse of time even as they confirm their submission to the circularity of renewed desire. Li's works may not be reminiscent of any specific late Qing depravity model, but her penchant for retelling old "decadent" stories drives home the rationale of the late Qing genre's snarled, repetitive narrative structure, one nurtured on recycled narratives of desire and recycled desires for narrative.

In the wake of the relative liberation from Maoist ideological constraints, many mainland writers have explored the "forbidden zone of sexuality," *xing jinqu* 性 禁 區, a trend that culminated in the late 1980s, with examples such as Wang Anyi's "Three Love" ("Sanlian" 三 戀) trilogy (1988): *Love in a Small Town* (*Xiaocheng zhi lian* 小 城 之 戀), *Love on a Barren Mountain* (*Huangshan zhi lian* 荒 山 之 戀), and *Love in the Jinxiu Valley* (*Jinxiugu zhi lian* 錦 繡 谷 之 戀). Of course, this new tendency to explore the sexual awareness of mainland Chinese can be described as depraved only by the old "revolutionary" standard. Its daring exposés and brazen rhetoric cannot hide a basic absence of the leisure and self-indulgence that generate a decadent culture, much less the post-modern awareness that lets decadence interplay with the rest of culture. One does not see works in the vein of new depravity fiction as I define it, till most recently, for example Su Tong's 蘇 童 selected works and Jia Pingwa's 賈 平 凹 *Abandoned Capital* (*Feidu* 廢 都, 1993).

Su Tong's best stories on the subject of decadence always take place in the days before the Communist revolution. Novellas and novels such as *The Family of Poppies* (*Yingsu zhi jia* 罌 粟 之 家, 1988), *The Diaspora of 1934* (*Yijiusansi nian de taowang* 一 九 三 四 年 的 逃 亡, 1988), *Rouge* (*Hongfen* 紅 粉, 1990), *Rice* (*Mi* 米, 1991), and *The Fall of the South* (*Nanfang de duoluo* 南 方 的 墮 落, 1992) deal with a historical moment when totems and taboos are disintegrating and orthodox thought is in shambles. This is the moment in which the flowers of evil begin to bloom: effeminate landlords, licentious concubines, languorous prostitutes, fervent revolutionaries, all are thrown together in the social space reserved for adultery, incest, drug addiction, madness, conspiracy, riot, and death. Revolution is seen as nurtured on these elements.

Su Tong's most remarkable achievement to date, however, is his novel *My Life as an Emperor* (*Wode diwang shengya* 我的帝王生涯, 1992). Dealing with the rise and fall of the last emperor of a fictitious Chinese dynasty, the novel first appears to be an exposé of royal life written in a nostalgic manner. A close reading shows, however, that Su Tong accumulates and rearranges anecdotes and legends from all the dynastic chronicles. With such devices, he turns the novel into an acrobatic extravaganza of all the "last dynasty" syndromes: imperial conspiracies, wars, power struggles are interwoven with sex scandals, love tragedies, and romantic schemes—less a royal melodrama than a celebration of the human capacity for degeneracy.

The internationally acclaimed writer Jia Pingwa scandalized the whole of China in the summer of 1993 with his novel *The Abandoned Capital*. Unlike Su Tong, who refines his narrative of a declining civilization with a lyrical style, Jia Pingwa forces readers to witness the raw aspect of contemporary Chinese society in a naturalist immediacy. *The Abandoned Capital* depicts a group of modern-styled literati's futile pursuit of vanities, ranging from fame to flesh, against the backdrop of the ancient city, Xi'an. An instant bestseller, the novel has won its popularity—or notoriety—mainly for its flagrant erotic scenes and its exposés of dissipation in a socialist country. Critics have identified *Golden Lotus* (*Jin Ping Mei* 金瓶梅) as Jia's model (Wu Liang 1994); they have overlooked the fact that, besides consuming lust, characters in *The Abandoned Capital* are capable of love. To explain this effect, one must draw on the erotic discourse of late Qing depravity fiction, in which characters assume the roles of both Jia Baoyu 賈寶玉 and Ximen Qing 西門慶, both Lin Daiyu 林黛玉 and Pan Jinlian 潘金蓮. The games of love and lust are so mixed that one can no longer distinguish their boundaries. Moral judgment aside, no other mainstream PRC writer has dared to go so far in exploring desire and its horrible consequences. Jia Pingwa literally plays out the "hard-core" realism first initiated by the May Fourth writers and presents a society well on its way to the edge of the carnal abyss.

Critics of an ideologically hygienic sort may see in *The Abandoned Capital* the last sign of capitalist degeneration, the final commodification of the socialist body and subjectivity by evil forces emanating from post-modern

Taiwan and Hong Kong. But one may equally argue that the lack of a discourse of depravity in mainland Chinese fiction as defined above does not reflect a purer state of its body politic, as much as it indicates an unclosed gap in its dialogical system between the normative and the transgressive, procreativity and expenditure, the inhuman and the all too human. But then, can the hundred thousand words of *The Abandoned Capital* compare to the billion words uttered in the name of Chairman Mao during countless movements, purges, and self-abasements? Living and writing in a society that still puritanically keeps the discourse of depravity separate from other discourses and enjoying the furtive debasements of hidden social terrains, mainland authors and readers have yet to enter into a social space in which discourses mix to flaunt their inherent hybridity and provide a more sophisticated exposé or critique of the power of depravity.

I conclude this survey with an examination of contemporary Chinese science fantasy. Compared with the other three genres discussed above, science fantasy has a relatively smaller market share. But it supports a group of writers and readers whose creative force and loyalty are never to be underestimated. By "science fantasy," I mean fiction that derives its power from narrating outlandish elements and illusory beings, in such a way as to stimulate a reader's fancy at both the imaginative and epistemological levels.[7] Science fantasy is at its most tantalizing when it impresses one as having united two seemingly conflicting discourses: that of knowledge and truth and that of dream and fabulation. For all its avowed departure from present-day reality, the genre engages us because it nevertheless gravitates toward reality. In practice, science fantasy finds manifestations in various subgenres: odysseys in space, time travel, robots and robotics, bionic wars and mechanized paradises, utopias and dystopias, to mention only a few.

The May Fourth literary tradition never paid serious attention to science fantasy, even though *science* was a major slogan of the enlightened intelligentsia. With the mimetic devices newly learned from the West, writers of mainstream May Fourth fiction were busy representing the real as it was

7. For more definitions of science fantasy, see Suvin 1988 and Malmgren 1991. For a general introduction to the rise of modern Chinese science fiction, see D. Wu 1989. I use the term "science fantasy," rather than the more common term "science fiction," intentionally, so as to stress a wider range of non-realist genres as incorporated by modern Chinese writers into their works.

represented in the best Western examples. They endorsed realism because it was the only "modern" and "scientific" way of writing and thinking, and therefore it was the only solution for China. Witness Mao Dun's advocacy of naturalism, the offspring of realism, as a "literary science" in the late twenties (Wang 1992a: 69–78). As a matter of fact, science fantasy arose in early nineteenth-century Europe almost at the same time as conventional European realism. In many ways the two genres formed a dialogue in regard to nineteenth-century Western writers' exploration of the boundaries of reality, actual and potential.

By the end of the nineteenth century, science fantasy had developed to become one of the most popular genres among Western readers; its presence in China can be demonstrated in newspaper serializations of Edward Bellamy's *Looking Backward, 2000–1887*, appearing from 1891 to 1892, followed by translations of works by such authors as Jules Verne and H. G. Wells. The turn of the twentieth century (the late Qing) witnessed a surge of writing and translation of science fantasy among Chinese writers. Liang Qichao, Wu Jianren, and Lu Xun all learned either to create their own science fantasy works or to translate European successes.[8]

Few writers of the post–May Fourth generation tried their hands at science fantasy. Lao She's *City of Cats* (*Maocheng ji* 貓城記, 1933) and Shen Congwen's *Alice's Travels in China* (*Alisi Zhongguo youji* 阿麗思中國遊記, 1932) are two of the handful of examples from that generation. This, however, does not mean that science fantasy completely vanished from modern Chinese fiction. As Rudolf Wagner's meticulous research indicates, the genre actually enjoyed a short-lived bloom in the PRC from the mid-1950s to the early 1960s, as part of the campaign for "marching toward science" (1985: 37). The pedigree of the genre can also be traced back to the late 1930s and 1940s, as illustrated by the founding of the popular-science journal *Taibai* 太白, by Chinese translations of Russian science fantasies, and by the publication of science fantasy writings from both the leftist and rightist camps (Wagner 1985: 37).

8. Wu Jianren wrote *A New Story of the Stone* (*Xin Shitou ji* 新石頭記) in 1904, a fantastic sequel to Cao Xueqin's 曹雪芹 classic; in the novel, Jia Baoyu visits the utopian "world of civilization," *wenming jingjie* 文明境界, through a time tunnel. Based on a Japanese translation, Lu Xun translated, or rather rewrote, Jules Verne's *De la terre à la lune* into *Yuejie lüxing* 月界旅行 in 1903. He also translated *Voyage au centre de la terre*.

Science fantasy enjoyed a brief comeback in late 1970s China, following the fall of the Gang of Four; it assumed, as Wagner argues, a new role as "lobby literature," a literature "presenting scientists' group aspirations in the form of the fantasy future, and portraying how scientists would operate in the larger framework of society if their demands were met" (1985: 44). To expand Wagner's thesis a little more, one may very well argue that this mode of science fantasy as lobby literature has always occupied a space in PRC fiction. Be it called socialist realism, revolutionary realism, or revolutionary romanticism, early PRC fiction can be readily seen as science fantasy of the most outrageous kind, one about the sublation of all sciences through the Marxist-Maoist "science," about the realization of a socialist utopia in the present as if in an ever regressive future.

If science fantasy of the early 1980s served as a "lobby literature" in anticipation of a brighter political and intellectual future, science fantasy of the early 1990s has taken on a much more ambiguous dimension. Writers from both Taiwan and mainland China have sent mixed signals when looking backward or forward. Although the ongoing murk of politics is still the primary concern of their works, these writers surpass their predecessors from the May Fourth to the early 1980s by lavishing production values on their daydreams and nightmares. They have brought us back to the late Qing era, when science fantasy first fascinated and stimulated Chinese writers and readers. By envisioning China on the verge either of a miraculous rejuvenation or of an eternal destruction, or by prophesying China either as a post-nuclear wasteland or as instigator of a new "yellow peril," contemporary Chinese science fantasy writers create different temporal and spatial zones through which to ponder the possible futures of their nation. Their endeavors should look familiar. It is in the steps of late Qing science fantasy writers, such as Liang Qichao (*The Future Of New China* [*Xin Zhongguo weilai ji* 新中國未來記, 1902]) and Biheguan zhuren 碧荷館主人 (*New Era* [*Xin jiyuan* 新紀元, 1910]), that these writers are again exploring the frontiers of the genre.

Just as in the late Qing, the utopia and the dystopia remain the favorite subgenres of contemporary Chinese science fantasy writers. By imagining a future landscape for Taiwan or China, these writers test out their political anxieties or desires. Yao Jiawen's 姚嘉文 *Taiwan Straits: 1999* (*Taihai 1999* 台海一九九九, 1992), for example, is a prophecy about what would have happened to Taiwan by the end of the twentieth century. By 1999, according to Yao, Taiwan will have already declared independence from China and rejoined the stage of world politics. While on its way to becoming the most democratic and prosperous state of Asia, Taiwan maintains a relationship of friendly rivalry with China. The novel centers around a plot in which Taiwan businessmen and politicians help the Chinese government to develop the Yangtze dam project, solve ecological problems, and even avert a political coup.

A veteran politician for the cause of Taiwan independence, Yao Jiawen wrote *Taiwan Straits: 1999* with a clear agenda: to lay out an ideal blueprint for a future Taiwan. In so doing, Yao has inherited a literary model from early modern China, with which he would probably wish to have as little to do as possible. Both Kang Youwei's 康有為 (1858–1927) *A Book About the World Of Commonwealth* (*Datong shu* 大同書, 1902) and Liang Qichao's *The Future of New China* were written as idealist accounts of a future China. One especially remembers how, in 1902, Liang wrote about the China of 1962: a model country with a constitutional monarchy, a revitalized utopia of Confucianism, and a supreme world power. Yao shares with Liang the same kind of earnest historical re-revisionism and nationalist yearning. A reader used to Western science fantasy would complain that, their futurist tenses notwithstanding, Yao's and Liang's works fall short of any scientific and fantastic elements. But insofar as they are ideologues turned into novelists, the "science" of politics is that which concerns Liang and Yao; and there can be no subject more "fantastic" than that of the founding of a new Taiwan or China. The irony is, if Yao's novel has only managed to reiterate the tenor of Liang's *The Future of New China* almost a century ago, one wonders how new his knowledge of the future of a new Taiwan would really be.

The mainland writer Liang Xiaosheng 梁曉聲 recaptures the other, darker side of late Qing sociopolitical science fantasy. Liang's *Floating City* (*Fucheng* 浮城, 1992) deals with the disastrous consequences that ensue when a metropolis of southeastern China (Shanghai?) is mysteriously disconnected from the mainland. The floating city drifts aimlessly, seeking a new country to attach itself to, while it confronts numerous threats at sea, including attacks from thousands of vicious birds, which seem to have flown in from the movie *The Birds* by Alfred Hitchcock. The residents of this floating city, nevertheless, have not been truly affected by their forced exile; they carry on their lustful affairs, sordid deals, petty fights, "overseas" fever, and bureaucratic corruption just as before.

A gloomy satire of life in contemporary China, *Floating City* bears the imprint of Lao She's *City of Cats*, a bitter allegory about an astronaut's visit to a corrupt Cat Country on the eve of its total destruction. But Liang's novel is even closer to the dystopian moments in late Qing novels, particularly the two allegories that respectively open Liu E's *The Travels of Lao Can* and Zeng Pu's *A Flower in the Sea of Sins*. In the prelude of *The Travels of Lao Can*, Liu E introduces a sinking ship, whose crew and passengers can never agree on how to save their own lives except for throwing Lao Can, their only hope, into the sea. Zeng Pu starts *A Flower in the Sea of Sins* with a story about a Happy Slave Island (Nule dao 奴樂島), whose citizens happily enjoy life in the face of a miserable destiny. Mix these two images of late Qing China, the sinking ship and the intoxicated island in "the sea of sins," and one gets Liang Xiaosheng's metaphor for late twentieth-century China.

Liang Xiaosheng's dystopia appears only too mild, nevertheless, when compared with the devastating plot of the novel *The Yellow Peril* (*Huang huo* 黃禍, 1991) by Bao Mi 保密 ("Confidential"—allegedly the pseudonym of a well-known writer in hiding after the Tian'anmen Incident). In this stupendous novel of more than half a million words, China is described as finally split into parts after Tian'anmen. Worse, nuclear power is employed as a weapon as warlords and politicians fight an internal war. The war accelerates quickly, involving first Taiwan and then America and Russia, to the point where nuclear bombs are fired en masse and the whole world is ruined.

As China enters the first stage of the world war, some scientists and politicians have launched a secret plan of emigrating Chinese overseas. More than a billion Chinese are sent to the rest of the world; wherever they go, they cause immediate political and economic crises. The Chinese exodus has become a true Yellow Peril. In the aftermath of the nuclear holocaust, however, it is the Chinese survivors, now everywhere, who are most ready to clean up the earth. But can they really do it?

Combining eschatological prophecy and political satire, the formula of the science disaster novel and the formula of the war epic, *The Yellow Peril* must be regarded as one of the more powerful science fantasies to emerge from the PRC. But Bao Mi is not the first modern Chinese writer inspired by the idea of a second Yellow Peril. As early as the first decade of the century Biheguan zhuren's *New Era* depicted a devastating world war started by China. In that novel, around 1999, China wages a war against the West on behalf of her own colonial territories and wins an overwhelming victory. Describing China as the supreme power in military and scientific scribing China as the supreme power in military and scientific technologies, *New Era* brings to a new plateau the apocalyptic vision of *The Future of New China*, as opposed to the rapidly precipitating political status quo. Bao Mi's end-of-the century vision is a bleak one: the "new era" so anticipated by late Qing writers might come in the long run, but only after China has managed to ruin, not rule, the world. What lingers in *The Yellow Peril*, nevertheless, is the nationalist fervor that underlies *New Era*. Bao Mi foresees that China will become the redeeming power for the world, for all the disasters it has brought to its own people and its own land. In doing so, he makes himself an accomplice rather than a critic of the Yellow Peril syndrome.

The Yellow Peril syndrome has also been treated in more a light-hearted, but no less poignant, way by Ping Lu 平路, an acclaimed Taiwan woman writer based in the United States. Ping Lu's "The Taiwan Miracle" ("Taiwan qiji" 台灣奇蹟, 1990) is a wild fantasy about the invasion of a monstrous "virus" called the "Taiwan miracle" into the States. The virus is so formidable that in a short time it transforms the American public's consciousness, making them as greedy, corrupt, and violent as people in Taiwan. Its power is further manifested by a new system of American democracy, mixing votes with fists; a new religious belief, celebrating the virtues of greed and opportunism; an incipient disease, whose symptoms can first be detected by the patients' insatiable desire for Chinese food and speculative activity; and an ecological mutation, which drastically changes the weather pattern and agricultural landscape in America. The "Taiwan miracle" will lead the world to a nuclear-free "new era," but one just as disastrous as that predicated by *The Yellow Peril*.

Using America as the most unlikely locale for its events, "The Taiwan Miracle" ridicules the degradation of Taiwan as its economy takes off, while it shouts aloud an island-nation's humiliated desire to marginalize the center, to empower all dwarfed countries. Years after being denied political legitimacy, Taiwan is now staging a comeback and regaining its national pride in the most fantastic and unbecoming ways. In a carnivalesque mode, Taiwan dominates the world by degrading and disintegrating first itself and then the world. Be it called corrupt or insidious, Taiwanization is a global movement that reshuffles the world order; it even proves to be an effective means to bring every country together in a single world order. Nevertheless, the victory in "The Taiwan Miracle" is a victory in fantasy and a victory of fantasy. If Taiwan's pride can be restored miraculously by means of self-debasement,

"The Taiwan Miracle" recalls Ah Q logic, a mode of thinking that turns real humiliations into "spiritual victories."

Any survey of contemporary Chinese science fantasy would not be complete without a reference to works by Zhang Xiguo 張系國, a versatile overseas Chinese writer who has won much acclaim among readers in Hong Kong, Taiwan, and overseas Chinese communities. A computer science professor, Zhang finds in fiction, especially science fantasy, his second vocation. For years Zhang has tried to produce a science fantasy with a "Chinese flavor": a work that engages readers not only through China-related subject matters but also through a distinctive Chinese narrative style. Zhang's trilogy, *City Trilogy: Five-Jade Sutra, Heroes of the Dragon City, A Feather* (*Cheng sanbuqu: Wuyu die, Longcheng feijiang, Yiyumao* 城三部曲：五玉碟，龍城飛將，一羽毛, 1981–91), represents the outcome of such an endeavor.

Zhang starts his trilogy with a Suolun City in the Huhui world of the Super G galaxy, a city famous for a gigantic and continuously growing bronze statue. For thousands of years, politicians, rebels, and outer space aliens have fought for ownership of the statue and therefore the city; the statue changes its looks to resemble those of the new ruler of the city. The fourth star war breaks out as the bronze statue cult, the snake people, the leopard people, and the Huhui citizens are engaged in a new battle for the city of Suolun. The war culminates in the mysterious vaporization of the great bronze statue by a dragon spaceship belonging to the monstrous Shan people.

This is only the beginning of Zhang Xiguo's novel. In the rest of the trilogy, the awesome statue reappears, growing at ever faster speed and even moving in and out of the city. It triggers endless conspiracies, wars, resurrections, and revolutions. It is not difficult to discern the allegory embedded in the bronze statue; what fascinates one more is the way by which Zhang Xiguo weaves his political allegory into an intricate narrative sequence; this narrative sequence comprises sources drawn from Western star war fantasies, classical Chinese chivalric and fantastic fiction, historical saga, and military romance. Never has there been a modern Chinese novel like the *City Trilogy* that ushers its readers into a world in which chivalric warriors encounter extraterrestrial creatures, and old magical devices compete with super-computerized spectacles. One finds a remote model, however, in a mid-nineteenth-century novel. Yu Wanchun's 俞萬春 *Quell the Bandits* (*Dang kou zhi* 蕩寇志, 1851), a belated sequel to *The Water Margin* (*Shuihu zhuan* 水滸傳), renders a full-scaled conflation of modern military technologies and classical wizardry against an epic background (Wang 1993). *Quell the Bandits* has been debunked as a novel spreading the corrupt thought of imperial loyalism,[9] but it introduces nineteenth-century Western scientific discourse to a military saga supposedly taking place in the twelfth century, which betokens a departure from traditional Chinese fantastic formulae. Given the historical context in which is was produced, the novel's blatant anachronism becomes a telling sign indicating the opening up of the temporal and narrative horizons of classical Chinese fiction.

In the afterword to the *City Trilogy*, Zhang Xiguo mentions that his writings have always been motivated by a deep historical concern and that the Taiping Rebellion, especially the rise and fall of a Taiping general like Shi Dakai (1831–863), is one of the historical moments that fascinates him (1991: 203). It is not entirely a coincidence that Zhang Xiguo puts his science fantasy in the historical perspective of mid-nineteenth century China. The mid-nineteenth century is the moment when modernity inscribed its first sign in Chinese historical dynamics as well as in literature about those dynamics. Zhang Xiguo's futurist epic may have revitalized a forgotten source of Chinese science fantasy. Although situated in the remote future, the chronotope, or the temporal-spatial context, of *City Trilogy* still never takes us too far from the Taiping Rebellion era, an era in which foreign beliefs and technologies, utopian and dystopian thoughts, reformers and revolutionaries, were preparing the Chinese for an odyssey in search of the new China.

With examples drawn from mainland China, Taiwan, Hong Kong, and overseas, I have ventured along four of the pathways that have appeared in the development of contemporary Chinese fiction: grotesque exposés, chivalric cycles, depravity romance, and science fantasy. I postulate that, for all the novelty they have indicated, these four directions in contemporary Chinese fiction have their antecedents in the late Qing era.

First, in their effort to represent reality in the full, contemporary Chinese writers must come to terms with a paradoxical result: that their mimetic intent can best be realized when couched in a narrative scheme of the bizarre and the uncanny. The May Fourth–oriented realism can no longer recapture

9. This view has been widely held by Chinese Communist critics since the 1950s. See, for example, Dai 1980.

the horrors and abuses contained in the history of China, because it has exposed itself as a complicit factor, encouraging the horrors and abuses. Late Qing grotesque exposés, with their endless parade of "strange things" and "ghosts, monsters, goblins, and devils," their outrageous reversal of values, and their ambiguous laughter, have resurfaced to facilitate contemporary writers' staging of the repertoire of the real. These late twentieth-century Chinese writers have found in flirtation, rather than obsession, a figuration of the circumstances in which they write and a strategy with which to negotiate these circumstances.

Second, through fictional inquiries into the terms of justice and order, contemporary Chinese writers have reopened a dialogue with late Qing chivalric and court-case fiction. Despite its apparent endorsement of established authorities, late Qing chivalric and court-case fiction contains a subtext, one that questions the agency of justice at both public and individual levels. The majority of writers inspired by the progressive thoughts of the May Fourth era see writing as a way to unite the pen and the sword; the way they carry out their mission, however, unexpectedly recapitulates the conservative aspect of late Qing chivalric idealism. By contrast, contemporary writing foregrounds the darker and more radical subtext of late Qing chivalric and court-case fiction, by producing works where neither political nor poetic justice is seen as possible. These writers have again addressed the polemic of writing and the representation of justice, even as they refuse to settle the polemic with an easy solution.

Third, through exploring the territory of desire and passion, contemporary Chinese writers are developing a discourse of depravity, touching on an aspect of Chinese imagination that has so far been regarded as either indecent or at least irrelevant to literary modernization. While echoing the late Qing discourse of depravity in depicting the libertine manners and morals of an overripe civilization, the new depravity fiction is aware of the moral ambiguity its subject matter can generate. It highlights the traditional boundaries of desire and its repression and circumscribes a new, wider social and literary space in which the politics of eros conflate with the erotics of the polis. Its openness to all discourses, no matter how forbidden, is the mark of its profoundly post-modern respectability.

Fourth, writing in an era of "post-History," contemporary Chinese writers have tried to "make sense" of history by evoking its fantastic other. Through science fantasies, they revisit the past and prefigure the future.

Quite apart from the mainstream realist discourse of modern Chinese fiction, this fantastic inclination seems to take us full circle to the point almost one century before, when the forerunners of modern Chinese fiction imagined a new China by means of utopian constructs, fantastic adventures, and futurist encounters. But unlike their predecessors, who posited a collective historical subjectivity—in the name of China—as the goal of their works, contemporary writers are learning to diversify "the future of the new China" by conjuring up various political and scientific possibilities.

All four directions have significantly undermined the traditional (May Fourth) approaches to modern China and modern Chinese literature, approaches that were bound by a mimesis-oriented canon of realism, a yearning for a total equation between ink and blood, a censorious impulse to redirect libidinous consciousness into an ideologically sanitized space, writing and revolution, and a reinforcement of History and Truth at the expense of an understanding of individual dreams and fantasies.

In stating these new directions by tracing their genealogies to the late Qing, I am not offering a transcendental view of the nature of end-of-century Chinese fiction, much less prescribing what paths it should take next. All that I want to do is to open up the horizons of modern Chinese literature by looking into the repressed modernities of late Qing fiction and by registering their imprints in late twentieth-century Chinese fiction. However preliminary it may be, I hope this study has conveyed the sense of wonder and pleasure that any reader must feel when suddenly aware that a literature is on the verge of recovering itself, of letting all its voices speak as if the departing century had at last learned from its painful experiments and was ready to begin again—*without* the illusion of a wholly new beginning.

Works Cited

Anderson, Marston. 1990. *The Limits of Realism: Chinese Fiction in the Revolutionary Period.* Berkeley: University of California Press.

Bakhtin, Mikhail. 1968. *Rabelais and His World.* Trans. Helene Iswolsky. Cambridge, Mass.: MIT Press.

Calinescu, Matei. 1987. *Five Faces of Modernity.* Durham, N.C.: Duke University Press.

Chang, Hao. 1971. *Liang Ch'i-ch'ao and Intellectual Transition in China, 1890–1907.* Cambridge, Mass.: Harvard University Press.

———. 1989. *Chinese Intellectuals in Crisis: Search for Order and Meaning.* Berkeley: University of California Press.

Chow, Rey. 1990. *Woman and Chinese Modernity.* Minneapolis: University of Minnesota Press.

Clark, Katerina, and Michael Holquist. 1984. *Mikhail Bakhtin.* Cambridge, Mass.: Harvard University Press.

Cohen, Paul. 1984. *Discovering History in China: American Historical Writing on the Recent Chinese Past.* New York: Columbia University Press.

Cohen, Paul, and Merle Goldman, eds. 1990. *Ideas Across Cultures: Essays on Chinese Thought in Honor of Benjamin I. Schwartz.* Cambridge, Mass.: Harvard University, Council on East Asian Studies.

Compagnon, Antoine. 1994. *The Five Paradoxes of Modernity.* Trans. Franklin Philip. New York: Columbia University Press.

Dai Hongsen 戴鴻森. 1980. "Preface." In Yu Wanchun 俞萬春, *Dang Kouzhi* 蕩寇志 (Quell the bandits), pp. 3–5. Beijing: Renmin wenxue.

Doleželová-Velingerová, Milena. 1980. *The Chinese Novel at the Turn of the Century.* Toronto: University of Toronto Press, 1980.

Hsia, C. T. 1971. "Obsession with China." In idem, *A History of Modern Chinese Fiction*, pp. 535–40. New Haven: Yale University Press.

Huters, Theodore. 1993. "The Authorial Self in Modern Chinese Literature." In Ellen Widmer and David Der-wei Wang, eds., *From May Fourth to June Fourth: Fiction and Film in Twentieth-Century China*, 231–53. Cambridge, Mass.: Harvard University Press.

Lau, Joseph. 1980. "Tilei piaoling de xiandai wenxue" 涕淚飄零的現代文學 (Modern Chinese literature in tears and sniveling). In idem, *Tilei piaoling de xiandai wenxue*, pp. 1–8. Taibei: Yuanjing.

Lee, Leo Ou-fan 李歐梵. 1973. *The Romantic Generation of Modern Chinese Writers.* Cambridge, Mass.: Harvard University Press.

———. 1985. "The Solitary Traveler: Images of the Self in Modern Chinese Literature." In Robert E. Hegel and Richard C. Hessney, eds., *Expressions of Self in Chinese Literature*, pp. 282–307. New York: Columbia University Press.

———. 1990. "In Search of Modernity: Some Reflections on a New Mode of Consciousness in Twentieth-Century Chinese History and Literature." In Paul Cohen and Merle Goldman, eds., *Ideas Across Cultures: Essays on Chinese Thought in Honor of Benjamin I. Schwartz*, 109–36. Cambridge, Mass.: Harvard University, Council on East Asian Studies.

———. 1993. "Mantan xiandai Zhongguo wenxue zhong de tuifei" 漫談現代中國文學中的頹廢 (On the decadent mode of modern Chinese literature). *Jintian* 11: 37–46.

Liu Binyan 劉賓雁. 1985. *Renyao zhi jian* 人妖之間 (People or monsters). Hong Kong: Yazhou.

Liu Kang, and Tang Xiaobin, eds. 1993. *Politics, Ideology, and Chinese Literature: Theoretical Interventions and Cultural Critique*. Durham, N.C.: Duke University Press.

Lu Tonglin, ed. 1992. *Gender and Sexuality*. Albany: State University of New York Press.

Lu Xun. 1976. *A Brief History of Chinese Fiction*. Trans. Gladys Yang and Xianyi Yang. Beijing: Foreign Languages Press.

Malmgren, Carl D. 1991. *Worlds Apart: Narratology of Science Fiction*. Bloomington: Indiana University Press.

Metzger, Thomas A. 1990. "Continuities Between Modern and Premodern China: Some Neglected Methodological and Substantive Issues." In Paul Cohen and Merle Goldman, eds., *Ideas Across Cultures: Essays on Chinese Thought in Honor of Benjamin I. Schwartz*, 263–92. Cambridge, Mass.: Harvard University, Council on East Asian Studies.

Peng Hsiao-yen 彭小妍. 1992. "Zhang Jingsheng de xing meixue" 張競生的性美學 (The sexual aesthetics of Zhang Jingsheng). *Lianhe wenxue* 112: 83–98.

Průšek, Jaroslav. 1980. *The Lyrical and the Epic: Studies of Modern Chinese Literature*. Edited by Leo Ou-fan Lee. Bloomington: Indiana University Press.

Schwartz, Benjamin. 1964. *In Search of Wealth and Power: Yan Fu and the West*. Cambridge, Mass.: Harvard University Press.

Semanov, V. I. 1980. *Lu Xun and His Predecessors*. Trans. Charles Alber. Armonk, N.Y.: M. E. Sharpe.

Suvin, Darko. 1988. *Positions and Presuppositions in Science Fiction*. Kent, Ohio: Kent State University Press.

Wagner, Rudolf G. 1985. "Lobby Literature: The Archaeology and Present Functions of Science Fiction in China." In Jeffrey C. Kinkley, ed., *After Mao: Chinese Literature and Society, 1978–1981*. Cambridge, Mass.: Harvard University Press.

Wang, David Der-wei. 1990. "Radical Laughter: Lao She and His Taiwan Successors." In Howard Goldblatt, ed., *Worlds Apart*, pp. 235–56. Armonk, N.Y.: M. E. Sharpe.

———. 1992a. *Fictional Realism in Twentieth-Century Chinese Fiction: Mao Dun, Lao She, Shen Congwen*. New York: Columbia University Press.

———. 1992b. "Fin-de-siècle Splendor." *Modern Chinese Literature* 5, no. 4: 45–65.

———. 1993. "Jia Baoyu zuo qianshuiting: Wan Qing kehuan xiaoshuo xinlun" 賈寶玉坐潛水艇：晚清科幻小說新論 (Jia Baoyu and submarine: a reappraisal of late Qing science fantasy). In *Xiaoshuo Zhongguo: Wan Qing dao dangdai de Zhongwen xiaoshuo* 小說中國：晚清到當代的中文小說 (Narrating China: Chinese fiction from the late Qing to the contemporary era), pp. 137–60. Taibei: Maitian.

———. 1994a. "Edifying Depravity: Three Late Qing Courtesan Novels." In Eva Hung, ed., *The Paradox of Virtue*, pp. 231–56. Hong Kong: Chinese University of Hong Kong Press.

———. 1994b. "Justice Undone: A Preliminary Study of Late Qing and Court Case Fiction." *Studies in Language and Literature* 6: 1–35.

Widmer, Ellen, and David Der-wei Wang, eds. 1993. *From May Fourth to June Fourth: Fiction and Film in Twentieth-Century China*. Cambridge, Mass.: Harvard University Press.

Wu, Dingbao. 1989. "Looking Backward: An Introduction to Chinese Science Fiction." In Dingbao Wu and Patrick D. Murphy, eds., *Science Fiction from China*. New York: Praeger.

Wu Liang 吳亮. 1994. "Tan *Feidu*" 談廢都 (On *The Abandoned Capital*). *Lianhe wenxue* 114: 23–25.

Zhan Hongzhi 詹宏志. 1990. "Yizhong laoqu de shengyin" 一種老去的聲音 (A kind of aging voice). Foreword to Zhu Tianwen 朱天文, *Shijimo de huali* 世紀末的華麗 (Fin-de-siècle splendor). Taibei: Yuanliu.

Zhang Ailing 張愛玲 (Eileen Chang). 1983. *Haishang hua* 海上花 (Singsong girls from Shanghai). Taibei: Huangguan.

Zhang Xiguo 張系國. 1991. *Yi yumao* 一羽毛 (A feather). Taibei: Zhishi xitong.

PART IV

Neither Renaissance nor Enlightenment

CHAPTER EIGHT

Neither Renaissance nor Enlightenment: A Historian's Reflections on the May Fourth Movement

Ying-shih Yü

In recent years the May Fourth movement has generally been identified as the Chinese Enlightenment. When Chinese authors first gave the movement this new identity in the late 1930s and early 1940s, it was clearly intended as a tribute of the highest possible order by way of analogy. However, now that the twentieth century is over, the honor originally implied in the identity is fast becoming a dubious one. For now it is the dark side of the Enlightenment that is occupying the attention of historians, philosophers, and cultural critics alike. As a result, the Enlightenment project centering on the idea of rationality is often perceived as a "failure" or, even worse, as a form of "domination." It is therefore only natural that the post-modern rage against Enlightenment rationality is also beginning to cast a shadow on the May Fourth project.

I shall return to the question of Enlightenment below. Right now I consider it important to call attention to the fact that before the identity of the Enlightenment was established, the May Fourth movement had been more widely known in the West as the "Chinese Renaissance." To begin with, I propose to explore the historical implications of each of these analogical concepts as well as explain why eventually "Renaissance" gave way to "Enlightenment."[1]

---

1. Chow Tse-tsung (1960) discusses briefly the concepts of "Renaissance" and "Enlightenment" and their applicability to the May Fourth movement. He takes both as representative

More than anyone else, Hu Shi 胡 適 (1891–1962) was responsible for propagating the idea of the "Chinese Renaissance" in the West. While on a lecture tour in Great Britain in November 1926, he lectured on the "Chinese Renaissance" repeatedly in academic institutions such as the Royal Institute of International Affairs (Hu 1926), Trinity College (Dublin), Oxford University, University of Liverpool, and Woodbrooke Settlement. One of the lecture posters even introduced him as "The Father of the Chinese Renaissance" (see Hu 1990: vol. 5, Nov. 9, 18, 23, 25, 28, 1926). When he arrived in New York in January 1927, the New York–based magazine *Nation* reported: "Hu Shi has returned to the United States. . . . Boldly advocating the use of a despised vernacular tongue, he did for Chinese what Dante and Petrarch had done for Italian: he opened the doors of literacy to millions who could never have mastered the intricacies of the involved classic tongue" (Hu 1990: vol. 6, Jan. 20, 1927). This is simply another way of identifying him as the "Father of the Chinese Renaissance."

In one of his Haskell Lectures at the University of Chicago in 1933, Hu Shi explained in no uncertain terms what he meant by the notion of "Chinese Renaissance":

The Renaissance was the name given by a group of Peking University students to a new monthly magazine which they published in 1918. They were mature students well trained in the old cultural tradition of the country, and they readily recognized in the new movement then led by some of their professors a striking similarity to the Renaissance in Europe. These prominent features in the movement reminded them of the European Renaissance. First, it was a conscious movement to promote a new literature in the living language of the people to take the place of the classical literature of old. Second, it was a movement of conscious protest against many of the ideas and institutions in the traditional culture, and of conscious emancipation of the individual man and woman from the bondage of forces of tradition. It was a movement of reason versus tradition, freedom versus authority, and glorification of life and human values versus their suppression. And lastly, strange enough, this new movement was led by men who knew their cultural heritage and tried to study it with the new methodology of modern historical criticism and research. In that sense it was a humanist movement. (1934: 44)

---

of "the liberals' views" (338–42). However, Vera Schwarcz (1968) identifies May Fourth with the "Enlightenment" without mentioning the "Renaissance," as does Li Zehou (1987: 7–49) in a well-known essay on the May Fourth movement originally published in 1986.

A few observations may be made with respect to this account of the origin of the idea of "Chinese Renaissance." First, it is indeed true that the English subtitle of the student magazine *New Tide* (*Xin chao* 新 潮) of Peking University was suggested by a founding member of the New Tide Society in 1918. However, Hu's self-effacing modesty prevented him from revealing the important fact that he himself has been the patron saint of this influential publication from its conception (Fu Sinian 1952). Second, it was Hu Shi who in 1917 drew the analogy between the literary revolution he was then advocating and the European Renaissance. During his return to China in June 1917, he read Edith Sichel's *The Renaissance* (1915) as his train rolled across the Canadian Rockies toward Vancouver (Hu 1939: 4.240–47). Much to his gratification he found his advocacy of the vernacular as opposed to the classical language as the medium of Chinese literature historically justified by the rise of vernacular literature in Renaissance Europe. Dante and Petrarch, Hu Shi noted, began to use the vernacular language in their writings. His attention was particularly drawn to the fact that although Leon Battista Alberti openly declared Latin "a dead language," Cardinal Pietro Bembo eventually settled the question by coming down on the side of the vernacular in his *Prose della volgar lingua*.[2] There can be no question that the adoption of "The Renaissance" as the English subtitle of the student magazine was due to Hu Shi's inspiration. Third, of the three prominent features listed in the passage quoted above, the second one, defined in terms of "reason versus tradition," "freedom versus authority," is clearly more characteristic of the Enlightenment than the Renaissance. This, however, should occasion no surprise. With all his talk of Renaissance, Hu Shi after all was more directly an intellectual heir of the French Enlightenment than of Italian humanism. In more ways than one, he reminded his Western contemporaries of Voltaire (Fairbank 1982: 45–46; Yü 1984: 62–63). Moreover, from many of his public lectures on cultural trends in the modern world, we get an unmistakable impression that Hu Shi took the Renaissance as the true beginning of modernity in the West and viewed all subsequent developments, such as the

---

2. Subsequent research on Renaissance vernacular literature has much softened this strict dichotomy between vernacular and Latin literatures. In the late fifteenth and the early sixteenth centuries, the relationship between the vernacular and Neo-Latin was one of coexistence and cross-fertilization. Had Hu Shi followed Renaissance scholarship after 1917, he would have abandoned his Renaissance analogy on these grounds. For a detailed discussion, see Yü 1976: 305–8.

Reformation, the scientific revolution, the Enlightenment, industrialization, the democratic revolutions, and even the socialist movements, as if they were elements in a linear progression of modernity following the Renaissance. It was probably because of his emphasis on the continuity of the Enlightenment with the Renaissance that he sometimes failed to draw a line between the two, as shown in the characterization quoted above.[3]

At this juncture we need to examine a little more closely the notion of Enlightenment as applied to the May Fourth movement. As far as I know, it was the Marxists who first interpreted the May Fourth movement in Enlightenment terms. In 1936, several underground Communists launched a "New Enlightenment" movement in Beijing and Shanghai. In the *Great Dictionary of Philosophy* (*Zhexue da cidian* 哲學大詞典), published in 1985, this movement is defined as follows:

> The New Enlightenment movement is also known as the "New Rationalist" movement. It was an intellectual and cultural movement that unfolded in response to the national struggle against Japan during the 1930s. It was also the continuation and development of the May Fourth Enlightenment movement. In September and October of 1936 it was first suggested in two articles—"The Mobilization of Philosophy for National Defense" and "New Culture Movement in Present-day China"—by the members of the Chinese Communist Party. They proposed that a joint effort be made to promote the spirit of the May Fourth revolutionary tradition; they made a clarion call to the patriots to start . . . a large-scale new enlightenment movement in order to awaken the masses to the need for a war of resistance and democracy. . . . The New Enlightenment movement lasted for a year until the complete breakout of the war of resistance against Japan and the formation of the anti-Japanese united front for national salvation at the end of 1937. It played a positive role in clearing ignorance as well as disseminating anti-Japanese propaganda. (676–77)

From this account it is clear that the Communists reinterpreted May Fourth as "Enlightenment" because they needed a "New Enlightenment" movement to carry out the party line of a new "united front." It is important to know that the authors of the two articles referred to above are none other than Chen Boda 陳伯達 (1904–89) and Ai Siqi 艾思奇 (1910–66), two leading

---

3. According to Peter Gay, however, although the affinity between Renaissance and Enlightenment is fundamental, the difference is also undeniable. As Gay says, "Like the Enlightenment, the Renaissance turned to the distant past to conquer the recent past, but unlike it, the Renaissance founded its radicalism in despair. Indeed, one cannot read Erasmus or Machiavelli without feeling that it also ended in despair: neither of them shows much confidence in the eventual victory of reason and humanity" (1966: 269).

party ideologues active in Beijing and Shanghai educational and cultural circles under disguises. I must also emphatically point out that, of the two, Chen was a more senior and far more important member of the Communist Party. It was Chen who initiated the New Enlightenment movement. At first it may seem very puzzling that a man practically unknown in the Chinese intellectual world could launch a movement single-handedly that was immediately and enthusiastically received by many leftist magazines in Beijing and Shanghai. However, once we know who Chen Boda really was, the puzzle disappears. In early 1936, when Liu Shaoqi 劉少奇 (1898–1969) arrived in Tianjin to head the underground North China Bureau of the Communist Party, Chen was appointed chief of its Department of Propaganda. It was in this new official capacity that Chen utilized the May Fourth legacy in the name of "Enlightenment" to fulfill the task recently assigned by the party. In his own words, "We want to form the broadest possible united front with all individuals loyal to the fatherland, all patriots, all liberals, all democrats, all rationalists, all natural scientists" (quoted in He 1947: 207). Here, it must be noted, the word "we" is not an editorial usage, but a coded reference to the Party. Needless to say, all the initial positive responses from leftist journalism were orchestrated by the Party through its underground network.

Moreover, the New Enlightenment movement was closely related to the famous December Ninth movement of 1935. The latter has been viewed by some of its participants as "a direct outgrowth and fulfillment of the aspirations of the original student movement of 1919" (Schwarcz 1986: 218). But in a crucial aspect, December Ninth of 1935 is different from May Fourth of 1919. As Fu Sinian 傅斯年 (1896–1950) recalled in 1946: "Many people said that during the May Fourth movement of 1919 we students were manipulated by certain politicians in the North. This was definitely nonsense. I was involved centrally in that movement. I know for a fact that nobody manipulated me, nobody asked me to rise against the unpatriotic government that was about to sign the Treaty of Versailles" (Fu Lecheng 1969: 62–63). In the case of the December Ninth student demonstration of 1935, however, we now know that it, like the New Enlightenment movement, was carefully planned and implemented by the underground cells of the Communist party. According to the firsthand account of Gao Wenhua 高文華 (fl. 1930s), party secretary of the North China Bureau: "Student unrest culminated in the December Ninth movement. We in the North China Bureau supported and led this patriotic movement. Within the party, leadership was assumed by Comrades Zhao Shengyang, Ke Qingshi, Chen Boda, and others. Those who directly led it in the open included Comrades Li Chang, Jiang Nanxiang (party secretary of the Qinghua University branch), Lin Feng, Yao Yilin, Xu Bing, Xu Deheng, and others" (Gao 1982: 187; Ye 1990: 102). Moreover, Lu Cui 陸璀 (fl. 1930s), a student leader of the December Ninth demonstration described by Edgar Snow in 1935 as "China's Joan of Arc," now openly admits, in a collection of her propaganda writings published in commemoration of the sixtieth anniversary of this historic event, that she was then working under the direct guidance of the party's underground organization (Lu Cui 1995: 7, 19). Obviously, the two movements—the December Ninth and the New Enlightenment—were ingeniously masterminded to support each other in a way very much reminiscent of the relationship between May Fourth in its narrow sense (student demonstration of 1919) and May Fourth in its broad sense (what Hu Shi and the New Tide Society called the "Renaissance"). Now, with the origins of the December Ninth and New Enlightenment thus traced to the underground Communist organizations of the North China Bureau, it does not seem to make much sense to say that the former was "a direct outgrowth and fulfillment of the aspirations of the original student movement of 1919" and that the latter was "the continuation and development of the May Fourth Enlightenment movement."

Since the New Enlightenment movement was conceived from the beginning to serve the needs of a hidden political agenda,[4] its proponents did not even bother to justify why, on intellectual grounds, "Enlightenment" was a

---

4. According to a confidential document of the Communist Party datable to late 1936, the Communist Party changed its line in September 1936 in two important ways. First, instead of proletariat revolution it now adopted a moderate strategy to push for a "Democratic Republic" in China. Second, tactically it made an appeal for an end to the civil war and to establish a "united front" in the broadest possible way with all parties and groups in China. This document came into Hu Shi's possession in 1940, when he was ambassador to the United States (see "Zhonggong de celüe luxian" 中共的策略路線 in vol. 6 of Hu 1990: unpaginated). This document is authenticated by Mao Zedong's report of May 1937 (1969: 1.233, 246–47*n*6). It cannot be a mere coincidence that Chen Boda and Ai Siqi launched the New Enlightenment in September 1936, exactly at the same time when the new party line began. Moreover, it is also extremely revealing that, according to Wang Yuanhua 王元化, who was then working for the party as a young writer, around 1938 the party suddenly decided to ban the term "Enlightenment" and thus brought the New Enlightenment movement to an abrupt end (Lin et al. 1989: 3).

better appellation for May Fourth than "Renaissance." From the political point of view, they linked both May Fourth and New Enlightenment to patriotism. Chinese Enlightenment, old and new, according to Ai Siqi, must take patriotism as its main task (He 1947: 209). But anyone familiar with European Enlightenment knows how absurd it is to relate patriotism to Enlightenment. With the possible exception of Rousseau, the *philosophes* were all cosmopolitans who took as their calling, not to exalt the interest of country, but to cultivate, enlighten, and ennoble mankind (Gay 1966: 13–14).

It is interesting to note that Chinese Marxists as a rule preferred Enlightenment to Renaissance. Whenever a period of Chinese history was compared to the Renaissance by earlier authors, they would change the analogy to Enlightenment. There is another example in addition to the May Fourth case. Liang Qichao 梁启超 (1873–1929), early and late in his career, insisted on characterizing the intellectual history of the Qing period as China's "age of Renaissance" (1959: 14). But the Marxist historian Hou Wailu 侯外廬 (1906–88) rejected Liang's analogy and instead made a sustained and systematic effort to reinterpret the same period as "early Enlightenment" (1956). Now, we must ask: Why were Chinese Marxists so obsessed with the idea of Enlightenment? I would like to hazard a few suggestions. First, according to the Marxist theory of history, as China entered the historical stage of capitalism, it had to experience a large-scale social expression of bourgeois consciousness similar to the French Enlightenment. May Fourth as an intellectual movement fits nicely into this scheme. Second, Diderot once wrote to Voltaire praising him for exciting "in our hearts an intense hatred of lying, ignorance, hypocrisy, superstition, tyranny" (quoted in Becker 1932: 92). Much of iconoclastic and anti-Confucian writings by May Fourth intellectuals can be similarly characterized (He 1947: 122–33). It was this destructive side of May Fourth that particularly appealed to Chinese Marxists. Third, Chinese Marxists were advocates of revolution. Since, as they noted, the Enlightenment movement often preceded political revolution in European countries, they needed an Enlightenment to justify their advocacy of revolution in China (He 1947: 97). In light of the above analysis, I am inclined to think that Chinese Marxists' persistence in redefining May Fourth in terms of Enlightenment did not arise out of a whimsical reading of history. On the contrary, they probably made a deliberate and calculated choice out of the conviction that their political radicalism would be much better served by

Enlightenment than by Renaissance, which was, in any case, too remote as well as too mild to be of immediate, practical relevance.

By the same token, we must also take Hu Shi and other liberals' espousal of Renaissance very seriously. From 1917 on, Hu Shi always insisted that May Fourth as an intellectual or cultural movement must be understood as the Chinese Renaissance. This is not only because of his advocacy of the vernacular language as the modern literary medium but, more important, also because of his profound sense of historical continuity. To him "Renaissance" suggests renovation rather than destruction of the Chinese tradition (Hu 1970b). In spite of his often severe criticisms, Hu Shi's rejection of the Chinese tradition, including Confucianism, was far from total. Central to the notion of Renaissance was his belief in the possibility of breathing new life into the old civilization of China. As early as 1917, he clearly stated the problem as follows: "How can we best assimilate modern civilization in such a manner as to make it congenial and congruous and continuous with the civilization of our own making?" The solution he then offered was that it "will depend solely on the foresight and the sense of historical continuity of the intellectual leaders of New China, and on the tact and skill with which they can successfully connect the best in modern civilization with the best in our own civilization" (quoted in Grieder 1970: 160–61). This sounds a far cry from a total break with the Chinese past. Later, in 1933, he stated in concrete terms what was "best" in each civilization and how the two could be skillfully "connected": "Slowly, quietly, but unmistakably, the Chinese Renaissance is becoming a reality. The product of this rebirth looks suspiciously occidental. But, scratch its surface and you will find that the stuff of which it is made is essentially Chinese bedrock, which much weathering and corrosion have only made stand out more clearly—the humanistic and rationalistic China resurrected by the touch of the scientific and democratic civilization of the new world" (Hu 1934: ix–x). In hindsight we cannot help but laugh at the premature optimism of this "incurable optimist," as Hu Shi was known to his friends. However, he remained undaunted even at the very end of his life. In "The Chinese Tradition and the Future," his speech to open the Sino-American Conference on Intellectual Cooperation held at the University of Washington in July 1960, he made his final attempt at a systematic application of the concept of Renaissance to Chinese history. He distinguished altogether three Renaissances in Chinese history before the May Fourth one. The first was the Renaissance in Chinese literature in the eighth and ninth centuries when the vernacular language began to appear in poetry and recorded conversations of Chan monks. The second Renaissance occurred in philosophy. By this he referred primarily to the rise of Neo-Confucianism in the eleventh and twelfth centuries. The third Renaissance was the "Revival of Learning" in the seventeenth and eighteenth centuries when humanist scholars began to use "scientific method" to study classical and historical texts on a large scale. Here, obviously, he was following Liang Qichao's interpretation of Qing intellectual history, as mentioned above (Hu 1960: 17–18).[5] It is beside the point whether we can accept his grand narrative of Chinese history woven around the central thread of "Renaissance." The important point is that, contrary to his popular image as a radical anti-traditionalist, Hu Shi, early and late in his career, always needed some parts of the Chinese tradition to justify the Chinese Renaissance of which he was a leading participant. Thus at the end of his speech, he emphatically concluded: "In short, I believe the tradition of 'the humanistic and rationalist China' has not been destroyed and in all probability cannot be destroyed" (Hu 1960: 22). It was indeed an expression of his personal faith, not an established historical fact, to make this claim in 1960 for the Chinese tradition he particularly cherished. But he had no choice but to keep that faith alive. For if that particular tradition were destroyed, so would be the Chinese Renaissance of the May Fourth era, which was nothing if not the alpha and omega of his own identity.

To conclude this part of my discussion, let me begin by suggesting that Renaissance and Enlightenment must not be taken lightly as two different analogical concepts randomly borrowed to characterize the May Fourth movement. Instead they must be taken seriously as representing two incompatible projects, each leading to a course of action of its own. Simply put, Renaissance was originally conceived as a cultural and intellectual project, whereas Enlightenment was essentially a political project in disguise. Central to the Renaissance project was the notion of intellectual autonomy. Knowledge and art must be pursued primarily as ends in themselves, not to serve some other higher purposes, whether they be political, economic, religious, or moral. It was precisely for this reason that Hu Shi often regretted that the student movement of May Fourth 1919, though laudable for its patriot-

---

5. Hu Shi first developed the theory of three Renaissances in premodern Chinese history in 1923, but his periodization with regard to the first two changed considerably over the next decades; see Hu 1990: Apr. 3, 1923.

ism, was nevertheless an unwelcome interruption as far as the Chinese Renaissance was concerned. For it marked the beginning of the politicization of Chinese academia, thereby undermining intellectual autonomy before it could be securely established in modern China (Hu 1970a). In contrast, the Enlightenment project designed by Chinese Marxists was ultimately revolution-oriented. With the emphasis placed squarely on patriotism and national salvation, Marxist advocates of New Enlightenment only recognized in culture and thought an ideological function in the service of revolution. The idea of intellectual autonomy was by and large alien to them. No wonder Mao Zedong's 毛 澤 東 (1893–1976) view of May Fourth was diametrically opposed to Hu Shi's. His highest praise was reserved for the student movement of May Fourth 1919, which, in his view, led to the revolution of 1925–27 (Mao 1969: 2.659–60; Li Changzhi 1946: 38–39). Ironically, even the New Enlightenment itself turned out to be no more than "false consciousness." No sooner had it served the purpose of the formation of a united front than it fell into oblivion. The idea of Enlightenment did not resurface until the end of the 1970s, when the Communist Party needed a "reliberation of thought" to turn itself around under completely new circumstances.

Renaissance preceded Enlightenment by two decades but gave way to the latter eventually. This was due, perhaps, less to the intrinsic merit of Enlightenment as a descriptive term for the May Fourth movement than to the radicalization of the Chinese mentality. The Renaissance project was deeply rooted in Anglo-American liberalism, which found China less than habitable as national crisis continued to deepen in the 1930s. Wedded to nationalism on the one hand and veiled behind Enlightenment on the other, Marxist radicalism became extremely attractive to student activists all over China. Renaissance could no longer find as many sympathetic ears in the new generation of university students as it had in 1918.

Above, I have delineated two contrasting projects in the May Fourth movement represented by Renaissance and Enlightenment. Although the term "Enlightenment" was not applied to May Fourth until 1936, the Marxist project itself was already set in motion in 1920, at the latest, when Chen Duxiu 陳 獨 秀 (1879–1942) moved the powerful magazine *New Youth* (*Xin qingnian* 新 青 年, also known as *La Jeunesse*) from Beijing to Shanghai and transformed the magazine into "a Chinese version of *Soviet Russia*," the New York Communist weekly pictorial (Chow 1960: 250). It resulted in the split in the New Youth Society between the left wing under Chen's leadership and the liberal wing in Beijing headed by Hu Shi. From this time on, the left wing began to direct May Fourth toward political revolution by actively engaging in ever-broadening mass organization and mobilization, whereas the liberal wing continued to expand the original Renaissance project in the cultural and intellectual realm.

A further clarification with regard to the Enlightenment project is in order. The substitution of Enlightenment for Renaissance as a description of May Fourth in recent years is primarily due, as shown earlier, to the efforts of Chinese Marxists traceable to the 1930s. It is for this reason that I find it useful to draw a sharp contrast between the Marxist interpretation of May Fourth as Enlightenment, on the one hand, and the liberal interpretation of it as Renaissance, on the other. What I refer to as the "Enlightenment project" is therefore, in truth, the Marxist project. But I am not suggesting even in the slightest that anyone who understands May Fourth in terms of Enlightenment must subscribe to the Marxist point of view. As I have already indicated above, there are indeed many valid reasons to argue for an analogy between May Fourth and the Enlightenment, if an analogical approach is to be followed in historical research, which, of course, is highly problematical. It is interesting to note that Luo Jialun 羅家倫 (1896–1969), Hu Shi's leading disciple and founder of *New Tide* (*Renaissance*), also compared May Fourth to the Enlightenment many years later. He said: "May Fourth, first and foremost, represents the awakening of a new culture consciousness . . . and is very similar to the eighteenth-century European Enlightenment. . . . Enlightenment figures such as Rousseau and Diderot used fierce criticism to break through the confines of old thought. Moreover, they used a scientific attitude and the spirit of freedom not only to reconsider prevailing literary tendencies . . . but also to undertake a thorough inquiry into the political and social system as well" (quoted in Schwarcz 1986: 256).[6] Luo's use of Enlightenment instead of Renaissance as analogy was in all probability influenced by Li Changzhi 李長之 (1910–78), who was on the faculty of the Central University in the early 1940s when Luo served as its president.

Equally at home with the literary and philosophical traditions of China and Europe, Li Changzhi developed penetrating observations on May

6. Xu Xiaoyan 許孝炎, who was a student at Peking University from 1920 to 1926, also characterized the May Fourth cultural movement as the "Enlightenment" in a speech given on May 4, 1973, in Hong Kong (see Zhou 1979: 679-85).

Fourth as a cultural movement. He weighed carefully and on intellectual grounds the pros and cons of the two analogies as applied to May Fourth and came to the conclusion that May Fourth bore a family resemblance not to the Renaissance but to the Enlightenment. He arrived at this conclusion independently of the Marxist New Enlightenment movement and for completely different reasons. He meant to exalt Renaissance and downgrade Enlightenment. According to him, to the extent that the May Fourth mentality was rational, critical, skeptical, iconoclastic, practical, scientific, and antimetaphysical, it is justifiable to identify May Fourth with Enlightenment. However, the main trouble with this Enlightenment mentality is its shallowness; it cannot appreciate anything intellectually profound. As a result, in philosophy, Dewey, Huxley, Darwin, and Marx became fashionable while Plato, Kant, and Hegel were little discussed. He further pointed out that the May Fourth spirit is antithetical to the Renaissance, which by definition implies both a return to and a revival of the classical tradition. May Fourth intellectuals showed neither an appreciation of their own early tradition nor an understanding of the classical culture of the West. Confucius was ferociously attacked as an apologist of the "feudal order," whereas Plato was dismissed as a mere "metaphysician." It was a classic case of a misnomer when Western scholars labeled Hu Shi the "Father of the Chinese Renaissance." Despite his scathing criticism, I must hasten to add that Li was not wholly negative about May Fourth as a cultural movement. May Fourth cleared the old cultural ground through its destructive work and thereby opened up China for the real possibility of cultural reconstruction, but the important thing was, he concluded, to start a true Chinese Renaissance by going beyond the Enlightenment (Li Changzhi 1946: 14–22). His revised version of a "Renaissance project" does not seem to have evoked much enthusiastic response in the Chinese intellectual world during the warridden and politically polarized 1940s, but it has begun to strike a sympathetic chord in a new generation of Chinese intellectuals who are moving away from the positivistic mode of thinking of the Marxist variety toward an "interpretive turn" in the human sciences (see Li Zhensheng 1995; Hiley et al. 1991).

What I find particularly interesting in Li Changzhi's re-evaluation of May Fourth is his open acknowledgment that May Fourth as a cultural movement must be clearly recognized, first of all, as a movement of cultural borrowing, or, as he puts its, the transplantation of Western culture to

China without ever taking roots in its soil (1946: 12–13, 19–20). In a sense, this is an obvious fact. Why should I find such a truism interesting? It deserves attention, I believe, for several reasons. First, as far as I know, no one has stated this plain truth so emphatically and with such a degree of seriousness. Second, this statement, though basically true, is nevertheless somewhat misleading if understood in the sense that those Western ideas and theories that had stirred up so many Chinese intellectuals of the May Fourth generation were completely without basis in the cultural reality in which they found themselves. Elsewhere I have tried to show that during the late nineteenth and early twentieth centuries Chinese intellectuals, generally speaking, responded with genuine enthusiasm only to those Western values and ideas that struck chords in their own tradition (Yü 1995). Finally, this plain fact undermines the very foundation on which the analogy between May Fourth on the one hand and Renaissance or Enlightenment on the other is built. The reason is not far to seek: in their own historical context, neither the Renaissance nor the Enlightenment was a result of cultural borrowing; each was the flowering of internal development and growth over many centuries of European culture. It is on this last point that I wish to comment further in order to clarify the nature of May Fourth as a cultural movement.

To begin with, I propose to discard analogy in the study of Chinese history altogether. If we can neither recognize general laws in history nor take the unique pattern of European historical experience as the universal model for all non-Western societies, why must we bother even to raise the question whether there was a Renaissance or an Enlightenment in Chinese history in the first place? We would do well to see the May Fourth movement as it really was. It was, as Li Changzhi rightly observed, first and foremost a cultural movement in response to the stimulus of Western ideas. May Fourth intellectuals did consciously borrow ideas from the Renaissance and the Enlightenment. That is precisely why one can interpret May Fourth in terms of either with some justification. But May Fourth was neither the Chinese Renaissance nor the Chinese Enlightenment for the simple reason that a great variety of Western ideas and values other than Renaissance and Enlightenment were also introduced into China during the same period. If we carry analogical thinking to its logical extreme, then we would have to crowd many centuries of European history into the brief space of one or two decades of twentieth-century China which, needless to say, amounts to monstrous absurdity.

Once we are free of the obsession with rigid analogy, we can begin to understand May Fourth in its own terms. In my earlier study of the radicalization of China in the twentieth century, I pointed out that "during the May Fourth era beginning with the literary revolution of 1917, a paradigmatic change took place in the development of radicalism in modern China. From this time on, whether in criticizing the tradition or advocating changes, Chinese intellectuals would almost invariably invoke some Western ideas, values or institutions as ultimate grounds for justification" (Yü 1993: 130). Now, in the context of the present discussion, I would add that the same principles also held true for Chinese conservatives during the May Fourth period. More often than not, they, too, appealed to Western authors in defending the Chinese tradition. Li Changzhi's definition of May Fourth in terms of the transplantation of Western culture to China must also be understood in this light. If we take the notion of "enlightenment" as a metaphor, rather than an analogy, we may say that May Fourth is different from the European Enlightenment in a very fundamental way. When the Enlightenment *philosophes* attacked Christianity, scholasticism, and the "Dark" Middle Ages, they were armed with the classics of Greek and Roman antiquity. In other words, they were guided by an inner light. By contrast, May Fourth intellectuals had to go out of their darkened cave—China—in order to see the light of day; they were guided by a light from outside—the West. Or, to borrow Mao Zedong's famous saying, China has been "seeking truth from the West since the end of the nineteenth century."

In its early days, May Fourth was also popularly known in China by the names "New Culture" or "New Thought," which seem to be more descriptive and less misleading than either Renaissance or Enlightenment. As a matter of fact, the identity of May Fourth with the term "New Culture" has been more firmly established than with any other term, at least in Chinese writing. In this connection, I propose to use Hu Shi's definition as the point of departure to re-examine the idea of New Culture and its place in the intellectual history of twentieth-century China. His 1919 article "The Meaning of New Thought" ("Xin sichao de yiyi" 新思潮的意義) begins by pointing out that "the fundamental significance of the new thought lies simply in a new attitude," which may be called the "critical attitude." It then goes on to list three specific tasks to be carried out under the guidance of this critical spirit: the first is to "study problems." There are many concrete problems in China—social, political, religious, literary—that require our immediate attention. They must be critically studied so that solutions may be found. The second is to support new ideas, new learning, new literature, new faith from the West. They not only meet the spiritual needs of Chinese intellectuals but also can provide them with theoretical guidance in their search for solutions of China's concrete problems. The third is to apply the critical spirit to the study of the Chinese intellectual tradition under the catchphrase of "systematic reorganization of the national heritage," *zhengli guogu* 整理國故. In the interest of self-understanding, China's old tradition must be critically and systematically re-examined. Only then can we develop an objective understanding of the various parts of our own intellectual heritage in historical perspective and determine their value. Finally, it concludes by suggesting that the ultimate goal of the new cultural movement is the reconstruction of Chinese civilization (Hu 1930: 41–50).

Here Hu Shi presented a New Culture project formulated in its broadest possible terms and at a higher level. Defined in this way the New Culture is not just about advocacy of Western values and ideas such as democracy, science, autonomy of the individual, emancipation of women, and the like. Nor is its central significance limited to the denunciation of the Chinese tradition including, especially, the theory and practice of Confucianism. From his point of view, all the above matters of a practical nature—the list is endless—can likely be included in the category of "study problems." However, in promoting simultaneously the importation of Western thought and scholarship on the one hand and the "systematic reorganization of national heritage" on the other, he seems to have returned to the theme he had set forth in 1917, namely, how to "connect the best in modern civilization with the best in our own civilization." It is not my purpose here to offer a detailed commentary on Hu Shi's essay. Instead I merely wish to use it as a starting point to suggest a new way of looking at the intellectual history of the May Fourth era.

If the New Thought or New Culture is definable in terms of a critical spirit under the guidance of which both Western and Chinese learning are to be pursued with the purpose, explicit or implicit, of illuminating each other in order to achieve, ultimately, a creative synthesis, then the very concept would have to be stretched to the extent of including every active member of the May Fourth intellectual world as a participant of the New Culture movement. For the simple truth is that those who are often labeled as "conservative" critics of the May Fourth movement turned out to be no less critical and no less Westernized than their "progressive" rivals. To illustrate my point, let me give one or two examples. By general consensus, Liang Shuming 梁漱溟 (1893–1988) was a cultural "conservative" *par excellence*. But is his justly famous *Eastern and Western Cultures and Their Philosophies* (*Dong xi wenhua ji qi zhexue* 東西文化及其哲學) of 1920 part of the New Culture or not? Surprisingly, the following is what Hu Shi had to say about it in his 1926 lecture on "The Renaissance in China":

> For the first time in history we begin to recognize a new attitude, a desire to understand the basic meaning of modern civilization, to understand the philosophy behind the civilization of the West. As the best example of this new consciousness I may cite the work of a Chinese scholar, Liang Sh[o]u-ming. . . . He is voicing the yearning of a new age. His book was widely read and much has been written since on the same subject. . . . May I suggest that in these discussions we find a completely new attitude, an attitude on the one hand of frank admission of our own weaknesses, all the weak points in Oriental civilization; and on the other hand, the attitude of a frank, genuine understanding of the spirit, not only the material prosperity, but also the spiritual possibilities of the Western civilization. (Hu 1926: 273–74; see also Feng 1984: 201)

I have quoted Hu Shi at some length because his words bear importantly and directly on my point. The "new attitude" he recognized in Liang's work is exactly what he had described as "the fundamental significance of the new thought" in 1919. Thus, by Hu Shi's own admission, Liang's study of Eastern and Western cultures and philosophies is very much a constituent part of the so-called Chinese Renaissance.

Next, I would also like to cite the example of Mei Guangdi 梅光迪 (1890–1945) in support of my contention. Mei, as is generally known, was one of Hu Shi's most intimate friends in their younger days, but in 1917 they became bitter intellectual rivals as a result of Mei's violent opposition to the literary revolution.

In 1922, Mei and Wu Mi 吳宓 (1894–1978), both leading Chinese disciples of Irving Babbitt, founded the *Critical Review* (*Xueheng* 學衡, 1922–33), which, as a Chinese writer vividly described in 1934, stood "for everything that Dr. Hu Shi [was] against. The avowed aim of the *Critical Review* . . . was to fight the *baihua* (白話) movement, and to strive to maintain the old ways of writing. It was a losing battle, but the effort was heroic" (Wen 1934: 27). So Mei and the *Critical Review* were contemptuously dismissed as conservative nonsense by May Fourth leaders including Hu Shi and Lu Xun 魯迅

(1881–1936) (Chow 1960: 282; see Lu Xun 1973: 2.98–101, 114–16). It would seem unquestionable that Mei not only placed himself outside the New Culture of the May Fourth era but also was its most relentless enemy. However, recently, 45 of Mei's letters to Hu Shi have been published for the first time, and they throw a wholly different light on his relationship to the rise of the New Culture as later promoted by Hu Shi. Without going into details, let me report a few of what I consider to be significant findings.

First, from October 1911 on, Mei wrote Hu Shi several long letters discussing the problem of Confucianism in modern China. At this time, probably due to the lingering influence of his father, Hu was still very much a believer in Cheng-Zhu 程 朱 Neo-Confucianism. Mei severely attacked the Cheng-Zhu orthodoxy and urged Hu Shi to move on to the learning of Yan Yuan 顏 元 (1635–1704) and Li Gong 李 塨 (1659–1733), which emphasized the central importance of social and political practice in the original teaching of Confucius and Mencius as opposed to the idle speculation of Cheng-Zhu Neo-Confucian philosophy (Geng 1994: 33.313–22, 327–33, 398–99). At first, Hu resisted the suggestion (1927: 73, 75); however, it sowed the seed of his ardent advocacy of the Yan-Li school a decade later (1927: 3–8).

Second, Mei was not only equally dissatisfied with Han and Song Confucianism but also highly critical of the National Essence (Guocui 國 粹) school then very much in vogue in China, which, he thought, still uncritically followed traditional commentaries on the Confucian classics (Geng 1994: 33.387–89). He was aiming at a higher synthesis of the Confucian tradition and Western culture. This could be accomplished only in two stages: a thorough purification of the Confucian tradition of the past two thousand years and a firm grasp of European learning with special emphasis on its classical beginning. Old Chinese texts, said he, must now be studied in light of the Western system of organizing human knowledge such as literature, philosophy, law, and the like (Geng 1994: 33.334–36).

Third, in his letter dated March 19, 1916, Mei wrote:

> In the future if I could introduce Western literary knowledge to China and provide a new point of view for the study of our traditional literature and thereby set some examples for younger scholars to follow, I would feel my wish more than fulfilled.... am much enlightened by your discussions of Song and Yuan literature in your letter. It goes without saying that the [present] literary revolution ought to begin with 'people's literature' (such as folklore, popular poetry, spoken language, etc.). However, it must go through a great war. For the sudden talk of vernacular literature will

inevitably be ridiculed and attacked by conservative men of letters. But on our part we rather welcome their ridicules and attacks. (Geng 1994: 33.436–37).

In view of this letter, Mei was actually an enthusiastic participant of Hu's literary revolution in its early days, even though he disagreed strongly with Hu's literary taste. Moreover, I have also carefully checked Mei's letters as quoted by Hu Shi against the original. There can be little doubt that Mei has been made a villain of the literary revolution by being quoted out of context. In these letters Mei repeatedly tried to make his position clear to Hu Shi: that he was sympathetic to the literary revolution but could not go with him so far as to glorify the spoken language (*baihua* 白話) beyond its limit. He told Hu in no uncertain terms that he was not necessarily less iconoclastic than Hu (Geng 1994: 33.450); he refused to embrace the "new currents" in literature and art not because he was "conservative" but because he was "too skeptical, too independent" (Geng 1994: 33.443). In light of this new evidence, we can say almost with certainty that it was Hu Shi's ever-growing radicalism in the subsequent debates that eventually pushed Mei to extreme conservatism. However, had Mei lived until 1952, he would have felt fully vindicated when Hu Shi, in his turn, became thoroughly disgusted with the "new poetry" and "new literature" in American colleges (1990: vol. 17, Feb. 25, 1952).

Finally, in political and social views, Mei was always a moderate liberal, just as Hu was. He was from the beginning on the side of the republican revolution and, later, when Yuan Shikai 袁世凱 (1859–1916) betrayed the republic, his sympathy was wholly with the Nationalist Party. His deep differences with Hu Shi in literature and philosophy did not prevent him from expressing his admiration for Hu's published statements against Yuan in American magazines. He even volunteered to write the revolutionary leader Huang Xing 黃興 (1874–1916) to recommend that Hu be appointed the spokesman for the republican cause. In his own words, "Hu Shi, being equally fluent in Chinese and English, is the only person among Chinese students in America who can use his pen to turn around the public opinion of this country" (Geng 1994: 33.437–38). In a letter dated December 28, 1916, in which he continued his debate with Hu Shi on the literary revolution, he nevertheless tried, in a rather reconciliatory tone, to seek a basic agreement with Hu on general "views of life." He suggested to Hu in earnest that his Babbittian humanism and Hu's Deweyan experimentalism shared more in common than they differed from each other. Both were in favor of reform, with only one major difference: Babbitt held that it should begin with the individual and then gradually spread to the whole society, whereas Dewey seemed to take an opposite view with regard to the process of reform (Geng 1994: 33.464–66). Moreover, although deeply committed to the moral faith of Confucius and Mencius, Mei's repudiation of imperial Confucianism as a political ideology was complete. He condemned both Han and Song Confucians for distorting Confucian teachings in the service of autocracy and social inequality and repeatedly denounced the theory of "three bonds," *san gang* 三 綱 (Geng 1994: 33.374–75, 384–87). Anti-traditionalist outbursts such as these could have appeared in the pages of the *New Youth* without their author ever being suspected of being a founding member of the *Critical Review*. This explains why he did not hesitate to praise Hu Shi for his liberal political views as late as 1922 (Hu 1924: 61).

The case of Mei Guangdi and his *Critical Review* raises a serious question about the true identity of the New Culture of the May Fourth era. If the New Culture consisted, first and foremost, of the importation of Western ideas to China, as Hu Shi's definition suggests, then Babbittian humanism was clearly just as "new" as Deweyan experimentalism to the intellectual world of May Fourth China. In a sense the conflict between Hu Shi and his followers on the one hand and Mei Guangdi and the *Critical Review* on the other may well be viewed as the rivalry between Deweyan experimentalism and Babbittian humanism transferred from America to China.[7] This is only natural because in cultural borrowing it is hardly possible to pick up a foreign idea without at the same time also calling someone else's attention to its opposite. Can we then consider Babbittian humanism part and parcel of the New Culture of the May Fourth era? At least this question was answered in the affirmative by both Liang Shiqiu 梁 實 秋 (1901–87) and Lin Yutang 林 語 堂 (1895–1976), whose credentials as members of the May Fourth move-

---

7. Thomas R. Nevin contrasts Babbitt with Dewey as follows: "His stress upon will, attended by its helpmate the rational intellect, might have given him a basis for rapport with dominant philosophical trends of his time, notably those influenced by Dewey. But Babbitt's focus was defiantly internal and individual. He scorned the problem-solving techniques of the sciences while he dreaded their inroads into humane values. He regarded the optimism of a generation of 'instrumentalists' and engineers as ill-founded and misguided, because no society, however adroitly planned or subjected to experiment, would ever escape the human frailties documented in the works of Sophocles, Dante, and Goethe, and revealed to the wisdom of the humanely balanced individual" (1984: 147). This passage applies perfectly to the intellectual tension between Mei and Hu Shi, including the former's attempt to reconcile his Babbittian humanism to Hu Shi's Deweyan experimentalism.

ment are impeccable. Having studied under Babbitt in 1924–1925, Liang returned to China convinced of his classical humanism. In the late 1920s, he edited a collection of Chinese articles on Babbitt, mostly from the pages of the *Critical Review*, and published it under the title *Babbitt and Humanism* (*Baibide yu renwenzhuyi* 白璧德與人文主義). The publisher, it may be noted, was none other than the Crescent Moon Society in Shanghai, a stronghold of the New Culture with Hu Shi as its patron saint (Liang Shiqiu 1963: 57–64). Lin Yutang, who studied with Babbitt at Harvard from 1919 to 1920, also wrote to Hu Shi that during his conversation with Babbitt he sensed some misapprehension, on the part of the latter, of Hu's points of view. However, he added that Babbitt, though against everything modern, was nevertheless right in his criticism of the neoteric mentality, which takes what is the newest to be the best. To Lin, it was the good fortune of the Chinese literary revolution to find a conscious and reflective opposition in people like Babbitt and Mei Guangdi (Geng 1994: 29.314–15). Clearly, both Liang and Lin did not, to say the least, share the partisan spirit of Hu Shi and Lu Xun in dismissing Mei Guangdi and the *Critical Review* as completely external to the New Culture. Interestingly, just as there has been some renewed interest in Babbitt in America since the 1980s (Nevin 1984; Schlesinger 1986), Mei Guangdi and the *Critical Review* have also been rediscovered by Chinese intellectuals since the 1970s (Hou Jian 1974; Lin 1979; Li Funing et al. 1990). There seems to be a growing trend of placing the cultural conservatism of Mei Guangdi and Wu Mi along with the radicalism of Chen Duxiu and Lu Xun and the liberalism of Hu Shi in the same discursive structure of May Fourth New Culture (Lin 1979: 396–402; Yue 1990: 255, 264–66).

Before bringing my reflections to a close, I wish to say a few words about the other part of Hu Shi's New Culture project—"the systematic reorganization of the national heritage." In this vast field of, essentially, historical studies of the Chinese tradition in all its aspects, there is even a greater need to enlarge the concept of New Culture in order to accommodate some of the leading "national heritage" (*guogu* 國故) scholars. A few examples will suffice for the purpose of illustration. Wang Guowei 王國維 (1877–1927), universally acknowledged as one of the most "scientifically minded" and original historians of ancient China, was politically a Qing loyalist and culturally an ultra-conservative. Chen Yinke 陳寅恪 (1890–1969), the leading medievalist, was both politically and culturally conservative and never wrote a single sentence in the vernacular. And yet he freely admitted that China has been inferior to the West since classical antiquity, not only in science but in philosophy and art as well (Wu 1992: 9–13). Tang Yongtong 湯用彤 (1893–1964), a great authority on the history of Chinese Buddhism and philosophy, was a contributor to the *Critical Review*, and, like Chen Yinke, always used the classical language in his writings. All three, needless to say, were unsympathetic to the May Fourth movement in both its narrow and its broad senses. But in the *guogu* field, Hu Shi admired them all and found in them kindred spirits. The compliment was sometimes reciprocated, though not always. If we measure *guogu* scholars by such narrowly and rigidly defined May Fourth standards as vernacular language, positivist mentality, anti-traditionalism, political radicalism or liberalism, ethical relativism, social egalitarianism, individualism, and the like, then a great majority and easily the best of them would have to be excluded from the New Culture of this era. As a result, what is left of the New Culture would be a linguistic world of conflicting ideological parodies but intellectually very much impoverished.

Daniel Bell once described himself as "a socialist in economics, a liberal in politics, and a conservative in culture" (Bell 1978: xi). I believe many Chinese intellectuals of the May Fourth period can be characterized in a similar way with, of course, a great variety of possible combinations. May Fourth has always been and still is many different things to different people. To me, it is primarily an age of cultural contradictions, and contradiction is by definition multidimensional as well as multidirectional. I can never bring myself to see it as a single coherent movement leading to a predetermined destination as if governed by an iron law of history. Each May Fourth intellectual not only seems unique, but many of them changed their minds quickly and sometimes drastically. Like the Russian intellectual before the Revolution who "could be a Westernizer in the morning, a Slavophil in the afternoon, and criticize after dinner" (Greenfeld 1992: 270), the May Fourth intellectual was also capable of shifting his position constantly within a period of months, if not days and weeks. Surely, some larger intellectual types and certain patterns of ideas may be vaguely discerned in the May Fourth movement in its broad sense. But, on the whole, it is extremely hazardous to generalize about these types and patterns. The Enlightenment republic of letters was described by Samuel Johnson as demonstrating "community of mind" because there was some kind of common core in that republic (quoted in Gay 1966: 39). Therefore, it may be permissible to speak of "the Enlightenment project"

(MacIntyre 1984: 117–18; Bernstein 1992: 202–8). By contrast, the May Fourth intellectual world consisted of many communities of changing minds. Consequently, not only were there several May Fourth projects constantly undergoing changes and often conflicting with one another but each project also had different versions. Perhaps the safest generalization one can make about May Fourth is that it must always be understood in terms of its multidimensionality and multidirectionality.

Works Cited

Becker, Carl L. 1932. *The Heavenly City of the Eighteenth-Century Philosophers*. New Haven: Yale University Press.

Bell, Daniel. 1978. *The Cultural Contradictions of Capitalism*. New York: Basic Books.

Bernstein, Richard J. 1992. *The New Constellation: The Ethical-Political Horizons of Modernity/Postmodernity*. Cambridge, Mass.: MIT Press.

Chow, Tse-tsung. 1960. *The May Fourth Movement*. Cambridge, Mass.: Harvard University Press.

Fairbank, John K. 1982. *Chinabound: A Fifty Year Memoir*. New York: Harper & Row.

Feng Youlan 馮友蘭. 1984. *Sansong tang zixu* 三松堂自序 (My autobiography). Beijing: Sanlian.

Fu Lecheng 傅樂成. 1969. *Fu Mengzhen xiansheng nianpu* 傅孟真先生年譜 (A chronological biography of Fu Sinian). Taibei: Zhuanji wenxue she.

Fu Sinian 傅斯年. 1952. "*Xin chao* zhi huigu yu qianzhan" 新潮之回顧與前瞻 (*New Tide*: retrospect and prospect). In *Fu Mengzhen xiansheng ji* 傅孟真先生集 (Collected works of Fu Sinian), vol. 1 (*shangbian, jia*), pp. 210–11. Taibei: Taiwan daxue.

Gao Wenhua 高文華. 1982. "1935 nian qianhou Beifang ju de qingkuang" 1935年前後北方局的情況 (The North China Bureau around 1935). In *Zhonggong dangshi ziliao* 中共黨史資料 (Source materials on the history of the Chinese Communist Party), pp. 184–88. Beijing: Zhonggong zhongyang dangxiao.

Gay, Peter. 1966. *The Enlightenment: An Interpretation; The Rise of Modern Paganism*. New York: Knopf.

Geng Yunzhi 耿雲志, comp. 1994. *Hu Shi yigao ji micang shuxin* 胡適遺稿及祕藏書信 (Hu Shi's unpublished manuscripts and private correspondence). 42 vols. Hefei: Huangshan.

Greenfeld, Liah. 1992. *Nationalism: Five Roads to Modernity*. Cambridge, Mass.: Harvard University Press.

Grieder, Jerome B. 1970. *Hu Shih and the Chinese Renaissance*. Cambridge, Mass.: Harvard University Press.

He Ganzhi 何幹之. 1947. *Zhongguo qimeng yundong shi* 中國啓蒙運動史 (History of the Chinese Enlightenment). Shanghai: Shenghuo.

Hiley, David R., James F. Bohman, and Richard Schusterman, eds. 1991. *The Interpretive Turn: Philosophy, Science, Culture*. Ithaca: Cornell University Press.

Hou Jian 侯健. 1974. *Cong wenxue geming dao geming wenxue* 從文學革命到革命文學 (From a literary revolution to revolutionizing literature). Taibei: Zhongwai wenxue yuekan she.

Hou Wailu 侯外廬. 1956. *Zhongguo zaoqi qimeng sixiang shi* 中國早期啓蒙思想史 (A history of early Chinese Enlightenment thought). Beijing: Renmin.

Hu Shi 胡適. [1924] 1986d. *Women de zhengzhi zhuzhang* 我們的政治主張 (Our political views). Reprinted—Taibei: Yuanliu.

———. 1926. "The Renaissance in China." *Journal of the Royal Institute of International Affairs* 5 (Nov.): 266–83.

———. [1927] 1986a. *Dai Dongyuan de zhexue* 戴東原的哲學 (The philosophy of Dai Dongyuan). Reprinted—Taibei: Yuanliu.

———. [1930] 1986c. *Hu Shi wenxuan* 胡適文選 (Selected works of Hu Shi). Reprinted—Taibei: Yuanliu.

———. 1934. *The Chinese Renaissance*. Chicago: University of Chicago Press.

———. [1939] 1986b. *Hu Shi liuxue riji* 胡適留學日記 (Hu Shi's diary while studying abroad). 4 vols. Reprinted—Taibei: Yuanliu.

———. 1960. "The Chinese Tradition and the Future." In *Sino-American Conference on Intellectual Cooperation: Report and Proceedings*, pp. 13–22. Seattle: University of Washington, Department of Publications and Printing.

———. [1970a] 1986e. "Wusi yundong shih qingnian aiguo de yundong" 五四運動是青年愛國的運動 (May Fourth is a patriotic movement of the youth). In *Hu Shi yanjiang ji* 胡適演講集 (Hu Shi's lectures), 2: 133–34. Reprint. Taibei: Yuanliu.

———. [1970b] 1986f. "Zhongguo wenyi fuxing yundong" 中國文藝復興運動 (The Chinese Renaissance movement). In *Hu Shi yanjiang ji* 胡適演講集 (Hu Shi's lectures), 1: 178. Reprinted—Taibei: Yuanliu.

———. 1990. *Hu Shi de riji* 胡適的日記 (Hu Shi's diary). 18 vols. Photographic reproduction of original manuscript, unpaginated. Taibei: Yuanliu.

Li Changzhi 李長之. 1946. *Ying Zhongguo de wenyi fuxing* 迎中國的文藝復興 (Welcome to the Chinese Renaissance). Shanghai: Shangwu.

Li Funing 李賦寧, Sun Tianyi 孫天義, and Cai Heng 蔡恆, eds. 1990. *Diyi jie Wu Mi xueshu taolunhui lunwen xuanji* 第一屆吳宓學術討論會論文選集 (Selected papers from the first scholarly conference on Wu Mi). Xi'an: Shaanxi renmin jiaoyu.

Li Zehou 李澤厚. 1987. *Zhongguo xiandai sixiang shi lun* 中國現代思想史論 (Essays on modern Chinese intellectual history). Beijing: Dongfang.

Li Zhensheng 李振聲. 1995. "Jingwei lishi, zunzhong lishi" 敬畏歷史尊重歷史 (Stand in awe of history, respect history). *Dushu*, July, p. 27.

Liang Ch'i-ch'ao. 1959. *Intellectual Trends in the Ch'ing Period*. Trans. by Immanuel C. Y. Hsü. Cambridge, Mass.: Harvard University Press.

Liang Shiqiu 梁實秋. [1963] 1969. *Wenxue yinyuan* 文學因緣 (Essays on literature). Reprinted—Hong Kong: Wenyi shuwu.

Liang Shuming 梁 漱 溟. [1920] 1977. *Dong xi wenhua ji qi zhexue* 東 西 文 化 及 其 哲 學 (Eastern and Western cultures and their philosophies). Reprinted—Taibei: Wenxue.

Lin Liyue 林 麗 月. 1979. "Mei Guangdi yu Xin wenhua yundong" 梅 光 迪 與 新 文 化 運 動 (Mei Guangdi and the New Culture movement). In Wang Rongzu 王 榮 祖, ed., *Wusi yanjiu lunwen ji* 五 四 研 究 論 文 集 (Collected studies on May Fourth), pp. 383–402. Taibei: Lianjing.

Lin Yu-sheng 林 毓 生 et al. 1989. *Wusi: duoyuan de fansi* 五 四：多 元 的 反 思 (May Fourth: pluralistic reflections). Hong Kong: Sanlian.

Lu Cui 陸 璀. 1995. *Chenxing ji* 晨 星 集 (A collection of morning stars). Beijing: Renmin ribao.

Lu Xun 魯 迅. 1973. *Lu Xun quanji* 魯 迅 全 集 (Collected works of Lu Xun). 20 vols. Beijing: Renmin wenxue.

MacIntyre, Alasdair C. 1984. *After Virtue: A Study in Moral Theory*. 2nd ed. Notre Dame, Ind.: University of Notre Dame Press.

Mao Zedong 毛 澤 東. 1969. *Mao Zedong xuanji* 毛 澤 東 選 集 (Selected works of Mao Zedong). 4 vols. Beijing: Renmin.

Nevin, Thomas R. 1984. *Irving Babbitt: An Intellectual Study*. Chapel Hill: University of North Carolina Press.

Schlesinger, Arthur M., Jr. 1986. "Democracy and Leadership." In idem, *The Cycles of American History*, pp. 419–36. Boston: Houghton Mifflin.

Schwarcz, Vera. 1986. *The Chinese Enlightenment: Intellectuals and the Legacy of the May Fourth of 1919*. Berkeley: University of California Press.

Wen Yuanning 溫 源 寧. [1934] 1990. "Mr. Wu Mi: A Scholar and a Gentleman" (in English). In Huang Shitan 黃 士 坦, ed., *Huiyi Wu Mi xiansheng* 回 憶 吳 宓 先 生 (Reminiscences of Mr. Wu Mi), pp. 24–28. Xi'an: Shaanxi renmin.

Wu Xuezhao 吳 學 昭. 1992. *Wu Mi yu Chen Yinke* 吳 宓 與 陳 寅 恪 (Wu Mi and Chen Yinke). Beijing: Qinghua.

Ye Yonglie 葉 永 烈. 1990. *Chen Boda* 陳 伯 達 (Biography of Chen Boda). Hong Kong: Wenhua jiaoyu.

Yü Ying-shih 余 英 時. 1976. "Wenyi fuxing yu renwen sichao" 文 藝 復 興 與 人 文 思 潮 (The Renaissance and humanism). In idem, *Lishi yu sixiang* 歷 史 與 思 想 (History and thought), pp. 305–37. Taibei: Lianjing.

———. 1984. *Zhongguo jindai sixiang shi shang de Hu Shi* 中 國 近 代 思 想 史 上 的 胡 適 (Hu Shi in modern Chinese intellectual history). Taibei: Lianjing.

———. 1993. "The Radicalization of China." *Daedalus* 122, no. 2 (Spring): 125–50.

———. 1995. "Confucianism in the Modern World: A Retrospective and Perspective Study" (in Japanese). *Chūgoku: shakai to bunka* 10 (June): 135–79.

Yue Daiyun 樂 黛 雲. 1990. "Shijie wenhua duihua zhong de Zhongguo xiandai baoshouzhuyi" 世 界 文 化 對 話 中 的 中 國 現 代 保 守 主 義 (A survey of

Critical Review: Modern Chinese conservatism in the dialogue on world cultures). In Li Funing 李賦寧, Sun Tianyi 孫天義, and Cai Heng 蔡恆, eds., *Diyi jie Wu Mi xueshu taolunhui lunwen xuanji* 第一屆吳宓學術討集會論文選集 (Selected papers from the first scholarly conference on Wu Mi), pp. 253–75. Xi'an: Shaanxi renmin jiaoyu.

Zhexue da cidian 哲學大詞典 (Great dictionary of philosophy). 1985. Shanghai: Cishu.

Zhou Yangshan 周陽山, ed. 1979. *Wusi yu Zhongguo* 五四與中國 (May Fourth and China). Taibei: Shibao wenhua.

Index

Index

Harvard East Asian Monographs
(* out-of-print)

- *1. Liang Fang-chung, *The Single-Whip Method of Taxation in China*
- *2. Harold C. Hinton, *The Grain Tribute System of China, 1845–1911*
- 3. Ellsworth C. Carlson, *The Kaiping Mines, 1877–1912*
- *4. Chao Kuo-chün, *Agrarian Policies of Mainland China: A Documentary Study, 1949–1956*
- *5. Edgar Snow, *Random Notes on Red China, 1936–1945*
- *6. Edwin George Beal, Jr., *The Origin of Likin, 1835–1864*
- 7. Chao Kuo-chün, *Economic Planning and Organization in Mainland China: A Documentary Study, 1949–1957*
- *8. John K. Fairbank, *Ching Documents: An Introductory Syllabus*
- *9. Helen Yin and Yi-chang Yin, *Economic Statistics of Mainland China, 1949–1957*
- *10. Wolfgang Franke, *The Reform and Abolition of the Traditional Chinese Examination System*
- 11. Albert Feuerwerker and S. Cheng, *Chinese Communist Studies of Modern Chinese History*
- 12. C. John Stanley, *Late Ching Finance: Hu Kuang-yung as an Innovator*
- 13. S. M. Meng, *The Tsungli Yamen: Its Organization and Functions*
- *14. Ssu-yü Teng, *Historiography of the Taiping Rebellion*
- 15. Chun-Jo Liu, *Controversies in Modern Chinese Intellectual History: An Analytic Bibliography of Periodical Articles, Mainly of the May Fourth and Post–May Fourth Era*
- *16. Edward J. M. Rhoads, *The Chinese Red Army, 1927–1963: An Annotated Bibliography*
- 17. Andrew J. Nathan, *A History of the China International Famine Relief Commission*
- *18. Frank H. H. King (ed.) and Prescott Clarke, *A Research Guide to China-Coast Newspapers, 1822–1911*
- 19. Ellis Joffe, *Party and Army: Professionalism and Political Control in the Chinese Officer Corps, 1949–1964*
- *20. Toshio G. Tsukahira, *Feudal Control in Tokugawa Japan: The Sankin Kōtai System*
- 21. Kwang-Ching Liu, ed., *American Missionaries in China: Papers from Harvard Seminars*
- 22. George Moseley, *A Sino-Soviet Cultural Frontier: The Ili Kazakh Autonomous Chou*

Harvard East Asian Monographs

23. Carl F. Nathan, *Plague Prevention and Politics in Manchuria, 1910–1931*
*24. Adrian Arthur Bennett, *John Fryer: The Introduction of Western Science and Technology into Nineteenth-Century China*
25. Donald J. Friedman, *The Road from Isolation: The Campaign of the American Committee for Non-Participation in Japanese Aggression, 1938–1941*
*26. Edward LeFevour, *Western Enterprise in Late Ching China: A Selective Survey of Jardine, Matheson and Company's Operations, 1842–1895*
27. Charles Neuhauser, *Third World Politics: China and the Afro-Asian People's Solidarity Organization, 1957–1967*
28. Kungtu C. Sun, assisted by Ralph W. Huenemann, *The Economic Development of Manchuria in the First Half of the Twentieth Century*
*29. Shahid Javed Burki, *A Study of Chinese Communes, 1965*
30. John Carter Vincent, *The Extraterritorial System in China: Final Phase*
31. Madeleine Chi, *China Diplomacy, 1914–1918*
*32. Clifton Jackson Phillips, *Protestant America and the Pagan World: The First Half Century of the American Board of Commissioners for Foreign Missions, 1810–1860*
33. James Pusey, *Wu Han: Attacking the Present through the Past*
34. Ying-wan Cheng, *Postal Communication in China and Its Modernization, 1860–1896*
35. Tuvia Blumenthal, *Saving in Postwar Japan*
36. Peter Frost, *The Bakumatsu Currency Crisis*
37. Stephen C. Lockwood, *Augustine Heard and Company, 1858–1862*
38. Robert R. Campbell, *James Duncan Campbell: A Memoir by His Son*
39. Jerome Alan Cohen, ed., *The Dynamics of China's Foreign Relations*
40. V. V. Vishnyakova-Akimova, *Two Years in Revolutionary China, 1925–1927*, tr. Steven L. Levine
*41. Meron Medzini, *French Policy in Japan during the Closing Years of the Tokugawa Regime*
42. Ezra Vogel, Margie Sargent, Vivienne B. Shue, Thomas Jay Mathews, and Deborah S. Davis, *The Cultural Revolution in the Provinces*
*43. Sidney A. Forsythe, *An American Missionary Community in China, 1895–1905*
*44. Benjamin I. Schwartz, ed., *Reflections on the May Fourth Movement.: A Symposium*
*45. Ching Young Choe, *The Rule of the Taewŏngun, 1864–1873: Restoration in Yi Korea*
46. W. P. J. Hall, *A Bibliographical Guide to Japanese Research on the Chinese Economy, 1958–1970*
47. Jack J. Gerson, *Horatio Nelson Lay and Sino-British Relations, 1854–1864*
48. Paul Richard Bohr, *Famine and the Missionary: Timothy Richard as Relief Administrator and Advocate of National Reform*
49. Endymion Wilkinson, *The History of Imperial China: A Research Guide*
50. Britten Dean, *China and Great Britain: The Diplomacy of Commercial Relations, 1860–1864*
51. Ellsworth C. Carlson, *The Foochow Missionaries, 1847–1880*

52. Yeh-chien Wang, *An Estimate of the Land-Tax Collection in China, 1753 and 1908*
53. Richard M. Pfeffer, *Understanding Business Contracts in China, 1949–1963*
54. Han-sheng Chuan and Richard Kraus, *Mid-Ching Rice Markets and Trade: An Essay in Price History*
55. Ranbir Vohra, *Lao She and the Chinese Revolution*
56. Liang-lin Hsiao, *China's Foreign Trade Statistics, 1864–1949*
*57. Lee-hsia Hsu Ting, *Government Control of the Press in Modern China, 1900–1949*
58. Edward W. Wagner, *The Literati Purges: Political Conflict in Early Yi Korea*
*59. Joungwon A. Kim, *Divided Korea: The Politics of Development, 1945–1972*
*60. Noriko Kamachi, John K. Fairbank, and Chūzō Ichiko, *Japanese Studies of Modern China Since 1953: A Bibliographical Guide to Historical and Social-Science Research on the Nineteenth and Twentieth Centuries, Supplementary Volume for 1953–1969*
61. Donald A. Gibbs and Yun-chen Li, *A Bibliography of Studies and Translations of Modern Chinese Literature, 1918–1942*
62. Robert H. Silin, *Leadership and Values: The Organization of Large-Scale Taiwanese Enterprises*
63. David Pong, *A Critical Guide to the Kwangtung Provincial Archives Deposited at the Public Record Office of London*
*64. Fred W. Drake, *China Charts the World: Hsu Chi-yü and His Geography of 1848*
*65. William A. Brown and Urgrunge Onon, translators and annotators, *History of the Mongolian People's Republic*
66. Edward L. Farmer, *Early Ming Government: The Evolution of Dual Capitals*
*67. Ralph C. Croizier, *Koxinga and Chinese Nationalism: History, Myth, and the Hero*
*68. William J. Tyler, tr., *The Psychological World of Natsume Sōseki*, by Doi Takeo
69. Eric Widmer, *The Russian Ecclesiastical Mission in Peking during the Eighteenth Century*
*70. Charlton M. Lewis, *Prologue to the Chinese Revolution: The Transformation of Ideas and Institutions in Hunan Province, 1891–1907*
71. Preston Torbert, *The Ching Imperial Household Department: A Study of Its Organization and Principal Functions, 1662–1796*
72. Paul A. Cohen and John E. Schrecker, eds., *Reform in Nineteenth-Century China*
73. Jon Sigurdson, *Rural Industrialism in China*
74. Kang Chao, *The Development of Cotton Textile Production in China*
75. Valentin Rabe, *The Home Base of American China Missions, 1880–1920*
*76. Sarasin Viraphol, *Tribute and Profit: Sino-Siamese Trade, 1652–1853*
77. Ch'i-ch'ing Hsiao, *The Military Establishment of the Yuan Dynasty*
78. Meishi Tsai, *Contemporary Chinese Novels and Short Stories, 1949–1974: An Annotated Bibliography*
*79. Wellington K. K. Chan, *Merchants, Mandarins and Modern Enterprise in Late Ching China*

Harvard East Asian Monographs

80. Endymion Wilkinson, *Landlord and Labor in Late Imperial China: Case Studies from Shandong by Jing Su and Luo Lun*
*81. Barry Keenan, *The Dewey Experiment in China: Educational Reform and Political Power in the Early Republic*
*82. George A. Hayden, *Crime and Punishment in Medieval Chinese Drama: Three Judge Pao Plays*
*83. Sang-Chul Suh, *Growth and Structural Changes in the Korean Economy, 1910–1940*
84. J. W. Dower, *Empire and Aftermath: Yoshida Shigeru and the Japanese Experience, 1878–1954*
85. Martin Collcutt, *Five Mountains: The Rinzai Zen Monastic Institution in Medieval Japan*
86. Kwang Suk Kim and Michael Roemer, *Growth and Structural Transformation*
87. Anne O. Krueger, *The Developmental Role of the Foreign Sector and Aid*
*88. Edwin S. Mills and Byung-Nak Song, *Urbanization and Urban Problems*
89. Sung Hwan Ban, Pal Yong Moon, and Dwight H. Perkins, *Rural Development*
*90. Noel F. McGinn, Donald R. Snodgrass, Yung Bong Kim, Shin-Bok Kim, and Quee-Young Kim, *Education and Development in Korea*
91. Leroy P. Jones and Il SaKong, *Government, Business, and Entrepreneurship in Economic Development: The Korean Case*
92. Edward S. Mason, Dwight H. Perkins, Kwang Suk Kim, David C. Cole, Mahn Je Kim et al., *The Economic and Social Modernization of the Republic of Korea*
93. Robert Repetto, Tai Hwan Kwon, Son-Ung Kim, Dae Young Kim, John E. Sloboda, and Peter J. Donaldson, *Economic Development, Population Policy, and Demographic Transition in the Republic of Korea*
94. Parks M. Coble, Jr., *The Shanghai Capitalists and the Nationalist Government, 1927–1937*
95. Noriko Kamachi, *Reform in China: Huang Tsun-hsien and the Japanese Model*
96. Richard Wich, *Sino-Soviet Crisis Politics: A Study of Political Change and Communication*
97. Lillian M. Li, *China's Silk Trade: Traditional Industry in the Modern World, 1842–1937*
98. R. David Arkush, *Fei Xiaotong and Sociology in Revolutionary China*
*99. Kenneth Alan Grossberg, *Japan's Renaissance: The Politics of the Muromachi Bakufu*
100. James Reeve Pusey, *China and Charles Darwin*
101. Hoyt Cleveland Tillman, *Utilitarian Confucianism: Chen Liang's Challenge to Chu Hsi*
102. Thomas A. Stanley, *Ōsugi Sakae, Anarchist in Taishō Japan: The Creativity of the Ego*
103. Jonathan K. Ocko, *Bureaucratic Reform in Provincial China: Ting Jih-ch'ang in Restoration Kiangsu, 1867–1870*
104. James Reed, *The Missionary Mind and American East Asia Policy, 1911–1915*
105. Neil L. Waters, *Japan's Local Pragmatists: The Transition from Bakumatsu to Meiji in the Kawasaki Region*
106. David C. Cole and Yung Chul Park, *Financial Development in Korea, 1945–1978*

107. Roy Bahl, Chuk Kyo Kim, and Chong Kee Park, *Public Finances during the Korean Modernization Process*
108. William D. Wray, *Mitsubishi and the N.Y.K, 1870–1914: Business Strategy in the Japanese Shipping Industry*
109. Ralph William Huenemann, *The Dragon and the Iron Horse: The Economics of Railroads in China, 1876–1937*
110. Benjamin A. Elman, *From Philosophy to Philology: Intellectual and Social Aspects of Change in Late Imperial China*
111. Jane Kate Leonard, *Wei Yüan and China's Rediscovery of the Maritime World*
112. Luke S. K. Kwong, *A Mosaic of the Hundred Days:. Personalities, Politics, and Ideas of 1898*
113. John E. Wills, Jr., *Embassies and Illusions: Dutch and Portuguese Envoys to K'ang-hsi, 1666–1687*
114. Joshua A. Fogel, *Politics and Sinology: The Case of Naitō Konan (1866–1934)*
*115. Jeffrey C. Kinkley, ed., *After Mao: Chinese Literature and Society, 1978– 1981*
116. C. Andrew Gerstle, *Circles of Fantasy: Convention in the Plays of Chikamatsu*
117. Andrew Gordon, *The Evolution of Labor Relations in Japan: Heavy Industry, 1853–1955*
*118. Daniel K. Gardner, *Chu Hsi and the "Ta Hsueh": Neo-Confucian Reflection on the Confucian Canon*
119. Christine Guth Kanda, *Shinzō: Hachiman Imagery and Its Development*
*120. Robert Borgen, *Sugawara no Michizane and the Early Heian Court*
121. Chang-tai Hung, *Going to the People: Chinese Intellectual and Folk Literature, 1918–1937*
*122. Michael A. Cusumano, *The Japanese Automobile Industry: Technology and Management at Nissan and Toyota*
123. Richard von Glahn, *The Country of Streams and Grottoes: Expansion, Settlement, and the Civilizing of the Sichuan Frontier in Song Times*
124. Steven D. Carter, *The Road to Komatsubara: A Classical Reading of the Renga Hyakuin*
125. Katherine F. Bruner, John K. Fairbank, and Richard T. Smith, *Entering China's Service: Robert Hart's Journals, 1854–1863*
126. Bob Tadashi Wakabayashi, *Anti-Foreignism and Western Learning in Early-Modern Japan: The "New Theses" of 1825*
127. Atsuko Hirai, *Individualism and Socialism: The Life and Thought of Kawai Eijirō (1891–1944)*
128. Ellen Widmer, *The Margins of Utopia: "Shui-hu hou-chuan" and the Literature of Ming Loyalism*
129. R. Kent Guy, *The Emperor's Four Treasuries: Scholars and the State in the Late Chien-lung Era*
130. Peter C. Perdue, *Exhausting the Earth: State and Peasant in Hunan, 1500–1850*
131. Susan Chan Egan, *A Latterday Confucian: Reminiscences of William Hung (1893–1980)*
132. James T. C. Liu, *China Turning Inward: Intellectual-Political Changes in the Early Twelfth Century*

Harvard East Asian Monographs

133. Paul A. Cohen, *Between Tradition and Modernity: Wang T'ao and Reform in Late Ching China*
134. Kate Wildman Nakai, *Shogunal Politics: Arai Hakuseki and the Premises of Tokugawa Rule*
135. Parks M. Coble, *Facing Japan: Chinese Politics and Japanese Imperialism, 1931–1937*
136. Jon L. Saari, *Legacies of Childhood: Growing Up Chinese in a Time of Crisis, 1890–1920*
137. Susan Downing Videen, *Tales of Heichū*
138. Heinz Morioka and Miyoko Sasaki, *Rakugo: The Popular Narrative Art of Japan*
139. Joshua A. Fogel, *Nakae Ushikichi in China: The Mourning of Spirit*
140. Alexander Barton Woodside, *Vietnam and the Chinese Model.: A Comparative Study of Vietnamese and Chinese Government in the First Half of the Nineteenth Century*
141. George Elision, *Deus Destroyed: The Image of Christianity in Early Modern Japan*
142. William D. Wray, ed., *Managing Industrial Enterprise: Cases from Japan's Prewar Experience*
143. T'ung-tsu Ch'ü, *Local Government in China under the Ching*
144. Marie Anchordoguy, *Computers, Inc.: Japan's Challenge to IBM*
145. Barbara Molony, *Technology and Investment: The Prewar Japanese Chemical Industry*
146. Mary Elizabeth Berry, *Hideyoshi*
147. Laura E. Hein, *Fueling Growth: The Energy Revolution and Economic Policy in Postwar Japan*
148. Wen-hsin Yeh, *The Alienated Academy: Culture and Politics in Republican China, 1919–1937*
149. Dru C. Gladney, *Muslim Chinese: Ethnic Nationalism in the People's Republic*
150. Merle Goldman and Paul A. Cohen, eds., *Ideas Across Cultures: Essays on Chinese Thought in Honor of Benjamin L Schwartz*
151. James Polachek, *The Inner Opium War*
152. Gail Lee Bernstein, *Japanese Marxist: A Portrait of Kawakami Hajime, 1879–1946*
153. Lloyd E. Eastman, *The Abortive Revolution: China under Nationalist Rule, 1927–1937*
154. Mark Mason, *American Multinationals and Japan: The Political Economy of Japanese Capital Controls, 1899–1980*
155. Richard J. Smith, John K. Fairbank, and Katherine F. Bruner, *Robert Hart and China's Early Modernization: His Journals, 1863–1866*
156. George J. Tanabe, Jr., *Myōe the Dreamkeeper: Fantasy and Knowledge in Kamakura Buddhism*
157. William Wayne Farris, *Heavenly Warriors: The Evolution of Japan's Military, 500–1300*
158. Yu-ming Shaw, *An American Missionary in China: John Leighton Stuart and Chinese-American Relations*
159. James B. Palais, *Politics and Policy in Traditional Korea*
160. Douglas Reynolds, *China, 1898–1912: The Xinzheng Revolution and Japan*
161. Roger Thompson, *China's Local Councils in the Age of Constitutional Reform*
162. William Johnston, *The Modern Epidemic: History of Tuberculosis in Japan*

Harvard East Asian Monographs

163. Constantine Nomikos Vaporis, *Breaking Barriers: Travel and the State in Early Modern Japan*
164. Irmela Hijiya-Kirschnereit, *Rituals of Self-Revelation: Shishōsetsu as Literary Genre and Socio-Cultural Phenomenon*
165. James C. Baxter, *The Meiji Unification through the Lens of Ishikawa Prefecture*
166. Thomas R. H. Havens, *Architects of Affluence: The Tsutsumi Family and the Seibu-Saison Enterprises in Twentieth-Century Japan*
167. Anthony Hood Chambers, *The Secret Window: Ideal Worlds in Tanizaki's Fiction*
168. Steven J. Ericson, *The Sound of the Whistle: Railroads and the State in Meiji Japan*
169. Andrew Edmund Goble, *Kenmu: Go-Daigo's Revolution*
170. Denise Potrzeba Lett, *In Pursuit of Status: The Making of South Korea's "New" Urban Middle Class*
171. Mimi Hall Yiengpruksawan, *Hiraizumi: Buddhist Art and Regional Politics in Twelfth-Century Japan*
172. Charles Shirō Inouye, *The Similitude of Blossoms: A Critical Biography of Izumi Kyōka (1873–1939), Japanese Novelist and Playwright*
173. Aviad E. Raz, *Riding the Black Ship: Japan and Tokyo Disneyland*
174. Deborah J. Milly, *Poverty, Equality, and Growth: The Politics of Economic Need in Postwar Japan*
175. See Heng Teow, *Japan's Cultural Policy Toward China, 1918–1931: A Comparative Perspective*
176. Michael A. Fuller, *An Introduction to Literary Chinese*
177. Frederick R. Dickinson, *War and National Reinvention: Japan in the Great War, 1914–1919*
178. John Solt, *Shredding the Tapestry of Meaning: The Poetry and Poetics of Kitasono Katue (1902–1978)*
179. Edward Pratt, *Japan's Protoindustrial Elite: The Economic Foundations of the Gōnō*
180. Atsuko Sakaki, *Recontextualizing Texts: Narrative Performance in Modern Japanese Fiction*
181. Soon-Won Park, *Colonial Industrialization and Labor in Korea: The Onoda Cement Factory*
182. JaHyun Kim Haboush and Martina Deuchler, *Culture and the State in Late Chosŏn Korea*
183. John W. Chaffee, *Branches of Heaven: A History of the Imperial Clan of Sung China*
184. Gi-Wook Shin and Michael Robinson, eds., *Colonial Modernity in Korea*
185. Nam-lin Hur, *Prayer and Play in Late Tokugawa Japan: Asakusa Sensōji and Edo Society*
186. Kristin Stapleton, *Civilizing Chengdu: Chinese Urban Reform, 1895–1937*
187. Hyung Il Pai, *Constructing "Korean" Origins: A Critical Review of Archaeology, Historiography, and Racial Myth in Korean State-Formation Theories*
188. Brian D. Ruppert, *Jewel in the Ashes: Buddha Relics and Power in Early Medieval Japan*
189. Susan Daruvala, *Zhou Zuoren and an Alternative Chinese Response to Modernity*

Harvard East Asian Monographs

190. James Z. Lee, *The Political Economy of a Frontier: Southwest China, 1250–1850*
191. Kerry Smith, *A Time of Crisis: Japan, the Great Depression, and Rural Revitalization*
192. Michael Lewis, *Becoming Apart: National Power and Local Politics in Toyama, 1868–1945*
193. William C. Kirby, Man-houng Lin, James Chin Shih, and David A. Pietz, eds., *State and Economy in Republican China: A Handbook for Scholars*
194. Timothy S. George, *Minamata: Pollution and the Struggle for Democracy in Postwar Japan*
195. Billy K. L. So, *Prosperity, Region, and Institutions in Maritime China: The South Fukien Pattern, 946–1368*
196. Yoshihisa Tak Matsusaka, *The Making of Japanese Manchuria, 1904–1932*
197. Maram Epstein, *Competing Discourses: Orthodoxy, Authenticity, and Engendered Meanings in Late Imperial Chinese Fiction*
198. Curtis J. Milhaupt, J. Mark Ramseyer, and Michael K. Young, eds. and comps., *Japanese Law in Context: Readings in Society, the Economy, and Politics*
199. Haruo Iguchi, *Unfinished Business: Ayukawa Yoshisuke and U.S.-Japan Relations, 1937–1952*
200. Scott Pearce, Audrey Spiro, and Patricia Ebrey, *Culture and Power in the Reconstitution of the Chinese Realm, 200–600*
201. Terry Kawashima, *Writing Margins: The Textual Construction of Gender in Heian and Kamakura Japan*
202. Martin W. Huang, *Desire and Fictional Narrative in Late Imperial China*
203. Robert S. Ross and Jiang Changbin, eds., *Re-examining the Cold War: U.S.-China Diplomacy, 1954–1973*
204. Guanhua Wang, *In Search of Justice: The 1905–1906 Chinese Anti-American Boycott*
205. David Schaberg, *A Patterned Past: Form and Thought in Early Chinese Historiography*
206. Christine Yano, *Tears of Longing: Nostalgia and the Nation in Japanese Popular Song*
207. Milena Doleželová-Velingerová and Oldřich Král, with Graham Sanders, eds., *The Appropriation of Cultural Capital: China's May Fourth Project*